Broadcasting Politics in Japan

Broadcasting Politics in Japan

NHK and Television News

ELLIS S. KRAUSS

Cornell University Press

First published 2000 by Cornell University Press

Printed in the United States of America

Library of Congress Cataloging-in-Publication Data

Krauss, Ellis S.
   Broadcasting politics in Japan : NHK and television news /
Ellis S. Krauss.
      p.   cm.
   Includes bibliographical references and index.
   ISBN 0-8014-3748-2 ISBN: 978-0-8014-3748-9
   1. Television broadcasting of news—Japan—History.
2. Nihon Hōsō Kyōkai—History.   3. Government and
the press—Japan—History—20th century.   I.   Title.

PN5407.T4 K73 2000
070.1'95—dc21

                                        00-021391

Cornell University Press strives to use environmentally responsible suppliers and materials to the fullest extent possible in the
publishing of its books. Such materials include vegetable-based,
low-VOC inks and acid-free papers that are recycled, totally
chlorine-free, or partly composed of nonwood fibers. Books
that bear the logo of the FSC (Forest Stewardship Council) use
paper taken from forests that have been inspected and certified
as meeting the highest standards for environmental and social
responsibility. For further information, visit our website at
www.cornellpress.cornell.edu.

Cloth printing   10   9   8   7   6   5   4   3   2   1

FSC FSC Trademark © 1996 Forest Stewardship Council A.C.
      SW-COC-098

To Hisamori Tetsuo

and

Hisamori Kazuko [née Matsukata]

and

Matsukata Saburō

Contents

Preface and Acknowledgments

My interest in NHK television news began when I touted its neutral broadcasting of information about policy making to an American
friend visiting me in Japan in 1975; after watching it for a while, he pro-
nounced it boring. We were both right. In 1983, thanks to a Japanese friend,
I gained access to the NHK News Center to explore why it had those characteristics. Gradually the research expanded into a book. Its completion
was delayed through (and because of) 15 years that encompassed publishing several edited books and numerous articles on related and unrelated
subjects, two transcontinental moves, a divorce, and other large and small
"distractions"; throughout, it remained an important, if too often subor-
dinated, professional interest. In a separate article I've described the whole
process: initial interest, access, methodologies employed, and delayed publishing gratification, and their trade-offs and lessons.[1]

The primary and secondary materials I used in researching this book
are voluminous, but only part of all that has been written about NHK. The
description and analysis of the news process itself, particularly chapter 3,
was initially based on intensive field research in 1983 and 1985, including
interviews with and observation of NHK reporters and executives at the
News Center and in reporters' clubs, and on many shorter subsequent follow-up visits and discussions up until 1995. To encourage frank and
detailed imparting of information in my interviews, I promised anonymity
to most of the respondents. I generally refer to them by the initial of their

---

[1] See my "Doing Media Research in Japan" in Theodore Bestor, Patricia G. Steinhoff, and
Victoria Lyons-Bestor, eds., *Field Research in Japan: Methods in Context* (Honolulu: University
of Hawaii Press, forthcoming).

family name only, and also provide some general but not necessarily identifying information about their position within the organization.

My concern for the actual organizational and institutional processes of, and influence on, NHK news is reflected in the way the book is organized. After an introduction to themes and questions, part I explores the broadcasting of politics—coverage of public affairs in the postwar period in comparative perspective (chap. 2) and the news gathering and editing process that produced it (chap. 3).

In part II, the book moves to the politics of broadcasting and to NHK's relationship to the state and the market that has shaped the organization's development. Chapter 4 explores NHK's legal and regulatory framework and financing, and how these furnish the opportunity for political pressures. The next chapter looks at management and especially at how NHK's president has been involved with the political world. Chapter 6 deals with personnel relations in NHK, from how reporters are recruited and socialized, through labor-management relations, to NHK's and the state's use of personnel to influence each other.

Chapter 7 focuses on how NHK's strategy concerning new media technology involved NHK in state industrial policy and the building of a conglomerate of commercial subsidiaries in the 1980s, with what current consequences. The last chapter of part II describes the transformations in Japanese television news in the 1990s, brought about by commercial television's challenge with a new, politically controversial news style. Finally, chapter 9 brings together the evidence, assessing its implications and significance for Japanese politics and the media's relationship to it. Throughout, Japanese names are given in their indigenous order, family name first, unless in a reference to an author who published in English and whose name appeared in print in the Western order or in the case of a Japanese living in the United States.

In 15 years of research, one accumulates an enormous number of debts to many individuals and organizations. Sakakura Kōichi, a former managing director of NHK, was instrumental in helping me gain access to the News Center. Special thanks also go to Tsugawa Tōru, Ōbata Masami, and Katō Kazurō, all of NHK, who were patient and informative mentors and facilitators through the years. Arai Mikio, Jurg Gassman, and Okada Hideichi aided in large and small ways with access to persons in Japan. Sachie Noguchi, Eiji Yutani, and Sanae Isozumi in the United States and Koide Izumi in Japan are wonderful librarians who gave me much assistance. Akuto Hiroshi, Joanne Bauer, John Condry, Ehud Harari, Jeffrey Hart, Isao Kawasaki, Kodama Miiko, Greg Noble, John Ratliff, Okamatsu Sōsaburō, Christena Turner, Kurt Steiner, and Watanabe Kōjirō also provided important primary or secondary materials or information concerning NHK, the commercial networks, and related matters. I also thank the Public Relations Offices at NHK and TV Asahi and Sunohara Shuichiro and Makino Hideyuki for giving me many of the photographs used in this book.

Doris Graber, Mina Hsiao, Jon Pierre, Monika Djerf Pierre, Alison Preston, Kate Stables, Eleanor Westney, the participants in the Media and Democracy project at Ohio State University (especially Max Kaase), and Ann Waswo and several people I met during a trip to England in 1990 (including John Cain, Rebecca Goodhart, Martin Harrison, Peter Hennessey, Jackie Morris, Colin Shaw, David Shukman, and Sir Anthony Smith), aided in various ways with comparative materials or insights concerning Western European or American broadcasters.

Many research assistants over the years efficiently accomplished the tedious but essential work of content analysis, interview tape transcription (and occasionally translation), and bibliographic searching, including the late Maki Yasuoka, John Nylin, Yoshiko Koda, Son-min Kim, Fumiko Carraro, Randy Soderquist, Eiji Kawabata, "Emo" Matsuda, and Brett Sheppard.

Financial support was provided at various times by a Fulbright Fellowship, and grants from the Joint Committee on Japanese Studies of the ACLS-SSRC, the Japan Iron and Steel Federation endowment funds and a Central Research Development Fund Grant at the University of Pittsburgh, the Swedish-America Foundation, and the Woodrow Wilson International Center for Scholars. The Wilson Center, Tokyo University's Institute of Social Science and Ishida Takeshi, Keio University's Faculty of Law and Sone Yasunori, and the Japan Center for Michigan Universities and Marty Holman, hosted me for various periods, enabling me to conduct initial and follow-up research. The International House of Japan was a comfortable base on several research trips.

Individual conversations and communications about the book with various individuals and groups, and the moral support of colleagues, helped me to hone my ideas and encouraged my persistence: Akiko Hashimoto and my other former colleagues in the Japan Council, University of Pittsburgh, T. J. Pempel, Michael Reich, and Eleanor Westney about Japan politics, organization, and media; my IR/PS colleagues Ulrike Schaede and John Mcmillan about aspects of organizational behavior; and the questions and comments of participants in various conferences, symposia, and presentations, such as the *Media and Politics* book project led by Susan Pharr, and university audiences at North Carolina Research Triangle, Cornell, Pittsburgh, Indiana, Berkeley, Virginia, and San Diego.

For intellectual influence in the book's final stages, I owe the greatest debt of gratitude to colleagues who read all or parts of earlier versions and gave me their suggestions and criticism. Gary Allinson, Peter Katzenstein, Pat Steinhoff, Greg Kasza, and Harvey Feigenbaum provided invaluable feedback on the entire manuscript. Susan Pharr, Dick Samuels, and Michio Muramatsu all helped greatly with parts of it. My editor, Roger Haydon at Cornell University Press, did an excellent job of guiding the work through the production process and pestering me to shorten and improve an overly wordy draft.

On more personal notes, I am especially grateful to my wife, Martha Anne Leche, for her unwavering support, loyalty, and love in this and everything else. My daughter, Rachel, and my ex-wife Carol Krauss-Bostick were patient, if sometimes skeptical, through the earlier years of this long project.

Finally, this book is dedicated to Hisamori Kazuko and Tetsuo, my oldest friends in Japan, and her father, Matsukata Saburō. The Hisamoris have always aided and supported my research in Japan, and it was Kazuko and her late father's contacts that enabled me to gain access to NHK and the News Center. Saburō, prewar journalist and head of Kyōdō News Service after the war, and a true renaissance man, spent his years in journalism trying to steer his own personal way between the realities of state power and ideological confrontation and the ideals of a free press. It is therefore particularly appropriate that this book is dedicated to them, with affection, respect, and gratitude.

I was not always able to use all the materials or information provided by these many gracious people, but all of them made this book better: without their professional or personal aid, feedback, encouragement, and inspiration this book would have never existed, or been however complete or informative it is. I am grateful. Thank you.

ELLIS S. KRAUSS

Encinitas, California

Abbreviations

APSR	*American Political Science Review*
DBS	Direct Broadcasting Satellite
HKTC	*Hōsō Kenkyū to Chōsa* [Broadcasting Research and Surveys], a respected journal of research on broadcasting and public opinion published by NHK HBCK.
JBC	Japan Broadcasting Corporation (English translation of "NHK")
JJS	*Journal of Japanese Studies*
JT	*Japan Times* (newspaper)
LDP	Liberal Democratic Party
MITI	Ministry of International Trade and Industry
MPT	Ministry of Posts and Telecommunications
NC9	*News Center 9 P.M.*
NHK	Nippon Hōsō Kyōkai. See also JBC
NHK BCRI	Broadcasting Culture Research Institute, NHK's research organization
NHK HBCK	NHK Hōsō Bunka Chōsa Kenkyūjo. Same as BCRI (its English translation) NHK's research organization. See also NHK RTVCRI
NHK HYC	NHK Hōsō Yoron Chōsajo. Broadcast Survey Research Institute. Part of RTVCRI or BCRI
NHK RTVCRI	Radio and TV Culture Research Institute, the earlier name for BCRI, NHK's research organization
Nippōrō	Nippon Hōsō Kyōkai Rōdō Kumiai, the Japan Broadcasting Company [NHK] Labor Union

NYT   *New York Times* (newspaper)
NKS   *Nihon Keizai Shimbun* (newspaper)
STF/CEC   Subcommittee on Telecommunications and Finance of the Committee on Energy and Commerce, U.S. House of Representatives

Broadcasting Politics in Japan

CHAPTER 1

NHK and Broadcasting Politics

Either neoclassical economists have ignored (or missed) an essential ingredient of every society; or if they are correct, the enormous investment that every society makes in legitimacy is an unnecessary expenditure.

—DOUGLASS C. NORTH, *Structure and Change
in Economic History*

Once it was said that "the pen is mightier than the sword," and newspapers and journalism functioned as an institution that watched over authority with the support of the people. However, today when television is widely diffused, the circumstances now are being created in which "television is mightier than the pen."

—SHIMA NOBUHIKO, *Media kage no kenryokusha-tachi*
[Media's Powerful Shadow People]

Where's the television cameras? Where's NHK? I won't talk to newspaper reporters. I want to talk directly to the people. . . . I hate the biased newspapers!

—PRIME MINISTER SATO EISAKU AT HIS FINAL PRESS CONFERENCE
AFTER SERVING SEVEN YEARS, EIGHT MONTHS IN OFFICE,
JUNE 17, 1972

The two most powerful institutions affecting the lives of citizens in advanced industrialized democracies today may well be the state[1] and the mass communications media. The relationship between these two, and how

[1] I adopt a variation of Eric A. Nordlinger's definition of the state in his *On the Autonomy of the Democratic State* (Cambridge: Harvard University Press, 1981), 11: all those roles that are authorized to make and apply binding decisions upon any and all segments of society. I take the *state* to mean political authority in its broadest manifestations, including, but not exclusively confined to, government. In contrast to Nordlinger, I emphasize "roles." The state is composed of more than just bureaucratic officials. Politicians who derive influence from

that relationship affects society, are thus among the worthiest topics in comparative social science research. This book is about these subjects in Japan, the world's second-largest economy and a democratic nation with some of the most developed mass communications institutions anywhere. More postwar Japanese citizens may have learned about what their government does and how it does it from their public broadcaster, NHK (Nippon Hōsō Kyōkai), the Japan Broadcasting Corporation, than from any other mass media source.

To explain television news's long-neglected contribution to political life in postwar Japan requires analyzing NHK as an organization, a deserving goal in its own right given that it is one of the world's largest broadcasters and one of Japan's most influential institutions. Specifically, I will explore NHK's news organization and process that has produced a news product different from that of any other industrialized democracy, one with significant consequences for how citizens view their state. I demonstrate how NHK's organization and its processes, in turn, resulted from the relationship that developed between NHK and the state. I will thus show how the institutionalized interaction of the state and the media over time ultimately, indirectly, and often inadvertently, fashioned the information Japan's citizens receive, and upon which the kind of support they give that state depends.

The dominance of NHK's television news from the 1960s through the 1980s helps to explain how Japan's democratic state became legitimized and thus stabilized following the instability and polarized political conflict immediately after the war. The form that legitimation took, combined with NHK news's relative decline in the 1990s and the rise of a new form of commercial broadcast news, helps to explain why the state has recently been experiencing rising public cynicism, alienation, and demands for reform.

NHK NEWS

Television news is the prime source of information for the average Japanese. Although Japanese consume more newspapers per capita than almost any people in the Western world, public opinion surveys confirm that Japanese are as dependent, and in some cases more reliant, on television news for information. Television is preferred over the other media as an information source for knowing things more quickly and as the most useful and the most frequent source of news.[2]

---

their roles in the authoritative policy-making process are considered part of the state even when their behavior is motivated by the desire to attain reelection.

[2]Terebi Hōdō Kenkyūkai, "Terebi hōdō hyōka no kenkyū—Phase II" (Tokyo, May 1979), 1, based on NHK HYC surveys conducted between 1975 and 1978. Similar information from the same source in 1983 also indicates that television news is the most trusted source of news.

NHK has been the primary source of television news in Japan for most of the postwar period. NHK is a public service broadcasting (*kōkyō hōsō*) organization, like the British Broadcasting Corporation (BBC) in England; it is not a national broadcasting (*kokuei hōsō*) agency. There is some governmental purview exercised by having its Board of Governors appointed by the prime minister, and its overall yearly budget and any receiver's fee increases must be approved by the Minister of Posts and the National Diet. On the other hand, it obtains its revenue from receivers' fees rather than from central government allocation and the government has no direct control over its daily administration. NHK is an independent broadcast agency, and on paper at least, perhaps the freest in the democratic world. Autonomous from, but somewhat accountable to, government may be a good way to characterize the position of NHK. Equally apt to NHK would be Tom Burns's characterization of the BBC as a "quasi-autonomous, non-governmental organization."[3]

Currently, NHK operates one general and one educational over-the-air broadcasting channels, two 24-hour direct broadcast satellite channels, one high-definition television station, two AM and one FM radio stations, and overseas television and radio services. Its combined television and radio broadcasts total more than 1,100 hours per week. All programs on its broadcast and satellite services are completely commercial-free. Among other activities, it has its own symphony orchestra, technical laboratories, and 28 related commercial firms.

In the mid-1980s NHK employed as many as 16,000 employees; by the late 1990s the number had dropped to about 13,000. It is one of the two largest broadcast agencies, along with the BBC. These personnel work at 54 domestic stations, including the giant Tokyo headquarters, and 27 overseas locations. In the mid-1990s NHK commanded an annual budget of about half a billion dollars, with almost all of it coming from receivers' fees collected directly from those who own television sets. More than 35 million households in Japan have contracts with NHK to pay receivers' fees, with more than 75 percent for color television sets and most of the remainder for satellite color service.[4]

NHK competes with a full range of private, commercial (*mimpō*) stations and "networks." This mixed system of public service and private broadcast-

[3]Tom Burns, *The BBC: Public Institution and Private World* (London: Macmillan Press Ltd., 1977), 192.

[4]NHK HBCK,ed., *NHK nenkan '96* (Tokyo: NHK, 1996), 42, gives the total number of employees as 13,113 persons; pages 66-67 give the 1996 budget (operating income) as ¥587,832,417,000 which at ¥120 to one dollar equals $4.9 billion. Of this amount, the dollar equivalent of about $4.7 billion, almost 97 percent, was derived from receivers' fees. Operating expenses were slightly lower. Most of the remaining 2.5 percent of contracts (about 900,000 households) are for black-and-white and satellite black-and-white receivers.

ing, recently becoming the norm in other industrialized democracies, has been in place since the early 1950s in Japan. For most of the postwar period, however, NHK tended to dominate the commercial competition, especially in television news. In the early 1980s about one-third of its entire programming (40 hours) fell into this category, with NHK broadcasting more than two and a half times as much news on a weekly basis on its general over-the-air television channel as the commercial stations. By the early 1990s, nearly half (47 percent) of all its general channel time was spent on news and information. NHK broadcasts, in terms of number of programs and total minutes per day, provide more television news than any other major (non-"all news") news organization in the West or in democratic Asia and Oceania.

On an average weekday during the early 1980s, between a third and three-quarters of viewers were watching NHK's major morning, noon, and evening (7 P.M.) news broadcasts, rather than those of the competing commercial networks. Asked in surveys to compare their trust in NHK television news with commercial stations' news, an overwhelming majority trusted NHK news as much, and usually more, than that of the private stations. This trust in television news is reflected in the generally favorable orientations of the public toward NHK: the broadcasting agency, according to a 1997 survey, was considered to be more trustworthy than newspapers, the courts, commercial broadcasting, and the National Diet and the government, especially outstripping the latter three by a factor of more than 2:1 or greater. Whereas, for example, 38 percent of respondents said that they more or less trusted commercial broadcasters, 79 percent trusted NHK. This high level of trust has been consistent since at least the 1970s, even while in the United States in the late 1960s and early 1970s, television news elicited less confidence than almost any other major institution.

If Japan is an information-oriented society, television is the primary means of dissemination of information to the Japanese citizen, and NHK news is the primary and most trusted source of television information

By the early 1980s, NHK was broadcasting 15 news programs per day: four major national news programs, numerous five-minute hourly news broadcasts, and also local news programs. Its 7 P.M. evening news in the mid-1980s received about one-third of the nationwide viewing audience at that time slot and has always been considered the prime news of the day for broadcast journalists, as the network evening news programs are in the United States.[5]

[5]NHK Sōgō Hōsō Kenkyūjo, Hōsō jijō chōsabu, "Dēta de miru Nihon no masukomi no idō to genjō" (Tokyo: March 1983); NHK HBCK, ed., *NHK nenkan (Radio and Television Yearbook)*, '91 (Tokyo: NHK, 1991), 523. See also *NHK nenkan '96*, inside front page. Terebi Hōdō Kenkyūkai, eds., *Terebi nyūsu no kenkyū* (Tokyo: NHK, 1980), 11. On ratings, see, e.g., NHK HYC, *Terebi-rajio bangumi shichōritsu chōsa* (November 1982), 31–32; also, NHK HYC, "Zenkoku hōsō iko chōsa" (Tokyo: NHK Broadcasting Culture Research Institute, 1975). On trust, see Takahashi Kōichi, "Public Opinion Survey Report: The Public Nature of Broadcasting

Fig. 1. Televisions on show outside the old NHK broadcasting building, 1953.

NHK AND JAPAN'S POSTWAR STATE

What do Japanese see on the prime evening news program in their country? As the next chapter will demonstrate, they have seen strictly factual news accounts about governmental activities, especially about their national bureaucracy and its related advisory organs. As I will further demonstrate later in the book, this large amount of coverage of the civil service is unique among the industrialized democracies where elected politicians, presidents, prime ministers, cabinet officials and legislators tend to dominate news of governmental and political affairs.

This unusual content of NHK news may help us answer a huge riddle at the core of postwar Japan's politics: how did a state with an almost entirely new democratic political framework based on principles of authority and

---

and the Audience—From the 'Role of Broadcasting' Survey" [*Yoron chōsa repōto: Shichōsha to hōsō no kōkyōsei—[Hōsō no yakuwari] chōsa kara*], *Hōsō Kenkyū to Chōsa,* no. 5 (May 1998): 15; see also, in English, *Broadcasting Culture & Research,* no. 3 (spring 1998): 4; NHK HYC, "Nihonjin no Terebikan Chōsa" (Tokyo: NHK Broadcasting Culture Research Institute, 1978). On the United States, see Gabriel A. Almond and Sidney Verba, eds., *The Civic Culture Revisited* (Boston: Little, Brown and Company), 190, based on a U.S. Senate Committee on Government Operations subcommittee report in 1973. On 7 P.M. news ratings, see NHK HYC, *Terebirajio bangumi shichōritsu chōsa: Zenkokusōbetsu kekkahyō* (Tokyo: NHK Yoron Chōsajo, November 1982), 1314, 2728.

sovereignty previously alien to its people, imposed by a foreign occupying power, and riven by a fundamental ideological conflict over the values and meaning of that framework, become legitimized and thus stable over time after 1960?

Today we tend to forget that between 1947 and at least 1960, Japan could not be considered a stable democracy. Despite the provision of a democratic constitution and political structure and a great deal of effort expended in the resocialization of the Japanese people into democratic values, the fate of the United States's experiment with imposed democracy in Japan was by no means a foregone conclusion. Polarized into two conflicting camps, left and right clashed. They fundamentally disagreed on the meaning of democracy, the suitability of the imposed constitution and political structure for the Japanese people, and the past and future Japanese identity. In the streets and in the Diet, Japan's parliament, these confrontations were intense and sometimes violent.

The United States itself was partially responsible, if unintentionally so, for this situation. At first, the United States enthusiastically filled the vacuum left by the defeat in war and the discrediting of Japan's prewar, Emperor-centered institutions with new democratic ideas and structures based on popular instead of imperial sovereignty, and the reform of almost all Japan's social institutions. The United States also attempted to give Japan a new identity as an unarmed and peaceable member of the community of nations.

Starting in 1947, however, the United States seemed to backtrack from these goals and values. With the onset of the Cold War, the consolidation of an ambitious program of reform mostly completed in only two years of occupation, and then the fall of China to the Communists and a war on the Korean peninsula, it became more important to achieve security rather than reform, rearmament rather than demilitarization, and alliance rather than democratization. In the process, the United States highly exacerbated the division between the political left and right in Japan and stimulated a reversal in those who supported and those who opposed its policies. The left had totally accepted the Occupation's original vision of a democratized and demilitarized Japan, whereas the right had always thought the Americans had gone too far in depriving Japan of its tradition and its sovereignty as a nation. Now the most fervent supporters of the new, American-inspired Constitution and its rights and processes, the left, became the most fervid critics of American hegemony, alliance, and the perceived attempt to backtrack toward the authoritarian past. At the same time, the most recalcitrant resistors to the Americans and their reforms, the right, now became the United States's most loyal and supportive allies in the war against Communism and the push for national security and social stability.

Thus, the very meaning and terms of democracy and Japan's political system were very much in question for 15 years after the end of the war as left and right each accepted part, but rejected other provisions, of the Constitution and political system. A series of violent clashes in the 1950s between the conservative-dominated government and the Marxist-dominated leftist opposition culminated in the Security Treaty (*Anpo*) crisis in 1960, the severest and most intense political crisis in postwar Japanese history. Ostensibly, it originated as a question of whether a revised military treaty with the United States should be ratified. Ultimately, however, when incumbent Prime Minister Kishi Nobusuke and his conservative Liberal Democratic Party unilaterally rammed the treaty through the Diet over the fierce resistance and blockade of the leftist opposition parties, it became a veritable "crisis of democracy" that mobilized hundreds of thousands of previously passive but concerned citizens.

Two of the most preeminent political scientists on either side of the Pacific, Robert A. Scalapino and Junnosuke Masumi, argued that this climactic event indicated that the new democratic institutions had not meshed well with the patterns of socioeconomic change in an increasingly mass society and that the political parties and the Diet had shallow roots among the people. They questioned whether Western-style democracy was compatible with Japanese cultural values and procedures.[6]

Flash-forward 30 years from the 1960 crisis. By the end of the 1980s, Japan is widely seen as a stable and successful parliamentary democracy. Indeed, it is so stable that Karel van Wolferen questions whether it even has the open conflict characteristic of democracy.[7] Even with allowances for Scalapino and Masumi's concentration on such a major conflictual event and for van Wolferen's tendency to concentrate on the oppressiveness and hypocrisy of Japanese culture, the contrast is striking. How has the vulnerable and threatened parliamentary democracy of the 1950s and early 1960s become, in such a short historical span, the stable—perhaps even overly stable—democracy of the 1990s? After more than a decade of the severest economic downturn since the Great Depression of the 1930s, there has been political change in Japan in the 1990s, but not a hint of fundamental political instability. Clearly, the democratic state in Japan has become legitimated.

Despite the dramatic nature and central importance of the fundamental question of the sources of legitimacy of this democratic regime, the literature on Japanese politics pays almost no attention to the question of *how* le-

[6]Robert A. Scalapino and Junnosuke Masumi, *Parties and Politics in Contemporary Japan* (Berkeley: University of California Press, 1971), chap. 5, esp. 145–53; on the fundamental value conflict, see Joji Watanuki, "Patterns of Politics in Present-Day Japan," in Seymour Martin Lipset and Stein Rokkan, eds., *Party Systems and Voter Alignments* (New York: Free Press, 1967), 447–66; on *Anpo*, see George R. Packard III, *Protest in Tokyo* (Princeton: Princeton University Press, 1966), for the most complete analysis of the crisis.

[7]Karel van Wolferen, *The Enigma of Japanese Power* (New York: Alfred A. Knopf, 1989), esp. chaps. 2 and 16.

gitimation occurred. A burgeoning literature on Japanese politics since the early 1980s has produced no work that directly addresses the problem of the legitimation of the state.[8] Instead, whereas Scalapino and Masumi were specifically concerned with questions of citizen support for the new democratic state, once the state had been legitimized, most political scientists assumed such support and concentrated on questions of whether bureaucrats or politicians have had more influence on policy making, particularly economic policy making. For example, current rational choice explanations that argue that the politicians are in charge, and the bureaucrats merely their "agents," do not deal with the legitimacy question at all. Instead these explanations assume that authority relations are established by the constitutional arrangements and that these arrangements accurately distribute power within the state.[9]

Almost lost in the intense left-right confrontation of 1960 was that this year represented a dividing line of a more subtle sort: the beginning of the television age in Japan. In 1955, less than one percent of Japanese households had a television set. Three years later, the distribution rate was 10 times that amount. Between 1958 and 1959, the distribution rate doubled and by 1961, doubled again—half of Japan's households now had television sets. In 1963, three quarters possessed them.[10] In other words, in the five short years from 1958 to 1963, nearly all Japanese acquired television. By comparison, it took radio more than 30 years to go from less than one percent to an almost 75 percent distribution rate, something television accomplished in less than a decade between 1955 and 1963.[11] It was also during this same period that NHK came to dominate the market for news in Japan, a position it was to retain until the mid- to late-1980s.

Is it a coincidence that the mass distribution of television sets and NHK's rise as the dominant source of television news in Japan coincided almost exactly with the beginning of the stabilization and legitimation of Japan's de-

[8] Ibid's chap. 12 is a partial exception, but only a very brief (17 pages), meandering sojourn through three hundred years of Japanese history, with no real evidence of how or why his asserted patterns came about.

[9] For example, J. Mark Ramsayer and Frances McCall Rosenbluth, *Japan's Political Marketplace* (Cambridge: Harvard University Press, 1993); Mathew D. McCubbins and Gregory W. Noble, "The Appearance of Power: Legislators, Bureaucrats, and the Budget Process in the United States and Japan," and "Perceptions and Realities of Japanese Budgeting," in Peter F. Cowhey and Mathew D. McCubbins, eds., *Structure and Policy in Japan and the United States* (Cambridge: Cambridge University Press, 1995). It is ironic that rational choice explanations in political science ignore the legitimacy question since this approach's intellectual origins did not. See, e.g., Douglass C. North, *Structure and Change in Economic History* (New York: W. W. Norton, 1982), esp. 43–58.

[10] All data from Hidaka Ichirō, *Nihon no hōsō no ayumi* (The Path of Japan's Broadcasting) (Tokyo: Ningen no kagakusha, 1991), fig. 2, p. 163.

[11] Ibid.

Fig. 2. NHK live coverage of the 1964 Tokyo Olympic Games. This coverage led to the building of NHK's new Broadcasting Center and also the initial development of Hivision (HDTV).

mocratic regime? Although there can be no conclusive way to prove that
television was definitely responsible for this change, I will argue that it is
highly likely that it is not a coincidence: television, especially NHK television
news, played some role in that transition.

Similarly, although Japan's democratic political system remained legitimate and fundamentally stable after the 1950s, the late 1980s through the
1990s witnessed some of the most important evolutionary changes in decades. Most especially, rates of political cynicism, always high in Japan, went
higher than they had been in 20 years, and public disgust with official corruption and malfeasance reached a peak, culminating in more pressure for
reform than Japan had witnessed since the Occupation. These changes in
Japan also coincided with the first major challenge to NHK news in the postwar period, its relative decline in importance, and the shattering of its dominance by a commercial broadcaster featuring news of a much different type
from NHK's. Another coincidence? Again, I shall argue that here too television news played a role in this more recent form of political transition.

WHY SUCH COVERAGE?

How do we explain such coverage with its important potential consequences? Why is NHK different from the private and public broadcasters

Fig. 3. NHK's huge Broadcasting Center, next to the site of the 1964 Olympic Games.

in the other industrialized democracies? One possible answer to these questions may be the simplest one: the bureaucracy plays a greater role in Japanese politics and policy making than in the politics and policy making of other democracies. In short, television news in Japan is merely a "mirror" reflecting the reality of each country's politics—in this case that the bureaucracy's power is such that it actually "rules" Japan.[12]

The national bureaucracy in Japan certainly plays a greater role in policy making than in the United States, for example, but there are several difficulties with the view of media as mirror of reality. The first problem is that there are industrialized democracies other than the United States where public officials also have long been seen as powerful and heavily involved in policy making and politics, often in ways equivalent to Japanese bureaucracy. France, for example has often been paired with Japan on the "strong state" side of the continuum of industrialized democracies.[13] Yet French public television coverage, as we shall see, differs from that of Japan. Why should television news merely reflect reality in one case but not the other?

---

[12]Chalmers Johnson, *MITI and the Japanese Miracle* (Stanford: Stanford University Press, 1982); see also Clyde V. Prestowitz, Jr., *Trading Places* (New York: Basic Books, Inc., 1988).

[13]For example, John Zysman, *Governments, Markets and Growth: Financial Systems and the Politics of Industrial Change* (Ithaca: Cornell University Press, 1983).

Another difficulty with the media-as-mirror view is that, even if we assume that bureaucrats are more influential in Japan, we have no way to measure with certainty *how much* more powerful they are than in other countries. Therefore, there is no way to know if television news covers bureaucrats in proportion to their relative influence compared to other political actors in Japan or to bureaucrats elsewhere.

In fact, however, the assumption that such extensive news coverage merely reflects the role of the bureaucracy in Japan is highly tenuous. In the 1980s, almost all observers of Japanese politics, academics and journalists alike, saw an increasing trend toward more influence by politicians in Japanese policy making.[14] Yet, as we shall see, NHK's news has remained fairly consistent in its more extensive coverage of the bureaucracy.

Furthermore, other aspects of the findings do not seem to fit either the reality or the image of Japan held by Japanese or foreigners. For example, although Japan does have a lower crime rate than the United States and is widely believed to be a less conflictual society, it is also believed to be a society in which courts play only a minor role in resolving disputes, compared to the legalistic and crime-ridden U.S. society. And yet, as we shall see, crimes, scandals, and investigations occupy a surprising percentage of the stories on NHK news, nearly as much as on American news, with the courts featuring as much in NHK coverage as on American network news, and the police more so.[15]

If news organizations must impose a televised "reality" on external reality by making choices in selection and presentation, and if the television news seems to reflect reality in some ways, but not in others, then "reality" cannot be used as an explanation of all that is found on the news. We must look elsewhere for our explanations. Unquestionably, events "out there" define the daily pool of stories that might potentially be presented on the news, but within that very broad and not very helpful limit, "reflections of reality" can-

[14]Discussions of this trend among scholars of Japanese politics may be found in Michio Muramatsu, *Sengo Nihon no kanryōsei* (Tokyo: Toyo Keizai Shimposha, 1981); Michio Muramatsu and Ellis S. Krauss, "Bureaucrats and Politicians in Policymaking: The Case of Japan," *American Political Science Review* 78 (March 1984); Inoguchi Takashi, "Politicians, Bureaucrats and Interest Groups in the Legislative Process," paper presented at the Workshop on One-Party Dominance, Cornell University, April 7–9, 1984; Sato Seizaburo and Matsuzaki Tetsuhisa, "Jimintō etchoki seiken no kaibo," *Chūō Kōron* (November 1984). Even the printed press in Japan has come explicitly to acknowledge this scholarly trend. See "Theories of the LDP's Ascendancy over the Bureaucracy Become Stronger," *Asahi Shimbun* (evening edition), September 14, 1985.

[15]Kobayashi's 1981 study of all NHK programs also found that criminals follow only ordinary citizens and government agencies in numbers of appearances in the news, appearing in almost one out of ten news items in his study. See Kobayashi Yoshiaki, "Terebi nyūsu no hōdō ni kansuru naiyō bunseki," *Keiō Daigaku Hōgaku Kenkyū* 55, no. 9 (September 1982), table 3, p. 35.

not completely explain our findings, which indicate that television news coverage may be at least somewhat independent of the reality it is reporting. This is precisely the conclusion of almost all media studies of the news process conducted in the United States.

No news organization—even one with the great resources and manpower of NHK—can cover everything that happens in society. Choices have to be made concerning what to cover; which stories will be featured on that night's newscast; what priority, order, and time they will be given; and how they will be portrayed visually. In short, we are no longer dealing with reality itself, but with how a news organization has chosen to portray reality. Austin Ranney has cogently restructured the "mirror" metaphor, describing television news as not so much an "electronic mirror" as a "flashlight in the attic," illuminating briefly whatever it shines its beam on and leaving the rest in the dark.[16] The structure and process of news organizations tell us why the beam focuses on which parts of the attic, accounting for many of the characteristics of the news product.

Going beyond the naive assumption that the "media is only the messenger," merely transmitting an objective reality of "news," a stream of scholarly work has emphasized the news as the product of the news organization and process. The titles of some of these works indicate more sophisticated assumptions: it is not *News from Nowhere* that appears on our TV screens nightly, but a question of *Deciding What's News*, of *Putting "Reality" Together*, and sometimes even of *Creating Reality*.[17] In Japan, Michael Reich finds, what gets defined as newsworthy in newspapers is the result of a complex bargaining process within the news company and between it and its sources.[18] A closely related type of media study has concentrated less on the organization and more on the beliefs and norms of individual journalists themselves, including their backgrounds and the formative impact of professional norms on what constitutes "news."[19]

[16]Austin Ranney, *Channels of Power: The Impact of Television on American Politics* (New York: Basic Books, Inc., 1983), 19.

[17]Edward J. Epstein, *News From Nowhere: Television and the News* (New York: Vintage Books, 1973), 172–73; Herbert J. Gans, *Deciding What's News: A Study of CBS Evening News, NBC Nightly News, Newsweek and Time* (New York: Vintage Books, 1980); Philip Schlesinger, *Putting "Reality" Together: BBC News* (Beverly Hills: Sage Publications, 1979); David L. Altheide, *Creating Reality: How TV News Distorts Events* (Beverly Hills: Sage Publications, 1976).

[18]Michael Reich, "Crisis and Routine: Pollution Reporting by the Japanese Press," in George DeVos, ed., *Institutions for Change in Japanese Society* (Berkeley: Institute for East Asian Studies, 1984), 148–65.

[19]Studies of journalists' norms include the work of Gaye Tuchman, for example, "Objectivity as Strategic Ritual: An Examination of Newsmen's Notions of Objectivity," *American Journal of Sociology* 77, no. 4 (1972): 660–79; Philip Elliott, "Professional Ideology and Organizational Change: The Journalist Since 1800," in George Boyce, James Curran, and Pauline

These works are concerned, in other words, with "the effect of the processes of a news organization on the news product"[20] that produces a "structural bias" in the news. Obviously, what does happen in the world defines the universe of potential news stories; within that rather wide sample, however, *which* stories get selected as "news," what priority or non-priority they are given, and how they are presented are very much functions of the information gathering and decision-making process of the news organization. Among the many organizational factors that may help mold that process are the relationships of journalists to their sources, perceptions of the audience and its values and preferences, economic factors, the political and legal environment, the structure of the decision process, the organization's professional ideology, and the shared organizational and professional norms concerning the definition of "news" and of the role of the journalist, among others.

So, our attempt to address why NHK covers politics and government in Japan the way it does must at least include a consideration of the organizational structure of the news division and the news processes of NHK itself, and the norms of what constitutes "news" for the journalists who work there.

SHAPING THE NEWS ORGANIZATION AND PROCESS

But what has shaped the organization that produces the news product? Here the literature in all fields is relatively silent. News organizations form, grow, and are molded by the context in which they operate: similar to all organizations, they are embedded in a web of relationships, structures, norms, and conventions—in other words, an institutional context—that helps determine the nature of that organization and how it operates.

At a time when the movement in all social science disciplines is toward the study of institutions, including a focus on the state as an institution,[21] the media have not been the subject of that attention. This book will analyze

---

Wingate, eds., *Newspaper History* (Beverly Hills: Sage Publications, 1978), 172–91, and also many of the TV news studies cited above.

[20] Epstein, *News From Nowhere*, xvii–xviii.

[21] Kathleen Thelen and Sven Steinmo, "Historical Institutionalism in Comparative Politics," in Sven Steinmo, Kathleen Thelen, and Frank Longstreth, eds., *Structuring Politics: Historical Institutionalism in Comparative Analysis* (Cambridge: Cambridge University Press, 1992): "include both formal organizations and informal rules and procedures that structure conduct"; Walter W. Powell and Paul J. Dimaggio, eds., *The New Institutionalism in Organizational Analysis* (Chicago: University of Chicago Press, 1991), especially the Introduction with its review of the literature in various social science disciplines (1–38); for specifically political applications, see James G. March and Johan Olsen, *Rediscovering Institutions* (New York: Free Press, 1989) and their "The New Institutionalism: Organizational Factors in Political Life," *American Political Science Review* 78, no. 3 (September 1984): 734–49.

NHK and its activities in television news using a "new institutionalist" approach. In the rational choice variant of this approach, the preferences of actors are supplied, intended, and can be rationally deduced, and the strategies adopted to pursue them shaped and constrained by the incentives of the institutional context in which they find themselves.[22] The historical institutional version, by contrast, puts more emphasis on "goals, strategies, and preferences as something to be explained" and sees institutions as also providing actors with "strategic openings" to modify and manipulate institutional procedures, and alternatives that are not obvious from the "rules" themselves.[23] Thus, institutions channel, not determine, behavior; offer strategic opportunities to the skillful, as well as constraints; may contain nonrational elements; and are the product of past choices as much as producing present preferences.

I adopt the latter approach in studying NHK, assuming that actors' incentives are structured by institutions, but that actors' interests also may lead them to attempt to manipulate institutions. I also presume outcomes can be unexpected or may not conform to the ideal preference of any of the actors involved.

The mass media and their relationship to the state has received little attention in any discipline. In political science the almost exclusive concern of media studies has been the media's product and its *effects* on the audience—impact on voter choice in elections and the rise of political cynicism—while ignoring the state's impact on media.[24]

The organizational sociology of mass media also has tended to give relatively little attention to the state, instead focusing on the news organization, process, and personnel, emphasizing the internal organization of news gathering and editing and the political or professional beliefs and norms of journalists and how these affect the product.[25] The state enters in as only a

[22]For a concise description of rational choice in political science and a comparison with the "historical institutionalism" approach, see Kathleen Thelen and Sven Steinmo, "Historical Institutionalism in Comparative Politics," in Steinmo, Thelen, and Longstreth, eds., *Structuring Politics*, 7–10.

[23]Ibid., 9–10; March and Olsen, "The New Institutionalism"; Ellen Immergut, "The Rules of the Game: The Logic of Health Policy-making in France, Switzerland, and Sweden," in Steinmo, Thelen, and Longstreth, eds., *Structuring Politics*, 85; Herbert A. Simon, "Human Nature in Politics: The Dialogue of Psychology with Political Science, *American Political Science Review* 79, no. 2 (June 1985), esp. 302–3.

[24]See, e.g., the collection of articles in Kathleen Hall Jamieson, ed., "The Media and Politics," a special issue of *Annals of the American Academy of Political and Social Science* 546 (July 1996): esp. 34–119.

[25]Epstein, *News from Nowhere;* Gans, *Deciding What's News;* Mort Rosenblum, *Coups and Earthquakes* (New York: Harper Colophon Books, 1981). One might also include here a few of the more perceptive "insider" accounts of the news process, such as Av Westin, *Newswatch* (New York: Simon and Schuster, 1982).

minor part of the general context in which the media organization operates, mostly in terms of how the legal environment of a broadcaster affects its internal routines and news selection or how major events have affected its corporate stance.[26] Much less attention is given to informal and longitudinal influences, including the way specific organizational practices of news gathering and editing may have evolved from interaction with the state.

Journalists have focused on the latter in their studies of press-government relations and the direct relations of journalists with officials, usually emphasizing how reporters try to gain access to stories despite officials' attempts to control information by manipulating, managing, and intimidating news personnel and organizations.[27] If sociological and political science studies have neglected the state to focus on how internal organizational processes produce a news product or how that product affects the audience, journalism has concentrated almost completely on the state's attempted manipulation of reporters without going beyond to see how broader relations with the state may also affect the evolution of the internal organization.

Each discipline then has taken a fragmented and piecemeal approach to the state and the mass media organization. News gathering routines, internal media organization processes and products, and effects have been examined as isolated phenomena. In this book I attempt to see each of these dimensions as part of a broader integrated and institutionalized pattern of historical state-media relations, one that affects the news product and thus the media's impact on a given society, including its effect on the state. Put another way, this study will bring the state back in as *both* an independent and dependent variable, treating the mass media institutions as the crucial intervening variable.

In most nations, the linkage between state and society and between political authorities and citizens is vicarious, mediated by mass communications shaped by media organizations. Analyzing the state and its impact on contemporary society without dealing with the institutional relationship that may contribute most to the state's capacity to influence society seems a bit like discussing food without considering cooking, reproduction without mentioning sex.

---

[26] Epstein, *News from Nowhere;* Tom Burns, *The BBC,* 186–210; Schlesinger, *Putting "Reality" Together,* 14–46, 163–204. The latter, BBC-related works come closest, but also tend to concentrate on the influence of legal restrictions or public events such as Reith and the 1926 General Strike.

[27] Most obvious, during the Nixon administration: Carl Bernstein and Bob Woodward, *All the President's Men* (New York: Warner Books, 1974); Timothy Crouse, *The Boys on the Bus* (New York: Ballantine Books, 1972); but also Mark Hertsgaard, *On Bended Knee* (New York: Farrar Straus & Giroux, 1988), and many others before and since. In Britain, see, e.g., Michael Cockerell, *Live from Number 10* (London: Faber and Faber, 1988).

Mass media are the major societal institutions that may help or hinder state actors in propagating an ideology, enhancing their autonomy, and increasing their capacity to act vis-à-vis society. How and how successfully do state actors attempt to manage such important institutions and enhance state goals? How and how successfully are media actors able to resist state institutions to serve independent purposes? How has the relationship between state and media organizations over time affected the development of the media's organization and of institutionalized linkages between the media and the state? How have these relationships contributed to the molding of what citizens learn about political authority? These are but a few of the questions that have been given short shrift in the state-society literature but which will be among the issues addressed in this book.

Most studies of state-society linkages have concentrated on the state's relations with private economic organizations. Yet in terms of economic and social impact, public service organizations, such as public broadcasting organizations, occupy an important and interesting relationship in state-society relations. Chartered by the state for public purposes, yet ostensibly independent of the state, public service organizations have an intentionally ambivalent role as non-nationalized but also noncommercial organs, seemingly bridging the division between public and private. This duality would appear to make them interesting vehicles for advancing our knowledge about the democratic state and its capacity to affect society.

How does the state influence the media organization? All states regulate, and to a certain extent state actors attempt to control or manipulate, their mass media organizations. Because the media divulge information they consider detrimental to state goals, or to their own organizational and personal status, state actors usually desire protection from media scrutiny. Its popularity, immediacy, audio and/or visual impact, and limited number of channels[28] gives over-the-air broadcasting the greatest potential to reach the widest and least segmented audience with the most immediate results. It therefore also has the greatest potential influence on most citizens' values, attitudes, and perceptions. For these reasons, state actors have tended to see it as the most potentially influential and threatening of organizations, providing the greatest incentives for regulation and interference.

---

[28]I am hypothesizing here a direct relationship between the extent to which a particular medium is "mass" and the degree to which the state is motivated to regulate it: states have less motivation to regulate (in terms of access and content) media whose individual organizations have the narrowest or most segmented audience than those with a wider and less segmented audience. Thus, broadcasting (and television more than radio because of the greater scarcity of channels) will be more regulated than newspapers, which will be more regulated than film, books, videocassettes, or the Internet.

What distinguishes democratic states are the limits placed on the owner-ship and/or control of media organizations and the norms or legal bound-aries that inhibit state actors' ability to intervene in the process and prod-uct of the media. Different democratic states have established a multitude of devices for drawing the boundaries between mass media organizations and the state's powers of control and interference. The questions become: What limits? What norms or legal boundaries? And how effective are these in creating autonomous media organizations in practice? These boundaries themselves may become subjects of contention.

All is not conflict and tension, however, for also built into the interfacing roles of state and media actors is a mutual dependency. The media in its news function need to acquire and disseminate information that state actors possess, while state actors need the news media to broadcast information to build support for their policy preferences and regime. Media organizations also depend on the state for the legal and sometimes financial framework within which they operate, while the state often may require the media or-ganization, especially broadcasting, for the development of telecommuni-cations systems, industries, or products the state considers a priority for eco-nomic, defense, or other reasons.

One of the most crucial political dilemmas of the modern democratic state is how to ensure both a free expression of information through the au-tonomy of mass media organizations and their accountability to the public, in whose name and for whose purposes they are supposed to operate. Insti-tutions that need some autonomy to serve the public's interests may also have to be controlled on behalf of the public.

This dilemma is acute in the case of public broadcasters. The democratic state is supposed to be society's only authoritative agent pursuing the col-lective interests of citizens. The establishment of a non-state body with the same primary function to serve the public, but also bearing enormous con-sequences for the self-interests of those who run the state, immediately es-tablishes a potential conflict of interests and jurisdiction between the state and the public broadcaster.

Much of the political science literature on the state and the private sec-tor looks primarily at the formal process of policy formation from the per-spective of the state, rather than at indirect and informal state influences or its implementation from the perspective of societal actors affected by those policies.[29] Such analyses miss not only the interactive nature of the state-society relationship, but also the possibility both that the state's methods of

[29]Richard Samuels's *The Business of the Japanese State* (Ithaca: Cornell University Press, 1987)—a work that looks equally at business and state interests, formal and behind-the-scenes behavior in energy policy through time—is one of the rare exceptions.

leverage may not be overt and that the affected societal actor may be able to modify or mitigate state intent. Power is not a static characteristic of the state, but always part of a two-way and more dynamic relationship encompassing formal-legal and informal channels.

Japan is a particularly interesting case of both accountability versus autonomy and formal and covert influence issues. Almost all democratic nations have legal prohibitions on state interference with the content of programming and some institutional means of protecting the organizational autonomy of the broadcaster. In Japan, however, this gap between legal ideal and reality is particularly large. The legal and financial arrangements of NHK are the least subject to direct state control of any public broadcaster in the industrialized democracies, and thus NHK should be the most autonomous public broadcaster. It is difficult to understand then why it so uniquely covers the state bureaucracy to such an extent. Clearly, we may have to go beyond formal-legal aspects of institutions to answer these questions.

A growing literature has pointed out the frequent disparity in Japan between formal institutions and informal processes and between legal principles and actual applications: John Owen Haley has focused on "extralegal, informal mechanisms of social control"; Richard J. Samuels has shown how the Ministry of International Trade and Industry (MITI) was willing to trade "jurisdiction for control" in energy policy and to engage in a process of "reciprocal consent" in privatized channels of conflict; Frank K. Upham has analyzed the tendency in Japan to avoid the use of specific laws and litigation in favor of bureaucratic discretion and elite control over the processes of social change and conflict; in the area of the handling of political protest, Susan J. Pharr has found a style of decision making and dealing with protest of "privatizing social conflict"; conceptualizations of Japanese politics as a "network state"[30] often have similar characteristics in mind.

I assume here that if states influence societal organizations, they do not do so by simply mandating laws, policies, and regulations that necessarily ac-

---

[30] John Owen Haley, *Authority without Power: Law and the Japanese Paradox* (New York: Oxford University Press, 1991), 14; Samuels, *Business of the Japanese State*, esp. 258–90; Frank K. Upham, *Law and Social Change in Postwar Japan* (Cambridge: Harvard University Press, 1987), 16–27, for a general statement of the argument; Susan J. Pharr, *Losing Face: Status Politics in Japan* (Berkeley: University of California Press, 1990), 207–31; Daniel I. Okimoto, "Political Inclusivity: The Domestic Structure of Trade," in Takashi Inoguchi and Daniel I. Okimoto, eds., *The Political Economy of Japan*, vol. 2, *International Context* (Stanford: Stanford University Press, 1988), 314. For more cultural approaches, see Takeshi Ishida, "Conflict and Its Accommodation: Omote-Ura and Uchi-Soto Relations," in Ellis S. Krauss, Thomas P. Rohlen, and Patricia G. Steinhoff, eds., *Conflict in Japan* (Honolulu: University of Hawaii Press, 1984), 16–38; and Karel van Wolferen, *The Enigma of Japanese Power* (New York: Alfred A. Knopf, 1989).

complish what state actors intended. Reality is both less and more efficacious. State policies are not always implemented as expected, but state actors may influence society in ways that transcend the formal-legal policy outputs of the state. The actual consequences of state policy depend upon how those policies and the other more informal state influences impinge upon and are handled by the societal organizations affected.

This book's perspective then is that of NHK, with the state treated as one, albeit the primary, dimension of the NHK environment that affects its behavior and organization. We thus will be as interested in NHK's interpretation of its legal mandates as in its formal broadcast policy, in how NHK copes with the state as much as how the latter deals with NHK, and in NHK's strategies as much as those of politicians. Most especially, the state-media relationship will be explored by looking at the central dimensions of the organization over time, processes that are crucial for any organization and that, according to economists and organization theorists, affect outcomes and behavior. These include *resources and production processes* (gathering and editing of information that results in NHK's product, the news); *capital* (how NHK is financed); *management* (especially NHK's chief executive officer, the president); *labor* (personnel structures, policies, and labor-management relations); *technology* (new media development and strategy); *and markets* (changing competition in television news).[31] These are the aspects of organization that matter to NHK and are crucial for its operation and survival. If the state actually influences the behavior and outputs of NHK, it is upon these dimensions that it will exert such influence, formally and informally, directly and indirectly. It is here we will find the answers to our questions about the state-media relationship and about the nature of NHK's news coverage.

This book is about the way in which state and journalistic institutions combine to produce a particular mass media product that in turn has important consequences for the capabilities of the state. In the process of exploring this theme, we will see how Japanese citizens formed images and gained knowledge about their state through NHK television news; how the state directly and indirectly, formally and informally, has tried to influence its activities despite and because of democratic legal prohibitions against political interference; how the media organization has coped with these attempted influences; and how this two-way relationship has affected the news and thus the state's legitimacy. The extent to which, and how, NHK television news has contributed to the state's authority vis-à-vis society is the result—sometimes

---

[31] See, e.g., North, *Structure and Change*, 4–5.

not the intended result for either party—of the way NHK's relationship with the state has affected its organizational structure and processes.

Through this study of a critical Japanese organization at a particular time and place in postwar political history, we are reminded again that the people who serve in such organizations and pursue its best interests must inevitably perform dual roles as victims and perpetrators of that politics and that history.

Part I

THE BROADCASTING

OF POLITICS

CHAPTER 2

Portraying the State

In this sense publishers and broadcast licensees are telling the exact truth when they excuse their poor performance with the plea that they give the public what it wants. It wants symbols and not news. . . .

The themes a society emphasizes and re-emphasizes about its government may not accurately describe its politics; but they do at least tell us what men want to believe about themselves and their state.

—MURRAY EDELMAN, *The Symbolic Uses of Power*

NHK is not an organ of opinion [*genron kikan*]; it is a news organ that transmits the facts as they are.

—FORMER NHK PRESIDENT MAEDA YOSHINORI QTD.
IN YAMAMOTO BUHEI, *NHK Kokueika no inbō*

What does the average Japanese viewer see and hear about political authority when she turns on her television set to watch NHK's 7 P.M. news, the flagship program of the most watched and trusted television news network in Japan? How has the state[1] been portrayed on NHK television news, and how typical or unique has that portrayal been compared to broadcasting in the other industrialized democracies?

I focus on the extent to which the state actors and activities are covered, and how—visually, orally, and in terms of news style—Japan's citizens received and still receive from NHK news an image of government and pub-

---

Portions of this chapter first appeared in different form in Ellis S. Krauss, "Portraying the State: NHK Television News and Politics in Japan," in Susan J. Pharr and Ellis S. Krauss, eds., *Media and Politics in Japan* (Honolulu: University of Hawaii Press, 1996), 89–129.

[1] The state can be conceived of both broadly, as all public officials involved in making and implementing authoritative policy, or narrowly as only the executive and national bureaucracy. See Eric A. Nordlinger, *On the Autonomy of the Democratic State* (Cambridge: Harvard University Press, 1981), 10. I explore news coverage of both in this book.

lic affairs quite different from that of viewers elsewhere in the democratic world. In this stringently neutral and noninterpretive image, the state is ubiquitous and its bureaucracy more omnipresent than any other aspect of the state.

The 7 P.M. news is the most widely watched news on NHK. Its ratings place it among the network's most-watched programs and as one of the two most viewed in Japan. Between the early 1960s and mid-1980s, it was by far the dominant news program in Japan. In the early 1980s, its average weekday ratings (proportion of all potential viewers) topped 15 percent, and its audience share (proportion of viewers watching TV at that time) was between 33 and 39 percent during one of the most popular prime time slots. It consistently listed among the top 10 NHK programs broadcast on its general channel and among the 20 most watched shows on Japanese television in greater Tokyo. No commercial network's evening news approached its ratings until the late 1980s.[2]

All NHK personnel I interviewed asserted that the 7 P.M. news was the core news program, usually comparing it, in pre-CNN days, to the evening news on American networks. The rest of the day's news slots were mainly news "briefs," which appeared during working hours. Two were longer and termed "news shows" to distinguish them from regular news programs: the 7–8:30 A.M. *Morning Wide* show, and *News Center 9 P.M.* (often referred to as *NC9*).[3] These two news shows, however, existed *because* the 7 P.M. news was central: *Morning Wide* and *NC9* differentiated themselves from the 7 P.M. news format, and they assumed the centrality of the latter as the "flagship" and "straight news" program for NHK. The news process existed primarily for the 7 P.M. news, and around it much of the day's news flow revolved.

A "TYPICAL" 7 P.M. NEWS PROGRAM

To give the flavor of the of the 7 P.M. news, I briefly describe a broadcast from the night of August 22, 1996.

[2]NHK HYC, *Terebi-rajio bangumi shichōritsu chōsa: Zenkoku-sōbetsu kekka hyō* (*Television, Radio Programs Audience Rate Survey: Charts of Findings Nationwide and by Strata*), November 1982, pp. 8, 42–50, 71. See also NHK HBCK, "Shichōritsu dēta bukku 90, shiryōhen" ("Audience Ratings Databook 90—Edited Documents"), March 1991, a document for internal use at NHK, pp. 8–11, 70–71, and 160–61. Yoron Chōsabu Shichōritsu Renzoku Chōsa Gurūpu, "Haru no bangumi kaihen to shichō jōgen" ("The Spring Program Revisions and the Audience Situation"), *HKTC* (August 1984), tables 2–10, pp. 33–37.

[3]See chapter 8. NHK journalists considered the similarly rated morning program to be the news people watched while doing something else. Surveys confirm this. See Yoron Chōsabu, "Spring Program Revisions," fig. 6, p. 39, and Fujiwara Norimichi and Miya Eiko, "Terebi hōdō was dō uketomerarete iru ka" ("How Have You Been Reacting to Television News—From a 'Television and the News' Survey"), *HKTC* (July 1987), figs. 5, 7, pp. 5, 6.

Dominating the news are scandals, particularly that involving the much vaunted Japanese bureaucracy and pharmaceutical firms that knowingly sold untreated blood products even though safer, heated products were available. Disasters, especially an epidemic of E. coli (0-157 strain) food poisonings, also receive a good deal of attention. It is a depressing but certainly not an undramatic or uninteresting time.

The 7 P.M. news, probably in conscious emulation of BBC practice, begins with a clock on the screen at five seconds before the hour. A syncopated, ticking music plays as the second hand sweeps up to the hour. As it does, the clock dissolves into a slick computer graphic of a globe, accompanied by a lively tune replete with trumpets, and "News 7" is superimposed over the graphic, which then disappears to reveal a pleasant, average-looking Japanese woman. She wears a conservative white, collarless suit and sits behind a desk in a modern but featureless studio set softly lit in tan, blue, and green pastels. A large metal and glass globe, close to her left hand, slowly revolves.

The announcer bows and tells the viewers that it is Thursday, August 22. The program begins with brief descriptions, accompanied by video clips, of the day's headline stories. As she introduces each one, a small window in the upper right-hand corner of the screen displays a still picture or graphic with the subject of the story beneath it. Set aside the bow, the written characters below the story pictures, and perhaps substitute a "working newsroom" backdrop popular in several countries, and this could be TV news almost anywhere.

After the headlines, the announcer returns to the lead story of the day. The first half of the program contains ten segments. In the top three stories tonight, the governor of Miyagi Prefecture announces new measures to prevent misappropriation of public funds by officials and punitive action against those who falsified travel expense reports; public prosecutors assert that the Green Cross pharmaceutical company told its salespeople to sell its unheated blood products despite the risk of AIDS infection and the availability of a treated substitute, and officials carry out a second raid for documents on the company's offices; and a Sanyo Corporation executive kidnapped in Mexico returns to Japan, with the Baja California police chief saying that arrests of his kidnappers are imminent.

The items continue:

- Prime Minister Ryutaro Hashimoto visits Mexico and meets with the Mexican president;
- Hatoyama Yukio, a young politician from a famous political family, is dissatisfied with party leaders' proposals to form a new party and is threatening to bolt the Sakigake (Harbinger) party;

- Minister of Health Kan visits Osaka Prefecture to discuss with the local officials the continuing investigation of food poisoning that contaminated school lunches;
- a Ministry of Education advisory council report proposes that school lunches be examined twice a year for contamination;
- a food service association holds an emergency session to discuss countermeasures to prevent a further decline in sales following the outbreak;
- police report a five-year-old girl, left unattended in a parking lot, was killed by a hit-and-run driver while her mother played pachinko, and the measures that pachinko parlor operators are taking;
- a high Liberal Democratic Party (LDP) official reports that there is no need for the LDP secretary-general, Katō Kōichi, to attend an investigation by the Ethics Committee of the House of Representatives into allegations of his receiving illegal contributions.

Almost all these items relate to scandals, accidents, and incidents involving Japanese at home or abroad. Several characteristics of major news stories are noteworthy. First, almost all involve political authority: cabinet officials, elected and appointed local government officials, political party leaders, bureaucratic advisory councils, public prosecutors, police. These public authorities—as well as any private groups shown—are involved in responding to problems, scandals, and incidents. Second, the visuals show those public or private sector association officials in meetings, going into meetings, or holding discussions or press conferences, though often the voices of the speakers are not heard.

Finally, the narrative is strikingly neutral in tone and content. Factual description characterizes the presentation. Even the reporters on location seem lacking in distinctive personality: they supply bland commentaries about the situation or problem. Unlike their counterparts elsewhere, they provide no undertone of skepticism, no interpretation for the audience, and add little sense of color, depth, or alternative perspective to the facts of the story.[4]

Are these impressions merely subjective? Have we become so accustomed to news served up by attractive anchors and wisecracking reporters, around whose personalities the program revolves, and so habituated to dramatic and often violent visuals that these differences seem greater than they really are? Quantitative data below helps answer these questions.

---

[4]To see how little has changed since the early 1980s, compare this description with the one on 1983 programs in Ellis S. Krauss, "Portraying the State in Japan: NHK Television News and Politics in Japan," in Susan J. Pharr and Ellis S. Krauss, eds., *Media and Politics in Japan* (Honolulu: University of Hawaii Press, 1996), 93–96.

COVERAGE OF GOVERNMENT AND POLITICS

What do Japanese viewers see and hear about public affairs on NHK news? Is it different from what earlier postwar generations experienced? After all, television news in many countries has been altered recently, at least in style and sometimes in content, in response to changes in technology, market competition, and audience tastes.

My first sample of programs is from four weeks of weekday broadcasts, 10 programs in August 1996 and nine in April 1997.[5] These programs contained 322 separate items, an average of almost 17 per program.

I also analyzed a sample of weekday programs from the early 1980s: a three-week period in June–July 1983, a total of 15 programs, and 10 weekday programs from January 16 to January 29, 1985. This five-week sample contained 365 separate news segments (193 in 1983, 172 in 1985). The average number of items per broadcast changed; in 1983 about 12–13 real news items took a bit more than 23 minutes of a slightly longer total program (I omitted sports and weather). By 1985, the 7 P.M. news format had been revamped to allow for more but shorter news items: an average of more than 17 per daily newscast.

Each sample contains a period when the Japanese parliament, the National Diet, was in session, and a period when it was not. In the 1996 sample, the Diet was not in full session, and there were only six stories about it, mostly about the Ethics Committee hearings. The 1997 sample, by contrast, contained more than 20 stories about the Diet, including debate about the American military in Okinawa, organ transplants and the legal definition of death, and health care.

In the 1983 sample period there were no plenary sessions of the Diet. In the only real political news, the Socialist Party was in the preliminary stages of finding a new chairman. The 1985 sample encompasses a more politically active period. The Diet was in session; the most important Diet story was the resignation of the Speaker of the House of Representatives and the appointment of his successor. Moreover, the Japan Socialist Party and the ruling Liberal Democratic Party were holding their annual conventions.

[5]The specific dates of the analysis were the 10 weekday programs between August 19 and August 23, and August 26 and August 30, 1996, and the nine programs between April 7 and April 11, April 14 to 16, and April 18, 1997. Unfortunately, technical difficulties prevented us from receiving the April 17 program. John Nylin, then a student at my school, conducted the initial analysis under my supervision for both periods. I checked his work to ensure that the procedures and definitions followed were consistent with the intent of the analysis and my own categorizations. Consistency across samples is more important than any unattainable exact, objective measurement of the data.

In presenting data on the NHK 7 P.M. news, I occasionally make comparisons to U.S. television news. Such comparisons are inexact: the American networks are commercial broadcasters, and the United States is a presidential, not a parliamentary, system. The U.S. data do not allow us to judge the uniqueness or universality of NHK news. Nevertheless, American news is, most likely, the news most familiar to readers of this book, so it is useful for illustrative purposes.

How much attention and time are devoted to news about politics and government in general—to the state in its broadest conception? Listed below are the percentages of items for stories related to different categories of subjects during the two sample periods. Stories could be classified in up to two, but no more than two, categories; because of multiple codings, the totals add up to more than 100 percent:[6]

	Politics/ Government	Society	Economy	Foreign/ Defense
1996/97	52%	55%	17%	30%
1983/85	53%	56%	13%	27%

The samples were separated by 11–14 years and conducted at various times of the year. The extent of political activity varied, yet there are only minor differences in type of subjects covered and time devoted to them. The similarities are remarkable. In both sampling periods, slightly more than half of the items each related to politics and government and to society. Stories involving foreign countries or national defense ran a distant third. Least frequent were items related to economics (including business and labor, as well as general economic trends and events).

To appreciate the remarkable visibility of the state on the evening news, however, we must look more closely at stories in other categories. In "society" stories, for example, 52 percent in 1983 and 45 percent in 1985 had some connection to politics and government. Only about half of the total items during these weeks were "purely" about society. By 1996–97, the percentage of society items also involving government drops to 40 percent, nonetheless still a substantial proportion.

In the case of economics stories, the role of government and politics is even greater in 1983: nearly two-thirds of the stories involving economics also involved politics or government, although in the later samples the per-

---

[6]The "politics/government" category was defined to include stories involving governmental authority, thus national or local governmental officials, politicians, processes, or decisions, opposition or protest related to these, courts and police, and elections. The "society" category included the activities, interactions, problems, or concerns of individuals or groups not normally engaged in political or governmental activities.

centage drops significantly to 30 percent in 1985, and then to 22 percent by 1996–97. Similarly, about a quarter (1983) to two-fifths (1985 and 1996–97) of the items devoted to foreign countries or defense matters also had connections to Japanese government and politics.

The state is very salient in NHK's news, and although its salience had decreased in stories about society and especially about economics by the 1990s, it remains a formidable presence in reporting about nonpolitical news events.

POLITICAL ACTORS AND ACTIVITIES

When portraying state actors, who is featured? Is it the elected politicians, the "core" state of national executive and bureaucracy, local officials, or the criminal justice system of courts and the police? Figure 4 shows all items grouped into 11 subcategories of subjects related to governmental authority. Each item's content could be counted in up to three subcategories, and so percentages add to more than 100 percent. The prime minister and the cabinet, the "government" or "executive leadership" in a parliamentary regime, are found in less than 15 percent of each sample. The National Diet is the subject of 9 percent of items in the earlier sample and 16 percent in the 1996/97 sample. Coverage of political parties and their factions increases from one-fifth to one-third of the number of items. Elections, local government, courts, and police each account for less than 15 percent of each sample.

It is striking that in both samples the national bureaucracy accounts for the largest proportion of political subjects, appearing in 35–38 percent of all items about government and politics. In addition, nearly all advisory councils are attached to bureaucratic ministries and agencies and are designed to give "expert" advice to the administrative arm of government; they appear in 5–14 percent of items. Add the advisory councils category to the bureaucracy group—there was little overlap in these categorizations—and the proportion of items increases to nearly one half in 1983/85 and more than two-fifths in 1996/97. The national bureaucracy, with or without its affiliated advisory councils, was and continues to be the most salient political subject covered on NHK television news.

Another major focus of public affairs stories, policy change, was seen in 16 percent (1980s) to 28 percent (1990s) of items. Here too bureaucracy is involved in 37 percent of such stories, compared to 27 percent for political parties and politicians, 12 percent for the Diet, and only 2 percent for the prime minister.

In this disproportionate focus on the national bureaucracy, NHK political coverage differs substantially from that of U.S. networks. I reanalyzed

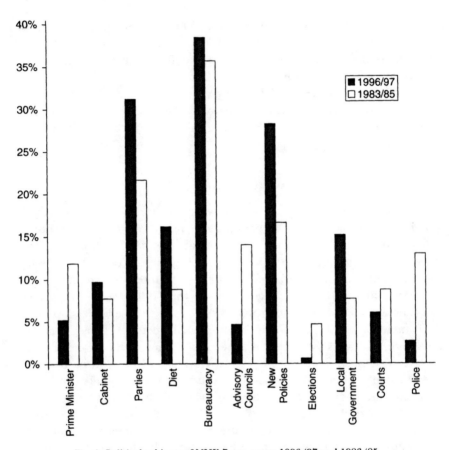

Fig. 4. Political subjects of NHK 7 P.M. news: 1996/97 and 1983/85.

one month of data on ABC's evening news coverage from a 1976 study conducted by Doris Graber, recalculating these data into the categories used for
the NHK data.[7] I found little or no substantial difference in general subjects
in the news and both covered government and politics extensively.[8] The two

[7] Doris A. Graber, *Mass Media and American Politics* (Washington, D.C.: Congressional Quarterly Press, 1980), table 3-2, pp. 66–67; this same table also appears in the second edition
(1984), pp. 82–83; raw data courtesy of Professor Graber. The NHK data are for a three-week
period, July–August 1983, week nights only; the ABC data are for a month, December 1976.
The N is the total number of categorizations in this sample. The ABC data are a percentage
of mentions of the domestic political topics for the month's national evening news programs.
The N is the total number of mentions in this sample, with up to three possible. Despite the difference between "mentions" and "categorizations," because both allowed for multiple classification, it is roughly equivalent. A more detailed analysis of this comparison can be found in
Ellis S. Krauss, "Portraying the State," table 3.1, pp. 99–100.

[8] Almost exactly: politics and government (45 percent on both), followed by economics,
society, and other stories as a combined category (39 percent on both), and least of all to for-

networks differ enormously, however, on stories related to the bureaucracy. Only 2 percent of U.S. news stories involved the bureaucracy; instead, predominant attention is given to the president and his cabinet (41 percent of total political mentions). Thus, broadcast news focuses the most attention on the executive "core" of the state in both countries and makes it central to news coverage. In the United States, however, that core is the chief executive, an elected politician; in Japan, it is the national bureaucracy.

Other data confirm this finding. Kobayashi Yoshiaki conducted a content analysis of several NHK news programs and those of commercial stations in Japan in 1981 and found that NHK covered domestic politics and government, particularly bureaucratic agencies, more than the commercial stations, but society and individual citizens less.[9] The great emphasis on the bureaucracy in Japan may be an integral aspect of NHK coverage of politics.

Another way to analyze news content is by kinds of activities portrayed. In 1967, Herbert J. Gans analyzed a month of CBS evening news in this way. I classified my NHK data according to the types of activities in Gans's sample. NHK data for 1983 and 1996/97 and the U.S. comparison data are found in figure 5.[10] Most of the categories show only a few differences: the U.S. news pays a bit more attention to crimes, scandals, and investigations, and to births, weddings, and deaths. Some differences appear in two categories related to conflict: U.S. news gives greater attention to conflict both within the government and against the government and in society (protests and strikes). The 1983 NHK news paid a lot more attention to the unusual and bizarre, and this is due to the existence of a regular feature in the middle of each 1983 NHK news program entitled "naigai no wadai" (domestic and foreign themes), which featured unusual human interest stories from Japan and abroad.

By far, the greatest difference is in the category of "government decisions, proposals, and ceremonies." Nearly two of every five NHK news stories in 1983 and in 1996/97 featured these basic state activities—at least three

eign affairs (about 16 percent on both, although the NHK category also included defense-related stories, it is not clear whether ABC's did, too).

[9]Kobayashi Yoshiaki, "Terebi nyūsu no hōdō ni kansuru naiyō bunseki," *Keiō Daigaku Hōgaku Kenkyū* 55, no. 9 (September 1982), 32ff. NHK also focused more on the government rather than the individual in stories about the prime minister.

[10]Herbert J. Gans, *Deciding What's News: A Study of CBS Evening News, NBC Nightly News, Newsweek and Time* (New York: Vintage Books, 1980), table 4, p. 16. Gans's data categories appear to be mutually exclusive, whereas in the NHK analysis, it was possible for the same item to appear in up to three categories (although most actually fit into one or two at the most) and thus adding up to more than 100 percent. The CBS sample was 392 news stories; the NHK 1983 sample, 143 news stories; and 1996/97 was 283 news stories, in all cases domestic stories only. A similar analysis on the 1985 NHK data also showed little change in the basic proportions and rankings on these dimensions.

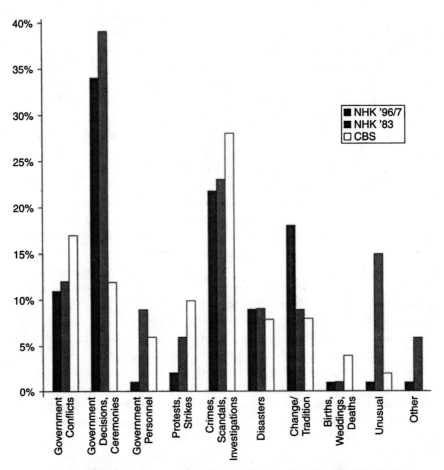

Fig. 5. Types of activities in the news: NHK, 1996/97 and 1983; CBS, 1967.

times as much attention as on U.S. news! Whether one analyzes the subjects or the activities in the news, NHK's coverage in both the 1990s and the 1980s focused disproportionately on the government, especially on the national bureaucracy and the decision-making process.

Priority Stories

The order in which stories are presented further demonstrates the major role played by the core bureaucratic state on NHK evening news. Thirty-five headline stories appeared during the three weeks analyzed in 1983, 58 in the four weeks in 1996/97, for an average of two to three per program. The announcer mentions these stories at the outset of the program and a brief headline is displayed, the equivalent of "page one" stories in a newspaper. Approximately four out of every five such stories in both 1983/85 and more than half of them in 1996/97 involved politics and government. Of these, 48 percent in 1996/97, 32 percent in 1985, and 36 percent in 1983 involved the bureaucracy, the largest proportion of all the political actors, and 18 percent in 1983 and 14 percent in 1985 involved bureaucratic advisory councils, with none appearing in 1996/97.

A look at the relative rank of the stories in the program reveals a similar emphasis. The first segment on almost all programs in 1983 (93 percent) and 1985 (100 percent), and 79 percent in 1996/97, was about the state. Such stories appeared in the second segment in 84 percent of the broadcasts in 1996/97, 80 percent in 1983, and 70 percent in 1985. In each case, this was a much higher proportion than societal, economic, or foreign and defense items.

Political Party Bias?

Were particular political parties favored in coverage? Of the stories involving political parties in 1983, 25 percent concerned primarily the LDP only, 37.5 percent the opposition parties primarily (just the Japan Socialist Party in this sample), 31 percent both government and opposition parties, and 6 percent smaller parties in the upper house. Activities related to the selection of a new Socialist party chairman during this period undoubtedly accounts for the slightly greater coverage given to the opposition parties. In 1985, primarily LDP stories composed 39 percent; primarily opposition parties stories, 35 percent (of which half were about the Socialists, half about other opposition parties); and 26 percent involved both. The situation was complicated in 1996/97 because two former opposition parties, the Social Democratic Party of Japan and the Sakigake (Harbinger) Party, were in actual or de facto coalition with the LDP. Nevertheless, results reveal no major bias in terms of party combinations. Although the LDP alone featured in twice as many stories as the opposition by itself, the overwhelming number of items involved more than one party, with almost exactly the same number of stories about the coalition as about all the parties, including the opposition.

Thus, I found no consistent bias in extent of coverage in favor of the governing party or the opposition parties. This is a finding confirmed by the 1981 Kobayashi study of NHK and Japanese commercial networks.[11] This study found that NHK gave more equal treatment to the LDP and opposition parties than did the commercial networks and was the *only* network to cover all the political parties. Kobayashi's sample, it should be noted, included *all* news programs on each station and was not confined to the main

[11]Kobayashi, "Terebi nyūsu no hōdō," 35–36.

evening news programs. This study, combined with our findings, offers substantial reason to believe that NHK television news is quite even-handed in the extent of its coverage both of government and opposition parties and of the ruling party and its coalition partners.

Images of the State and the Journalist

Going beyond the extent of coverage, how are political subjects treated? Are specific actors portrayed in particular ways? Are there common themes associated with public affairs news? And what is the journalist's approach to political actors?

We see the most ubiquitous national actor, the bureaucracy, formulating rather than implementing policy. Coverage emphasizes the public rituals involved in the process of making goals and rules for society. Although reporters sometimes speculate about the implications of decisions, these consequences are rarely shown. Politicians and government officials are usually not depicted as individuals or in spontaneous situations. Rather, they are shown almost invariably in a group context, giving speeches in meetings, meeting in a group or as representatives of groups in the performance of their official roles, and carrying out ritual activities, such as ceremonies.

The bureaucratic state is portrayed as guardian of the public's interests, taking care of problems, considering new policy or changing old policy, or pursuing the culprits of scandal or criminal activity.

As the theme of a story, conflict, such as disagreement between parties or bureaucratic agencies, protests, strikes, or crime, is not uncommon—if less common than in U.S. news. The state is almost inevitably portrayed as moving to solve or manage such conflict: party leaders meet to try to resolve a stalemate in the Diet over legislation, a bureaucratic agency issues a warning to the public about a problem, an advisory council presents a report recommending changes to the law, or the police capture a suspect and take him into custody.

Journalists' approach to political news is in most cases strictly factual, straight descriptions of what occurred, accompanied by a bit of background. Often appearing at the bottom of the screen is a concise sentence summarizing the news item's content. In cases where an advisory committee presents a report, a bulleted list of the major points will be presented. Reporters provide less commentary from location than on U.S. network news. Announcers narrate many stories in voice-over. This is especially the case in stories concerning meetings of governmental bodies. Few governmental actors are interviewed or speak in their own voice on camera.

Viewers are not aware of the reporter as an individual professional with a personality mediating between the audience and a source or functioning as a representative of the viewer, as in American television news.[12] On NHK news, an omniscient but extremely neutral and impersonal narrator states just the facts of the story. Only occasionally does either the journalist or the source become an individual personality speaking in their own voice. Reporters give comments or analysis in only a minority of stories—about 10 percent in 1996/97. The percentage of commentary or analysis on items concerning government and politics is even less (8 percent).

In NHK's news coverage of public affairs, both in the 1980s and 1990s, government administrative agencies as active agents of the public represents the most dominant theme and the highest priority story, and these stories are treated in an extremely factual, neutral, and impersonal way.

VISUALS

Television is a visual medium, and much of its power lies in its ability to communicate events, impressions, and symbols through images. Yet too many analyses treat television news as if it were only a narrative, ignoring its potential visual impact.

I analyzed and summarized the visual images telecast in each story of the samples, and from this description I classified type of visuals. I used four general categories of visuals, each containing several specific visual types:[13]

1. *Nonmoving visuals:* still photos of people; graphics (e.g., cartoons); still photos or videos of building exteriors.
2. *Moving visuals of staged action:* journalists reporting; people entering or leaving a building; people posing for cameras; speeches and various kinds of meetings; press conferences; and interviews.
3. *Moving visuals of limited action:* Ordinary scenes or activities from daily life; unusual or bizarre activities or scenes.
4. *Moving visuals of drama, conflict, or violence:* arrests or scenes involving courts or crime evidence; armed forces or weapons not in combat; dra-

---

[12]See Daniel C. Hallin and Paolo Mancini, "Speaking of the President," *Theory and Society* 13, no. 6 (November 1984): esp. 839–44.

[13](1) "Nonmoving visuals" portray people and events statically, without human action. (2) "Staged action" visuals portray people and events in action, but in contrived situations purposely arranged in advance. This type of television visual has sometimes been called "pseudo-events" or "medialities" because they might not have occurred in the same way, or at all, had the cameras and reporters not been present. (3) "Limited action" visuals show people acting in situations not covered by the preceding category and not involving great drama, conflict, or violence. (4) "Drama, etc." visuals have as their common denominator the showing of confrontation and tension with and without actual violence. On "pseudo-events" see for example, Austin Ranney, *Channels of Power: The Impact of Television on American Politics* (New York: Basic Books, Inc., 1983), 22–23; Timothy Crouse, *The Boys on the Bus: Riding with the Campaign Press Corps* (New York: Ballentine Books, 1972), 149–50.

matic but nonviolent scenes; nonviolent conflict or confrontation, such as protests, debates, or altercations; and actual violence, brutality, or combat or their consequences.

The visuals used in each of the news items were classified in up to three of the types above. All but four of the 322 items in the 1996/97 sample and all but seven of the 193 news items in the 1983 sample, contained a visual. Usually this included the use of videotape or film. Thus, NHK evening news is quite visual and does not have as many of the frequent "tell" stories found each evening in U.S. network news, when the anchorperson merely reads a short news item without an accompanying videotape.

In the 1996/97 sample, 25 percent of all items contained a nonmoving visual, the least exciting form of visual portrayal, with another 30 percent involving moving visuals of limited action. By far, the most common type of visual, however, was the staged event, comprising 61 percent of all the classifications. The least frequent type of visual was related to drama, conflict, or violence: 12 percent were in this category. Half of these were found in foreign, not domestic, stories, for example, the Japanese hostage crisis in Peru, a terrorist bombing abroad, the hijacking of an airline in Sudan, or an oil spill from a Korean tanker. In domestic news, four out of five dramatic visuals appeared in society segments, usually those concerning arrests, courts, or crime evidence or natural or human-made disasters or accidents. Another study also has found that, compared with Japan's commercial networks, NHK emphasized visuals least and talk most.[14]

Drama enters into visuals related to politics or government news items as little or even less than it does in other themes. Items related to the Japanese state contained a higher proportion of staged visuals (77 percent), and a lower proportion of dramatic or conflictual visuals (7 percent) than in the sample as a whole.

The most common type of visual used in stories about government and politics depicts meetings. Nearly half (47 percent) of all the domestic political classifications involved videos of meetings in progress or their participants sitting around a table, of visits of a person or delegation to meet another person, and of speeches being made at formal meetings. Other staged events, such as interviews, were also quite common.

By far the most frequent single subcategory of conflictual visual involving politics or government related to crime or courts. Usually, however, what is depicted is not crime per se, or its consequences, but rather prosecutors dramatically raiding an office building and hauling off boxes of evidence, or a

---

[14]Kobayashi, "Terebi nyūsu no hōdō," 37, 40–41.

criminal suspect being arrested, or a defendant in or coming into or out of court. Twelve of the 21 classifications in this category included these kinds of scenes.

Finally, the data indicate a disparity between the content of political news items and their visual portrayal. According to our analysis of the activities in the 1996/97 news sample, nearly a third of all items involved some sort of conflict: governmental conflicts and disagreements; protests or strikes; and crimes, scandals, or investigations. Only 7 percent of all items, however, and only a bit more than half of the items classified in those categories, had dramatic or conflictual visuals. The translation of conflictual political items to the screen loses the drama inherent in the events.

Comparing visual patterns at NHK to U.S. news is difficult as most content analyses of U.S. news focus on the story contents rather than the pictures. However, all analyses of U.S. network news have emphasized that one of the chief criteria for selecting national news in the United States is the value placed upon drama, conflict, and violence, especially when videos of these are available. Gans, for example, found that stories about citizen versus government combined with intragovernmental conflict were the most frequent items portrayed in the news, and Graber argues that one of the most important elements of U.S. media "newsworthiness" is *"violence, conflict, disaster, or scandal."*[15] Producers of U.S. network news assume "that the home audience is more likely to be engrossed by visual action than a filmed discussion of issues, or 'talking heads,' and so they place high value on action film," with "visually identifiable opponents clashing violently" as the best type of action film.[16] One unpublished study shows that television is much more likely than local newspapers to cover noncriminal violence.[17] Yet by contrast, although pictorial images accompany almost all NHK news items, the images are not dramatic, but visually staid, staged, or nonconflictual. There is one exception to this visual dissimilarity: foreign news. When violence, conflict, drama, and the military appear, it is often elsewhere, not in Japan: only 7 percent of domestic news items contains a visual with conflictual or dramatic elements. U.S. network news also tends to have the same characteristic.[18]

---

[15]Gans, *Deciding What's News*, 17; Graber, *Mass Media and American Politics*, 63; italics in original.

[16]Edward J. Epstein, *News From Nowhere: Television and the News* (New York: Vintage Books, 1973), 172–73.

[17]Cited in Michael J. Robinson, "Public Affairs Television and the Growth of Political Malaise: The Case of the 'Selling of the Pentagon,'" *American Political Science Review* 70 (June 1976): 428.

[18]Gans, *Deciding What's News*, 35.

THE STATE PORTRAYED

Watching NHK news, the Japanese viewer would have assumed that the media's proper role is to transmit what the state is doing in a staid manner, through scrupulous attention to nonpartisan and neutral conveyance of facts, usually from information derived from official sources. The image of the state that the citizen receives from this kind of coverage is a distinctive one.

The Japanese state is first a *salient* one in that it is omnipresent; involved in most aspects of social and economic life. The typical viewer could not be blamed for receiving the impression that the most important events in his world involved political authority in all of its manifestations and that this authority was interwoven in a seamless web with all other dimensions of society.

Most especially, this omnipresent state was primarily an *administrative* one. It is not the elected leaders—neither representatives nor the nominal heads of state and executive, the prime minister and the cabinet—that dominate the news, as they do in the United States, but the elite national higher civil service, the bureaucracy or its related advisory councils. At the core of the state lies its administrative organs of appointed officialdom and, to a lesser extent, those experts from whom it seeks advice.

The activities of this administrative state, as depicted in the news, are primarily the holding of meetings and rituals and the formulating of policy and goals and rules for society. The state is portrayed as, among other things, a *ritualized rule and decision maker*.

It is also depicted as a *conflict manager*. Conflicts between or among state actors are reported, but with no interpretation beyond that which those actors themselves give to the situation and certainly with no criticism implied. Almost inevitably, some state actor—both representative and, as often as not, administrative—is shown as trying to remedy or control the situation and bring about a change toward unity, consensus, or order.

The state carries out these activities on behalf of the public and is thus presented as a *paternal and active guardian of the public's interests*, taking care of the problems that arise in society. Bureaucracy and advisory councils are constantly shown considering new policy, changing old policy, or pursuing the culprits of scandal or criminal activity. The visual images of criminals almost inevitably in or being taken into custody is one example, as are those depicting a government agency "saving" the average citizen from himself or from unscrupulous others. If, as Edelman argues, one of the functions of politics is as a symbolic "reassurance" ritual,[19] in Japan, television news un-

---

[19] Murray Edelman, *The Symbolic Uses of Politics* (Urbana: University of Illinois Press, 1964), 41–43.

derlines the bureaucratic state performing this function. It is not the journalist who is the watchdog of the public's interests against the state, as American journalists so often like to portray themselves; rather, it is the state itself that acts on behalf of the public, helping to uncover, manage, and
respond to the faults, foibles, and frictions inherent in human society.

Finally, the state—especially its bureaucratic component—is portrayed as
impersonal and collective. Politicians and government officials rarely appear as
private individuals or in spontaneous situations, but instead in the performance of their official roles and usually in the carrying out of a ritual activity.
Typically, they are shown in a group context, giving speeches to meetings,
meeting in a group, or representing groups. Further, whereas the voices of
party politicians and Diet members will sometimes be broadcast in debates,
speeches, or interviews, bureaucrats and advisory council members are generally shown without a soundtrack. This only serves to reinforce the image
of impersonality and individual anonymity of administrative state actors.

It needs to be emphasized that such patterns of coverage and presentation
are not confined to the 1980s and 1990s, even though I do not have content
analysis for earlier periods. There is much evidence that these patterns have
existed at least since the building up of NHK's news services in the early
1960s. First, the reporters and news directors interviewed in the early to mid-
1980s all indicated that the news style and process had not changed since
the 1960s. Indeed, it was the continuance of this very old-fashioned, traditional style of news that prompted dissatisfaction and the desire for change
in some NHK reporters and news executives by the 1970s and 1980s.[20]

Second, even in the 1960s and 1970s, external critics of NHK news were
complaining about the strict neutrality, the lack of criticism of government,
and the "self-regulation in covering events." One magazine survey showed
that NHK news was disliked because it was "turning broadcasting into
official business and siding with the government too much."[21]

Not only was there virtually no difference between coverage in the early
1980s and late 1990s, the evidence is strong that the coverage and style of

[20]There was even some dissatisfaction as early as the 1960s. See "Sokuhō kyōsō" ("News
Flash Competition"), May 9, 1968; "Nyūsu no enshutsu" ("News Production"), *Asahi Shimbun*
May 10, 1968, and pp. 34 and 37 of *AS* series on NHK put together for internal use; the *NHK
terebijyon bangumi seisaku handobukku, 1963* (*NHK TV Program Production Handbook, 1963*)
(Tokyo: NHK, 1963), the basic reference for program production, on p. 235 argues that in
producing news programs, all aspects will "needless to say, be made with speed, properness,
fairness, and public interest," and on p. 236, news editing orders that "no matter what, avoid
adding fixed judgments with a comment (subjectivity)."

[21]"Goyōka shite, seifu no kata o mochisugiru." Minami Shinjirō, "Nayameru kyojin-NHK
no uchimaku" ("Behind the Scenes at the Troubled Giant NHK"), *Bungei Shunjū* (May 1976),
276; see also 288 on "fairness and neutrality," leading to "not saying anything"; and Shiga
Nobuo, *Hadaka no NHK* (Tokyo: Seimondō, 1969), 138, 142, and *Terebi uraomote no jitsuzō* (*The
Real Image of the Both Sides of Television*) (Tokyo: Hakuma Shuppan, 1972), 219, 231–33.

the news broadcasts, and the organization that gathered, edited, and produced them, had not substantially changed since at least the early 1960s. *That is, the findings about NHK news since the early 1980s also represent news programming since the early 1960s and reflect the type of news about the state seen by more Japanese during the postwar period than any other.*

Perhaps the characteristics of NHK 7 P.M. news are different only from U.S. network news with its private broadcasters and its dissimilar journalistic traditions operating in a much different political system. It may be U.S. commercial news that is unique, and NHK's news may well be typical of, for example, public broadcasters in European democracies with parliamentary regimes. Or, perhaps the much greater attention NHK allots to the bureaucracy may be a reflection of the realities of different political systems: the bureaucracy has been generally accepted by many political scientists and Japan experts to be more influential in policy making in Japan than in the United States. We might expect to find more similar coverage of the bureaucracy in European countries where, as in Japan, administrative agencies also play a more active and influential role in the formulation of policy. These issues can only be resolved by comparison.

Comparing NHK's news product to those of other countries also provides us with a start toward explaining the factors that have shaped NHK's news. If NHK's news product is common to all public broadcasters in industrialized democracies, but not to private broadcasters, then universal factors in the relationship between the state and public broadcasters are producing a particular kind of news product. On the other hand, if NHK is more like other industrialized democracies with reputations for strong bureaucracies, then NHK's news product, like theirs, probably just reflects political reality. If the public broadcaster's style and content of news are just like those of commercial broadcasters in Japan but different from those of public broadcasters elsewhere, then idiosyncratic aspects of media organization and journalism in Japan are the likely explanation.

Because of the difficulty of securing samples of television news coverage from several different nations and the tedious and time-consuming nature of content analysis, these comparisons are necessarily to small samples of two to four weeks. The selection of the data was purely random, based on availability of other researchers' work or on access to programs in that country. In each case of comparison, I either recalculated other researchers' data to accord with the categories of my NHK content analysis or conducted a content analysis in the same manner as I had done on NHK news. Thus, while the length of the samples or the time period in which they were conducted may not match exactly,[22] the methods used in the content analysis were as equivalent as I could make them. Although there is no way to determine for certain that the samples are not systematically biased in a particular direction, there is also no apparent reason to suspect that they are.

I first present some general indications, based on other researchers' work, of whether NHK television news is similar to or different from the broadcasters of Italy, Germany, and Sweden. Then I offer a more specific, detailed comparison of French and British public broadcaster news, based on my conducting the same type of content analysis as I did with NHK. I singled out these for more detailed and systematic comparison because France, with its similarly central national bureaucracy, is a key case for ascertaining whether coverage is merely a reflection of the reality of a strong administrative state, and the British Broadcasting Corporation is the public broadcaster NHK most resembles in legal structure and organization. In each case, I use the NHK data from the 1980s or 1990s that are closest in time to the data in the other country.

Italy, Germany, and Sweden

Daniel C. Hallin and Paolo Mancini analyzed one week of the daily newscasts of Italy's public broadcaster, Radiotelevisione Italiana (RAI), noting how it covered important political actors in 1982 and comparing it to U.S. coverage. I included only the domestic coverage of political actors and recalculated their percentages, comparing them to NHK's 7 P.M. news in 1983. Hallin and Mancini combined coverage of the cabinet with a general category of "administration" and I've collapsed several of NHK's more specific categories accordingly for a similar comparison.[23] The results are shown in figure 6. The data show that NHK covers the prime minister more than RAI covers Italy's premier or president, and Parliament somewhat less, but that neither is significant as a proportion of coverage. Parties and the cabinet/administration are the two most covered subjects, but in opposite ways: about 70 percent of RAI's coverage concerns political parties; almost the same proportion on NHK is devoted to the cabinet and all forms of national

[22]Domestic news varies across countries in any case, and thus equivalent time periods are less important than in comparing different countries' media of the same international events.

[23]Daniel C. Hallin and Paolo Mancini, "Speaking of the President," 832. The Italian data are based on 10 newscasts, July 7–11, 1982. See p. 831. "Administration" includes the combined categories from the original NHK analysis—see, for example, figure 4—of bureaucracy, advisory councils, police, courts, and local administration. Because the Italian data were based on mutually exclusive categories, for comparison I used the total number of categorizations, rather than items, as the basis for calculation, thus also enabling the NHK data to total 100 percent.

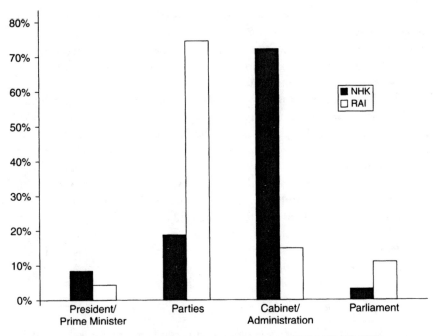

Fig. 6. Political subjects in Japan's and Italy's news: NHK, 1983; RI, 1982.

and local administration. NHK allocates less than a fifth of its coverage to political parties, only slightly more than RAI devotes to the cabinet and administration.

According to these analysts, RAI's style of coverage also is distinctive, focusing on debate and party activity—rather than on government as in U.S. (and NHK) news—and on domestic social and political conflict. Despite its similarity to NHK news in its lack of attention to visual drama, Italian television news differs from both U.S. and Japanese news in the roles played by its journalists. "The Italian television journalist is, both in training and in terms of actual power relations, a party functionary," who tends to pass on the views of particular political parties "objectively" but with a more personalized connection with his audience. The American journalist, on the other hand, stands apart from the audience and provides comment and context.[24] As discussed, NHK's news is like neither of these styles, focusing on the administrative state, rather than on party views or social and political conflicts, and featuring journalists as neutral conveyors of facts in impersonal, impartial reports.

A comparison of NHK to Germany's public and private broadcasters in 1985 shows fairly similar results with a slightly different classification (see

[24]Ibid., 834–44; quotation from p. 842.

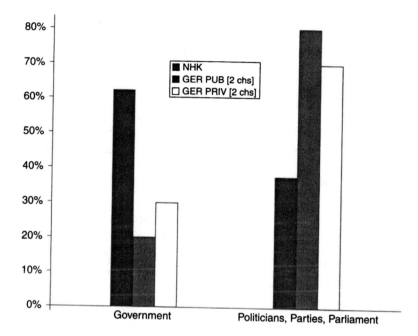

Fig. 7. Political subjects in Japan's and West Germany's news: NHK, 1983/85; W. Germany, 2 public, 2 private channels, 1985.

fig. 7). "Government," encompassing in our NHK data the categories of prime minister, cabinet, and the bureaucracy and its related advisory councils, occupies a larger percentage of classifications than does "politicians, parties, and Parliament," composed of the "parties/faction," "Diet," and "elections" categories. West Germany's private and public channels show politicians, Parliament, and parties more than government. According to media specialists in West Germany, however, the networks are scrupulous in their neutrality toward political parties,[25] the only way in which the German case resembles NHK more than Italy.

Unable to obtain actual programs from Swedish public television, I used a written summary of programs for two weeks (10 programs) of weekday newscasts of (then-called) Sveriges Radio (or SR; now called Sveriges Television, or SVT) for early June 1983, just a month before the NHK 1983 sample.[26]

[25] Max Kaase, "Germany," paper presented at the Battelle-Mershon Conference on "Mass Media Technologies and Democracy," October 8–11, 1992, Ohio State University, p. 62; the data are taken from Barbara Pfeftsch, "Politische Folgen der Dualisierung des Rundfunk systems in der Bundesrupublik Deutschland: Konzept und Analysen zum Fernsehangebot und zum Publikkum sverhalten" (Baden-Baden: Nomos Verfagsgesellschaft, 1991), 105–7. "Politicians" includes the "politicians," "parliamentary debates," and "party meetings."

[26] The dates were June 1–3, 6–10, 13–14, 1983. I am grateful to Monika Djerf-Pierre, of the University of Gothenberg, for providing me with this data from an ongoing project to "log" the main topic and a summary of all news items on television.

Although a majority of the 1983 NHK segments concerned government and politics, running a close second to society, these types of stories were the *least* prevalent in Sweden, accounting for only 21 percent of all items. This compared to 23 percent for economic segments, 30 percent for society stories, and 49 percent, almost half the total, for foreign and defense items.

The bureaucracy, a major political actor in Sweden, is one of the two most covered subjects in the news. Still, Swedish coverage of the bureaucracy— 21 percent of domestic political stories, the same percentage that the cabinet receives—does not compare to NHK's coverage of that subject. About two out of every five stories about government concern the prime minister and his cabinet, approximately double that of the national bureaucracy. Similarly, the number of stories about political parties and the Rikstag, the Swedish parliament, exceed the number of stories about the civil service. Although the bureaucracy is featured more prominently in television news in Sweden than in Italy and Germany, this coverage does not approach the bureaucracy's prominence in NHK's 7 P.M. news.

France

With its tradition of elite government bureaucracy and *dirigisme* (i.e., state direction and involvement in the economy), and thus what some have seen as its ostensible similarity to Japan's "strong state,"[27] France provides the best comparative test of the extent to which NHK's coverage of the bureaucracy may reflect merely the transmission of "reality." If French television news is similar, then perhaps both are depicting extensive bureaucratically-influenced polities.

The sample covers two weeks of the public broadcaster France 2's news on its major evening program, *Le Journal*, in late 1996.[28] With 136 individual segments, about 14 per day, France 2's average was fairly close to that of NHK. Although the average time per France 2 segment was a bit less than two minutes, the segments varied more in length than those on NHK, ranging from under 10 seconds to 10-minute segments composed of different aspects of the same news story.

The data showed that in coverage of subjects in the news, France 2 does not differ much from NHK: on politics and government, 57 percent (France 2)

[27]On the similarity of France's and Japan's "strong state," see John Zysman, *Governments, Markets, and Growth* (Ithaca: Cornell University Press, 1983). I am grateful to Peter Katzenstein for emphasizing the importance of France as a comparative test.

[28]Friday, November 15; Monday, November 18 to Friday, November 22; and Monday, December 16 to Thursday, December 19. I used these dates to get as "normal" a news coverage as possible. A terrorist bombing attack dominated the news immediately following the early November dates, and Christmas either would have dominated the news later in December or caused a dearth of news.

to 52 percent (NHK); on society, 63 percent to 55 percent; on the economy, 18 percent to 17 percent; and on foreign and defense, 36 percent to 30 percent. If we look only at strictly domestic political segments their numbers match almost exactly (46 percent to 47 percent).

However, the content of those domestic political stories differed between the two broadcasters, as becomes clear in figure 8. Some are minor, such as France 2 covering some subjects more than NHK: the cabinet (14 percent to 10 percent); the courts (14 percent to 6 percent); the police (17 percent to 3 percent); local government (23 percent to 14 percent); and elections (8 percent to 1 percent). On the other hand, NHK covers political parties (31 percent to 22 percent) and the parliament (16 percent to 8 percent) more.

The greatest differences between the two broadcasters, however, are the much greater extent to which NHK covers the bureaucracy (38 percent to 2 percent) and new policies (28 percent to 8 percent) and the overwhelming coverage France 2 gives to the French executives compared to NHK's coverage of Japan's prime minister (33 percent to 5 percent). Each of the French executives, the president (16 percent) and the prime minister (17 percent) receives more than three times the coverage of the Japanese leader.

French television news differs in other respects. The French network focuses more on crime, scandal, and investigation, one of the reasons that courts and police are represented more in news about the state in France. Among types of activities in the news, crime composes 26 percent of the segments on the French program, the highest category, compared to about 22 percent on NHK. In stories about domestic government and politics only, crime constitutes a full 39 percent on the French news, compared to about 33 percent on NHK. Instead, NHK pays far more attention to government decisions, proposals, and ceremonies, both in all segments (34 percent to 23 percent) and in domestic political stories only (34 percent to 27 percent). The French television news is striking for the number of stories that seem to involve criminal or ethical accusations against national and local officials or that concern criminal prosecutions and court cases.

Some of these differences are reflected in the types of visuals each broadcaster emphasized.

	France 2	*NHK*
No or nonmoving visuals (still photos, graphics)	18%	25%
Staged visuals (meetings, interviews, speeches)	68%	61%
Limited action visuals (ordinary life scenes)	46%	30%
Dramatic visuals (conflict, violence, weapons)	32%	12%

Fewer segments on France 2 than NHK use only stills or no visuals, while there are between two and three times the proportion of dramatic visuals on

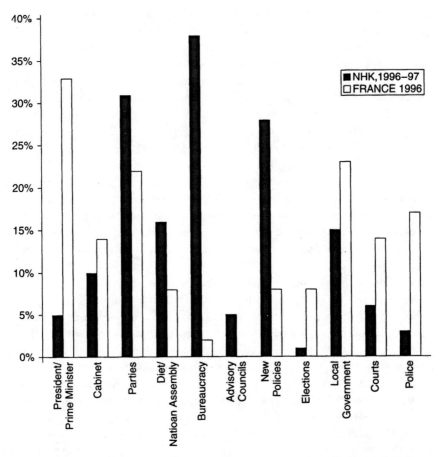

Fig. 8. Political subjects in Japan's and France's news: NHK, 1996–97; France 2, 1996.

France 2 news as on NHK. On the other hand, a higher proportion of all NHK's items are broadcast with limited action or staged visuals. Looking at only stories of domestic government and politics, the number of dramatic visuals on France 2's news increases from the total's average to 38 percent of segments; for NHK, however, it decreases to only 5 percent. One reason for this is that on France 2, 58 percent of all, and 62 percent of domestic government, stories involving crime, scandal, and investigation contained dramatic visuals.

Finally, France 2 also differs markedly from NHK in the extent to which its reporters offer analysis and commentary and to which a particular point of view is represented in the story. Of all the segments, 28 percent contain some analysis or commentary by a journalist, compared to NHK's 8 percent. Although the percentage of such interpretation on France 2 decreased for domestic government and politics stories to 23 percent, this was still almost three times the 8 percent finding for the same type of segments on NHK. Furthermore, in several France 2 items, the point of view of the story, with or without overt commentary, is clearly one-sided. For example, a segment on the workers of France's giant electrical firm, Thomson, offered only the fears and complaints of the workers, who were demonstrating against privatization, with no retort or opinion from the government or management side. A balanced viewpoint was also missing from an item about a book fair honoring an immigrant author in a city with a far right-wing mayor. The mayor boycotted the proceedings, but the Minister of Culture attended. The reporter's words left little doubt as to which side he was on: "Three culture ministers sat side-by-side in a denunciation of cultural censorship, which leads to fascism." He added: "We know where it starts, but not where it ends."

Despite France's reputation for having as influential and elite a bureaucracy as Japan's, in contrast to NHK, France 2 news emphasizes not this part of the state but the president and prime minister, and crime, scandal, and investigation, offering more dramatic visuals and a frequently more interpretive, and occasionally quite partial, journalistic approach.

Britain

The British Broadcasting Corporation is one of the world's largest, and has always been the model for, public broadcasters in the democratic world. In many dimensions of the public broadcaster's organization and relationship to the state, NHK and the BBC are the most similar. We might therefore expect their news products to be similar as well, offering the final test of NHK's uniqueness. I conducted a full content analysis on three weeks of BBC television news, one week each from the years 1991, 1994, and 1997.[29] As with the NHK data, the sample contains periods both when Parliament was in session and when it was not.

Both the BBC and NHK provide a substantial amount of coverage of society and government and significantly less coverage of economic news. In all three cases NHK provided more of each than the BBC. The coverage of society by both surpasses that of politics and government, but not by much, and between two-fifths and half of their items contain some political theme:

	BBC: 1991/94/97	*NHK: 1996/97*
Government/politics	44%	52%
Society	49%	55%
Economics	13%	17%
Foreign/defense	43%	30%

[29]The exact dates were in 1991, August 28 to August 30 and September 2 to September 3; in 1994, May 16 to May 20; and in 1997, November 17 to November 21. Weeks were selected primarily on the basis of availability or to ensure a balance between periods when parliament was in session or not.

The major difference is the more extensive coverage of foreign affairs and defense matters by the BBC. This is a finding we also found in the case of Sweden and France, and may be a common characteristic of all European broadcasters because their countries, unlike Japan, are partially integrated, militarily, economically, and politically with other nations in their geographical proximity.

Figure 9, however, indicates several differences in coverage of the state. Among the more minor differences: the BBC devoted far more attention to the police than NHK, whereas NHK devoted more to the courts; the prime minister and elections appeared more often on British television than on Japanese television, but local government and parliament were more prominent subjects on NHK; and items in the "other" category show up much more in the British than in the Japanese data, primarily because all but one of the these "other" stories are about the royal family (the Queen and Prince Philip celebrated their fiftieth wedding anniversary during one of the weeks in our sample).[30] There are also some similarities, primarily in the nearly equivalent attention given to new policies and policy change, appearing in a quarter of all items in both countries.

The greatest disparity in the data, however, is found in the coverage of the cabinet and the bureaucracy. The cabinet is the subject of domestic public affairs news that receives the most attention in Britain: about a third or more of all political news in Britain involves the cabinet. Indeed, "cabinet government" is more than just a phrase in the BBC's reporting on government and politics. And, once again, we see that NHK's attention to the bureaucracy is not found in other industrialized democracies.

I found other significant differences in visuals and in the extent of commentary and analysis. The contrast between the two broadcasters in the visual aspects of the news can be seen below:

	BBC	NHK
No or nonmoving visuals (still photos, graphics)	35%	25%
Staged visuals (meetings, interviews, speeches)	67%	61%
Limited action visuals (ordinary life scenes)	45%	30%
Dramatic visuals (conflict, violence, weapons)	33%	12%

The BBC has a higher percentage of each kind of visuals in its segments, indicating a more visually-oriented program. The greatest difference though lies in the use of the least staged visuals: the BBC has 50 percent more visuals showing limited action, such as scenes of daily life, and nearly three times more visuals involving dramatic elements, such as conflict, weaponry, or vi-

[30]The one "other" story in Japan was omitted from figure 4.

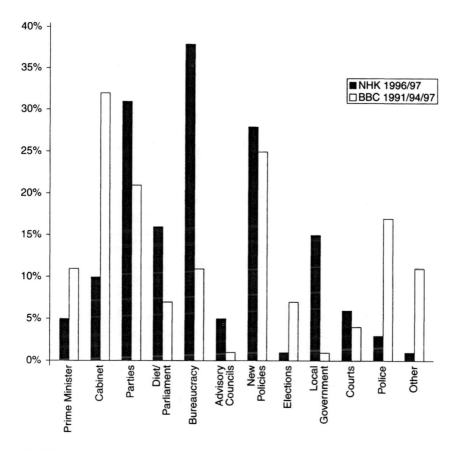

Fig. 9. Political subjects in Japan's and Britain's news: NHK, 1996–97; BBC, 1991, 1994, 1997.

olence. Also, the dramatic visuals also were not as prevalent on foreign stories as they were on NHK. Almost three-quarters (73 percent) of all the items with these types of pictures were domestic stories, compared to half on the Japanese broadcaster.

Perhaps most interesting, 36 percent of all dramatic visuals on the BBC (5 percent for NHK) accompanied stories involving domestic politics and government, and the proportion of domestic government stories (31 percent) with accompanying dramatic visuals is quite close to the percentage (33 percent) of these types of visuals for the sample as a whole, unlike NHK. Among these visuals on the BBC were protests by the disabled and by students; several crime scenes—not just of the police taking a suspect into custody or searching for evidence, as in Japan; displays of weaponry by the British military; and a British soldier killed in Northern Ireland. Clearly, the BBC has a much more visual approach to the news.

Britain also is similar to France in its inclusion of interpretive comments on the news. Recall that on NHK only 8 percent of all news segments included commentary or analysis by journalists, with about the same percentage for government and politics segments. On the BBC, on the other hand, a full 38 percent of all items included some analysis or commentary, and the percentage was higher (45 percent) on domestic government and politics items. Indeed, government and politics items constituted nearly half (45 percent) of all the segments that included interpretation by journalists.

The type of commentary made by journalists often is also of a different type. Any analyses or comments made by NHK journalists are usually fairly close to the facts of the story, sometimes almost insipid in its reinforcement of the information already presented. For example, in a story about the coalition government discussing health care reform but with a specific proposal, the reporter merely added that the plan so far had nothing concrete. Another segment on a report that business confidence was down elicited a journalist's "analysis" that the report "showed a lack of vigor in the private sector."

BBC comments are both much more informative and interpretive, although not to the extent of that found on Japanese commercial television news and described in chapter 8 and not as one-sided as some France 2 segments. Some BBC comments could limit the impact, or counteract the intended public effect, of a governmental proposal. For example, the proposal to arm more policemen in London because of a wave of violence against the police prompted a correspondent to comment that such a measure might not be enough if violent crime continued to rise. A BBC reporter tacked on the comment "that many people feel the new plan is overdue" to a story about the Department of Health's publication of new standards for treating cancer patients. Not only do the BBC journalists' comments often add new information or provide an alternative view, occasionally they verge on the editorial, as when the reporter on a story about a government policy for better air pollution warnings aimed at respiratory disease sufferers commented that better information would not do anything to reduce air pollution or keep it from getting worse.

Public broadcasting of the news varies not only in content, but in approach, style, presentation, and the role of the correspondent.

THE DISTINCTIVENESS OF NHK TELEVISION NEWS

Our data indicate strongly that NHK television news is different from the major public broadcasters of Europe and the private broadcasters of the United States and Germany. All broadcasters pay significant attention to government and politics and less so to economic stories, but NHK seems to place a heavier priority on public affairs than some and less of a priority on international stories than European broadcasters. More significantly, only NHK of all the broadcasters in the democratic world we surveyed covers the national bureaucracy, rather than elected politicians like a prime minister or president, or a cabinet, more than any other political subject and to such a great extent. This is true despite the fact that some of these other democratic countries, especially France and Sweden, reputedly have policy processes in which the bureaucracy is as influential as some purport it to be in Japan. This does not accord with the idea that NHK pays attention to the bureaucracy so much because it is merely covering Japan's political reality.

NHK covers the state with fewer interesting visuals and in a more descriptive fashion than the other broadcasters. Although all broadcasters, especially public ones, must preserve some degree of "neutrality" from party and ideological perspectives because of their status, the way in which broadcasters accomplish this varies greatly. Many conform to a type of journalistic "objectivity," with the journalist taking no overt ideological stance but rather attempting either to represent the public or to convey the views of different sides. Within this approach, however, different forms of journalistic interpretation may enter the broadcast. The U.S. network version is the correspondent as cynical, populist interpolator, representing the public but presenting different points of view through the sources interviewed. The BBC features serious, added-on commentary that transcends the facts of the piece, while French television occasionally uses ad hoc direct opinions and one-sided stories. At the far extreme are the Italian reporters' straightforward transmission of whatever particular partisan view they are covering (and thus some "balance" is achieved across reports, rather than within single ones). Only NHK, however, adopts an almost completely noninterpretative, transmission of only-the-facts style of reporting in which the story is often narrated by an announcer who merely gives information or a reporter weighing in but taking no perspective and adding little real interpretation.

These findings argue against an explanation based on the commonalities of public broadcasters. None of the other public broadcasters in England, France, Germany, or Sweden covered the administrative state to the extent or in the way that NHK did. Thus, it is not sufficient to explain the differences in broadcasters' coverage of public affairs by noting that they are each merely reflecting varying political processes or structures, or that their differences are due to their common public (or common commercial) nature. Further, note that despite the BBC's similar formal and legal arrangements, its news product is different from that of NHK. We must therefore look more closely at how the specific institutional arrangements operate in practice, as well as at the development of broadcasting organizations, their political context, and the informal relationship between journalistic and political institutions in Japan for possible explanations.

The rest of this book is devoted to attempting to explain why NHK is different from other broadcasters in the industrialized democratic world—and also in important respects from commercial broadcasting in Japan—and the potential political consequences of those differences.

CHAPTER 3

The 7 P.M. News

A news story is also in the business of giving instruction for desired operations within a going concern. The news story informs its readers about politics, but in a specific way. Its meaning lies in the instructions it tacitly gives about what to attend to, and how to attend, within the going concern of American political life. It asks readers to be interested in politics, but politics as the community of journalists conceives it.

—MICHAEL SCHUDSON, "The Politics of Narrative Form"

If television news is not quite an "electronic mirror," what is it? Some have suggested that a more appropriate metaphor would be that of a flashlight blinking on and off in a dark attic. . . . Metaphors aside, the point is that selection and editing, while significant in producing newspapers, are the very essence of television news. This is the case, not because television news people are dishonest or eager to slant the news, but because of the basic nature of their medium.

—AUSTIN RANNEY, *Channels of Power*

How journalists collectively define "news," the procedures they use to collect, select, and mount a program, and the structure and incentives of the context in which they work, all shape the news the viewer sees.

NEWS ORGANIZATION

Among the most important factors that influenced the 7 P.M. evening news organization and process was its use of Japan's "Big 3" national newspapers as a model.[1] As it changed from a government-controlled mo-

[1] The *Yomiuri, Asahi,* and *Mainichi* newspapers are often collectively referred to as "The Big 3." Among the largest mass circulation newspapers in the world, they have a combined nationwide circulation of more than 22 million copies just for their morning editions alone. Japan also enjoys a thriving large circulation "block" or regional press, as well as a local press.

53

nopoly that merely announced news gathered by others to an independent news agency with commercial competition in a postwar democratic Japan, radio and, later in the 1950s, television news had few models to draw upon. Thanks to the American and British occupiers who "reformed" it, NHK's general structure came to resemble its overseas counterpart, the BBC. However, there was little concrete knowledge at NHK about the internal operation of the news media in Western countries. Further, NHK did not emphasize news during the radio era. So it was not until the rise of television broadcasting and the rapid build-up of NHK as a news organization between the late 1950s and late 1960s that NHK needed any examples for its news organization.

At that time, the appropriate model seemed to be Japan's great mass circulation press, with their similar nationwide news organizations that set the standard for news. Because almost all American newspapers were local, they influenced network news less and it quickly developed its own style of news. In Japan, however, the national newspapers, not other television stations, were NHK's major competitors.[2] Of this crucial period in the development of NHK as a news organization, a top News Department executive said, "I'm sure I can say that the newspaper was the only model available to us. Newspapers were the focus of output for the Japanese news and the system for providing information. We were a latecomer, so we were not in a position to do something different."[3]

Further, many of the top news people and those who trained the new reporters for NHK came from the press.[4] As the *Asahi Shimbun,* one of the "Big 3" papers, described the origin of NHK's news functions in the postwar era in a 1968 series, "Reporters' training was carried out with newsmen lecturers using newspapers as teaching materials. They expanded their news gathering net by competing with newspapers using newspaper companies as models. It was catchup and surpass them."[5]

From this original newspaper model of news organization flowed several other important characteristics of NHK's news organization. Like the giant newspapers, the 7 P.M. evening news relies completely on its own vast news gathering apparatus for material, making it very much a vertically integrated organization. Also, news gathering was highly dependent on the "reporters' clubs." Whereas in prewar Japan these clubs were restricted to the

[2]Interview with T2, a leading reporter at the political desk, August 16, 1983.

[3]Interview with T, a top executive of the News Department, December 18, 1991.

[4]Shima Nobuhiko, *Media no kage no kenryokusha-tachi* (*The Powerful People of Media's Shadow*) (Tokyo: Kōdansha, 1995), 105.

[5]"Genron no jiyū" ("Freedom of Expression"), *Asahi Shimbun,* May 8, 1968. This series on NHK was published between May 1 and May 27, 1968. I consulted it in the form of a book put together for internal use by NHK. The above quote is from p. 30 of that book.

Fig. 10. NHK News broadcast, 1967.

reporters of newspapers, after the war they were opened first to NHK reporters and later to those of the commercial stations. Broadcasting journalists, like newspaper journalists, would gather news from specialized "beats."
News editing organization also followed that of the newspapers, with specialized "desks" (*bu*) [6] for each type of news. Discussing the expansion of the
News Division during this period, the same high News Center executive said:

> And there was no model that we could look to, so we used the newspaper
> and created the political section, the economics section, and . . .
> (Interjected Question: Were you very conscious of the fact that you were
> using the newspaper as a model?)
> It is more than a matter of whether we were conscious of it or not . . . for
> example, in the case of the Prime Minister's Office, or if we wanted to send
> reporters to the Foreign Ministry, there were already reporters' clubs, and
> all newspapers assigned political reporters there. . . . [7]

Finally, the newspaper model would influence not only the organization
for the news, but the values, norms, and standards of the news itself. What
was defined as "news," how it was to be reported, and the priorities given to

[6] Although *bu* is usually translated as "department" and is a standard part of a Japanese organization, above a "section" (*ka*) and below a "division" (*kyoku*), I have translated it here as
"desk" because this corresponds to the usage of the term in U.S. news organizations.

[7] Interview with T, December 18, 1991.

different types of news—in other words, the news judgments that permeated the news organization and process reflected those of Japanese newspapers. Whatever distinctive technological or market imperatives television news had, these would operate within the organizational and journalistic framework of a "newspaper news" model in Japan.

Some changes occurred during the early to mid-1980s, as forces within NHK pushed for a renovation of the news process to make it less like the newspaper model and more attuned to the age of video and videotape. My initial fieldwork between 1983 and 1985 on the 7 P.M. news coincided with these transitions. In chapter 8, I will indicate how the news process was being, and subsequently has been, revised somewhat, but not substantially, in accord with this trend. (Even though what follows thus applies to the program from the onset of the television age in the 1960s to the mid-1980s, I use the present tense to describe it.)

NEWS GATHERING

The Source-Reporter Relationship and the Reporters' Club

The interface between news organizations and the state is greatest at the point at which news organizations are most dependent and vulnerable, news gathering. What the state does is often the most important aspect of what is defined as news. State actions must be covered, and politicians and officials become prime sources of information for journalists whose careers depend on these sources. At the same time, without access to the news media—indeed, without the cultivation of relationships with the journalists—politicians and officials cannot attain the visibility (or conversely, invisibility) or the distribution (or suppression) of information to the public required to maintain their and their government's support. In democratic theory, press and government institutions are supposed to be separate so that citizens may have access to some information independent of that which the state wishes them to know. In reality, this source-reporter relationship adds elements of mutual dependence and potential mutual manipulation.

Consequently, in all democracies, (elected and appointed) officials and journalists have developed subtle, often complex, formal and informal rules and norms to regulate this relationship. These usually include rules and norms governing where, when, and how reporters may have (or not have) access to officials; reporters are organized (or not organized) to receive information; reporters will be given (or not be given) information that officials want the public to know; reporters may release (or not release) information for publication; reporters may possibly get (or not get) confidential information officials do not want the public to know; reporters may identify (or not identify) the officials giving the information; and reporters may be

Fig. 11. NHK's 7 P.M. News Center, early 1980s.

sanctioned (or not be sanctioned) when such rules and norms are violated. While norms governing these relationships are universal, the specifics vary greatly across countries.

One of the most distinctive aspects of Japan's reporter-source relationship is the *kisha kurabu,* or reporters' club. Journalists for the major newspapers and broadcast networks are assigned to a particular specialized "beat" to cover major governmental, political, and societal organizations.[8] At these institutions, reporters use the clubs as a home base and press room. Most of the major media's news gathering process are organized around these clubs, which originally began for social purposes.[9]

[8] Although reporters' clubs exist throughout Japan, NHK reporters in local bureaus are more generalists. So many of the "hard news" stories on the 7 P.M. news originate in Tokyo, however, that the generalizations made here still hold.

[9] On reporters' clubs in general, in English, see Ofer Feldman, *Politics and the News Media in Japan* (Ann Arbor: University of Michigan Press, 1993), 67–93; Ivan P. Hall, *Cartels of the Mind* (New York: W.W. Norton, 1998), 45–79; Young C. Kim, *Japanese Journalists and Their World* (Charlottesville: University Press of Virginia, 1981), 45–47; Nathaniel Thayer, "Competition and Conformity: An Inquiry into the Structure of a Japanese Newspaper," in Ezra F. Vogel, ed., *Modern Japanese Organization and Decision-Making* (Berkeley: University of California Press, 1975), 296–300; and Maggie Farley, "Japan's Press and the Politics of Scandal," in Susan J. Pharr and Ellis S. Krauss, eds., *Media and Politics in Japan* (Honolulu: University of Hawaii Press, 1996), 135–38. The most comprehensive study is Laurie Ann Freeman, "Ties that Bind: Press, State and Society in Contemporary Japan" (Ph.D. diss., University of California, Berkeley, 1995), which has a revised version published as *Closing the Shop: Information Cartels and Japan's Mass Media* (Princeton: Princeton University Press, 2000).

Fig. 12. NHK News Center in the early 1980s, drawn by Katō Kazurō, an NHK news producer. The program being aired is the morning news show. The 7 P.M. news was broadcast from a separate, soundproof booth next to the newsroom.

The Japan Newspaper Publishers Association officially sanctions and regulates clubs, but they are each quite autonomous in that rules and their enforcement depend largely on the club members themselves. These usually include provisions that regulate the competitive and cooperative relationships among the reporters representing different media organizations. For example, the rules specify when information obtained from a source may be considered a "scoop" and when it must be shared with other club members, as well as how and when it can, or cannot, be made public.[10]

Other informal regulations and norms govern relationships between reporters and journalists, and some of these rules can become quite detailed. For example, most major media organizations have their largest contingent covering the prime minister, with novice political reporters assigned to the job of *ban* (a watch or turn) *kisha* (reporter) to follow the prime minister constantly, ask questions, record verbatim the responses, and report with whom he meets and why.[11] One rule governing their task is that they can ask questions until the prime minister's hips are lower than his knees (in other words, when he sits), at which point questioning must cease.

[10]Freeman, "Ties that Bind," esp. chap. 4, pp. 161–238; Feldman, *Politics and the News Media*, 114–16; Thayer, "Competition and Conformity," 297–99; Farley, "Japan's Press," 136–37.
[11]On *ban kisha*, see Feldman, *Politics and the News Media*, 82–84.

In another example, Yamaguchi Akio describes how the meetings of the Executive Council (*Sōmukai*) of the ruling Liberal Democratic Party are closed to the press, but, by custom, the door is left open five centimeters so that reporters can hear the discussions. Only one person at a time can stand by the narrow opening, so reporters from different news organizations take 15-minute turns at the door, with each sharing the information overheard.[12]

Other countries also have established arrangements governing official-reporter relationships in key political institutions. In the "lobby system" in Britain, for example, political reporters based in Westminster have institutionalized access and relationships with Parliament.[13] The closest equivalent to reporters' clubs in the U.S. media, of course, is the White House press room.[14]

Major differences exist, however, between the British and American press organizations and the Japanese reporters' club. One key difference is that the clubs are far more ubiquitous in Japan than elsewhere. Their locations indicate just how pervasive and central they are to news gathering activities for both the printed and broadcasting media in Japan. Table 1 lists the reporters' clubs in Tokyo alone, with the dates of establishment in brackets for those founded after 1953.[15] These are situated in most of the major political, governmental, economic, and societal organizations, and some locations (indicated in parentheses) have two clubs. Most U.S. broadcast reporters are assigned to specific regions and cover all kinds of stories in those locales. Only if most American journalists, including broadcast reporters, were specialized, and the White House press room was reproduced in all of the institutions and organizations in government and society, would there be a U.S. equivalent to Japan's reporters' club. Additionally, American reporters would have to abandon their flexibility to pursue investigative reporting[16] and concentrate on the task of transmitting official information.

Reporters are assigned to these clubs by the media organization. Although reporters may express their wishes concerning their assignments, the organization makes the final decision in accord with the reporter's suitability for

[12]Yamaguchi Akio, "Za Seijibu" ("The Political Desk"), *Chūō Kōron* (February 1985): 170. For other examples, see also Feldman, *Politics and the News Media*, 116–20.

[13]Michael Cockerell, Peter Hennessey, and David Walker, *Sources Close to the Prime Minister: Inside the Hidden World of the News Manipulators* (London: Macmillan London Ltd., 1984), esp. 9–12 and 31–47; see also Feldman, *Politics and the News Media*, 196–97.

[14]See, e.g., the description of White House reporters in Michael Baruch Grossman and Martha Joynt Kumar, *Portraying the President: The White House and the News Media* (Baltimore: Johns Hopkins University Press, 1981), 36–38 and in Timothy Crouse, *The Boys on the Bus: Riding with the Campaign Press Corps* (New York: Ballentine Books, 1972), 203–12.

[15]For a similar chart, see Feldman, *Politics and the News Media*, table 4-2, pp. 70–71. Freeman, "Ties that Bind," 153–58, also has a comprehensive list.

[16]Farley, "Japan's Press," 136.

Table 1. Reporters' Clubs in Tokyo by Type and Specialty

Government Agencies	Haneda Airport (1975)
Prime Minister's Office	Narita Airport (1972)
Imperial Household Agency	
Hokkaidō Development Agency	*Local Government*
Defense Agency (2)	Metropolitan Police (3)
Economic Planning Agency	Tokyo Government (2)
Science and Technology Agency (1956)	Tokyo Fire Dept. (1960)
National Land Agency (1974)	Prefectural Association (1965)
Justice Ministry (1955)	
Foreign Ministry	*Political Parties*
Ministry of Finance (2)	LDP Headquarters
National Tax Agency	Socialist Party, HOR
Ministry of Education (2)	Clean Govt. Party, HOR
Ministry of Health (2)	Dem. Social. Party, HOR (1960)
Ministry of Agriculture, Forestry	Communist Party, HOR (1968)
and Fisheries (2)	
Food Agency	*Economic and Financial Organizations*
Farm Agency	Bank of Japan
Fisheries Agency	Tokyo Stock Exchange
Ministry of International Trade	Federation of Economic Orgs.
and Industry (2)	Commercial Broadcasters and Railroads
Ministry of Transportation	
Maritime Safety Agency	*Broadcasting*
Meteorological Agency	NHK (2)
Ministry of Posts and Telecommunications	
Ministry of Labor (2)	*Entertainment, Sports*
Central Labor Council	Tokyo Sports Reporters' Club (1970)
Ministry of Construction	Japan Sports Reporters' Club
Home Ministry	Tokyo Film Reporters' Club
Supreme Court	Japan Film Reporters' Club (1960)
Police Agency	Local Film Reporters' Club
Environmental Agency (1971)	Tokyo Theater Reporters' Club
Social Insurance Agency (1977)	Local Theater Reporters' Club
	Tokyo Sumo Reporters' Club
Public Corporations	Tokyo Horseracing Reporters' Club
Japan RR Group (2)	Leisure Reporters' Club (1974)
Government Monopolies Corps.	
Nippon Telephone & Telegraph	*International*
	Soviet Union/Eastern Europe—
	Issues Reporters' Club (1959)

Source: Yamamoto and Fujitake, *Zusetsu—Nihon no Masu Komyunikēshyon*, 2d ed. (1987), 42; translation by the author.

the post and the benefit for his career training. Many journalists might actually prefer to be a freelance *yūgun* (literally, "reserve corps"), not assigned a club, because this offers them both freedom from the fixed organizational schedules of the clubs and the opportunity to develop their own stories.[17] Thus, the organizational traditions and norms of the newspaper model determine the distribution and assignment of reporters, not journalists' preferences.

[17] See Kuroda Kiyoshi, *Shinbun kisha no genba* (Tokyo: Kodansha Gendai Shinsho, 1985), 70, 76–77. Kuroda discusses newspaper reporters here, but much applies to NHK as well.

Another characteristic of the Japanese reporters' club system is the extent to which they allow, even encourage, their reporters to become close to their sources through informal contact. Naturally, formal press conferences are held, but if the one I observed at the prime minister's office is typical, and I was told it was, little real information is imparted. At this press conference, the chief cabinet secretary (*kanbōchōkan*) was asked only two questions, and he responded to both in a relatively evasive fashion ("I will look into it"), and then left. The entire affair lasted perhaps 4 minutes, with nothing important disclosed to the media.[18] When I told a leading NHK political reporter about my impressions that both press conferences and briefings are mere formalities (*tatemae*), he responded, "That's right. That's why we need *yomawari*."[19]

"Night rounds" (*yomawari*), or "night attacks" (*youchi*), allow all the club reporters covering a government agency or political group to visit its higher executives' homes in the late evening. There, provided with food and drink, they can question the official in this more informal setting. Although most of the information is "off the record," reporters can obtain the background information needed to put events into perspective and to understand what is going on behind the scenes.[20] This is the kind of information an American reporter would get in one-on-one interviews with sources or in "deep background" press briefings. "Night rounds," however, are open to all the club reporters, so it is very difficult to get any sort of "scoop."[21] This leads the more ingenious reporters to invent surreptitious strategies for getting the source alone, or nearly alone. For example, one described a technique in which he pretends to leave but comes back. If there are still other journalists around, he repeats the process until he's alone with the politician and can encourage the source to be honest with him.

> For example, if there are ten reporters there, he can't say what he wants to. It's only show. But when it's one on one, the politician feels like he's betrayed me if he lies. I've created a situation where he can't lie."[22]

The "night rounds" and the frequent interaction during the one to two years the reporter covers the official leads to a close relationship. Indeed, a reporter's status among his fellow journalists can depend on how far into the private quarters of the source's residence he gains admittance.[23] Free ac-

[18]However, Feldman, *Politics and the New Media*, 80, says that others may last 15–20 minutes and that the chief cabinet secretary is otherwise considered a good information source.

[19]Interview with H, a veteran political reporter who had also served as "cap" of a reporters' club at an important political institution, May 28, 1985.

[20]Feldman, *Politics and the New Media*, 88–89, 90–91. There are also *kondan*, or informal chats, during the day. See pp. 88–89; Kim, *Japanese Journalists*, 51–53.

[21]Yamaguchi, "Za Suijibu," 177.

[22]Interview with H.

[23]Yamaguchi, "Za Seijibu," 176; Farley, "Japan's Press," 137.

cess to the official's refrigerator, for example, gains one more respect, but being able to use the official's bedroom telephone brings the most status as the ultimate sign of having the source's confidence.

Reporters' Clubs, Television News, and Predictability

For television news, the reporters' clubs perform specific additional functions. Perhaps the most essential is that of an "advanced warning system." Even though the visual nature of television gives audiences the impression that it is a more "spontaneous" news gathering medium than either print or radio news, being a visual medium actually makes it far more necessary and likely that it will cover predictable events. Covering a news scene for print and radio news requires only a reporter with pen and pad or microphone and tape recorder; in television news, because stories accompanied by visuals are more likely to be selected for broadcast, reporters need a camera crew on the scene.

Electronic news gathering (ENG) and the use of increasingly smaller videocassette recording equipment and now mobile satellite trucks have vastly simplified the problem of getting visual recording and sound equipment to the scene. Nonetheless, minicams and mobile trucks are scarce resources that must be rationed, so television broadcasters still require advance warning of what news will occur, and they must make decisions in advance as to how to apportion and where to assign cameras. This results in television news giving priority to and covering predicted, and predictable, news.

Thus, "staged events," such as press conferences and interviews play a large role in the presentation of television news. Edward J. Epstein, in his pioneering sociological study of American television evening news of the early 1970s, estimated that producers had at least one day's warning on 90 percent of all stories used and that only 2 percent of the filmed stories showed totally spontaneous or unpredictable events.[24] This is also true of NHK news. When I asked a veteran reporter with leading responsibilities at the political desk how many news items generally were predictable three hours before the 7 P.M. newscast, he estimated 80–90 percent, adding that unpredicted stories by that time are "very rare indeed."[25]

For U.S. television network news, the wire services function as an advanced warning system to enable the news organization to assign cameras to stories deemed in advance to be worthy of such visual coverage. In Japan, however, correspondents in the reporters' clubs perform this function for NHK news.

[24]Edward J. Epstein, *News from Nowhere: Television and the News* (New York: Vintage Books, 1973), 31, 133–34, 146–47; also Herbert J. Gans, *Deciding What's News: A Study of CBS Evening News, NBC Nightly News, Newsweek and Time* (New York: Vintage Books, 1980), 87–88.
[25]Interview with T2, August 16, 1983.

Through their close relationships to sources, broadcast reporters learn before the fact what is likely to occur in the near, and sometimes even relatively distant, future.

NEWS SELECTION, EDITING, AND PRODUCTION

Selecting Stories to Cover

Which of these predictable stories will be covered and developed are decisions the club reporter makes partially in conjunction with more veteran reporters back at their desks—the "city" or "society" desk (*shakaibu*),[26] the political desk (*seijibu*), the economic desk (*keizaibu*), and the foreign desk (*gaishinbu*), for example—at the News Center. All reporters belong to a desk and those stationed at reporters' clubs are directly responsible to it, with veteran reporters providing leadership and administration.[27] At the political desk, for example, six such experienced journalists function as "the desk" (the English term is used to refer to these people), including its director who has final decision authority and responsibility.

In addition to their own special assignments, two of the six "desks," in rotating shifts, are responsible for daily administration and for acting as supervising and assignment editors for the field reporters. Reporters and desks are in frequent communication, and it is to the desk that the club journalists report the up-and-coming news items.

The political desk records up to a month in advance the scheduled events that their reporters intend to cover, with more detail being added to schedules for the following week and the next day. Asked about the schedules, a veteran political desk reporter explained:

> So for events that are listed on the schedule, especially for major events, we make decisions about how it will be covered (*shūzai taisei*), how the cameras will be positioned, how many reporters to send, if one person is going to talk, and what he will say. These things are decided in advance. So the desk obviously is aware of this coming event.[28]

Reporters also consult with the desk about which events to cover. In large clubs, like that of the prime minister's office, a "*kapu*" ("cap" or "captain") will discuss this with the club reporter. Where there is only one NHK re-

---

[26] *Shakaibu* is literally "society desk," but to prevent confusion with "society pages" and because it covers crime, scandal, and human interest stories like a newspaper "city desk," I've used this term instead.

[27] Usually the head of a desk will have about 10 years of field experience before being appointed to that position. Interview with T2, August 16, 1983.

[28] Ibid.

porter, however, the journalist is given a fair amount of freedom to determine which stories to cover. Nevertheless, the reporter must still keep the desk informed, and the latter has the authority to reject or revise a story, as a leading political desk reporter indicated:

> Well, the desk decides if he doesn't need to do a story. Or he may tell the reporter, "Your story focuses on this point. But if you are going to write this story now, it's better to emphasize this point instead."[29]

The reporters request cameras from the desk editors for that day and make arrangements with the special section that assigns the cameramen. Club reporters and their supervisors at the desks therefore function as their own assignment editors.

Reporters have difficulty articulating norms of what they consider "newsworthy" because they place great store on experience and the development of something akin to a professional "instinct." There is no set "formula" for determining news value. Nevertheless, I was told by some experienced newsroom personnel that, to meet the simplest criteria of newsworthiness at NHK, the story must (1) be national, (2) have an impact on people's daily lives, and (3) be of concern to taxpayers.

The desk also checks the drafts of the reporters' stories for accuracy and balance. A leading desk reporter told me what he looks for when he checks stories:

> As you'd expect, whether or not it ought to be reported in NHK news now. Is it newsworthy or not? Simply, is it news? Is it not at all an old story? That's first and primary, isn't it? One more is really whether or not it's completely accurately captured the present political situation. This is important. The third is, well, is it fair? It's those kinds of things I pay attention to.[30]

Selecting and Editing the Stories for Broadcast

If the desk faces outward and is a key link with the field reporters in the clubs, it also faces inward and is one of the main starting points for the news order of that day, making decisions about the relative importance of expected stories for the evening news program. They thus serve as the important intermediary between reporters in the field and the News Center's main decision makers, the executives of the "coordination" desk (*seiribu*).

[29]Ibid.
[30]Interview with O2, political desk leader with extensive experience in reporters' clubs, August 4, 1985.

These executives determine what segments will be broadcast that evening from the pool of reports covered by the various desks.

The coordination desk and its more than one hundred members—former reporters who have been assigned to production work, directors, and editors—have responsibility for actually producing the entire program. Six senior reporters function as executives of the desk, chosen for their long experience and news value judgment. Each serves, on a weekly rotation basis, as the duty director, deciding what will be included in that evening's program. The duty director is called the "main desk," or just "main" for short, but I refer to him here as "the main producer" because he functions as the executive producer for that day's program. The main producer is assisted in this task by two other coordination desk personnel, "P.D.s," or program directors, who help with the coordination of visuals, text, and sound in the flow of the entire program, and by one of the other six coordination desk executives, who functions as the *shidanchō* or "division commander," the main, central script editor for the nightly news program.

As we have seen, the informal process of selecting which stories to cover begins as much as a month in advance with club reporters and desks. The final, formal process of selecting and editing the stories for that evening's broadcast, however, takes place in two major daily meetings in the News Center. One is the 10 A.M. final meeting for decisions about the noon news program; the other is the 4 P.M. final meeting for decisions about the 7 P.M. news. Leading people from the various desks tell the main producer what stories they have for broadcast, and how and why their stories are important.

The desks also will alert the main producer about what stories they will probably have lined up for the next day's evening news. On the following day, after discussion of the noon news items at the 10 A.M. meeting, they will again do this and relate how complete these stories are, for example, what kind of visuals they are getting and when. After the meeting, their proposals are put into writing for reference by the main producer. Gradually the main producer's preliminary decisions are being formed about the distribution of stories into that afternoon and evening's programs, including the 7 P.M. news.

Between the 10 A.M. meeting and the final editorial meeting at 4 P.M., these decisions are refined and revised through constant informal discussions with the desks, the item producers, and others about the composition of that night's program and the status of various reports. The main producer must constantly be calculating the likely stories that will be coming from the various desks, their news value, and the order and time to devote to each.

The 4 P.M. general editorial meeting formalizes the main producer's preliminary decisions as to which incoming stories to include in the 7 P.M. news; which to put into other, shorter five-minute news "briefs" later that evening;

Fig. 13. NHK producer deciding order of stories for 7 P.M. news, 1985.

and which to drop. He distributes a written list of his preliminary decisions as to what items will be broadcast, in what order, and in approximately what length. He also lists those items that have not yet arrived, either because the story is a late-breaking news event or because they are awaiting an overseas satellite transmission, but these items are indicated with judgment reserved as to whether they will be inserted later. As noted above, the next day's potential items are also briefly discussed.

The representatives of the various desks at this time may disagree with the priorities given their stories by the main producer's disposition of their desk's segments. Usually, however, this meeting is relatively formal and ritualized. If a desk wishes to lobby the main producer concerning a particular segment, he may do so informally before or after the meeting. A producer I queried as to whether this meeting really performed a function or was primarily for "show" said:

Yes, it's just show. With 20 people in the same room, nothing gets done. Each desk states what it thinks is important to report on the 7 P.M. News whereas they should, and do, already know which reporter will do what news, on which show. Nothing gets decided at that meeting. (Interjected Question: Are important decisions also made before that meeting?) Yes.

Before the information is released on the chart (distributed at the 4 P.M. meeting), everyone knows it anyway.[31]

Even if ritualized, the 4 P.M. meeting seems to perform two not inconsequential functions: it formally legitimizes and makes public to the representatives of all units the general content of the that evening's news; and it seems to provide a fixed demarcation in the news process between the preliminary and the final stages of preparation for the program.

Following the 4 P.M. meeting right up to air time, the main producer agonizes, sometimes with colleagues, about his tentative priority and time decisions, often making adjustments to them before the program. He will receive updates on the status of items, be told if an expected item fails to arrive, or consult with others informally about the order or length of an item. Once I clearly overheard the main producer reveal his doubts about his preliminary placement of an item to one of other main desk executives who reassured him he had made the right decision.

Many of these conversations occur by the news order machine that sits in a corner of the News Center. Standing about 3–4 feet high, it has two columns, each with several small white plastic boards. Next to each plastic board are two red electronic digital read-out columns, usually set at "00.00." As he makes his decisions about news order and time length for each item, the main producer will write the item titles on one of the white plastic boards, in descending order of appearance on the program. He will also set one of the red digital columns at, for example, "01.30," indicating one minute and 30 seconds estimated length for that segment. Linked to a computer, the second column automatically calculates and displays the cumulative total of minutes, providing the main producer with an immediate overview of the overall time composition of the program as he makes his news order and time decisions. This facilitates his shortening of some segments and lengthening of others, depending on the information he is receiving from segment producers and his judgments about news value. Small colored plastic indicators are also attached to the cards for various items to indicate which are "remotes" live from the scene, which are coming in from distant locations through "feed" lines, and even which items are to be read by the female and which by the male announcers. A television camera over the news order machine transmits this information to monitors throughout the News Center so that editors, desks, and producers can see if their items have been changed and thus if they need to make any revisions to their segments.

Certain fixed structural aspects help organize the main producer's decisions. The broadcast is 27 minutes long, about 25 minutes without the

[31]Interview with N, news producer, May 28, 1985.

weather report that always ends the program. Sports occupies perhaps two minutes, leaving about 23 minutes of "real news" per day. After a brief introduction of the headline stories, the program is divided into three fairly separate segments, even though obviously there are no commercial breaks, with the first 10-minute portion reserved for the most important, hard news of the day.

A shorter middle portion follows, made up of at least three to four brief "human interest" reports from around the country or the world.[32] These once usually consisted of rather bizarre and unusual "man bites dog" types of features, but by 1985 this type of story had been dropped in favor of up to seven segments of regional news from around Japan, often about some theme, such as how different regions were coping with a heat wave.

The goal of the middle portion is to break up the program with "softer" human interest stories to provide the viewer with a respite after being bombarded with 10 minutes of five or six important news items. This was considered to be the outer psychological limit for a viewer to stay tuned to such fast-paced, serious news, and thus the middle portion helped to retain viewer interest in the program.[33] Not coincidentally, these segments, drawn from all over Japan, have the added benefit of using the huge nationwide network of reporters NHK maintains and giving viewers from many regions the feeling that NHK serves them. The final portion of the program is made up of less important regular news items and features, followed by sports and weather.

Programming and audience considerations, such as the news "flow" of the day, also may enter the main producer's calculations. Before the 7 P.M. news, many of the day's major events have already occurred and been reported in NHK's frequent news programs, and both the morning and afternoon editions of Japan's major national newspapers have appeared. How "old" the news is and how likely it is that the viewer has already seen that information must be taken into account. Stories that are no longer new, but are somewhat important might appear lower in the order or not included as a headline story.[34]

Because the main function of the 7 P.M. news is to be the repository for the major hard news stories that occurred that day, however, the prime factor in the selection and order of the news on the program is news value. Indeed, it is this function that distinguishes the 7 P.M. news from NHK's early morning and late night "news shows" that place more emphasis on audience appeal considerations. One veteran main producer noted that television

[32]In 1983 it was called *naigai no wadai* or domestic and foreign topics of conversation.
[33]Both these reasons were given to me in an interview with A, an experienced coordination desk and main producer, June 4, 1985.
[34]A softer news feature sometimes may be included among the three "headlines" after the important hard news headlines to keep viewers watching until the end of the program. Ibid.

viewers can switch channels, but they cannot choose the stories of interest to them. Therefore, their interests must be taken into consideration. He added, however, that "basically we edit the entire news according to its news value. The news with news value tends to be included more, to become lengthier and to receive higher priority in the order."[35]

What does "news value" mean in this context? The traditional Japanese print journalist norms held by the club reporters and the desks permeated the entire news process and influenced the main producer's choices of headline stories and news order. In American TV news it is usually said that the basic division in a news organization is the one between "journalists (notably reporters) who judge a story from the perspective of sources and those, such as top producers and editors, who look at it from the viewpoint of the audience."[36] An NHK main desk reporter rephrased this dichotomy in simpler terms: the news "they want to have" (audience perspective) and the news "we want them to have" (journalist-source perspective). This also closely overlaps the distinction often made between "hard news" and "soft news." In reality, both must be taken into account, but they do represent different approaches to story and programming decisions.

The newspaper model of journalism and journalists dominates the entire 7 P.M. news process, meaning that traditional Japanese print journalism's "hard," factual news is given by far the greatest priority. Journalists gather the news at the clubs and, with other journalists at the various desks, make the crucial decisions about what pool of stories should be covered and proposed for inclusion in the programs. The main producer and many at the coordination desk are career journalists, and many of the producers of individual segments are reporters, too. It was the club reporters' draft, not the visuals collected, that formed the basis for the narrative of the individual segments. Other than very outstanding or unusual new stories (in other words, "page 1 stories"), which might come from any field, the priority in terms of news value is Japan's traditional newspaper order of "politics, economics, society."[37]

Production

After the 4 P.M. meeting is over, the pace and activity of the News Center becomes noticeably livelier. The main producer for the 7 P.M. program meets with his counterparts on the 6:30 P.M. local (Tokyo) news and the *News Center 9 P.M.* programs to discuss which items will appear on which programs and how much overlap will be in the "news flow" for the evening.

[35] Interview with K, news producer, August 31, 1983.
[36] Gans, *Deciding What's News*, 89.
[37] Shima, *Media no kage no kenryokusha-tachi*, 114.

Following this meeting, he will begin the final stages of deciding the order and time of the items to be included in the broadcast.

As the main producer puts his initial, tentative news order on the machine, producers and visual editors for the first time get an idea of the probable length of their segment. Each news story is produced *separately* by *different* control desk producers,[38] who are responsible for coordinating the script and the visuals together into a final story item. The producers are chosen each day by the two program directors under the main producer from among the large pool of such personnel on that desk. Some producers are career reporters; some have television news production and editing experience only.

The scripts are developed from the drafts produced by the field reporters in the clubs, again a legacy of newspaper news.[39] Reporters in the field fax in the drafts (*genkō*) of their stories, which are then edited by reporters at the various desks and also by the *shidanchō*. Meanwhile, the producer for that segment tries to cut the script and the visual editors under his supervision pare the video to fit the script, both to conform to the time constraints for the segment. The visuals are cut and used almost exclusively to support the story in the journalists' draft.[40]

Segment producers and their visual editors make decisions about transitions between visual scenes, or what written descriptions of the story will be displayed on the screen. These transitions and coordinations between the script and the video are implemented through color-coded plastic cards. Producers put these cards into a machine that indicates, for example, the camera number, the headline that will appear behind the announcer, the live remote line number, and so forth. In effect, these cards control the news item's technical production during broadcast.

Meanwhile, two women, almost the only females in the News Center for most of the afternoon, are translating interviews with foreigners or the video sometimes used in segments from the ABC news feed that, by arrangement, routinely enters NHK's News Center. The program directors under the main producer try to coordinate the technical requirements of the entire flow of the program as the main producer makes his order and time decisions.

About 5:30 P.M., two newcomers—conservatively but nattily dressed male and female—enter the News Center for the first time. They are the "announcers." NHK's 7 P.M. news always uses announcers, as opposed to "casters" (or broadcaster; the English terms are used). Casters more resemble

---

[38]The names for several roles at the News Center at this time were in transition. I have chosen consistently to use the term "producer" to refer to those individuals responsible for putting together a program or segment.

[39]Shima, *Media no kage no kenryokusha-tachi*, 105.

[40]Interview with K, August 31, 1983.

American "anchors," while announcers are essentially what the BBC once called "news readers."

The announcers are not journalists; they are specially hired for their news-reading ability and trained solely to read the news. Although they follow a similar rotation to reporters, they never gather news, edit reporters' drafts, or in any way participate in editorial decisions regarding the content of the program. Selected for their voice and speech qualities, trained to conform to the stringent NHK standard of proper and clear Japanese speech, and taught to read at the expected pace of news reading (300 characters a minute), the readers have only one task: to be, as reporters sometimes derogatorily call them, "talking machines." They begin to read the scripts as they are completed, rehearsing over and over their contents and timing themselves on stopwatches, occasionally consulting with the *shidanchō* about a possible change of a word here or there to be able to meet the standard pace.

As the time for the program approaches, the tension in the News Center grows palpable and activity becomes almost frenzied as the last-minute changes in time and order are made. When the occasional late-breaking story suddenly comes in, the pace becomes even more frenetic as space for the story must be made in the news order and the time allotted to all the other segments adjusted, with last-minute editing cuts made accordingly.

Finally, the announcers take their places in the small soundproof studio next to the main newsroom five minutes before the broadcast. All the producers of individual segments gather around the "T.D." (technical director) in the control area, sitting at a console facing a wall with a bewildering array of monitors that represent the different "feeds." A central monitor, labeled "on the air," is what the viewer sees; the monitor labeled "next" will be switched to following the current "on the air" visual. Then the NHK 7 P.M. news logo goes on the air with the clock counting off the last five seconds before the hour. The announcers bow and say, "Good evening."

As his segment appears, the responsible producer comes to stand next to and behind the T.D., tapping him on the shoulder as a signal that it is time to make a "switch" in the scene during the item. When the T.D. presses a button, the automatic feeding machine, with its plastic cards coded with the arrangement of scenes, will instantly feed into the "on the air" line the next scene. Then that segment producer is replaced by the next, and so on. As the program ends, especially if there have been no technical glitches, the normally silent crowd in the control booth area suddenly dissipates. Noisy chatter and noticeable relief fill the area as the segment producers and main desk executives scatter.

Often, following the program, the main producer calls a "response meeting" (*hansei kaigi*) to provide the opportunity for self-criticism and feedback about the program. He also meets privately with higher news executives,

Fig. 14. Program directors watch their segments being aired in the "control room" portion of NHK News Center during a 7 P.M. news broadcast, 1985.

usually the duty vice director of the News Center. I was allowed to observe this meeting one day. It was a short session, but very business-like, with the vice-director asking the main producer specific questions about the news judgments he made in terms of order and time, and the main producer giving his justification, always in news value terms. Occasionally, the main producer may express his dissatisfaction with a decision or reveal his conflicts about the choices he made. At the meeting I attended, the executive delivered no negative recriminations or orders about the future; it was clear, however, that the very existence of such a meeting means that the main producers know as they prepare a program that they will later have to justify their news choices to the satisfaction of higher-ups. The fact that every stage of this news process decision making is documented, in writing, on forms designed for that purpose undoubtedly also conveys the message that one must be able to justify decisions by professional values.

CHARACTERISTICS AND COMPARISONS: ORGANIZATION AND PROCESS

Characteristics of the 7 P.M. News

The first salient feature of NHK's 7 P.M. News process is its high vertical integration, with no reliance on external organizations for news gathering, assignments, or production. This makes it very personnel-centered with a huge number of reporters, editors, producers, technicians, and executives. Consequently, it allows for a broader coverage for the news than commercial networks can afford, but it also is highly expensive to produce.

Second, roles are highly specialized. News gatherers are mostly specialized reporters operating in reporters' clubs and responsible to other senior specialized desk reporters who loosely supervise and advise club reporters and edit their reports. Specialized coordination desk producers are in charge of producing each individual item on the news and coordinating the reporters' drafts and the visuals. Visual editors edit the videos in a separate specialized task. A special desk executive does final script editing, and the main producer, who has not been involved in assignments or coverage decisions, has the specific job of making final decisions about news order, time, and overall program pacing. The sole job of the announcers is to read the script; they have no involvement at all in the reporting and editing activities.

Third, the process is highly collective and standardized. Authority and task assignment is clear throughout the process. The numerous formal meetings; the many written forms to propose a month in advance items to be covered or included in the program, as well as to document the process completely; and a news order machine to communicate instantaneously changes in order or time—all these indicate a large, specialized, and compartmentalized organization and process that makes formal coordination necessary through fixed routines and overt procedures. Frequent rotation in roles but standardized training are characteristic of personnel policies. Responsibility for news content is collective, diffused, and subject to constant verification and accountability, according to universally shared norms of neutrality, fact orientation, trust, and accepted journalistic news values. If one had to sum up this aspect of the process in a single word, "bureaucratic" comes immediately to mind. A consequence of this process (and a cause?) is that news content also is highly standardized.

Fourth, the norms, organization, and process are highly reporter-centered. Journalists dominate the process from news gathering through editing to production of the segments. The only persons who are not reporters or do not have reporter backgrounds are a few producers, the visual and sound editors, and the announcers, all of whom are clearly subordinate to the journalists, who are clearly in charge of the content of the news and have the authority. News and news order judgments are consequently based on reporters' definitions and values, which in turn are based on the traditional values of Japan's national newspapers where "hard," national news that influences the citizen takes precedence, and political news is given priority.

Fifth, partially as a consequence, the news is "script-centered." Television news is very much like a newspaper with visuals used merely to illustrate the text. The announcers read directly from a script that is closely based on the original drafts of the reporters, who are primarily stationed in reporters' clubs in government, many in bureaucratic agencies, and are highly dependent on sources for information.

Comparisons: U.S. Television Network News

A brief comparison to the U.S. television network news process illustrates NHK's differences. In U.S. network news, the program's executives learn of forthcoming events primarily from the wire services (AP and UPI). Using a list of such scheduled events, the assignment editor assigns film crews to cover events. More than two-thirds of the stories on U.S. network news begin with the wire services. Only a small percentage of stories originate with correspondents or other "in-house" sources.[41] Choosing the stories to film for the evening news from the wide pool of wire service-provided possibilities allows for the potential inclusion of many different types of news.

Most American television correspondents (with the typical exception of those assigned to the president, the Supreme Court, or the State Department) are not assigned to specific beats." Rather, they cover all the news in a region. They thus tend to be generalists, lacking the expertise and background to cover particular topics in depth. At the same time, they are freer from the institutionalized, dependent source relationships of specialized beats.

In comparison to the structure of the huge, bureaucratized, and journalist-centered NHK news, U.S. news has only a few really important "gatekeepers": the executive and associate producers, who have responsibility for the major final decisions as to news inclusion, priority, and presentation; the anchorperson(s), who often participates in these decisions and also frequently edits the final copy of the script; and the assignment executive, who is responsible for the advance selection of stories for crew assignment.[42] The executive producers and assignment editors may have backgrounds in the entertainment divisions of the networks rather than in journalism and are therefore attentive to audience appeal. This is probably one major factor in the proclivity of U.S. news toward drama, action, and violence in visuals. As one former vice president of ABC indicated, U.S. television news is much more inclined to transmit what its producers think the viewers want to see

[41] Gans, *Deciding What's News*, 37, 141–44.
[42] Epstein, *News from Nowhere*, 134–51; Gans, *Deciding What's News*, 99; Doris A. Graber, *Mass Media and American Politics* (Washington, D.C.: Congressional Quarterly Press, 1980), 72–73, citing Malcolm Warner, "Decision-Making in Network News," in Jeremy Tunstall, ed., *Media Sociology* (Urbana: University of Illinois Press, 1970), 158–67.

and hear rather than what they ought to know,[43] as opposed to the "hard" and source-oriented NHK 7 P.M. news.

U.S. network news stories are either filmed first by the camera crew, then the story written by the professional story writers, or the correspondent writes the story and then, together with a producer, edits the visuals in the field before sending the segment package back to the studio.[44] The visuals and the story line, molded respectively by nonreporter producers and story writers, determine the visual production.

All these aspects make U.S. television news the product of a smaller, less bureaucratic, less specialized news gathering and news editing organization with norms and news judgments as inclined to audience, visual, and entertainment factors as journalist, script, and source considerations.

EXPLAINING THE 7 P.M. NEWS PRODUCT

Reporters' Clubs and Official Sources

The reporters' clubs possess definite advantages and disadvantages as a means of gathering news. On the positive side, the Japanese media defend the clubs, citing the collective nature of the club and its institutionalized rules as a way to protect the individual reporter from intimidation or manipulation by the source. This system also clearly encourages the reporters to become specialists on a particular organization or individual and to obtain more detailed information than would be possible without the clubs. A less frequently noted advantage is that, given Japanese media organizations' permanent employment systems and strong organizational identifications, the clubs are one of the few sites where journalists from different organizations can interact and develop and reinforce professional relationships and norms.

On the other hand, their negative attributes include complaints that the constant interaction among reporters of different papers at the clubs is one of the prime causes of the conformity in the Japanese press, especially in the major dailies because the reporters' daily contact with one another causes them to take a similar approach to a story and its importance.[45] In this sense, reporters' clubs represent an extreme and institutionalized form of "pack

[43]Quoted in Matsuda Hiroshi, "Ima terebi jyānarizumu no kōzō o tō" ("Questioning the Structure of Television Journalism Now"), *Hōsō Bunka* (August 1983): 57.

[44]Av Westin, *Newswatch: How TV Decides the News* (New York: Simon and Schuster, 1982), 83–88. Westin, an executive producer at ABC News, stresses the importance of words, but also says, "If a picture can do the work, let it. Narration should add to what the picture already tells us." See p. 89.

[45]See Thayer, "Competition and Conformity," 296–303.

journalism" common anywhere the same journalists cover the same events over a period of time.[46]

The most important aspect of these clubs for our purposes, however, is that they induce a dependence on sources and a tendency to report the news as these sources see it. Attached on a long-term basis to that organization, reporters know that if they alienate their sources they cannot do their job. "Beat" journalists who cover the same organization or person over time tend to come to see the world as their sources see it. Also, dependence on the source can make reporters less objective observers of what they cover, transmitting the "official facts" that sources prefer be communicated to the public. Investigative reporting becomes more difficult, and club reporters often can become "prisoners" of the source's official handouts and his leaked and released information.[47]

When I asked a leading political reporter for NHK about the difficulties in maintaining objectivity about a source with whom he has developed such a close relationship of mutual trust and dependence, his response indicated his own ethical concerns and noted that dependence can be mutual. He also, perhaps unintentionally, revealed more about the temptations and inducements club reporters face from sources than he intended:

> If you become so close that you become a member of the family, then when you turn around to report information you are causing the family damage. You have to set a line as to how far you can go. Even if you enter the family as a reporter, you must preserve your objectivity. Whether or not you preserve this becomes the source of a reporter's reputation. Sometimes the politician will represent his gratitude to the reporter by wrapping up some money and giving it to him. I won't accept that. I'm not his secretary, but at the same time I let him know that our relationship is one of mutuality. That's why I don't accept money.[48]

Ofer Feldman has argued that these close linkages actually make the reporter an integral part of the political process in Japan, providing vital ser-

[46]See Crouse, *The Boys on the Bus*, 7–8 and passim. Crouse coined the term "herd" or "pack" journalism in the context of U.S. presidential primary and election campaigns.

[47]See Koitabashi Jirō and Onose Kenjin, "NHK vs. Mimpō: Shiretsu na hōdō sensō no jittai," *Tsukuru* (June 1986): 85; for a case study of Japanese print reporters' relationship to their sources, see Michael Reich, "Crisis and Routine: Pollution Reporting by the Japanese Press," in George DeVos, ed., *Institutions for Change in Japanese Society* (Berkeley: Institute for East Asian Studies, 1984); for a good summary of the pernicious effects of reporters' clubs, see Hall, *Cartels of the Mind*, 73–74; for an American example of dependence on a source leading to vulnerability to manipulation, see Roger Morris, "Henry Kissinger and the Media: A Separate Peace," *Columbia Journalism Review* (May–June 1974). On U.S. reporters' relations to sources and beats, see also David L. Paletz and Robert M. Entman, *Media-Power-Politics* (New York: Free Press, 1981), 20–21, 55–56, 201–2.

[48]Interview with H, May 28, 1985.

vices and functions for the politician.[49] As we will see in subsequent chapters, this close and mutual relationship can often last a lifetime, providing the reporter with a continuing channel to lobby and ask favors for his news organization and the politician with a continuing channel into the news organization.

Reporters' Clubs, Predictability, and Political News

Partly as a consequence of reporters' clubs, predictable stories are more common in political news than in other kinds of news, a fact confirmed to me by a political desk reporter. One reason for this predictability is the number of reporters stationed at bureaucratic agencies:

> It is more difficult to predict societal news stories. Accidents, incidents—they're difficult to predict. In the case of the political section, it's possible to have an idea of what is to come by knowing what is going on right now. In other words, the ministries . . . the reporters work according to the pace of the ministries. So there are relatively few unpredictable stories.[50]

He went on to say that although there may be some unpredictable stories from the political parties or from foreign stories, they are a small percentage of the whole picture.

NHK's news flow during the day and the conception of the 7 P.M. news as the day's main news also contribute to the emphasis on predictable, factual, and "staged" news, with many political segments focused on predictable events, such as meetings. Asked about the distribution of political stories among the major news programs through the day, a leading political desk reporter confirmed that there are more stories on the 7 P.M. news about basic events, such as meetings, with any commentary and speculation about politics occurring on the morning or late evening programs.[51]

Reporters' Clubs and Coverage of the Bureaucracy

Another related consequence of reporters' clubs is that they tend to skew the numbers of likely news stories toward a high proportion involving the bureaucracy. Refer again to table 1 and note the large proportion of the clubs in Tokyo that are located within the bureaucratic agencies of government.

A similar distribution characterizes political desk reporters. Of the 40 NHK political desk reporters, six comprise the editing desk in the News Center;

[49]Feldman, *Politics and the New Media,* esp. 201–5.
[50]Interview with H, May 28, 1985.
[51]Interview with T, December 18, 1991.

the remaining 34 are stationed in the clubs. The largest single number, nine, are sent to the prime minister's office; the second largest number, to the LDP. Eleven reporters cover the political parties (the LDP and the opposition parties), and another two cover the chambers of the National Diet. An approximately equal number cover nine bureaucratic agencies.[52] Therefore, if the prime minister's office is excluded, almost half of all the political desk reporters assigned to clubs cover the civil service. Indeed, if one considers that the prime minister's office contains within it many bureaucratic agencies that function the same as the 12 line ministries and therefore are as administrative as political, then almost two-thirds of political desk reporters cover the executive rather than the legislative or party organs.

Numbers alone, however, do not reflect the extent of structural bias of the club system toward the executive branch and particularly toward bureaucratic agencies. Economic and city desk reporters are also assigned to the administrative agencies. Of the approximately 80 city desk reporters in the field (excluding those assigned to cover sports), almost half are assigned to some government agency, including the courts, the major ministries, the police, the Tokyo prefectural government, and even one to the Diet. The other half are either the *yūgun*, who go where needed or are developing a particular story on their own, or the reporters assigned to particular locales. The same is true for the much smaller economics desk: almost half of their approximately 30 reporters are assigned to government agencies. The remainder are assigned to a functional topic (e.g., energy, trade, stocks) or the major business trade association (Keidanren) or are troubleshooters, but many of these may also wind up gathering information at government agencies, depending on the story they are covering.

The different allocations of space and time in newspapers and television also ensure a greater proportion of political and governmental news at NHK. After the major "newsworthy" page one stories, Japanese newspapers follow a traditional, fixed format in which particular kinds of news appear on specific pages, and all articles begin and end on the same page. All types of news, then, will have a relatively fixed share of space.[53]

In NHK television news, however, with its mere 12–13 items on average each night and no fixed apportionment of these items, stories related to politics and government can appear in any proportion, subject only to "newsworthiness" and the desire for some "balance" among the various desks. As

---

[52]Foreign Affairs (3), Defense Agency (2), Home Affairs, Justice, Finance, Education, Health and Welfare, Posts and Telecommunications, and Labor. Interview with T2, August 16, 1983, and an NHK internal document on "Political Desk Club Distribution," dated August 8, 1983. For a similar lineup of political reporters at a Japanese newspaper, see Thayer, "Competition and Conformity," 293.

[53]See Thayer, "Competition and Conformity," 287–88.

we have seen, though, so many city and economic reporters are also assigned to cover government agencies that even their stories may have a connection to the state, particularly its bureaucratic agencies. The main producer responsible for assembling the program will attempt to include at least one item from each desk each day, but many of the stories that are suggested to him by other desks will involve government and politics anyway, and because this type of news has such a priority according to the traditional news value judgments, such items will appear frequently.

Finally, journalists' practices of coverage in the clubs multiply the likelihood that the bureaucracy will be covered even when a bureaucrat is not the source or that a bureaucrat will serve as a source for stories beyond those about the bureaucracy. For example, the reporter stationed at a government ministry or agency also will cover the Diet committee specializing in that policy area. The club journalist will often get information about the agency from the LDP veteran politicians who have specialized in that policy area (known as "policy tribes," *seisaku zoku*), while higher civil servants will often be used as sources for what is happening in the Diet committees, the LDP, and among the related *zoku* politicians with regard to specific policy.[54]

In summary, the need for an advanced warning to send cameras to cover stories for television news makes it more likely that predictable stories from reporters' clubs will be covered. Furthermore, the distribution of broadcast reporters to those clubs and the practices of coverage create a large pool of predictable news stories about the administrative agencies of the state.

News Values, Organizational Ideology, and Coverage of Government

Ascribing priority to national daily life and to taxpayers' concerns further reinforces the consideration of political stories as important "hard news." Such norms may be common in U.S. evening news,[55] but when combined with the reporters' club and desk system and the traditional Japanese print journalism norms of priority to governmental affairs, the result is a greater number of potential stories for broadcast related to the bureaucracy.

The connection between these news values and the emphasis on the bureaucratic elements of the state was clear in a veteran political desk leader's response when I asked him what was the subject with the highest political news value in Japan. After mentioning the prime minister and general political trends, he dwelt on the ministries because they affect the taxpayers.[56]

Because the broadcast generally had a fixed format (hard priority news, human interest, softer news), any other packaging, pacing, and audience

---

[54] Interviews with H, May 28, 1985, and T2, August 16, 1983.

[55] See, for example, Gans, *Deciding What's News,* 20.

[56] Interview with T2, August 16, 1983.

considerations were secondary to the most basic norm, that of news value: journalistic criteria, meaning source-perspective news, predominate over audience perspective news. Because of the club news gathering system, sources are more likely to be official, governmental, and bureaucratic. News "we want them to have" takes precedence over news "they want," and although the "we" means journalists, invariably it also must involve journalists' official sources.

A second factor reinforcing the consideration of political stories as "hard news" is NHK's ideology as a public broadcaster emphasizing reliability and trust. What kind of news most easily fits the criteria of being trustworthy and reliable? News from and about official government is a category of news that obviously may be considered national and reliable, and can be presented with directness and authority in the mere minute or two average allotted for each news item. Straightforward, "factual," and responsible presentation of hard news items originating in government agencies also is unlikely to engender controversy that might undermine the public image and political credibility of the broadcasting agency.

The News Process and Visuals about Politics

In a system where reporters' stories determine the visuals and journalists' norms guide the process of filming, visual editing, and production, visuals rarely had priority on their own merits, but merely served to illustrate the reporter's story. With the frequent news about bureaucratic policy making, visuals of "talking heads" at meetings tended to be a common sight on the evening news.

A particular problem is inherent in news emphasizing bureaucracy or policy making. Even when such news concerns conflict among rivals or adversaries, how does one portray this visually? Aside from Diet and Diet committee debates, what can illustrate a story on disagreements within the state? There is little that can be shown except the personnel involved, either in still photos or meeting together. Any film merely shows them prior or subsequent to their actual meeting, and they would rarely display overt conflict or hostility at such times. One of the visual editors at NHK complained about this:

> So that's why you see talking heads because cameras are allowed in the room for the first three minutes or the first few minutes. So the greatest difficulty . . . well, representatives of both the ruling and opposition parties become involved in fierce debate when it comes time to speak their minds, but they don't have any personal grudges against one another. . . . All the while, you see them smiling. That's why you get what you see on television. But then when you get the [news] script, it says something to

the effect that "there was a heated debate and it appears that no proposal will come out of this Diet session." It's natural that the script ends up this way. So there is a huge gap if you were to try to match the footage, taken before the meeting started, with the text. You must wonder why everyone looks like they're getting along; everyone's smiling in the video, while the script ends up the way it does. . . ."[57]

He added that sometimes the disparity is so awkward, they do not use video at all.

POLITICAL PRESSURE AND POLITICAL NEUTRALITY

To what extent are the participants in the news process protected from partisan and ideological pressure and imbued with a sense of strict neutrality? No journalist at NHK told me that he had ever been subject to any crude direct political pressure from a politician or an official. Several desk reporters did admit that they and club journalists "often" receive calls with "complaints" (*monku*) from politicians about stories or broadcasts. Many of these complaints are about why something the politician said was not covered, but there are also many about accuracy and bias.

In their response, they explain the reasons for their actions and how the approach was neutral, and that would usually resolve the matter. The reporters further acknowledged that offended sources would sometimes temporarily "freeze out" a journalist and deny him information, but they saw this as normal in media-government relations everywhere.[58] One main producer denied the existence of any policy that ensured a balance of appearances between the LDP and opposition parties on a given news program. He also denied ever hearing of a higher executive in the News Department conveying an official's complaint downward during his three years in the News Center.[59]

One could evince some skepticism about such total denials. Although there may not have been a strict attempt to "balance" government and opposition parties within the context of a single program, the remarkably equal coverage accorded these parties in NHK news compared to the commercial broadcasters described in chapter 2 argues for some consideration of balance across programs. Further, prime ministers' and higher LDP leaders' complaints to NHK news executives about particular programs are amply documented.[60]

[57]Interview with K, June 13, 1985. Michael Reich has suggested to me that behind these norms may lie implicit norms against portraying powerful political actors negatively and widely accepted routines for illustrating certain types of stories.

[58]For example, interview with O2, August 4, 1985.

[59]Interview with A, an experienced coordination desk and main producer, June 4, 1985.

[60]See Shima Keiji, *"Shima Geji" fūunroku—Hōsō to kenryoku, 40-nen* (*The Troubled Record of "Shima Geji": Broadcasting and Politics, 40 years*) (Tokyo: Bungei Shunjū, 1995), 168–70; Ni-

Nonetheless, the journalists portrayal of their independence is probably generally correct, as it is unusual for top LDP politicians to try to intervene directly and overtly into the actual news editing and selection process.[61] These processes are fairly well insulated from such direct attempts at influence: the very complex and large, collective nature of the news organization and process, their highly specialized and bureaucratic components, and journalist's strong norms of news value and independent news judgments all would make crude attempts to influence a working journalist within the News Center unlikely to succeed. One former reporter and newscaster with NHK, now with a commercial network, said that complaints from politicians almost never got down to him. He would only be told about them, he said, if the problem was due to "a mistake" he had made.[62]

The News Center is also protected by a specialized group outside the newsroom that deals with politicians. In response to a query about complaints, a News Center executive replied:

> There is a department at NHK that specializes in Diet measures (*kokkai taisaku*). Most of the people there are former political desk reporters, and they're there to listen to such opinions all day. They act as a buffer because they know through their directing or reporting experience whether the complaints are valid or not.[63]

This executive identified that body as the General Affairs Office (*sōmushitsu*), saying that it handled all the relationships with the Diet and the Ministry of Posts and Telecommunications (MPT). He, and almost every other journalist who told me of complaints from politicians, also noted that there were more complaints and pressure from the opposition parties than from the LDP, even when they did stories on the LDP.[64]

Thus officials' attempts at influence, when and if they do occur, may be more subtle, indirect, and filtered down to the News Center through the NHK bureaucratic chain. A former NHK newscaster and reporter, now working for a commercial network and with no incentive to defend NHK, told me that he did not think politicians were stupid enough to try to intervene directly into the News Center itself and that he personally had never seen an example of LDP interference directly into news content. He said that instead they may tell NHK's top management and expect that it would get down to the news room. Although he wasn't sure of the exact process, he

---

shizen Kazuo, "NHK ga abunai!" ("NHK in danger!"), *Asahi Jānaru*, June 17, 1988, 17; and chaps. 4 and 5 below.

[61]Shima, *"Shima Geji,"* 171.

[62]Interview with K2, former society desk reporter, March 27, 1995.

[63]Interview with A2, News Center executive, June 4, 1985.

[64]Ibid.; also interview with O2, August 4, 1985.

speculated that, for example, the director of the News Division might tell his vice-director to "be careful and report the facts," and the point would be made and transmitted to exercise more restraint in dealing with that issue in the future.[65]

We should also consider the paradox in the 7 P.M. news process: the very collective, bureaucratic process that insulates the News Center from direct political interference also makes such intervention rather unnecessary. NHK's organization, process, and norms make it highly unlikely that anything truly critical about a particular party, politician, or bureaucrat would ever make it into the 7 P.M. news. The media institutions that protect journalists from officials equally serve to protect officials from journalists.

NHK's organizational ideology also ensures neutral and noncontroversial news that will not offend officials. NHK news prides itself on presenting "news one can trust." This core principle of its policy and image derives in part from NHK being a public service broadcasting agency that collects fees from the public and whose budget is passed by the Diet. How this has permeated to the working journalist level is shown by the political desk executive who told me that because NHK is a "public entity" collecting subscriptions from the public, it has to be "responsible" and "more neutral":

> For example, the *Sankei Shimbun* or Fuji Television, you can tell just by reading or watching them that they take a clear position. NHK probably doesn't lean toward either. It's written in the Broadcasting Law. We are to be neutral in reporting about what the politicians are doing. Neutral doesn't mean that we are to challenge authority. Neutral literally means neutral. So it must be true that NHK reporters bear such things in mind more than reporters for commercial broadcasters. Unless they do, it wouldn't be right for them to get money and to say and do as they please.[66]

Later, in response to a general question about what the public expects of NHK, especially of the political desk, he immediately responded, "I would say trustworthiness. That reporters not be wrong. I think that the public believes we provide accurate information. . . . Compared to the others, we believe that we are the most trusted media in Japan."[67]

Executives at commercial television news stations feel indirect pressure to be responsible and sensitive to the public because of their stations' dependence on commercial sponsors, who are in turn dependent on the public to sell their products. Public service broadcasting agencies feel not only that they should not alienate the public, but indeed that they should actively cater to and reinforce a positive image with the public because only by pub-

[65]Interview with K2, March 27, 1995.
[66]Interview with T2, August 16, 1983.
[67]Ibid.

lic support can they rationalize their existence and expansion to the public's representatives who have some control over their finances. NHK is particularly sensitive to this need because any increases in its receiver fees (like the BBC) and its yearly budget (unlike the BBC) [68] must be approved by the Diet. To accomplish this, NHK has chosen an image of being the provider of the most accurate and responsible news possible. Philip Elliot has hypothesized a direct relationship between the extent of political control over media organizations and the degree to which they emphasize a style of "factual news."[69]

Audience factors reinforce both the national and trust norms of the evening news. The 7 P.M. news audience tends to be older, rural, female, and less educated. This is a function of an urbanized, commuter, and work-oriented society in which younger, educated, urban middle-class males usually do not return home until later in the evening, as well as the fact that NHK for many years was the only or one of the only television channels that residents in some rural areas could receive. The News Center knows their audience's expectations: news that has some relevance also to the non-urbanite, older, and less educated citizen and news with a simple, direct reliability, rather than flashy, sophisticated news.

"EXPLAINING" NEWS

News gathering, editing, and production, and the organization and norms that structure and guide them, help explain NHK's news product for most of the postwar period. Such an "explanation," however, only provides a partial and proximate understanding of the shaping of the news product. A fuller explanation must also delve into how the organization that produced that news has developed and been influenced by its relationship to the state. The next section of this book is devoted to showing how "the politics of broadcasting" provides a broader and deeper understanding of how NHK's particular "broadcasting of politics" came about.

[68] Yet the British government, through the Postmaster General and by means of the provisions of the BBC license, retains some latent power to interfere in actual programming. See Walter B. Emery, *National and International Systems of Broadcasting* (East Lansing: Michigan State University Press, 1969), 98–100.

[69] Philip Elliot, "Production and the Political Content of Broadcasting," in M. J. Clark, ed., *Politics and the Media: Film and Television for the Political Scientist and Historian* (Oxford: Pergamon Press, 1979), 20–21.

Part II

THE POLITICS OF

BROADCASTING

CHAPTER 4

Organization and Its Environment

Broadcast programs shall never be interfered with or regulated by any person, excepting the case where he does so upon the powers provided for by law. . . .

—*The Broadcast Law,* Article 3

. . . if the formal principles (*tatemae*) of the present Broadcast Law could be fully protected, NHK could be said to be an enterprise unparalleled among broadcast systems in the world.

—AOKI SADANOBU, *NHK sekai saidai no masukomi shudan*

(*NHK: The World's Largest Mass Media Company*)

To repeat, for NHK the most important barriers are fee increases and budget approval.

—SHIMA KEIJI, "*Shima Geji" fūunroku—Hōsō to kenryoku,*

40-nen (The Troubled Record of "Shima Geji":

Broadcasting and Politics, 40 Years)

A good place to look for explanations for how and why a broadcasting organization develops is the legal and regulatory environment in which that organization operates. Yet when we look at the formal legal regulatory environment established by the U.S. Occupation (1945–52) for NHK, it seems to provide fewer opportunities for direct political interference and more for autonomy than that of almost any other industrialized democracy with a large, influential public broadcaster.[1] How can such an apparently "free" regulatory environment provide an explanation for NHK's development and behavior? It is because this regulatory structure's framework for accountability, combined with the political context of postwar Japan, provided political elites with indirect means to attempt to modify NHK's policies and operations.

---

[1]That is, all except the Public Broadcasting Service (PBS), the U.S. public broadcaster, which is excluded from this analysis because of its very small audience.

THE U.S. OCCUPATION: "DEMOCRATIZING" BROADCASTING

One can discern three clear purposes in the decision making, policies, and actions of the U.S. Occupation of Japan regarding broadcasting. Each purpose was emphasized somewhat more in different periods of the Occupation: ensuring the Occupation's security (early period), resocializing the Japanese people to democratic values (mid-Occupation), and restructuring broadcasting in a democratic manner (later period).

In practice, however, these purposes overlapped a great deal and the Occupation often strove for all three simultaneously. Nevertheless, sometimes they were incompatible. For example, the attempt to maintain Occupation control to accomplish the democratic reorientation of the Japanese population often necessitated formal and informal controls that compromised the independence of Japanese broadcasting. This represented the fundamental but perhaps inevitable contradiction of the Occupation itself: democracy had to be imposed on the Japanese people from above.

The first purpose, security, had a simple, defensive intent—to ensure that radio broadcasting was not used to undermine the security or control of the Occupation and its democratizing and demilitarizing goals for Japan. On only the second day of the Occupation in 1945, the General Headquarters of the Allied Forces (GHQ) under General Douglas MacArthur, the Supreme Commander Allied Powers (SCAP),[2] assumed control of the broadcasting facilities of the prewar monopoly, Nippon Hōsō Kyōkai. Then just 10 days into the Occupation, SCAP issued a "Radio Code for Japan," which set forth guidelines for radio broadcasts: "Newscasts must adhere strictly to the truth," must be factual newscasts without distortion by propaganda of any kind, and must not criticize or cause trouble for the Allied Occupation's forces.[3]

To ensure these standards, a form of precensorship was imposed on both information and entertainment programs. All scripts were submitted in both Japanese and English to Occupation authorities, with special attention to any items involving the Occupation. Once a script was approved, it had to be followed exactly.[4] Despite the severity of the censorship, some Japanese journalists did not find it chafing, especially in comparison to wartime Japanese censorship, and relations with Occupation censors was generally not adversarial.[5] Nevertheless, precensorship continued until August 1947;

[2]Japanese and U.S. writings on the Occupation often refer to the Occupation authorities in general as GHQ or SCAP, and this practice will be followed here.

[3]NHK Radio and TV Culture Research Center (NHK RTVCRI), ed., *50 Years of Japanese Broadcasting* (Tokyo: NHK, 1977), 136–39.

[4]Ibid., 146–47.

[5]"NHK hōdō no kiroku kankō iinkai" ("Record of NHK News' Publication Committee") in *NHK hōdō no gojyū-nen: gekidō no Shōwa totomo ni (Fifty Years of NHK News: Along with the Convulsions of the Shōwa Period)* (Tokyo: Kondo Shoten, 1988), 74–75.

post-broadcast censorship was implemented until October 1949.[6] Despite the formal ending of censorship, Occupation supervision and guidance of radio content continued, reinforced by the sensitivity to leftist influences with the onset of the Cold War.[7] To the official censorship was added, in the later days of the Occupation, increased "self-regulation" by NHK.[8]

The second Occupation aim was more positive: to use radio, a powerful tool of mass information and education, to resocialize the Japanese people toward democratic norms and values. This goal had been incorporated into the U.S. government's earliest planning for post-surrender even before the end of the Pacific War. "Clearly, there was a massive propaganda effort underway in occupied Japan to effect American style democratization, and guidance of radio broadcasting was at the center of it."[9] Responsibility for such reorientation, including the broadcast area, belonged to the Civilian Information and Education (CIE) Section.

Restructuring Broadcasting

The third American purpose, in contrast to the first two, saw broadcasting as not only a means toward other ends, but also an integral part of democracy in itself. Broadcasting would undergo fundamental structural change and the institutionalizing of a new legal regime to ensure its future independence from the state. The "democratization" of the radio broadcaster Nippon Hōsō Kyōkai was the core of this policy.

There was good reason for the Occupation to be concerned about the structure and function of this broadcaster. The prewar Nippon Hōsō Kyōkai emerged from the idea that radio was to serve the public interests under careful state supervision. Although local private companies began the first radio broadcasts in mid-1925, within a short time the government's growing understanding of the new medium's importance and potential influence—in part stimulated by the role of the BBC in the May 1926 general strike in Britain—led to its exerting even greater control over the management and operation of a national radio system. Heavy pressure from the Communications Ministry, backed by key politicians and strongly resisted by the original private ownership, forced the merger of the local companies into a public interest national monopoly in August 1926. Soon after its establishment,

---

[6]NHK RTVCRI, ed., *The History of Broadcasting in Japan* (Tokyo: NHK, 1967), 150; "NHK hōdō no kiroku," 87; Hidaka Ichirō, *Nihon no hōsō no ayumi* (*The Path of Japanese Broadcasting*) (Tokyo: Ningen no Kagakusha, 1991), 107.

[7]Marlene Mayo, "The War of Words Continues: American Radio Guidance in Occupied Japan," in Thomas W. Burkman, ed., *The Occupation of Japan: Arts and Culture* (Norfolk, Va.: General Douglas MacArthur Foundation, 1988), 54, 69–70.

[8]See "NHK hōdō no kiroku," 86–87.

[9]Mayo, "The War of Words Continues," 52, see also 47–52, 55–56.

Nippon Hōsō Kyōkai was ordered by the Communications Ministry to establish within five years four more stations in other major cities and link them in a nationwide relay system. This network was rushed to completion in time for the broadcast of the Emperor Hirohito's enthronement ceremonies, which not coincidentally also resulted in a great boost to radio sales.[10]

The company maintained some distance from the state by continuing to involve private investment, becoming legally constituted as a *shadan hōjin* (a corporate juridical person), and gaining authorization to collect receivers' fees directly from the audience, thus not being dependent on direct state subsidies. The rest of its legal arrangements, however, betrayed the state's interest in control. The Communications Ministry, for example, chose many of the new nationwide public monopoly's executives and most of the positions went to retiring ministry officials. This control over personnel, transforming the broadcast corporation into something resembling a sub-agency of the ministry, was implemented over the strenuous objections of the original companies and succeeded only by the threat of complete state takeover. The broadcasting corporation also was deprived of any independent source of revenue, such as advertising, except receivers' fees sanctioned by the state. Budgetary plans, executive salaries, and definitions of duties, however, required ministry approval in advance.[11]

Prior censorship and the watchful eye of the Communications Ministry effectively prevented controversial or political argument, even while making radio available for government use.[12] After the Manchurian Incident of 1931, in which the Japanese military took over part of Manchuria and began to exert greater influence over Japan's government and foreign policy, the ministry broadened its attempt to ensure that no oppositional or extremist ideas entered into the increasingly influential medium of broadcasting. Further, the language and speech of broadcasters was to be neither excitable nor biased, but moderate, correct, and level in tone. In response, the broadcaster adopted a policy of promoting a common and standardized national language in speech, grammar, pronunciation, accent, and intonation. The grave, solemn, and "objective" style of NHK news readers, and the

---

[10] The history of the founding of radio in Japan is covered in broad descriptive terms in NHK RTVCRI, *50 Years*, 14–26, and analytically in Gregory J. Kasza, *The State and Mass Media in Japan, 1918–1945* (Berkeley: University of California Press, 1988), 72–88. See also Hara Kōjirō, *NHK: Kōkyō hōsō no rekishi to kadai* (*NHK: The History and Issues of Public Broadcasting*) (Tokyo: Kyōikusha, 1978), 67–68. The acronym "NHK" was not used for station identification until after the war. See NHK RTVCRI, *50 Years*, 148.

[11] Kasza, *State and Mass Media*, 85–86; NHK RCTVRI, *50 Years*, 16–17, 24–25; Kasza, 75, argues that banning advertising eliminates a broadcaster's economic self-sufficiency, and therefore "The end of advertising is the beginning of radio's dependence on officialdom."

[12] Kasza, *State and Mass Media*, 88–92.

goal of maintaining and diffusing a standardized national speech, continued into the postwar era.[13]

The increasing militarization of government and the fascist model, with its effective use of broadcasting, encouraged the government's control even more. In 1934 with the government's support, Nippon Hōsō Kyōkai carried out a reorganization that centralized authority and programming. It also established various advisory councils— on which government officials served —to advise executives on programming and internal committees to make the final selections of programs. The Communications Ministry supervised and monitored the reorganization process. Its underlying conception was revealed by a ministry official when he said, "Broadcasting, fundamentally a government service, is specially licensed to Nippon Hōsō Kyōkai in accordance with Article 2 of the Wireless Telegraphy Law, and therefore NHK should be considered as an extension of the (Communications) Ministry. The network acts as a surrogate for the government. . . ."[14]

Indeed, in news gathering in the prewar era, NHK hardly deserves the appellation "news agency" as it could not participate in the reporters' clubs (*kisha kura-bu*) that have been essential to the development of sources and news gathering in Japan. Until 1930, radio news consisted solely of the reading of reports supplied by 11 newspapers or wire service agencies; NHK was not even being permitted to edit the scripts. In November 1930, its national news finally obtained the right to select and edit these reports, but this only increased the surveillance of organs of the Communications Ministry. Ministry officials would indicate any errors in the broadcast and corrections would be announced on the air immediately, supposedly enhancing radio news' reputation for accuracy.[15] With increased military control over government and mobilization for war after 1937, whatever little independence NHK previously possessed was totally curtailed and it became a simple propaganda arm of the state.[16]

The Occupation meant fundamentally to change all this. The first of a series of pivotal memoranda that were to restructure broadcasting in a democratic direction was the so-called Hannah Memorandum of December 1945. This memo primarily set out the Occupation's intentions to re-

[13]Aoki Sadanabu, *NHK: Sekai saidai no masukomi shūdan* (*NHK: The World's Largest Mass Media Company*) (Tokyo: Asahi Sonorama, 1980), 61–63. NHK continues to be active in this area through its Radio and TV Culture Research Center (RTVCRI); see NHK RTVCRI, *50 Years*, 51.

[14]Quoted in ibid., 58. On the effect of militarization on broadcasting, see NHK RTVCRI, *The History*, 52.

[15]Ibid., 39, 52.

[16]Kasza, *State and Mass Media*, 252, and the rest of chapter 10 for details on wartime controls and the organization of radio. Also, Aoki, *NHK*, 64–67; and Hara, *NHK: Kōkyō hōsō no rekishi to kadai*, 76–80.

organize the corporation on a democratic basis while maintaining its monopoly.[17]

Simultaneously, within many Japanese organizations, workers were reacting to the defeat in war and responding to the new democratic environment being implemented by the Americans by taking the initiative in challenging their former bosses and democratizing their organizations. During the fall of 1945, employees and managers at Nippon Hōsō Kyōkai also demanded changes from both their executives and the government. They wanted broadcasting to be independent of the government; its content, democratized. Under this simultaneous pressure from above and below, prewar executives retired, and the corporation underwent several internal reorganizations.[18] As will be discussed in a later chapter, employees also organized a very active, leftist labor union.

As the Occupation progressed, policy making for a new legal broadcasting regime began. Many of the steps taken to democratize the organization—for example, establishing an advisory committee to help nominate a president or democratizing the program content—or to ensure its aims, such as Occupation censorship and guidance, were accomplished by GHQ fiat and had ambivalent legal status. As time progressed, the Occupation increasingly turned its attention from establishing its control and instilling democratic norms to the longer-range aim of installing a legal and institutional structure in broadcasting that would remain democratic even after the Occupation ended.

Two more Occupation memoranda were key in this development: one by V. L. Hauge, put together in August and September 1947,[19] and a more important one by C. A. Feisner in October 1947.[20] The Feisner memo especially spelled out four principles of broadcasting—freedom of broadcasting, political impartiality, service to the public, and maintenance of technical standards—that were to shape decisively some of the content of the Broadcast Law developed by the Japanese government in the following years. Both memos conceived of Nippon Hōsō Kyōkai becoming an independent public service broadcasting agency acting on behalf of the people.

[17]NHK RTVCRI, *50 Years*, 156; NHK RTVCRI, *The History*, 152; "NHK hōdō no kiroku," 78–79; Hanawa Tōru, "Nihon Hōsō Kyōkai no saishoki seifu kikan kara minshū kikan e: Hanna-memo no keisei katei" ("The Reorganization of the Japan Broadcasting Corporation from Government Organ to Democratic Organ: The Formation Process of the Hannah Memo"), *Broadcasting Research and Surveys* (November 1986), 29–35.

[18]"NHK hōdō no kiroku," 77–78; NHK RTVCRI, *50 Years*, 155–56; *The History*, 151–56.

[19]"Implementation of Policies Relating to Japanese Broadcasting." Hauge was a member of the staff of the Civil Communications Section (CCS) with responsibility for broadcast policy.

[20]"Memorandum for Record Concerning Conference Outlining SCAP's General Suggestion to a Japanese Broadcasting Law." Feisner was acting director of the Analysis Division of CCS of SCAP.

In both memos and in the planning for a new broadcast law, one of the chief means cited to accomplish these goals was to separate the body that made policy and supervised broadcasting from the organization that carried it out. In this way, the independence of broadcasting could be protected from administrative control and governmental interference in content.[21]

This conception was a rather unique combination of the American and British systems. Whereas Britain had an independent public broadcasting service, it did not have an independent supervisory agency. The United States, on the other hand, had an independent regulatory supervisory agency, the Federal Communications Commission (FCC), but it had no independent public broadcasting service. Japan was to have both. This aim led eventually to the establishment, under the Broadcast Law, of the *dempa kanri iinkai* (Radio Regulatory Commission). This attempt to install an American-style regulatory agency for broadcasting was to result in one of the bitterest conflicts between SCAP and the Japanese government. Viewing the establishment of independent regulatory commissions as incompatible with the principle of cabinet government, the Japanese government fought implementation of the Radio Regulatory Commission. The agency was established only after a direct order by MacArthur in a letter to Prime Minister Yoshida Shigeru in December 1949.[22]

Public Monopoly or Commercial Competition?

Another key issue in Occupation policy toward broadcasting was whether the broadcaster should retain its monopoly on standard broadcasting, or whether it should have private, commercial competition.

At first, SCAP's general policy was to support a public monopoly on broadcasting without commercial stations. This is reflected in the 1947 Hauge memo that first conceived of standard broadcasting as public monopoly, partially because Hauge did not see strong commercial broadcasting being realized in Japan soon, a view shared by many Japanese, even in the private sector, who did not think their country was ready for commercial radio broadcasting. Also, because the existing monopoly already had a "quasi"

---

[21] See Kondo Tsuneo, "GHQ Bunsho-shōgen ni yoru sengo hōsō seido no genten" ("The Starting Point of the Postwar Broadcasting System by GHQ Document, Testimony"), *Broadcasting Research and Surveys* (August 1994), 28–37; Hanawa Toru, "GHQ bunsho ni miru minkan hōsō shōnin no keii"("Details of the Approval of Commercial Broadcasting Seen in GHQ Documents"), *Broadcasting Surveys and Research* (February 1988), 16–21. On the Feisner memo in English see NHK RTVCRI, *The History*, 159.

[22] Kondo, "GHQ Bunsho-shōgen," 33, 35, 37; NHK RTVCRI, *50 Years*, 171–73; on U.S. and Japanese differences in conceptions of broadcasting, see NHK RTVCRI, *The History*, 159–60, 161–62.

public character, many believed that all that was necessary was to change it into an independent public service broadcasting agency.[23]

There was some division of opinion, however, within the Civil Communications Section staff as to whether Nippon Hōsō Kyōkai should maintain its monopoly. A key turning point in changing Occupation policy occurred in October 1947 when CIE chief D. R. Nugent came down strongly against a legal public monopoly and for the competing commercial broadcasters because to do otherwise might prompt criticism in the United States that their policy was socialistic. As Nugent's comments imply, the beginning of the Cold War also may have influenced some SCAP leaders.[24] Thus, when Feisner's memo came out in October 1947, it included, despite Nippon Hōsō Kyōkai's opposition, the establishment of commercial broadcasting and the notion of a dual system of public and private broadcasters. This became Occupation policy and was incorporated into the Broadcast Law then being written.[25]

On June 2, 1950, the day the new Broadcast Law went into effect, *shadan hōjin* Nippon Hōsō Kyōkai was dissolved, and the new *tokushu hōjin* (special juridical body or corporation) NHK was established.[26] Although NHK was one form of public corporation, it was neither established with government funds nor intended to conduct the state's business.

Two years after the new Broadcast Law was implemented, the Occupation ended. Almost immediately thereafter, on July 31, 1952, the newly sovereign Japanese government abolished the Radio Regulatory Commission, transferring its supervisory and policy functions for broadcasting to the Ministry of Posts and Telecommunications (MPT), ending Japan's brief experiment with an American-style independent regulatory commission for broadcasting.[27]

The Historical Legacy

With the omnipresent direct hand of the state in its prewar development, NHK developed from 1925–37 as a broadcasting organization in a limitedly democratic state without any liberal conceptions of the role of me-

[23]See Frank S. Baba, "Discussion" (of Marlene J. Mayo's "The War of Words Continues: American Radio Guidance in Occupied Japan"), in Thomas W. Burkman, ed., *The Occupation of Japan: Arts and Culture* (Norfolk, Va.: General Douglas MacArthur Foundation, 1988), 86–87). It was thought that commercial broadcasting should confine itself to services—such as FM, facsimile, and television broadcasting—then seen as serving the interests of a minority of people. See Kondo, "GHQ Bunsho-shōgen," 30–31.

[24]On Nugent's thinking, see ibid., 35. On such ideological influence, see NHK RTVCRI, *The History*, 160.

[25]Kondo, "GHQ Bunsho-shōgen," 35–36.

[26]Hōsō keiei hikaku kenkyūkai, *Hōsō gyōkai shuyō 11-sha no keiei hikaku (An Administrative Comparison of the 11 Most Important Broadcast Industries)* (Tokyo: Kyōikusha, 1981), 77.

[27]NHK RTVCRI, *50 Years*, 204.

dia in restricting state power. Its function was conceived by both bureaucracy and politicians to be a means to enhance state power, achieve public goals, and disseminate a homogeneous cultural standard.[28]

In postwar Japan, the American Occupation set out to substantially alter the role, function, and context of broadcasting and thus it sought to revamp NHK's structure and mission to reflect the democratic polity in which it was to operate. The autonomy of NHK and the media would be enshrined in law and come increasingly to be accepted as a value, with partisans of that autonomy found both within NHK and within government. NHK would develop an independent news gathering apparatus, and journalists would see their roles in terms similar to those in other industrialized democracies.

Yet, for all this change, the prewar era of state-Nippon Hōsō Kyōkai relations would leave an important legacy. The importance of public broadcasting in maintaining cultural standards and homogeneity would survive, albeit as only one of several motifs in broadcasting. Self-regulation, in response to criticism and pressure, and the devotion of considerable energy to maintaining credibility through an appearance of neutrality would reappear clearly as postwar patterns. Also, we will find a repetition of NHK's use of major events—particularly those involving the state or national symbols, often in cooperation with state agencies—to expand the distribution of new broadcasting technology products. Finally, some conservative politicians would have difficulty accepting NHK's transition from being a broadcaster controlled by and serving the purposes of the state to one responsible to the people.

As in many other areas of life in postwar Japan, neither the prewar nor the immediate postwar experiences would completely triumph: the historical legacy of the state-controlled broadcasting system would not reestablish itself once the Occupation ended. Nevertheless, the intention to establish Western-style democratic institutions would not remain completely unchanged either: the Occupation's aims would remain enshrined in law, principle, and partially in spirit. But as we shall see below, some conservative political elites, for whom the independence of broadcasting proved inconvenient to their or the state's interests, would constantly attempt to subvert the principle of broadcasting independence and use the Broadcast Law to accomplish their partisan ends.

LAW AND THEORY: BROADCASTING AND FREEDOM OF EXPRESSION

Constitutional and Legal Protection

The 1947 Constitution of Japan, written by the American occupiers and unamended to this day, clearly guarantees freedom of expression. Ar-

---

[28]Kasza, *State and Mass Media,* 111–18.

ticle 21 states, "Freedom of assembly and association as well as speech, press and all other forms of expression are guaranteed." It goes on to say that "No censorship shall be maintained, nor shall the secrecy of any means of communication be violated."[29] Note that this is a wider and more explicit formulation than that found in the U.S. Constitution's proscription against laws abridging freedom of the press. Indeed, whereas over-the-air broadcasting in the United States has always had to wage a legal battle to be recognized as part of the constitutionally protected press, no such legal issue has arisen in Japan.

On broad issues of the freedom of the press and journalism, the courts have been even more liberal than those in some other industrialized democracies, including the United States. Thus, courts in Japan have sometimes affirmed something close to a journalistic privilege not to reveal sources; have liberally interpreted the libel laws, issuing few convictions against media organizations for violations; and have rarely prosecuted broadcasters for obscenity. In the famous 1969 "Hakata Film Decision" involving an NHK station, the court affirmed the people's right to know and extended constitutional guarantees to the freedom to gather news.[30]

The Broadcast Law was promulgated as one of the "Three Radio Laws" (*Dempa Sampō*) on June 1, 1950, and is the primary legislation establishing the legal and regulatory regime of broadcasting in Japan.[31] The Law clearly establishes legal protection against interference in journalism, with its first article expounding three principles upon which the regulation of broadcasting for the public welfare is to be based. One of these is "To assure the freedom of expression through broadcasting by guaranteeing the impartiality, integrity and autonomy of broadcasting."[32] Article 3, quoted at the

[29]Robert E. Ward, *Japan's Political System*, 2d ed. (Englewood Cliffs, N.J.: Prentice-Hall, 1978), 231.

[30]Murata Kiyoaki, "Freedom of the Press: Appellate Court Upholds Reporter's Right Not to Reveal Source," *Japan Times*, September 22, 1979, 3; Lawrence Ward Beer, *Freedom of Expression in Japan* (Tokyo: Kodansha International, 1984), 294–302, 314–25, 338–39. Hakata also was notable both for the media companies' unified refusal to turn over news film to a court as evidence and for the Supreme Court's ultimate decision in the case that, while broadcast had to be turned over, unbroadcast film did not have to be relinquished. It should be noted, however, that the courts have allowed a prior injunction against publication of defamation against a politician, claiming this did not constitute censorship. See ibid., 324–25. And in the *Ishii* case, the same year as *Hakata*, the Supreme Court explicitly rejected giving the media immunity to testimony about sources when it is needed in judicial cases. See Young C. Kim, *Japanese Journalists and their World* (Charlottesville: University Press of Virginia, 1981), 128–30.

[31]The other two were the Radio Law and the Radio Regulatory Commission Law, the former was concerned with technical matters and the latter was abolished with the Commission at the end of the Occupation.

[32]JBC, *The Broadcast Law*, 1. The other two are "securing the maximum availability and benefits of broadcasting to the people," and "clarifying responsibility of those persons engaged in broadcasting" so that it can "contribute to the development of healthy democracy."

beginning of this chapter, prohibits interference in programming except with legitimate legal provisions. The broadcaster, in turn, is enjoined not to disturb public security and morals, be "politically impartial," "broadcast news without distorting facts," and give multiple perspectives on controversial issues (Article 3-2).[33]

NHK's Mission and Legal and Financial Status

Most of the rest of the Broadcast Law provides the general regulations governing broadcasters, and most of these concern the structure, mission, and operations of NHK. Indeed, so much of the original Broadcast Law passed in 1950 was about NHK, it was informally referred to as "the NHK Law."[34] Even with the addition of 18 amendments between 1951 and 1989, three quarters of all the articles (44 out of 59) in 1990 still concerned NHK (Articles 7–50). By contrast, only two articles (51 and 52) concern private broadcasters.

The ambivalent nature of public broadcasters in general is apparent in the provisions concerning NHK. On the one hand, the purpose of the corporation is "to conduct its domestic broadcasting with rich and good broadcast programs for the public welfare and in such a manner that its broadcasting may be received all over Japan." It is also enjoined to develop broadcasting reception and conduct international broadcasting.[35]

Almost all expert commentaries interpret this statement of mission to mean that NHK must respond to the public as a whole by providing programs that raise cultural standards for as many citizens as possible.[36] Its responsibilities to deliver *public* goods—both in the sense of providing goods in the public interest and to as much of the public as possible—is clear.

On the other hand, it was to be responsible to that public as directly as possible, and not to the state, the ostensible sole public authority. The U.S. Occupation's intent concerning NHK was to establish an independent public service broadcaster. NHK was to be different not only from state agencies but also from the other former government entities that were made into public corporations after the war. These entities, while independent of the state in management, were in fact state organs in funding and mission. NHK, in contrast, did not receive infusions of taxpayer funds, was conceived of as belonging to the public itself, and was established to be independent

[33] Ibid., 6 (Article 3-2).

[34] Hōsō keiei hikaku kenkyūkai, *Hōsō gyōkai*, 77.

[35] JBC, *The Broadcast Law*, 10 (Article 7).

[36] Kataoka Toshio, *Hōsō gairon: Seido no haikei or saguru (Introduction to Broadcasting: Searching for the Background of the System)*, rev. ed. (Tokyo: Nippon Hōsō Shuppan Kyōkai, 1990), 48; also, Nippon Hōsō Kyōkai Keiei Kikakushitsu (NHK Administrative Planning Office), *NHK to sono keiei (NHK and its Administration)* (Tokyo: NHK, 1968), 4–5.

of the state not only in management but also in mission. As an instrument of the people rather than the state, it was to be accountable to the people's representatives, but involvement by the state bureaucracy was to be kept to the necessary minimum.[37]

NHK's finances were to be funded by receivers' fees collected directly from the public. Article 32 of the Broadcast Law provides that anyone with equipment capable of receiving NHK's broadcasts "shall conclude a contract with the Corporation."[38] At the inception of the Law, the reception in this clause referred only to radio. Since that time, the Law has been amended specifically to exclude radio and apply to television. In the only provision for state funding, the Minister of Posts and Telecommunications can order NHK to conduct either international broadcasting or research on behalf of the government, in which case the expenses "shall be borne by the state" (Articles 33–35).[39]

NHK collects its own receivers' fees directly from television set owners; the money never goes through government hands or to the public treasury. These fees have provided between 97 percent and 99 percent of NHK's operating revenue during the postwar period. Government subsidies, primarily for international broadcasting as the Broadcast Law provides, have made up the small remainder.[40] NHK sees its financial base resting on receivers' fees, collected directly from the public, as an important factor in ensuring the independence of its broadcast programs.[41]

Legally, all who receive broadcasting provided by NHK are supposed to conclude a contract with NHK and pay the receivers' fees (Article 32).[42] The only legal penalties in the Law, however, apply only to broadcasters' violations, not to failure to pay the receivers' fees.[43] Despite some abortive attempts by NHK and the LDP to clarify the legal obligation to pay and to attach penalties for nonpayment,[44] there have been no criminal penalties for

---

[37]Kataoka, *Hōsō gairon*, 30. In English, see NHK RTVCRI, *The History*, 165–66; NHK, *NHK to sono keiei*, 3–5.

[38]JBC, *The Broadcast Law*, 23.

[39]Ibid., 23–24.

[40]Receivers' fees composed the following proportions of operating revenue at the beginning of decades: 1960, 98.7 percent; 1970, 98.3 percent; 1980, 97.2 percent; 1990, 98.1 percent. Government subsidies (*kōfukin*), for example, were about 0.44 percent in 1983 and 0.35 percent in 1990 of operating revenue. The remaining 1–3 percent of revenue comes from various miscellaneous or secondary sources. See NHK HBCK, ed., *NHK nenkan '84* (*NHK Radio and Television Yearbook, 1984*) (Tokyo: NHK, 1984), 64, 67; NHK HBCK, ed., *NHK nenkan '91* (*NHK Radio and Television Yearbook, 1991*) (Tokyo: NHK, 1991), 52.

[41]Nippon Hōsō Kyōkai, *NHK to sono keiei*, 4.

[42]JBC, *The Broadcast Law*, 23. The only exception provided is if the Ministry of Posts and Telecommunications approves standards for such exemptions in advance.

[43]Ibid., 54–57. Penal provisions are given in Chapter VI, Articles 54–59.

[44]Inaba Michio, *NHK jushinryō o kangaeru* (*Thinking about NHK's Receivers' Fee*) (Tokyo: Aoki Shoten, 1985), 106–7.

failure to pay the receivers' fee for public broadcasting,[45] and thus no state involvement in enforcement of fee collection.

It is perhaps to be expected that NHK's status as a public service broadcaster is often misunderstood in the United States. Our political economic ideology and lack of quasi-public bodies lead many to assume only the dichotomous existence of either government agency or private sector. It is more surprising, however, that much of the *Japanese* public also either is ignorant or has an erroneous impression of NHK's legal and financial status. Since the late 1970s, NHK has carried out surveys of the public's perceptions of NHK, including of its legal character, as shown in table 2. From 1980 to the late 1990s, at least two-thirds of the Japanese public did not understand NHK's status as a special public enterprise, and a majority believed it was half or fully a governmental agency. The figures also indicate no real improvement in public understanding through the 17 years covered by the surveys: the same percentages have the correct response in 1997 as in 1980 and there are actually small increases among those incorrectly believing NHK to be a state agency or a private company.

Table 3 indicates that by the early 1980s a majority correctly understood that receivers' fees constitute nearly all of NHK sources of funding. Additionally, those correctly understanding NHK's financial status increased by 10 percent in the three years between 1980 and 1983, undoubtedly due to the effects of a spot ad campaign conducted by NHK during that year that featured the phrase "NHK's programs are produced by receivers' fees from everyone."[46]

Yet after that brief spike between 1980 and 1983, correct knowledge on the part of the public about NHK's source of funding declined, until by 1997 it was at an even a lower level than in 1980. At their highest percentages, those who mistakenly thought that NHK was completely or partially dependent on the national treasury comprised two-fifths of the public (1980 and 1997) and they were never less than about a third (1983). If we include

---

[45]Michael Tracey, "Japan: Broadcasting in a New Democracy," in Raymond Kuhn, ed., *The Politics of Broadcasting* (New York: St. Martin's Press, 1985), 285, cites a 4 percent nonpayment rate, but more likely, between 90 percent and 95 percent of Japanese households with TV sets who sign a contract with NHK pay the fee despite the lack of criminal penalties. Higher estimates are 10–30 percent of the potential audience do not pay. See, for example, Shiga Nobuo, *Terebi eitei* (*Television '80*) (Tokyo: Kioi Shobō, 1980), 187–88; Shima Keiji, "*Shima Geji" fūunroku—Hōsō to kenryoku, 40-nen* (*The Troubled Record of "Shima Geji": Broadcasting and Politics, 40 Years*) (Tokyo: Bungei Shunjū, 1995), 78–80. On why it is so difficult to determine the number of nonpayers, see Inaba, *NHK jushinryō o kangaeru*, 119–23; There has also been a movement to mobilize people not to pay their fees and the popular author Honda Katsuichi has written a book entitled *NHK jushinryō kyohi no ronri* (*The Theory for NHK Fee Rejection*) (Tokyo: Asahi Shimbunsha, 1991), listing as reasons the political (including its conservative and pro-government bias) and other sins of NHK.

[46]Ise Akifumi, *NHK daikenkyū* (*NHK Big Research*) (Tokyo: Poru Shuppan, 1988), 106.

Table 2. Public Perception of the Nature of NHK (in percentages)

	1980	1983	1989	1997
A state-operated agency (*kokuei no kikan*)	26%	26%	25%	29%
Half governmental, half private (*Hankan hanmin no dantai*)	23	26	31	23
A special public enterprise (*Tokushu na kōkyōteki jigyōtai*)	34	32	29	35
A commercial company (*Minkan no kaisha*)	5	4	4	6
Don't know	12	12	11	7
	100%	100%	100%	100%

Source: Kataoka Toshio, *Hōsō gairon: Seido no haikei o saguru* (*Introduction to Broadcasting: Searching for the Background of the System*), rev. ed. (Tokyo: Nihon Hōsō Shuppan Kyōkai, 1990), table, p. 53; Inaba Michio, *NHK jushinryō o kangaeru* (*Thinking about NHK's Receivers' Fee*) (Tokyo: Aoki Shoten, 1985), 34–35; also in Ise Akifumi, *NHK daikenkyū* (Tokyo: Poru Shuppan, 1988), 105; 1997 data from Takahashi Kōichi, "Yoron chōsa repōto: Shichōsha to Hōsō no kōkyōsei—(Hōsō no yakuwari) chōsa kara" ("Public Opinion Survey Report: The Public Nature of Broadcasting and the Audience—From the 'Role of Broadcasting' Survey"), *HKTC*, no. 5 (May 1998): 15.

those who simply admit they don't know NHK's funding source, fully half of Japan's citizenry does not understand where NHK's money comes from.

Even though citizens are somewhat more aware of NHK's dependence on directly collected receivers' fees rather than on government subsidies, their numbers today constitute only a bare majority, and even some of these people do not seem to translate this knowledge into a correct evaluation of NHK as a nongovernmental agency. Possibly the high proportion of stories about governmental bodies on the news, as we have seen, may help create and maintain such a widespread public misconception about NHK's legal and financial status.

Accountability and Regulation

One of the most direct and crucial aspects of the relationship between a broadcaster and the state is the way in which the broadcaster is held accountable to the public through regulation by the public's representatives. Had the U.S. Occupation's effort to establish the Radio Regulatory Commission been maintained, in conjunction with its legal guarantees of noninterference in programming and its independent funding source, NHK would have been a public broadcaster with such minimal and indirect supervision by and reliance on the state as to have approached the autonomy of private broadcasters.

Even with license allocation and responsibility for broadcasting supervision vested in a governmental bureaucratic agency, NHK's direct accountability to government theoretically does not appear to be terribly onerous.

Table 3. Public's Perception of NHK's Funding Sources (in percentages)

	1980	1983	1997
Relies nearly completely on the national budget	6%	5%	5%
Relies nearly completely on receivers' fees	51	62	49
Government bears about half of NHK's budget	15	12	14
Government makes up insufficiencies in receivers' fees	19	14	25
Don't Know	9	8	6
	100%	101%	99%

Source: 1980 and 1983: Inaba Michio, *NHK jushinryō o kangaeru* (*Thinking about NHK's Receivers' Fee*) (Tokyo: Aoki Shoten, 1985), 33–34; also in Ise Akifumi, *NHK daikenkyū* (Tokyo: Poru Shuppan, 1988), 105–6. 1997: Takahashi Kōichi, "Yoron chōsa repōto: Shichōsha to hōsō no kōkyōsei—(Hōsō no yakuwari) chōsa kara" ("Public Opinion Survey Report: The Public Nature of Broadcasting and the Audience—From the 'Role of Broadcasting' Survey"), *HKTC*, no. 5 (May 1998): 15–16.

The Diet has most of the supervisory functions—most importantly, the ultimate veto power over the ability to increase revenues. First, NHK's annual overall budget must be approved by the Diet, as must its business plan. Unlike the budgets of other public corporations that are debated and approved along with the general governmental budget, NHK's budget is submitted and considered independently of any other budget.[47] Nor does the approval process for NHK's budget give government quite as much power as it may appear on the surface, for, by custom, NHK's budgets are voted up or down in the Diet in their entirety, and the parliament does not revise the details of the budget.[48] Second, the Diet also must approve any increases in the level of the receivers' fees. NHK's other obligations to parliament include nothing more than the submissions of financial statements and business reports.

Formal and direct bureaucratic supervisory authority is also intentionally rather minimal.[49] In fact, this authority is more a liaison function with the Diet than any real regulatory power. The Minister of Posts is thus responsible for passing on NHK's budget, business plan, and requests for increases in receivers' fees to the government with an advisory opinion, as well as for passing on its business reports and financial statements to the Cabinet. The minister and his agency have actual decision power only on technical matters, such as the approval of NHK undertaking voluntary projects to improve broadcasting, the transfer of broadcast equipment, and the exact terms of the receivers' fee contract.[50] The minister must also approve any provisional budget when the Diet cannot act on the actual budget for some

[47] Kataoka, *Hōsō gairon,* 80; NHK, *NHK to sono keiei,* 12.

[48] This provision is not in the Broadcast Law and there are various opinions as to whether the Diet has to follow this procedure. See Kataoka, *Hōsō gairon,* 80.

[49] Ibid., 79.

[50] For example, Articles 32, 42, 47. See JBC, *The Broadcast Law,* 23, 27, 30. Even the Postal Minister's approval of the transfer of broadcasting equipment is subject to Diet approval except under certain circumstances.

reason. Even here, however, the duration of such a temporary budget is limited to three months and the receivers' fee amount cannot be changed from the previous budget (Article 37-2).[51]

Any state's ultimate regulatory power in broadcasting lies in the authority to grant or deny a license to broadcast. Like commercial stations, each NHK station must apply to and be approved by the MPT for a license to operate. In the United States, the authority of the FCC to review licenses periodically and, if necessary, to revoke them, has always represented one of the prime potential political threats and governmental powers in broadcasting regulation. Of course, this threat is somewhat mitigated by the fact that it is an independent U.S. regulatory commission evaluating licenses ostensibly using rational and fair public criteria. MPT's licensing power and threat is actually much more restricted than that of the FCC. MPT policy is never to transfer a license once awarded.[52] This means that:

> . . . MPT's ability to enforce content restrictions either through administrative guidance or through formal procedures is limited, because the agency has relatively few sanctions to impose on broadcasters: the threat of relicensing denial is not credible, and the threat of licensing competitors is squandered once acted upon.[53]

Once again, in principle, regulation by appointed officialdom is highly constrained.

The Governing Board and the State

Aiming for an independent management, the Occupation, through the Broadcast Law, provided for authority, decision making, and such management prerogatives as the appointment of executives to be vested in an autonomous board. Article 13 of the Broadcast Law of Japan provides for a board of governors (*keiei iinkai*) for NHK, serving three-year reappointable terms and invested with "the powers and responsibilities to decide the management policy and other important matters relative to the operation of the business of the Corporation."[54] This arrangement is quite similar to that of the BBC in Britain, where such delegation of authority is seen as a means to ensure the public broadcaster's responsibility to Parliament even while establishing a buffer to make it autonomous from direct state control.[55]

[51] Ibid., 25; in English, see the handy chart in Tracey, "Japan: Broadcasting in a New Democracy," 278–80. In Japanese, see a similar chart in NHK, *NHK to sono keiei*, 6.

[52] Jonathan Weinberg, "Broadcasting and the Administrative Process in Japan and the United States," *Buffalo Law Review* 39, no. 3 (1991): 642.

[53] Ibid., 686–87.

[54] JBC, *The Broadcast Law*, 15.

[55] Ralph Negrine, *Politics and the Mass Media in Britain*, 2d ed. (London: Routledge, 1994), 83.

The board is selected by the prime minister with the consent of both Houses of the Diet, a system adopted to emphasize NHK's direct relationship to the people and to avoid giving the prime minister sole discretion in such appointments.[56] Board members elect a presiding chair from among themselves. Two-thirds of the members are subject to regional representation—eight must be chosen from among individuals resident in specified local areas—and overall appointments should be made ideally with "fair representation in the fields of education, culture, science, industry, and others." Directors may also not be staff members of political parties or government officials. No more than four shall have "come to belong to one and the same political party."[57]

Perhaps the most important feature of the organization of NHK is that the state does not directly appoint either its chief executive officer or his subordinates in management. By at least a three-quarters majority (9 of the 12 members), the Board of Governors selects the president (and may also dismiss him) for a three-year tenure with the possibility of reappointment. The president may attend meetings of the Board and, with their consent, appoints a vice president and a board of directors (*rijikai*), who are essentially specialized managing directors charged with advising the president and helping him administer the organization.[58] As in the case of regulatory supervision, NHK's relationship to the state is designed to be indirect and autonomous, with ultimate accountability to elected, not appointed, officials.

NHK IN COMPARATIVE PERSPECTIVE

No public broadcasting organization is completely independent of government, and all are held accountable in some way to it. One of the prime justifications for governmental regulation of broadcasting has always been the scarcity of airwaves that can be allocated and operated without interference in reception. Another has been the need to regulate broadcasting's tremendous potential to influence in order to prevent private exploitation of that power in democratic societies.[59] In the case of public broadcasters there is an additional rationale for some form of regulation and supervision: if the broadcaster is, in whatever form, receiving funds from the public, for whose benefit it was ostensibly established, then it should be accountable to the public. As individual members of that public cannot exercise such responsibility themselves, their elected or appointed represen-

[56]RTVCRI, *The History,* 166.

[57]Articles 15, 16, and Article 16-5; Article 20-2, JBC, *The Broadcast Law,* 16–18 and 18–19.

[58]Articles 23–29; ibid., 19–22.

[59]Weinberg, "Broadcasting and the Administrative Process," 616–17. Also see Kataoka, *Hōsō gairon,* 24.

tatives in government must be delegated the task. How do NHK's legal and regulatory arrangements compare with those of other democratic nations in dealing with this dilemma of giving a public broadcaster autonomy from the state while guaranteeing its responsibility to the public?

NHK's legal, regulatory, and financial environment contains some similarities with many, but not all, public broadcasters in the other industrialized democracies: principles of journalistic autonomy from censorship are buttressed through constitutional law and/or political norms; the broadcaster is neither owned by government nor managed by state bureaucracy; the public finances the operation, although not by direct disbursement from the government budget; a buffer from direct political interference is provided by vesting authority in a semiautonomous governing board, responsible to elected representatives rather than to the state bureaucracy.

Table 4 presents the various relationships of public broadcasters to the state for NHK and various Western European countries with public broadcasting. The first subcategory for each dimension represents the arrangement that, in theory, should give the public broadcaster the most autonomy from the state or from commercial influence with the most direct accountability to the public. As can be seen, NHK differs in several respects from other public broadcasters, especially in its cumulative combination of characteristics.

First, the state has no direct shares of ownership or capital stake in NHK, as is the case in, for example, France and Italy. Second, even where receivers' fees, rather than direct allocations from the state treasury (as in Canada), constitute all or part of the public broadcasters' revenue, the fee often is collected by government in European countries and transferred from the state to the broadcaster. For example, in Britain until the 1990s, the Ministry of Posts collected the fees and transferred the income to the BBC's budget from the general funds. The BBC often received less from the government than the full amount collected. The Home Office decided the level of the fees, thereby giving the state a potentially direct means of control over the public broadcaster.[60] NHK, in contrast, collects its own fees and therefore theoretically should be even more independent of government.

Third, NHK's budgets, like those of the BBC but unlike those of several Western European countries, are not approved as part of the general government budget, but as a separate decision. This uncouples NHK's finances

---

[60]Barrie MacDonald, *Broadcasting in the United Kingdom: A Guide to Information Sources* (London: Mansell Publishing Ltd., 1988), 12–13; Tom Burns, *The BBC: Public Institution and Private World* (London: Macmillan Press Ltd., 1977), 20; M. J. Moulds, *British Television Revealed: An Economic Study* (Coventry: Xray Books, 1983), 93. As Moulds puts it rather starkly: "Any organization that does not determine its own revenue is not a free organization. The BBC has its own Charter and in every other respect is free: but the BBC is in 'the pocket' of the Home Office when it comes to money—therefore the BBC is not free."

Table 4. Comparison of Major Public Broadcasters in the Industrial Democracies[a]

Dimension	Countries
Ownership	
Quasi-independent corporation	NHK, Britain, West Germany, Sweden
Government share in ownership or capital	France, Italy
Income Source	
Receiver fees only	NHK, Britain, Sweden
Receiver fees and advertising	West Germany, France, Italy
Government treasury and advertising	Canada
Method of Receiving Funds	
Public broadcaster directly collects, keeps	NHK, West Germany, Britain (post-1991)
Broadcaster collects, transfers to government	Sweden
Government collects, transfers	Britain (pre-1991), France, Italy
Directly from government treasury	Canada
Decisions on Fee Levels	
Government approval as separate decision	NHK, Britain
Government decides or is part of general government budget	France, Italy, West Germany (local govt.), Sweden
Which Governmental Actor Decides Fee Levels	
Parliament	NHK, France, West Germany[b]
Bureaucracy, executive	Britain (Home[c] and Finance Ministries)
Appointment of Chief Executive and Management	
CEO by governing body and management by CEO	NHK, Britain, Germany, France (post-1982), Sweden
CEO by government	France (pre-1982)
Level of Commercial Competition	
Full commercial competition	NHK, Canada
Limited commercial competition	Britain,[d] Sweden, (post-1992) France (post-1985)

[a]This table is an adaptation and extension of table 2, pp. 40–41, in Inaba Michio, *NHK jushinryō o kangaeru (Thinking about NHK's Receivers' Fees)* (Tokyo: Aoki Shoten, 1985); other sources consulted include: Tom O'Malley, *Closedown?: The BBC and Government Broadcasting Policy 1979–92* (London: Pluto Press, 1994); NHK, ed., *Sekai no rajio to terebijyon, 1984 (The World's Television and Radio—1984)* (Tokyo: Nippon Hōsō Shuppan Kyōkai, 1984). I am grateful to Professor Monika Djerf-Pierre of the University of Gothenberg for providing the information on Sweden.

[b]With the approval of local governments.

[c] In 1992, responsibility for broadcasting was transferred from the Home Office to the new Department of National Heritage.

[d]A semi-commercial network, Independent Television was begun in 1954; the more commercial Channel 4, in 1981.

from the zero-sum game of budgetary politics. Fourth, whereas NHK is not unique in having parliament decide its fee levels, in Britain this is done by bureaucratic ministries.

Fifth, public broadcasters that operate as monopolies may be especially vulnerable to the state because the state enforces that monopoly. This renders broadcasters dependent on the state, much as was the case in the early years of the BBC.[61] As the sole potential broadcasting influence over the public, monopolies especially may invite attempts at interference and control by politicians and bureaucrats. Operating with competition from a wide range of commercial broadcasters may help public broadcasters avoid becoming the exclusive target of political attention. In contrast to many other public broadcasters in the democratic world that operated as monopolies or quasi-monopolies for at least parts of the postwar era, NHK has competed with a full range of commercial broadcasters since the Occupation.

Finally, of all the broadcasters in the countries listed, only NHK appears in the first subcategory of all dimensions. Not even the BBC, the most comparable to NHK among public broadcasters in terms of size, function, and institutional and legal relationship to the state, appears in all. Theoretically, at least, even if accountable to public authority, NHK should have the most autonomy from the state of any public broadcaster in the industrialized democracies. Indeed, it was intended by Occupation reformers to be exactly that. To what extent, however, does reality match the legal ideals?

BROADCASTING REGULATION AND FREEDOM IN PRACTICE

In its very American way, the Occupation saw a society that could be divorced from the state that was supposed to serve it, intending to create in Japan a public broadcaster that was truly an expression of and responsible to the public, not the state. To a large extent, NHK's institutional arrangements seem to fulfill that intent.

Yet, as a competing legitimate representative of the public, challenging the monopoly on authoritative delegation and performing a function crucial to the self-interests of elected and appointed officials, all broadcasters, but particularly public broadcasters, are prime targets for politicians and bureaucrats who want to shape broadcasters' policies and products, whatever the institutional safeguards. Indeed, institutional rules and procedures can be both opportunities and constraints. They may channel attempts to exercise power, opening up probabilities that certain kinds of attempts may be made and not others. At the same time, rules and procedures cannot eliminate those attempts completely and may in fact be used by skillful politicians as a means of influence.

[61] Negrine, *Politics and the Mass Media in Britain*, 85.

In the case of Japan, there are especially good reasons for suspecting a more diverse reality behind the surface of legal principle. As discussed in the introduction, a consistent theme in the literature on politics and law in Japan is the disparity between formal-legal arrangements and actual behavior, authority and actual power, public responsibility and private exercise of influence, and public facade and behind-the-scenes decision making.[62] The attempts at political interference in prewar broadcasting by politicians and officials and in postwar commercial broadcasting, most notably the efforts of Tanaka Kakuei to use license allocation for political purposes,[63] also indicate NHK's potential vulnerability.

Finally, Japan's dominant party system for most of the postwar period of the conservative LDP (1955–93) and its predecessors (1950–55) might also have provided fewer incentives for political elites and public broadcasters to adhere to legal principles of autonomy from the state. It is logical to assume something of an implicit political "golden rule" in operation. That is, when influence over broadcasting is in the context of alternation in power, parties in power have to consider "the shadow of the future"—that gains achieved by interference are likely to be temporary because once one's opponents achieve power, they could easily reverse the gains and impose added costs in retaliation.

This "golden rule" also operates in reverse for the broadcaster. In an alternating party democracy, the broadcaster also has direct incentive to maintain some distance from the party in power. Never knowing when the party in power will change, the broadcaster in effect must be careful not to get too close to the current power, lest it be punished when administrations alternate.

Thus, alternating party regimes provide incentives against the temptations of interference for the political parties and the lure of sycophancy for the broadcaster and in favor of both supporting the broadcaster's neutrality and autonomy.[64] When the system is a de facto dominant party democracy, as in Japan, the inhibitive effects of the usual iterative game of holding power are highly mitigated. The perennial party in power need not be as inhibited from attempts to influence, and the broadcaster may have fewer incentives to completely resist such efforts. How the party in power attempts that influence, why, and with what success is the theme of the rest of this book.

---

[62]For institutional and political approaches to this disparity, see the references in p. 18n.

[63]For prewar examples, see Kasza, *State and Mass Media,* 88–100; on postwar, see Weinberg, "Broadcasting and the Administrative Process," 668–71, 682.

[64]My argument here is based on the logic of Sven Steinmo's institutional analysis of bureaucrats' incentives in alternating (Britain) versus dominant (Sweden) party systems. See his "Political Institutions and Tax Policy in the United States, Sweden, and Britain," *World Politics* 41, no. 4 (1989): 500–535.

In any political system, core questions of political control are often issues of financial control and thus a likely place to look for channels of influence.[65]

Directly collected receivers' fees seemingly provide NHK with a measure of autonomy from political interference. Nevertheless, the necessity of gaining Diet approval for its annual budget—even if in toto rather than for specific items—and for any increase in receivers' fees ultimately provides a major opening for politicians to exercise influence over the broadcaster's policies. In the formal process, neither the Diet nor the Ministry of Posts is supposed to have the opportunity to amend NHK's budget directly. In fact, however, after the budget is sent to the Minister of Posts, the LDP Policy Affairs Research Council's (PARC) Communications Division and the LDP in general have the opportunity to review the budget and have input into its substance, sometimes engaging directly in negotiations with NHK.[66]

The greatest vulnerability of NHK to pressure from the LDP comes at times of financial crisis when budget deficits make fee increases imperative. At such times, the LDP can investigate NHK, criticize it, and even hold approval of the needed policy "hostage" to promises of current or future good behavior as defined by the politicians. In his career autobiography, Shima Keiji, former NHK news executive and president, is critical of NHK's relationship to the LDP, a relationship in which he himself played a pivotal role, and stresses that "The greatest issue (for politicians) is trying to control the news and public opinion through NHK. And it is NHK's budget approval in the Diet which becomes the stage for that direct interference."[67]

Normally, such interaction may take place behind the scenes, in bargaining between NHK executives and important LDP politicians. Not only party leaders engage in these negotiations, but also those with long service and power on the LDP's Policy Affairs Research Council's Communications Division (*teishinbu*) and the Diet's Communications Committee (*tsūshin iinkai*)—usually the same influential politicians on each. It is the responsibility of these party and Diet committees to consider NHK's budget and fee increase requests, and the veteran leaders of these committees are sometimes called the "communications policy tribe" (*teishinzoku*) of the party, a subcategory of the "postal tribe" (*yuseizoku*) of LDP veteran Diet members who concentrate on the policy areas related to the Ministry of Posts and Telecommunications.

Some of these behind-the-scenes communications between broadcasters and "policy tribes" concerned with telecommunications and posts have been institutionalized. Annually, top executives from NHK and the com-

[65]Michael Tracey, "Japan: Broadcasting in a New Democracy," 276.

[66]Matsuda Hiyoshi, "NHK wa doko e iku—Nyū medeiya jidai o mukaete" ("Where NHK Is Going: Confronting the New Media Age), *Sekai* (November, 1986): 77–78.

[67]Shima, *"Shima Geji,"* 75.

mercial networks meet quietly in a hotel room, one broadcaster at a time, with more than 10 of the LDP "postal tribe" Diet members, including former Ministers of Posts and Telecommunications. These informal "broadcast discussions" were initiated in 1967 by a former LDP Minister of Posts and influential "communications tribe" leader, Hashimoto Tomisaburō. These meetings are supposedly off-the-record discussions and an opportunity for politicians and practitioners involved in broadcasting policy to exchange views; they are also, however, frequently the occasion for LDP politicians to warn and criticize broadcasters about the content of programs.[68]

NHK's budget process negotiations also are normally quite covert. In 1979–80, however, the process of Diet approval for NHK's annual budget and for a related proposal to raise the receivers' fees became unusually controversial and public, as did LDP criticisms of NHK. As such, that year's process provides an excellent case study of the actual politics surrounding NHK's budgets and financial condition, as well as of the legal constraints against state intervention and the opportunities for the state to intervene in broadcasting.

NHK'S BUDGET: A CASE STUDY

Background and Significance of the Case

Three specific conditions at NHK in the late 1970s were crucial to the LDP motivation and ability to interfere politically during this period. The first was NHK's precarious financial condition in the 1970s, a particularly vulnerable situation because personnel is the largest component of NHK's budget, and, as in many other Japanese organizations, the cutting of staff except by attrition has been taboo.

The timing of these financial problems was almost predictable. As each new broadcasting technology was introduced—first black-and-white television, then color television, and then direct broadcasting satellite transmissions—the number of contracts would rise dramatically, then stagnate and decline. Naturally, revenue patterns followed accordingly. Beginning in the mid-1950s, NHK's operating revenue skyrocketed along with the purchases of television sets, reaching nearly seven times the 1955 figure by 1965. Then, as the number of black-and-white television receivers' contracts declined precipitously, and the color TV market became saturated, revenue increases began to level off.[69]

---

[68]Shima Nobuhiko, *Media no kage no kenryokusha-tachi* (*The Powerful People of Media's Shadow*) (Tokyo: Kōdansha, 1995), 226–27.

[69]Thus, television contracts rose dramatically in the decade from 1956 (less than half a million) to 1966 (about 19 million). A color television fee was introduced (and radio fees abolished) and payers increased 10 times (2 to 20 million households) in 1968–1974. Then the rate of increase declined to only less than 50 percent (to about 29 million) in the next 11

Expenses, on the other hand, increased consistently. Between 1950 and 1971, NHK always showed a surplus of revenues over expenditures, reaching a peak in 1965. But all this changed as NHK grew. Between 1955 and 1980, the total number of employees almost exactly *doubled*. During this period, even if retirees are taken into account, NHK hired about 10,000 new employees alone.[70] Whereas all the commercial networks together had caught up with and then far outspent NHK on facilities and construction by the late 1960s, in the early 1970s, NHK's construction money nearly doubled and outstripped that of the commercial networks.[71] Production costs also mounted, and then a new News Center and new editing and news gathering technologies, such as the use of computers and electronic news gathering and videotape, added to expenses. All these costs of course were especially exacerbated in the 1970s by the inflation following the first oil shocks.

In 1972, for the first time since a one-year shortfall in 1953, NHK's operating expenses exceeded its revenues, and the problem grew consistently worse for the next three years. The interest burden on borrowing for its huge facility investments during the rapid growth era exacerbated the problem.[72] By 1975, NHK had a deficit equal to almost 14 percent of its income from receivers' fees.[73]

Something had to be done. In 1976, NHK asked for and received a massive increase in receivers' fees of 43 percent,[74] resulting in a large surplus that year, which diminished during the next two years. Then in 1979, a revenue deficit again emerged. The problem was beginning to appear structural. NHK was forced back to the Diet only three years after the large fee increase of 1976 to ask for another along with its annual budget approval.

The second background fact precipitating political intervention was that the Ministry of Posts and Telecommunications, broadcasting's legal regulator and NHK's nominal supervising agency, was being pushed by the LDP "communications tribe" to implement a change in the law regarding collection of receivers' fees. NHK's financial situation provided the opportunity. As noted, NHK's "contract obligation" system levied no real penalties for nonpayment of receivers' fees; NHK's only recourse was to take the re-

---

years. See Inaba Michio, *NHK jushinryō o kangaeru*, Document 3, p. 49. Accordingly, between 1958–1960, NHK's operating revenue was increasing between 25 percent and 50 percent yearly; then 5 percent in 1965–1966, 8–9 percent as color TV replaced black-and-white, but by 1974 and 1975 again around 5 percent. See Hōsō keiei hikaku kenkyūkai, *Hōsō gyōkai*, Documents 14, 15, pp. 266, 267.

[70] Tokunaga Masaki, *NHK fushoku kenkyū* (*Research on NHK's Rot*) (Tokyo: Seibunsha, 1981), 182.

[71] Ibid., fig. 3.1, p. 105.

[72] Matsuda, "NHK wa doko e iku," 72.

[73] Calculated from data in NHK HBCK, *NHK nenkan '84*, 64.

[74] Hōsō keiei hikaku kenkyūkai, *Hōsō gyōkai*, Documents 14 and 15, p. 266.

calcitrant to court for breach of contract, a burdensome and costly process. In 1966, MPT unsuccessfully proposed a revision of the Broadcast Law to the Diet, based on a report of an advisory committee to MPT, primarily for the purpose of clarifying the language concerning the legal requirement to pay.[75]

Things changed by the end of the 1970s, however. Confronting NHK's financial difficulties, another prospective fee increase, and an organized movement to encourage nonpayment of fees as a protest against NHK's alleged conservative bias, MPT and the "communications tribe" of the LDP became increasingly concerned about the inherent unfairness of asking those who dutifully paid their fees to pay more when others were not paying at all. Thus, they thought that, both for equity's and revenue's sake, NHK's ability to collect fees had to be backed up by the law and the threat of punishment for nonpayment. They proposed a revision to the Broadcast Law to change the basis for receivers' fees from an obligation to sign a contract to an obligation to pay the fee, with punishment for nonpayment. This became intricately involved with NHK's budget and fee increase proposals.

The third background fact to the case was the increasing sensitivity and hostility of the LDP to the media, and especially to NHK. In general, there had been intense coverage of a string of major scandals involving the ruling party, beginning in 1974 with the resignation of former Prime Minister Tanaka Kakuei over his money and business connections and culminating in the Lockheed scandal a few years later in which he was indicted for accepting bribes while prime minister. Additionally in the case of NHK, there was the issue of Ueda Tetsu, the former president of Nippōrō (Japan Broadcasting Union) in NHK and a Socialist Diet Member, and the power of the union, issues I will discuss further in chapter 6. During the late 1970s the LDP came to see Ueda's union as having given the NHK news division a decidedly "leftist bias."

The budget and fee increases and the Broadcast Law revision process of 1979–80 provide a good case to observe the informal and formal processes by which such matters are approved, and the various institutional means of pressure that the LDP can exert on NHK for its own purposes. These and the views prevalent among a portion of the ruling party about NHK's autonomy were unusually and strikingly revealed publicly when several issues concerning NHK particularly angered some important LDP politicians. And finally, it highlighted the respective roles of the MPT bureaucrats and LDP politicians over issues concerning broadcasting.

[75]The Provisional Investigation Committee on Legislation Related to Broadcasting (*Rinji hōsō kankei hōsei chōsakai*), chaired by Matsukata Saburō, respected prewar journalist and immediate postwar head of Kyōdō Wire Service. See Shiga, *Terebi eitei*, 191, concerning receivers' fees.

Budget and Fee Increase Proposals

By spring 1979, NHK's budget was ¥2.1 billion in the red, severe enough to require action. On April 4, 1979, NHK President Sakamoto Tomokazu held a press conference and announced the establishment of the Second NHK Basic Problems Investigation Council (*Dainiji NHK kihon mondai chōsakai*), an advisory organ of external experts, to report to him on NHK's difficulties and with recommended solutions. This, as the name indicates, was only the second time NHK had felt the need to establish such an organ to delve fundamentally into its way of operating. As the first had been only three years before in 1976, preceding NHK's request for its last fee increase, the press accurately saw the establishment of this new advisory organ as a preliminary step toward another fee increase.[76]

In its report, the 26-member committee, composed of scholars, business people, labor unions, and consumer groups, did just that, but only after real debate and disagreement among committee members. The committee report implied criticism of NHK in that it recommended that the public broadcaster needed to strengthen its ties to its audience, clarify its legal relationship to those who paid the fee, take steps to deal with nonpayers, and make its administration more efficient.

The group judged that although NHK had attempted to control expenditures after the last rate increase, the effort was not sufficient and costs had risen further. The committee recognized, however, that NHK had no other real sources of revenue outside the receivers' fees and that the broadcaster could neither achieve a balanced budget nor fulfill its mission by merely placing more limitations on expenditures. Therefore, even while concerned about the "deficit-fee increase" cycle that was developing, the committee recommended a 25 percent increase in the receivers' fee.[77]

With the committee's report legitimizing a fee increase, NHK prepared the draft of its budget. A month after the committee's report, as is customary, the budget went quietly and informally to the Radio-Broadcasting Issues Subcommittee (*denpa, hōsō mondai shoiinkai*) of the Communications Division (*tsūshinbukai*) of the Policy Affairs Research Council (*seimuchōsakai*), the main policy-making organ, of the LDP.[78] The purpose was to conduct *nemawashi*, or prior consultation, to prepare the ground for the budget's

[76]*Asahi Shimbun*, April 5, 1979, 2.

[77]See *Asahi Shimbun*, November 20, 1979, 3; Shiga, *Terebi eitei*, 191, 206; and the background article, "Doko e iku 'kokumin no NHK'" ("Where Is the 'People's NHK' Going?"), *Asahi Shimbun*, November 20, 1979, 4.

[78]Shiga, *Terebi eitei*, 206; Shiga's account is based on Inaba Michio, "NHK o kokuei hōsō ni sasete wa naranai" ("NHK Mustn't Be Made into a State Broadcaster"), *Masukomi Shimin* (April 1980), 8–17.

approval by the powerful LDP politicians specializing in broadcasting and communications policy. They would have to pass on it before it went to the full policy-making body of the LDP, the party leaders, the Cabinet, and finally the Diet and its committees. It should be noted that these are subdivisions of a (ruling) political party, not a legislative body, and that such deliberations precede the formal legislative process, are not public, and do not include representatives of minority or opposition parties. Nor is this stage in the process part of any legal or constitutional requirement—nowhere is it written that NHK's budget must go through the LDP PARC prior to going to the Minister of Posts.[79]

Indeed, NHK's budget had been negotiated with, and approved by, the LDP "communications tribe" even prior to formal approval by NHK's Board of Governors, legally the highest decision-making body of NHK. It was not until January 30, 1980, that a budget was to be presented to NHK's Board of Governors prior to being sent for approval to the MPT and then to the Diet.[80] This fact reflects the relative influence of LDP politicians and NHK's Board of Governors on NHK.

On January 29, after discussing NHK's budget, the LDP's PARC Communication Division approved NHK's budget proposal on condition of a fee increase. The next day, NHK publicly announced its proposal for a 24 percent increase in receivers' fees: from ¥710 to ¥880 for color televisions and from ¥420 to ¥520 for black-and-white sets. The same day the Board of Governors passed the NHK budget proposal based on such an increase, sending it to the Minister of Posts for his approval.

By the end of the first week in February, the formal proposal had cleared PARC's entire Communication Division, had been approved by PARC, and was in the Executive Council (*Sōmukai*) of the party. It was approved for submission to the Diet, but there had been enough strong opposition to any fee increase among party leaders to attach the condition that NHK "make efforts for administrative rationalization and be unbiased and nonpartisan in its programming." Dissatisfaction with the frequent fee increases had surfaced, as had, according to media observer Shiga Nobuo, displeasure with both NHK programming and the broadcaster's failure to cooperate in enhancing the LDP's image. He further observed: "Listening to the comments of Diet members knowledgeable in broadcasting administration you somehow can understand that they feel as if they want to make NHK into a possession of the government and LDP."[81]

[79]These criticisms are made by Inaba, "NHK jushinryō," 9–10.

[80]"Kara-jushinryō wa 880-en" ("Color Receivers' Fee 880 Yen"), *Asahi Shimbun*, January 24, 1980, 3.

[81]Shiga, *Terebi eitei*, 210–11. On this part of the PARC process, see also 207, and "NHK neage ryosho" ("NHK Increase Acknowledged"), *Asahi Shimbun*, February 9, 1980, 2, and

The Fee System, Videotape Evidence Issues, and LDP's Attacks

The secret and preliminary discussion of NHK's budget in the PARC Communications Division subcommittee, and the issue of equity, motivated several LDP members influential in the broadcasting field to push MPT to revise the fee system to one of obligation to pay, rather than merely contract obligation. By February 22, 1980, MPT had put together a draft proposal to revise Article 32 to make obligatory the reporting of the installation of a receiver that could provide reception for NHK broadcasts, the payment of a fee for that reception, and explicit penalties for failing to do so, including doubling of the fee if payment had not been made within 60 days. This proposal also had been approved by the LDP Communications Division and was to be sent to LDP PARC and Executive Council and the Cabinet, with expectation of submission to the Diet within three weeks.[82]

The *Asahi* newspaper, often a critic of government in its editorial stances, reacted the next day, questioning whether this would really make proving nonpayment any easier and raising the issue of whether the revised fee status would not make the fee more like a tax, thereby changing the nature of NHK and damaging the good will of citizens who pay their fees.[83] This was not the only proposal under consideration at the time that might have changed NHK's status. Just a few days before, in response to a scandal at the public telephone corporation, the government had begun to discuss expanding its supervision over many previously loosely controlled "Special Legal Entities" (*tokushu hōjin*), NHK among them, raising the issue of how this might interfere with broadcasting freedom.[84]

Another broadcasting issue then was thrown into this already intense situation. On March 3, the Chiba District Court ruled that news videotape, taken by media organizations, could be used as evidence in a case involving an invasion of the new Narita airport control tower two years earlier by people protesting the building of the airport. As they had in other such incidents, NHK and several other TV news organizations refused to hand over the tapes on media freedom grounds.[85]

"Kara-880-en o teishutsu" ("880 Yen for Color Submitted"), *Asahi Shimbun*, January 31, 1980, 22.

[82] "NHK jushinryō no fuharai" ("Nonpayment of NHK Receivers' Fees"), *Asahi Shimbun*, January 29, 1980, 3, and February 22, 1980, 2; Shiga, *Terebi eitei*, 206–7.

[83] "Me ni tsuku 'kōshisei'" ("The Conspicuous High Posture"), *Asahi Shimbun*, February 23, 1980, 4.

[84] See "Zentokushu hōjin o gyōsei kansatsu" ("All Special Public Corporations to be Administratively Inspected"), *Asahi Shimbun*, February 18, 1980, 1; on the complexities of *tokushu hōjin* (public entities), see Chalmers Johnson, *Japan's Public Policy Companies* (Washington, D.C.: American Enterprise Institute for Public Policy Research, 1978), 34–48.

[85] See Beer, *Freedom of Expression in Japan*, 298. On the resistance to the airport, see David E. Apter and Nagayo Sawa, *Against the State: Politics and Social Protest in Japan* (Cambridge: Har-

This action infuriated many LDP representatives, already hostile to NHK for its perceived bias against them and irritated by its frequent fee increases. At the LDP Executive Council meeting of March 4, consideration of the proposal to change the existing contract system provided the opportunity to vent that rage. Criticism ranged from the mild ("The Court's adoption of the evidence is reasonable and consistent also with the nature of public broadcasting. Why are they resisting?") to the enraged ("Is the public nature of NHK to be for radical organizations?"). Some LDP leaders labeled NHK's action as a "disgrace!" The denunciation in some cases revealed as much about how they viewed NHK's relationship to the state as anything else. Take, for example, these comments: "We are bound by contract with NHK. When there's a contractual relationship, doesn't one use at one's own discretion what one buys?" and "Based on taking a tax (receivers' fee) NHK is a public broadcaster. It's absurd to go against state control."

In addition to such verbal criticism, the LDP Executive Council retaliated, putting a hold on introducing the contract change proposal into the Diet. When NHK's president and other chief executives did not respond satisfactorily to their complaints, the chair of the Council (and later Prime Minister) Suzuki Zenkō, said, "It's necessary to clarify a bit more your posture as a public broadcaster, and today I'd like to defer the bill proposal."[86] The action was interpreted by the press to be motivated as much by the LDP's dissatisfaction with NHK's news program content as with its legal actions in the Narita tower incident. Discussing the fact that the LDP is concerned about the "rash" of fee increases of public service agencies, the *Asahi* goes on to say that the LDP's long-term criticism of NHK's "program bias" is also a motivation:

> The LDP has made demands on NHK, through unofficial channels, with regard to the content of certain (individual) programs. The LDP view is that despite doing their best as the governing party, whatever they do is given negative coverage. Its action probably comes from the hope (to get better coverage) at least from "public broadcasters" which they control in terms of subscriber fees and related legislation. . . .

It concludes that the LDP's aims are to make "public broadcasting" mean "state run broadcasting" (*kokuei hōsō*) and to exert control over its programming. Within a few days, it was clear that the *Asahi*'s interpretation was shared by opposition parties, their supporting groups, and some consumer

---

vard University Press, 1984); "Hōsōhō kaiseian no kokkai teishutsu—Jimin sōmukai ga 'Matta'" ("Broadcast Law Revision Bill Diet Submission: LDP Executive Council Says 'Wait'"), *Asahi Shimbun*, March 5, 1980, 2; Shiga, *Terebi eitei*, 192.

[86] All quotations in the last two paragraphs from *Asahi Shimbun*, March 5, 1980, 2, and Shiga, *Terebi eitei*, 193.

groups, all of whom saw all this as part of the LDP's pernicious strategy to put NHK on the road to becoming a "state broadcaster."[87]

Meanwhile, at another Executive Council meeting on March 8, NHK President Sakamoto meekly promised strictly correct, fair program content for NHK's nightly news programs. He even went so far as to promise that NHK was going to try "for broadcasting in a form that would not become a problem."[88]

An Investigative Committee and Denouement

The LDP Executive Council did not seem impressed with this promise. At the March 11 meeting, called to discuss the bill proposing the revision of the Broadcast Law to change the legal nature of receivers' fees, several LDP veteran politicians again criticized NHK's resistance to turning over videotapes as evidence to the Chiba District Court. This time, NHK President Sakamoto more explicitly defended NHK's action on broadcasting freedom grounds, explaining the need to protect the source-journalist relationship and the importance of freedom of information and pleading for understanding from the ruling party. But LDP executives retorted that "Providing evidence on the crimes of radical students is also in your public nature." And, "Freedom of broadcasting is ok but you ought not to complain about how things in the news are used." They then proceeded to attack NHK's alleged bias in favor of the opposition in the content of its news programs, including on issues of nuclear power generation, revealing the LDP's distrust of the mass media in general.

One LDP Upper House representative, Tamaki Kazuō, after criticizing both NHK and the *Asahi*'s news reporting, went so far as to ask, "Why should we politicians fold our hands to these kinds of mass media conceits? Why don't we thoroughly clean out the mass media with this good opportunity related to the problem of NHK?" Commenting on Tamaki's attack, Aoki Sadanobu has argued that this statement reveals the LDP's true motive in holding NHK's budget "hostage" to put through a revision in the Broadcast Law: the LDP wanted to make NHK, "the weakest link within mass media because its budget and management personnel are subject to Diet approval," into a "state broadcaster."[89]

LDP leaders, however, faced a dilemma. As some within the party argued, holding up the Broadcast Law revision seemed counterproductive. After all,

[87]Quotation from *Asahi Shimbun*, March 5, 1995, 2; on other criticism, see also "'Kakuei hōsōka' kenan no koe" ("Creating 'State-run Broadcasting' Voices of Concern"), *Asahi Shimbun*, March 6, 1980, 4.

[88]Shindō Ken, *Kenryoku toshite no NHK* (*NHK as Power*) (Tokyo: Sanichi Shobō, 1981), 26.

[89]Aoki, *NHK*, 170–71; see also "Jimin no chōsa iinkai" ("An Investigation Committee in the LDP"), *Asahi Shimbun*, March 12, 1980, 1, for these LDP verbal attacks.

the Broadcast Law revision was originally the idea of the party's own "communications tribe" representatives, not NHK, and changes in the receivers' fee structure might help resolve NHK's cycle of budget deficits and requests for fee increases. Further, the legal change seemed to make the fee more like a "tax," thus bringing the broadcaster closer to the model of a state agency. Also, because the Executive Council had already previously passed NHK's budget bill, it would be difficult to use the usual, ritualized threat to hold up its passage in the Diet.

The compromise solution was to pass the Broadcast Law revision with its change in receivers' fee status, but give the final decision to the top leaders of the LDP. Moreover, an investigative committee was to be established within the party with authority to explore the public nature of NHK. It was the first time the LDP had established internally an organ specifically to investigate NHK, and the action raised interesting and complicated issues concerning freedom of broadcasting.

NHK's budget was finally proposed to the Diet on March 17. Reportedly the delay of several weeks after being approved by the LDP and the Cabinet was due in part to the resistance of the opposition parties to the LDP's plan to consider both the budget and broadcast law changes.[90] The LDP finally was forced to propose the budget first, without the controversial change in the legal status of the receivers' fee.

Meanwhile, the opposition mobilized against both the Broadcast Law revision and the LDP investigative committee. On March 21, 1980, Sōhyō (Nihon Rōdō Kumiai Sōhyō Kaigi, the General Council of Trade Unions), the major leftist national labor union federation and support group of the Japan Socialist Party (now called Social Democratic Party of Japan), which includes NHK's Japan Broadcasting Union [*Nippōro*] as a member, established a Joint Struggle Council to Oppose Making NHK a State Broadcaster (*NHK no kokuei hōsōka hantai kyōtō kaigi*). The union opposed making the NHK receivers' fee a legal obligation, and they were also against the establishment of the LDP NHK investigative committee. Scholars also began weighing in with newspaper articles publicly raising constitutional issues and questioning whether the ruling party's means of expressing their dissatisfaction with news coverage by establishing an investigative committee was an overreaction.[91]

As the LDP moved to establish the NHK Investigation Committee (NHK Chōsa Iinkai, its provisional title), it soon became clear that the party itself might be divided on the issue. On March 22, LDP party executives decided

[90]On the establishment of the investigative committee, the issues it raised, and the opposition and the LDP compromise decision, see *Asahi Shimbun*, March 12, 1995, 1. Shiga, *Terebi eitei*, 208–9.

[91]See quotations in Shiga, *Terebi eitei*, 195–96; "Kōkyō hōsō to wa nani ka" ("What is Public Broadcasting?"), *Asahi Shimbun*, March 21, 1980, 22, and also March 26, 1980, 12.

to select quickly the personnel for the investigative committee concerning "the way NHK's public broadcasting ought to be." In response to demands for an entity with more authority, the party planned to make the committee a special organ directly under the party president, in other words, the prime minister.

Some party executives, however, were reportedly concerned that the committee would be perceived as an attempt at news suppression. Even a leader like Diet member and conservative writer Ishihara Shintarō, who had been one of the harshest critics of NHK among the party leadership at the Executive Council meetings, began publicly to wonder whether such a committee would work to the LDP advantage because, as a partisan organization, they would have difficulty persuading public opinion without the opinion of experts, too. One party leader was quoted in the press anonymously as insisting that the committee would not carry out daily supervision of NHK; rather "it will take up problems when they arise; but it's better not to draw the sword."[92]

By the beginning of April 1980, it had become clear that the former Minister of Posts Akagi Shutoku was the compromise candidate to chair the NHK Investigation Committee. He had been critical of NHK; but because he also had bureaucratic experience and had served as the prime minister's chief Cabinet secretary, the chief press liaison, he was seen as leaning toward the "doves" on the issues.

While all this was occurring, NHK's budget bill was still not passed, and it had became clear that it could not be passed by the Diet before the end of the fiscal year, March 31. On March 28, in accordance with the Broadcast Law's provisions for such an eventuality, NHK proposed to the Minister of Posts a one-month provisional budget to allow the broadcaster to continue operating until the bill could be passed into law. The budget, including the 24 percent fee increase, finally was passed by the House of Representatives' Communications Committee on April 10, but with a six-item supplementary resolution that included an admonition to NHK to maintain "freedom of expression and unbiased, nonpartisan broadcasting," as well as to attempt to reign in fee increases. The budget bill passed the full house on April 17 and then the House of Councilors on April 25, and the receivers' fees increase was scheduled to go into effect in May. The Broadcast Law revision died.

At their April 8 Executive Council meeting, LDP leaders had decided to cater to the anti-NHK elements in the party and to send a warning to NHK by establishing the Investigation Committee. By the end of the month, how-

---

[92] "Iinjinsen, kaishi e" ("Committee Selection, Toward a Start"), *Asahi Shimbun*, March 23, 1980, 1.

ever, concerned about criticism that it was trying to interfere in the mass media and that such a committee was meaningless without a broader mandate to investigate all mass media, LDP leaders had decided to let the committee quietly die without ever meeting.[93]

INSTITUTIONAL PROTECTION AND POLITICAL REALITY

The Occupation had attempted in a practical way to mitigate the potential for political interference in broadcasting by institutionalizing an independent regulatory commission to oversee broadcasting rather than have it supervised directly by the elected representatives in parliament. The Japanese government's subsequent abolition of this institutional buffer between the state and the broadcaster left Japan with state and broadcasting institutions potentially operating in contradiction. A British type of parliamentary state, with its locus of sovereignty and lines of accountability centralized in the national legislature, confronts a legally independent broadcaster, responsible ostensibly to the people rather than the state, in a constitutional regime that guarantees the freedom of a press.

The constitutional and Broadcast Law prohibitions on direct interference with the media have been legitimized enough to make many LDP party leaders worry about the appearance of news suppression and to prompt members of the opposition, its support groups, the intelligentsia, and not least of all the media itself, to rally to the defense of such norms when the LDP appears to violate them. When challenged on these grounds, the party and government understood that its best course was a quiet retreat once it had expressed its media criticisms. But it is also clear that a segment of the LDP defines "public broadcaster" very differently from the way intended by the Occupation and also from the spirit and purpose of the Broadcast Law, and this group will attempt to use their parliamentary sovereignty to intimidate NHK.

Because NHK is a public broadcaster receiving receivers' fees from the public and has its budget approved by the ruling party and the Diet, these LDP leaders and members perceive it as having a special responsibility to avoid news and information programming or policy actions that cast the ruling party in a bad light or that offend its sense of duty to the state. Such attitudes among the LDP seem to go beyond the antipathy to and claims of bias against the media found among ruling officials everywhere. As the statements

[93]Late March and April events are found in "NHK jushinryō" ("NHK Receivers' Fees"), *Asahi Shimbun,* March 29, 1980, 3; April 3, 1980, "Akagi-shi kiyō" ("Mr. Akagi Appointed"), 2; "Shūini de Shōnin-NHK no neage" ("NHK Fee Increase Approved in House of Representatives Committee"), April 11, 1980, 22; "NHK neage kaketsu" ("NHK Increase Approved"), April 18, 1980, 3; "Kōsō dake de, jitsugen miokuri?" ("Only in Conception, Farewell to Implementation?"), *Asahi Shimbun,* April 30, 1980, 3.

and actions of the "hawk" faction in the case study above indicate, these conservative politicians have a definite conception of NHK that is closer to the prewar conception of broadcasting's role as a servant of the state.

The case also reveals something about the process of budget and policy making concerning NHK and, more generally, about relationships among the key actors in the politics of broadcasting. Clearly, the dominant role in broadcasting politics is played by the LDP, and especially its "communications tribe" in the Communications Division of PARC. It was from among these latter specialized politicians that the initiative to revise the legal status of the receivers' fees stemmed, and it is they who have the greatest influence in the policy-making process for NHK's budget. Once the issues of NHK's alleged news program "bias" and its resistance to the court on the videotape evidence intensified, the role of the party leaders on the Executive Council became crucial. They put a hold on the receivers' fee change to punish NHK and also decided first to establish, then to let quietly die, the NHK Investigation Committee.

Although in some areas, such as economic policy making, the elite Japanese bureaucracy may play a more important role than the politicians, the LDP seems central in broadcasting policy and, more generally, in issues related to posts and telecommunications. This is not to say that bureaucrats have no role or do not attempt to influence NHK, too. For example, MPT often attempts to serve as intermediary between the politicians and NHK on its budget.[94] But this issue area of broadcasting provides more incentive, and the legal process more opportunity, to politicians than to bureaucrats to interfere. Elected officials hold the prior and predominant position even if— as can be seen in our case where the politicians proposed the revision to the legal status of the receivers' fees and MPT immediately took up the cause— they often cooperate and work together.

LDP politicians and the MPT are far more important in the budget and policy-making process than NHK's own Board of Governors. This is evidenced in the fact that it is standard practice for NHK's top management to consult with and get prior approval of its budget from the LDP "communications tribe" before the Board even sees it. Former President Shima Keiji's description of the Board indicates that it is probably fairly politicized in any event. He describes the chair as being in the pocket of the ruling party and that both the LDP and MPT have "spies" among Board members.[95] The fact that the Board does not serve its intended role as a buffer from political in-

---

[94]See Shima, "*Shima Geji*," 88–89, on saying one thing to NHK and another to the politicians.

[95]Ibid., 70–71.

terference and the above case study indicate that there is indeed a disparity between the legal theory and formal institutional norms of NHK's independence from the state and the political reality and also one between parliamentary power and constitutional freedoms.

The nature of these disparities are most interesting. The legal institutions concerning the regulation of broadcasting in Japan provide very limited channels for overt political pressure on NHK. Government, as we have seen, does not have the legal power to collect NHK's fees, provide any significant portion of its funds, own any portion of it, officially appoint its management, or interfere directly or through its governing board in its program content. Administratively, government has never used its power to revoke broadcast licenses. Almost no other public broadcaster in the democratic world can make this claim. One of the only legal powers government has over NHK is the Diet's power to pass its overall budget.

Former NHK President Shima considers the requirement that NHK's budgets be approved by the Diet to be one of the most important reasons for politicians' interference in NHK. The politicians essentially can and do warn, "If you don't listen to what I'm saying, we won't have the budget passed in the time limit."[96] Almost all observers of NHK agree that the ability to hold the broadcaster's budget "hostage" to the end-of-the-fiscal-year deadline is a power that the ruling party uses, and abuses, to its advantage. The case above is only one of many examples of how the timing of budget passage enabled the LDP to gain influence with NHK.

The nature of what the LDP politicians want may vary from the trivial to the important, but NHK executives always know that however much the law proscribes interference in program content, they will have to justify and perhaps answer for their news treatment of the LDP at budget time and that an alienated LDP can make it difficult to move NHK budgets through the Diet. For most of the postwar period, these executives also knew that the LDP would control the government and a majority in the Diet. With no alternation in power, being seen as critical of government meant alienating the LDP, which, in turn, meant long-range as well as short-term consequences.

Even if executives rarely explicitly convey this need for caution to their subordinates in the newsroom, no newsroom employee of NHK can fail to be aware of the dangers lurking in controversial or critical coverage of the party and government, a caution reinforced, as we saw in chapter 3, by the process by which the news is gathered, selected, and edited.

---

[96] Ibid., 84. The other reasons are the LDP's personnel control of the Board of Governors, and NHK's union and labor-management relations, which gives the politicians an excuse to intervene (66). On NHK labor-management issues, see chapter 6.

The legal and normative institutional constraints on political control over broadcasting deny Japanese politicians formal and overt means of interference in broadcasting content. The few means that do exist, however, have been exploited by the LDP to gain attention to its complaints and to try to induce limits on potentially negative coverage. As we shall see, the same legal and normative institutional constraints also have encouraged and channeled attempts at control into more informal and covert means.

CHAPTER 5

Leadership and Politics

The president shall be appointed by the Board of Governors.

— *The Broadcast Law,* Article 27

The biggest task for any president of NHK was to resist pressure from the LDP. The pressure was overwhelming.

—Kimura Tarō, former NHK newscaster,

qtd. in David E. Sanger, "Japan's Old Guard

Flails at the Talking Heads"

In a rather British way, the lines of both political pressure and political resolution (in Japanese broadcasting) tend to take place outside any legalistic structure.

—Michael Tracey, "Japan: Broadcasting in a New Democracy"

One of the most important channels for the government's indirect and covert influence on NHK is through its upper management, consisting of the Board of Governors, the president and vice president, and the directors (*riji*) and managing directors (*senmu riji*). Designed to make NHK indirectly accountable to government while preserving its independence from direct interference, the law specifies the relationships among these key actors; but the actual linkages among them, and between them and the ruling LDP, have developed rather differently.

The Board is formally the highest decision-making body of the organization, but in fact, it meets rarely and almost always approves the policies of the president who actually has the strongest influence in determining the direction and organizational culture of the institution. Further, as was indicated in the previous chapter, the Board and its personnel are hardly politically neutral as some members have close ties to the governing party and the Ministry of Posts and Telecommunications.

The process of selection of the president and the Board is nearly reversed from that specified in law. In reality, the prime minister and other leaders of the LDP approve the president, and in turn, the president and sometimes the MPT wield some influence over the Board selection.[1] The entire process of selection of the president has at times been highly politicized and wrapped up in the factional politics of the LDP, while at the lower levels, NHK management personnel have developed close and institutionalized relationships with the governing party and the MPT. The administrations of many postwar presidents of NHK have been marked by often embarrassing cases of public political controversy, which sometimes revealed political interference for partisan purposes.

After the late 1950s, two simultaneous trends were to make NHK and its presidents particularly vulnerable to political pressure. The first was the growing importance of television. With the 1960 Security Treaty crisis (*Anpo*), the LDP came to recognize the potential political power of this new medium. The ruling party increasingly became attentive both to personnel decisions, such as the selection of the president, and to programming content.[2] The second trend was NHK's increasing emphasis on television news. Strengthening its news-gathering operations and becoming dominant in television news programming after the late 1950s meant an ever more intimate involvement with politicians and officials. At the same time, increasing contact with and reliance on political figures as sources and subjects also meant more possibilities to offend and depend on the same powers that passed its budgets and selected its top management.

The result has been a nearly uninterrupted series of NHK presidential terms that have encompassed, indeed all too often been initiated by or terminated in, public political controversy or private political deals. The brief political chronicles of these presidential terms and issues reveal much about the usually behind-the-scenes world of NHK top management and its relationship with the state. What follows does not represent a definitive history of the successes and failures of these presidents or of the organization during their terms in office. I focus here only on the theme of this book—NHK and its involvement with the political world.

TELEVISION, *Anpo*, AND NHK

With the spread of television and the polarization of Japanese political culture into the rightist and leftist camps by the late 1950s, broadcast-

[1]Shiga Nobuo, *Buraun-kan no uragawa* (*The Hidden Side of the Television Tube*) (Tokyo: Nihon Kogyo Shinbunsha, 1977) 44; Yamato Buhei, *NHK kokueika no inbō* (*The Conspiracy to Nationalize NHK*) (Tokyo: PMC Shuppanbu, 1980), 92; Ise Akifumi, *NHK daikenkyū* (*Large Research on NHK*) (Tokyo: Poru Shuppan, 1988), 154; Hara Kōjirō, *NHK—Kōkyō hōsō no rekishi to kadai* (*NHK: History and Issues of Public Broadcasting*) (Tokyo: Kyōikusha, 1978), 58.
[2]Hara, *NHK—Kōkyō hōsō*, 126–27; Shiga, *Buraun-kan no uragawa*, 42–43.

ing became more closely scrutinized by politicians, and NHK came under increasing pressure from conservative governments. One issue was popular criticism of the harmful influence of vulgar and violent programs on children, with some critics claiming such programs contributed to higher juvenile delinquency and crime rates. Another was the dissatisfaction of conservative governments with the broadcasting laws and their attempt to gain more direct control over the NHK organization in particular and broadcasting in general. Some see the two issues as linked, the former providing the excuse for the latter.[3]

Although the conservatives had been trying to revise the Broadcast Law since the end of the Occupation, in 1957/58 Minister of Posts Tanaka Kakuei's renewed efforts became intertwined with the selection of a new NHK president. Tanaka was an especially active Minister, and the connections he developed to the mass media during this period would serve him well later in his career. During Tanaka's term, beginning in October 1957, he approved 36 commercial and seven NHK broadcasting stations' licenses—often over the objections of the Ministry of Posts bureaucrats—a record number for any minister.[4] He also formulated plans to revise the Broadcast Law, including a proposal to have the Cabinet appoint the president of NHK directly.

When NHK President Nagata Kiyoshi died in November 1957, Tanaka discussed his successor with Prime Minister Kishi Nobusuke and decided to appoint Nomura Hideo, a member of the State Public Safety Committee with a background in the *Asahi* newspaper organization. In the immediate postwar period, presidents of NHK tended to come from newspaper or academic backgrounds.[5] When the government's decision leaked to a newspaper, however, the Board of Governors and its chairman Abe Shinnosuke—a future NHK president—balked at quietly going along. They did not have any objection to Nomura, and governmental selection or approval of a new NHK president was not unprecedented. They objected, however, to the highhanded way Tanaka had made the decision without so much as consulting them.[6]

Nomura offered to withdraw to end the impasse, so Tanaka proposed a deal: if the Board accepted Nomura, Tanaka promised both to eliminate the provision about the government directly appointing the NHK president

[3]Matsuda Hiroshi, *Dokyumento—Hōsō sengoshi 2: sōsa to jyānarizumu (Document—Broadcasting's Postwar History,* vol. 2, *Manipulation and Journalism)* (Kanagawa: Sōshisha, 1981), 81–91, on the history of criticism of television and its linkages to broadcast law revision.
[4]Kenkyū shūdan, komyunikēshyon '90, eds., *Masu komi no myōnichi o tou—vol. 1: Hōsō (Questioning the Future of Mass Media,* vol. 1, *Broadcasting)* (Tokyo: Otsuki Shoten, 1985), 134–35.
[5]Yamato, *NHK kokueika no inbō,* 98.
[6]Matsuda, *Hōsō sengoshi 2,* 99–100, and footnote 9, p. 228. Matsuda cites statements from Nomura's biography confirming the Tanaka discussions with Kishi and the basic nature of the deal that brought him the presidency.

from his proposed revision of the Broadcast Law and to respect NHK's independence henceforth. Based on that agreement, the Board officially announced the appointment of Nomura as president in early 1958, more than two months after the death of the previous incumbent.

Several days later at a press conference related to the Nomura's appointment, Tanaka announced that he would introduce into the next session of the Diet a revision of the Broadcast Law. As he had promised, the proposed revision did *not* contain any provision changing the procedures for appointing NHK's president. Later, however, two MPT bureaucrats, including Tanaka's vice minister during this period, would parachute into NHK as director or managing director, the first post-retirement placements of high-ranking bureaucrats (*amakudari*) into NHK since the democratization of the organization after the war.[7]

Nomura's term would witness the most intense political crisis in postwar Japan's history, the confrontations between left and right over the ratification of the revised U.S.-Japan Security Treaty (*Anpo*) in 1960. Much attention has been paid to the role of the newspapers in both covering and exacerbating that crisis; less to the role of television. By 1960 there were 5 million television sets in Japan, a distribution rate of about 40 percent of households, and Anpo was to be the first major political event in Japanese history vicariously experienced by the public via television.[8]

NHK was in a difficult position. The government and ruling party were very critical of NHK and the media in general during this crisis, blaming newspapers, television, and intellectuals for opposition to the treaty. Then once the government rammed the treaty through the Diet in a "snap vote" (*kyōkō saiketsu*), it also faulted the media for the even larger anti-government, "crisis of democracy" movement that resulted. At one point, there was discussion in a Cabinet meeting about the possibility of the Minister of Posts "warning" NHK—a legal power that the Minister did not have, incidentally.[9]

Nomura's experience as a political reporter on close terms with LDP politicians may have enabled him to stand up to crude pressure. During the crisis, a delegation of LDP Diet members came to see Nomura to protest NHK's "leftist bias." After listening quietly for a while, he angrily responded that they should "go study politics more. It would be better to leave NHK mat-

---

[7]Ibid., 97–100. *Amakudari* literally means "descent from heaven."

[8]Matsuda, *Hōsō sengoshi 2*, 132, on television's distribution at the time. See Edward P. Whittemore, *The Press in Japan Today: A Case Study* (Columbia: University of South Carolina Press, 1961), and George R. Packard III, *Protest in Tokyo* (Princeton: Princeton University Press, 1966), esp. 242–25, 280–84, on the role of media in the crisis, including Packard's p. 27 on radio and television.

[9]The following discussion of NHK during the Anpo crisis is based on Matsuda, *Hōsō sengoshi 2*, 144–54, and Aoki Sadanobu, *NHK: Sekai saidai no masukomi shūdan* (*NHK: The World's Largest Mass Media Company*) (Tokyo: Asahi Sonorama, 1980), 127.

ters to me," and then he walked out on them. During his tenure, NHK also sometimes distinguished itself in its coverage, especially of the snap vote that pushed the treaty through the Diet, and in producing many special programs during the crisis.

At the same time, however, Nomura instituted a rigid system of checking programs concerning *Anpo,* with discussants carefully chosen to emphasize a middle-of-the-road conservatism. In response to a government media campaign to reverse public opinion after the snap vote and in anticipation of President Dwight Eisenhower's projected—later aborted—visit to Japan, NHK also began to eschew violence and extreme views, as did many other media organizations. Several programs about *Anpo* were either cut entirely or had portions cut if judged to be exacerbating the confrontation.

Long after the end of the treaty crisis, its media legacy would be the lesson that the new medium of television was a potentially powerful source of political information and imagery. The careful internal controls on controversial political content that had been established in this crisis would become an institutionalized feature of the news process.

MAEDA YOSHINORI AND THE "GOLDEN AGE"
OF TELEVISION NEWS (1964–73)

Many consider Maeda Yoshinori the most influential NHK president of the postwar era. His career as a higher executive at NHK and record three terms as president coinciding with the enormous expansion in the distribution and importance of television alone might have earned him that distinction; but Maeda also was greatly responsible for building the large NHK news apparatus that would become the vaunted core of the organization.

Born in Hokkaidō in 1906, he majored in Italian at Tokyo Foreign Language (University), graduated in 1927, and then went to Italy and studied politics at the University of Rome. Upon graduation in 1936, he entered the *Asahi* newspaper's Rome Bureau as a reporter. He covered Italy's fascist period—he is said to have known Mussolini quite well—and the invasion of Ethiopia, as well as the war. Soon after the end of the war he resigned from the newspaper and briefly started a publishing firm, but then, with the encouragement of a former mentor at the *Asahi,* he entered NHK in 1945 as a commentator. His rise was rapid: during the next 13 years he became head of the foreign desk, head of the News Bureau, head of the Editing Bureau, director, managing director, and vice president.

Finally, following the abrupt death of Abe Shinnosuke in 1964, the Board appointed him president, primarily because Maeda's supporting faction in the LDP emerged victorious over a rival faction. Both Prime Minister Ikeda

Hayato and his MPT minister backed the chairman of the Board of Governors for the presidential post. Ikeda's longtime factional rival, Satō Eisaku, however, supported Maeda, and the selection of NHK's new president became totally entwined in the LDP's internecine factional strife. Finally, former Prime Minister Yoshida Shigeru, the political godfather to both Ikeda and Sato, settled the matter in Maeda's favor. Because of continued resistance from the anti-Maeda faction, it was to take a 14-hour Board of Governors meeting to confirm him finally as president, reportedly including the condition that the next time there would have to be a "suitable" (*fusawashii*) president.

Maeda, however, had other plans. In the months following his selection, he purged his opponents and potential rivals from both the Board and from among the directors, appointing his own supporters in their place. Having consolidated his power, he had no trouble being reappointed the next term, and the one thereafter. Throughout, he had the backing of Satō Eisaku, whose term of office as the longest-running prime minister in postwar Japan was to be, some think not coincidentally, nearly coterminous with Maeda's as NHK president.[10]

Most important among Maeda's accomplishments during his three terms was his reversal of NHK's previous priorities in order to emphasize news and information over entertainment. Prewar NHK had no news-gathering capabilities at all, and even in the early postwar period, it was said "for information, commercial networks; for entertainment, NHK." In status, broadcast reporters stood several rungs below entertainment producers at NHK.[11] Maeda changed all this. Even before becoming president, Maeda had been active in strengthening the News Bureau. As director and managing director in the late 1950s, Maeda helped overhaul the Bureau into a more organizationally complex and important branch of NHK, building up specialized news-gathering and editing units with better equipment. NHK's extensive coverage of the *Anpo* crisis had been one immediate result of this strengthened organization.[12]

Believing that "the soul of public broadcasting is news" and that NHK had to "catch up to the newspapers and surpass them," Maeda continued as president to give priority to the News Division. In mid-1957, the News Division consisted of only four units: editing, domestic and foreign desks, and a local communications section. Up until that time even the radio and televi-

---

[10]On Maeda's early life, his career at NHK, and appointment as president, see Aoki, *NHK,* 81–85; Ise, *NHK daikenkyū,* 152–54; Yamato, *NHK kokueika no inbō,* 98–100, 102; Shiga, *Buraun-kan no uragawa,* 42.

[11]Aoki, *NHK,* 85; Ise, *NHK daikenkyū,* 154.

[12]Matsuda, *Hōsō sengoshi 2,* 140–41.

sion broadcasting functions were separated. In the next decade, the News Division became devoted to television, rather than radio, coverage.

As it became more important in the organization, it also became far more complicated organizationally. By 1959, the News Division had seven desks— including a politics-economics desk (*seikeibu*) and a TV news-gathering desk (*terebi nyūsu shuzaibu*)—a section, and an office, as units. A decade later it would have 8 desks, including separate politics-economics desks and a main desk (*seiribu*).[13]

Maeda also increased the quantity of news programs, augmented news-related equipment, and initiated satellite broadcasting for NHK's extensive coverage of the 1964 Tokyo Olympics, among other efforts. He changed personnel policy too, elevating the role of reporters. After Maeda, it became common for several directors and managing directors to have backgrounds in the News Division. For example, within two administrations after Maeda, the majority of upper managers (director class and above) had backgrounds in the news. The elevated status, quantity, and quality of news, both in the organization and in the programming, led to the pun among media people that NHK stood, not for Nippon *Hōsō* Kyōkai (Japan Broadcasting Corporation), but rather for Nippon *Hōdō* Kyōkai (Japan News Corporation).[14]

The improvements in the news division were buttressed by the growth in numbers of television sets in Japan during the 1960s, expanding the income from receivers. This enabled the news organization expansion and the rapid increase in personnel at NHK in general, with the organization taking on gigantic proportions.[15]

One of Maeda's other lasting influences was his construction of a huge new Broadcasting Center to house the mammoth organization. With NHK's coverage of the 1964 Tokyo Olympics becoming the focus of global attention, Maeda wanted a new physical plant to reflect NHK's newfound status in Japan and the world, and the Olympics afforded him that opportunity. He decided to move NHK from its cramped and dispersed quarters to a centralized, modern facility in a new Broadcasting Center on more than 80,000 square meters of land next to Yoyogi Park and the new Olympic sports complex that was to remain as part of the park after the games. In 1963 the land was acquired in a special deal and approved by the Cabinet, despite opposition

[13]*Nippon Hōsō Kyōkaihō* (*Japan Broadcasting Corporation Report*), June 1, 1957, 3 and 19; June 1, 1959, 7; NHK HBCK, *Hōsōshiryōshū—Shokusei (3): Shōwa 44-nen 8-gatsu-Shōwa 52-nen 7-gatsu* (*Broadcast History Documents Collection: Personnel System (3): August 1969 to July 1977*) (Tokyo: NHK Sōgō Hōsō Bunka Kenkyūjo, 1978), 27.

[14]Ise, *NHK daikenkyū*, 154, 152, for Maeda's quotes, and more generally on his building up the news organization and other policies, 154–56; Aoki, *NHK*, 85–90; Ise, *NHK daikenkyū*, 152; Shiga, *Buraun-kan no uragawa*, 6–10, 25.

[15]Aoki, *NHK*, 38–42, 79, 91–102.

from the Tokyo prefectural government. In this deal, NHK would get a special discounted price on 80 percent of the property, and the remainder in an equal swap for land NHK owned in Chiba Prefecture.[16]

Maeda had greater long-range influence in molding NHK than any other of its presidents. His significant accomplishments, however, were not without their limitations and critics who saw him as stifling creativity and judgment. In retrospect, some observers also have wondered whether the vaunted news division he created was imbued with sufficient spirit of investigative journalism and determination to defend freedom of expression. Even Maeda seems to have had some doubts on this score, saying after his retirement that "I was not able to nurture NHK as a news organ."[17] Indeed, the building of the new Broadcasting Center would come back to haunt NHK.

TWO PRESIDENTS AND THE SHADOW OF TANAKA KAKUEI

Maeda resigned in 1973 after three terms as NHK president, and in at least one version of the story he did so reluctantly. His friend and fellow former *Asahi* newspaperman Hashimoto Tomisaburō supposedly tried to secure Maeda a fourth term. Hashimoto, an influential LDP politician and member of the communications policy tribe, wielded such great influence in this field that he was sometimes called the "Shadow Minister of Posts." Maeda and Hashimoto were apparently stymied in their efforts, however, by an even more influential personage.[18]

Ono Yoshirō and Tanaka Kakuei

If Maeda had wanted a fourth term, it would have been difficult to attain because he had lost his chief political patron the year before when Satō Eisaku had left the prime ministership to be succeeded by Tanaka Kakuei. And Tanaka was the powerful patron of Ono Yoshirō, who followed Maeda as president of NHK.

When Tanaka was MPT minister in the late 1950s, Ono had been his administrative vice minister, a ministry's highest career official who really runs its daily affairs. Supposedly, the two got on quite well. In fact, Ono was the vice minister who "descended from Heaven" (*amakudari*) to NHK in 1959

---

[16]Yamato, *NHK kokueika no inbō*, 124–25.

[17]The rest of Maeda's regretful quote was ". . . What I did was only 'sentimental manufacturing.'" See Yamato, *NHK kokueika no inbō*, 102. Maeda's quotation at the beginning of chapter 2 was in response to such criticism. See also Aoki, *NHK*, 94–102.

[18]There are different versions of Maeda's relationship with Tanaka and Tanaka's personal view of him. See Ise, *NHK daikenkyū*, 157–58, cf.; Shiga, *Buraun-kan no uragawa*, 15; Ishii Kiyoshi, *NHK fukumaden no shinsō (The Truth About NHK Pandemonium)* (Tokyo: Jiyū Kokuminsha, 1983), 41.

after Tanaka abandoned his formal efforts to change the law regarding appointment of NHK presidents. Once there, Ono rose from managing director to vice president under Maeda.[19]

It was Ono who, as managing director, served as the NHK representative negotiating the 1963 land deal with the government to build the new Broadcasting Center. In 1972, in Maeda's waning years as President, the issue of the land purchase nearly a decade before resurfaced when a Diet committee investigated the purchase and discovered that the land NHK had swapped for the remaining 20 percent of the new Broadcasting Center land had been part of a Chiba City project until it had been sold to a private developer only six months before it was purchased by NHK. The Diet committee also had trouble accounting for about ¥300 million (more than $800,000 at the exchange rate at the time) of the transactions, although research by a media critic asserts that the missing money was in fact the handsome profit a second private developer made when he bought the land from the first developer and then sold it to NHK a few days later. Why hadn't the government just bought the land directly from Chiba City six months earlier or NHK from the first developer and each saved hundreds of thousands of dollars? Was all the money involved in the transactions really accounted for by the sales? The answers to these questions remain shrouded in mystery. One fact that is known, however, is that the then minister of finance who negotiated the land deals with Ono was his old MPT boss, Tanaka Kakuei.[20]

While the revelation of this potential scandal marred the record of Maeda's last years in office, it somehow never became a *cause celebre*. With Tanaka as prime minister, the disclosure also never harmed Ono's chances of succeeding Maeda. Ono, deeply obligated to Tanaka for much of his career, now became the object of his beneficence once again: Tanaka made him NHK's president in 1973.

Ono's attempt to succeed himself in 1976 was not to be as smooth as his initial appointment. His patron Tanaka was no longer prime minister and also was under increasing pressure because of the Lockheed scandal. The incumbent prime minister, Miki Takeo, the powerful Hashimoto, and a faction on the Board of Governors preferred someone other than Ono. So did Nippōrō, NHK's leftist labor union, because Ono had tried to curb the connections to and influence on top management that Nippōrō had developed during Maeda's terms.

[19] On Tanaka as Ono's patron, see Yamato, *NHK kokueika no inbō*, 103–4; Ise, *NHK daikenkyū*, 158–59; Matsuda, *Hōsō sengoshi 2*, 100–101.

[20] On the deals for, allegations about, and Diet investigation of the new Broadcasting Center land see Yamato, *NHK kokueika no inbō*, 123–52; also Tokunaga Masaki, *NHK fushoku kenkyū (Research on NHK's Rot)* (Tokyo: Seibunsha, 1981), 179–80.

The conflict over Ono's reappointment—with government, Governors, and NHK personnel choosing sides—was eventually decided in Ono's favor. Miki, leader of a weak faction and seen within the LDP as a caretaker prime minister, was unable to achieve a consensus on any of his favored candidates, whereas the powerful Tanaka faction and the MPT supported Ono. Miki finally gave his reluctant approval to Ono, who then proceeded to force one of his rivals into retirement, the first time an NHK vice president had resigned after only one three-year term.[21]

Unfortunately for Ono, the source of his success also proved the cause of his undoing. Almost immediately after Ono's reappointment, Tanaka was arrested in the Lockheed scandal, charged with accepting bribes to influence the procurement of military aircraft. Released on ¥200 million (more than half a million dollars at exchange rates then) bail, Tanaka retreated to his Mejiro estate in northern Tokyo, receiving hundreds of sympathy visits from loyal colleagues, supporters, and acquaintances. On August 24, 1976, one of those visitors was Ono Yoshirō, president of NHK. Soon the news appeared in the papers that the head of Japan's public broadcasting company, ostensibly responsible to the general public, had made a sympathy call on a politician just indicted for bribery by a court.

This news provoked immediate and intense criticism. NHK's switchboard was flooded with hundreds of negative phone calls, and Ono was called as a witness before the Lockheed Special Investigations Committee of the House of Representatives. He stated there that although a careless act, his visit was a personal sympathy call, not in his official capacity as NHK president. At a press conference later, he also indicated that, even if objectionable, his visit had not affected NHK mission.[22]

Why Ono, with his experience both as a government bureaucrat and in various high-level positions at NHK, would visit Tanaka, knowing that his house was under constant scrutiny by the press and that his visit might well be reported and cause an uproar, remains a puzzle. One knowledgeable and veteran critic and commentator of the media, Shiga Nobuo, however, offers an intriguing explanation. According to Shiga, Ono and Prime Minister Miki had been in negotiations over a program that would provide Miki the opportunity to express his views on the Lockheed scandal. Ono had ordered such a program, entitled "The Political Situation Hereafter and the Issues We'll be Confronting—Listening to the Prime Minister," to be produced and it was scheduled to be aired on the evening of August 24. Shiga hypothesizes that the Tanaka faction was angered when they found out

[21] On Ono's reappointment, see Ise, *NHK daikenkyū*, 159–61.

[22] On the infamous visit, see ibid., 161–62; Yamato, *NHK kokueika no inbō*, 104–5; Aoki, *NHK*, 33–34, 116–18; Shiga, *Buraun-kan no uragawa*, 18–20, 36–41, 50–53; Gōdo Shirō, *NHK shakaibu kisha* (*NHK Society Desk Reporter*) (Tokyo: Asahi Shimbunsha, 1986), 204–5.

about the program, and Ono had to visit Tanaka on the morning of the 24th to apologize and smooth things over with his old friend and patron.[23] In any event, both Ono and NHK stuck to the official version that it was merely a personal courtesy call.

The visit naturally put news personnel in an embarrassing position. The News Center had mobilized 40–50 reporters from the various desks in a special project team on the Lockheed incident, an almost unprecedented scale of special news gathering. Now their own president was caught visiting the leading figure in the scandal. Despite constant requests by newsroom personnel to management, neither they nor any other NHK employees were ever given either an explanation of the reasons for Ono's visit or an apology.[24]

This incident publicly revealed the close connections between the NHK president and the ruling party. Nipporo, and the major leftist national labor union federation Sohyo of which it was a part, and the mass media all clamored for Ono's resignation. Unable to resist the pressure any longer, he resigned on September 3, 1976, only two months after his reappointment.

The Board of Governors now faced the difficult choice of picking a successor in the midst of a highly charged political atmosphere. Nipporo, not content with just Ono's resignation but also hoping to forestall LDP interference in the decision of a successor, mounted a successful nationwide campaign to get one million signatures demanding that the next president of NHK be from within the organization. The LDP, in a turmoil over the Lockheed incident, couldn't get a consensus on a candidate. The Board of Governors thus was in a quandary over how to proceed, as well as under great pressure from both inside and outside NHK. Two weeks passed before, on September 20, they finally decided on a successor, Sakamoto Tomokazu, the man who had just become the new vice president under Ono two months earlier. The Board had given in to the pressure to name a "homegrown" president: Sakamoto was NHK's first president to have come up entirely within its ranks.[25]

Sakamoto Tomokazu and the Echoes of Lockheed

Sakamoto entered NHK in 1939 with a background in the performing arts, entertainment, and general broadcast management. In contrast to previous presidents, he had no news background and therefore few political connections. His policies centered on strengthening the audience

---

[23]Shiga, *Buraun-kan no uragawa*, 18–20, 37–41.

[24]Godo, *NHK shakaibu kisha*, 201–6.

[25]On the politics of Ono's resignation and Sakamoto's appointment, see Ise, *NHK daikenkyū*, 163–64; Yamato, *NHK kokueika no inbo*, 105; Aoki, *NHK*, 118–21.

appeal of programs, including news programs, stabilizing finances, and establishing various advisory organs to bring external input into NHK. He also took a cooperative stance toward Nippōrō, fresh from its role in the overthrow of Ono, during his first term. Certainly, compared to the chaos surrounding Ono's abbreviated second term, Sakamoto's tenure was relatively peaceful. Perhaps to forestall any possibility of a recurrence of overt political controversy or interference, the Board of Governors took the unusual step—both in terms of precedence and of independent action—of reappointing Sakamoto to a second term in July 1979, a full two and a half months before his term was up, an action that is said to have angered some LDP leaders.[26]

If comparably quiet, Sakamoto's terms nonetheless were haunted by the consequences of the Lockheed scandal and Ono's resignation. The Communications Committee of the House of Representatives discovered, not much more than a month after he took office, that Sakamoto had quietly made former President Ono an "emeritus advisor" (*meiyo komon*) at the same salary he had received as president. The controversy ended only when Ono resigned the honorary position a few days later. The story of Ono's honorary post and salary was not broadcast on NHK news, and the decision to kill the story apparently had been made higher than the newsroom. News personnel made several unsuccessful efforts to get it broadcast or, at least, to receive an explanation of why it would not be aired.

Throughout Sakamoto's tenure, the Lockheed scandal and NHK's role in covering it would be downplayed. Not once in his 40-minute New Year's speech to NHK personnel did President Sakamoto mention news gathering concerning Lockheed, the greatest domestic political news story of the year and the decade. The city desk that had been the center of the extensive news gathering about Lockheed was honored by President Sakamoto, but only privately and separately from the regular public awards ceremony, possibly because the Minister of Posts, a member of the Tanaka faction, attended the public rituals. (It is difficult to imagine the U.S. equivalent: the *Washington Post* honoring Bob Woodward and Carl Bernstein privately rather than offend a former member of the Nixon Cabinet invited to attend the awards dinner!)

Toward the end of his second term, Sakamoto encountered the Lockheed scandal and its aftermath again in other ways. One was the case of Ueda Tetsu, a Socialist Diet member and leader of Nippōrō, which will be discussed in more detail in chapter 6. Suffice it to say here that it appears that

[26]On Sakamoto and his tenure, see Aoki, *NHK*, 121–24; Ise, *NHK daikenkyū*, 66, 164; Yamato, *NHK kokueika no inbō*, 105–6; Shiga, *Buraun-kan no uragawa*, 26.

Ueda was pressured to resign his union post as a result of LDP pressure on Sakamoto.[27]

Another scandal-related incident occurred in 1981, when the News Center planned a special 10-minute fifth anniversary segment on Lockheed for *News Center 9 P.M.*, the mid-evening news show. The segment consisted of two parts: the first, on the trial itself, was the responsibility of the city desk; the second, on interviews with political leaders, especially former Prime Minister Miki, was the responsibility of the political desk. The head of the News Bureau, Shima Keiji, a veteran political correspondent with close ties to LDP leaders, wanted to cut the whole segment, but other News Bureau executives resisted. Shima finally ordered that the first part be broadcast but the political desk's part, including the interview with former Prime Minister Miki, be cut.

This decision aroused tremendous resistance, not only from predictable sources like the union, but also from among Shima's subordinate executives, a rare defiance that put the News Bureau in chaos for two weeks. Shima eventually defused the situation by writing a memo in which he took responsibility for the action and offered a form of apology. In the next regular personnel rotation at NHK, however, those who had resisted Shima in the incident, as well as those who had been identified with Ueda—approximately 40 persons—were purged and sent to local or other bureaus outside the News Bureau.[28]

THE KAWAHARA YEARS

Incidents like these apparently soured many people on the possibility of Sakamoto returning for a third term as president. The Board of Governors wanted someone who could further eliminate the power of the Ueda faction and the union and stabilize labor-management relations. After considering several outside candidates, the Board settled on another internal president—Kawahara Masato, head of the NHK Art Center, a subsidiary responsible for such things as set design. Kawahara, a former news reporter, had been a managing director for labor-management relations but had clashed with Nippōrō and, as a result, had been moved to Finance and then to the Art Center, an apparent demotion. The Board apparently

[27]On the Sakamoto incidents above, see Yamato, *NHK kokueika no inbō*, 105–6; Ise, *NHK daikenkyū*, 165, 170–71; Gōdo, *NHK shakaibu kisha*, 214–22.

[28]On the "Miki cut" incident, see Gōdo, *NHK shakaibu kisha*, 228–36; also Tokunaga, *NHK fushoku kenkyū*, 14–28, 37, 40; Ise, *NHK daikenkyū*, 167–68. On Shima's version of the transfers see, Shima Keiji, *"Shima Geji" fūunroku—Hōsō to kenryoku, 40-nen* (*The Troubled Record of "Shima Geji": Broadcasting and Politics, 40 years*) (Tokyo: Bungei Shunjū, 1995), 119–20.

now liked his past ability to stand up to Nippōrō. Just to make sure, however, they supposedly insisted on Shima's elevation to director as a condition of Kawahara's appointment.[29]

The Case of Yobisute

The final act of the drama of Tanaka Kakuei and NHK were to be played out during Kawahara's watch, and it involved the simple question of how to refer to Tanaka in the news during the years of his court proceedings. In Japanese newspaper journalism, it is sometimes the custom to omit the honorific (e.g., "-san" or "-shi," i.e., "Mr." or "Ms.") once a person is arrested for a crime, and refer to that person only by surname. Prior to Lockheed, if the indicted individual was a Diet member, the news organization would sometimes attach the appellation "Representative" (*daigishi*). However, at the outset of the Lockheed case, all the major newspapers and NHK omitted the honorific, a practice called *yobisute* (literally, "throwing out the calling").

NHK had followed this practice consistently throughout Lockheed, referring to Tanaka only as "Tanaka" in its reports concerning the case, but calling him the "former prime minister" in reports of his other activities. This infuriated Tanaka and his faction, and they accused NHK of "bias" and of being unduly influenced by Ueda and Nippōrō. When after his first public hearing in 1977 some media organs began to refer to Tanaka as "former Prime Minister Tanaka" or "the defendant Tanaka," the pressure on NHK increased, especially in times of Diet approval of NHK budgets or requested fee increases.

In 1982, a city desk committee recommended continuing omitting the honorific, but two years later, after the Tanaka verdict of "guilty" was brought in by the court in October 1984, a new committee was formed, this one drawn from the entire newsroom. It recommended reversing the previous practice and that, out of respect for human rights, all criminal defendants should have some honorific attached to their names. It was claimed to be a decision with no connection to Tanaka's case, but some remained skeptical, especially as the announcement that NHK was going to abandon the custom came at the same time the LDP was discussing an NHK request to raise its receivers' fees.[30]

Budget Crises, the Rise of Shima Keiji, and the Death of a Critic

Otherwise, Kawahara's two terms in office (1982–88) were to be dominated by the issues of rising expenses and stagnant revenues, budget

[29] Ise, *NHK daikenkyū*, 171–74; Shiga, *Buraun-kan no uragawa*, 29–31, 34–35.
[30] The history of *yobisute*, Tanaka, and NHK is found in Gōdo, *NHK shakaibu kisha*, 248–59.

deficits, and the need to raise receivers' fees, which left NHK vulnerable to
LDP pressure.

The Kawahara administration tried to cut expenditures. Severe austerity
measures were introduced. A more important device for reducing expenditures was to shrink the number of personnel. Because of the taboo regarding layoffs of full-time workers, the goal was to reduce NHK's staff by two
thousand employees through attrition within a few years.

Finding new sources of revenue was the second part of the plan to eliminate the deficits. This entailed the new media strategy, discussed in more
detail in chapter 7, centered on developing satellite broadcasting and eventually high-definition television to enable NHK to establish new categories
of receivers' fees instead of merely continuing to raise the standard ones on
color TVs.

Central to this new strategy was the rise of Shima Keiji as a power within
NHK after his elevation to director. A former political reporter with very
close ties to one faction of the LDP, Shima had further earned the gratitude
of NHK management and factions in the LDP with his decision regarding
the Miki cut and his resistance to the union. Shima now proceeded to consolidate his position both within NHK and in the political world. In the area
of personnel, he had in some ways replaced Ueda as a force to be reckoned
with. He could ship reporters off to the organizational equivalent of Siberia
if necessary. It was said around NHK that "if you glare at Shima, your neck's
in danger."[31]

Shima also was a late, but devout, convert to NHK's new media strategy,[32]
gradually becoming the most important force in the Kawahara administration pushing for NHK's investment in the new technologies as the center-
piece of its future role in broadcasting.

The third strategy for coping with the budget deficits of course was the interim one of raising receivers' fees. To do this required not antagonizing the
LDP and granting such concessions to the party as the elimination of the
yobisute custom in 1982 during the LDP's consideration of NHK's fee increase. The not coincidental combination of the rise to power within NHK
of former political reporters, such as Kawahara and Shima and their factions, and the increasing deference to LDP sensitivities in covering the news
did not go unnoticed by veteran reporters.

When I first met Godō Shirō in mid-1985, he was a recently retired veteran of the NHK newsroom. A colleague of both Shima and Ueda, he had
been head of the city desk during much of the Lockheed scandal. In his retirement, he was publishing in a weekly magazine a series of critical articles

---

[31] Ibid., 236. See also 224ff. on Shima, the Miki cut, and Shima's personnel power at NHK.
[32] "Nanmon sanseki no NHK Ikeda Taisei," *Asahi Shimbun,* June 16, 1988, 4.

Fig. 15. Shima Keiji, former NHK news executive and president.

about NHK's handling of the news during Lockheed, including details about the internal workings of the newsroom and NHK management that had previously not been made public.[33] The articles later formed the basis for his book, *NHK shakaibu kisha,* cited as a source in this chapter.

During my two-hour interview with him,[34] Gōdō was critical of such trends as the increasing entertainment value in, and the changing audience's expectations toward, the news. Although also critical of the real, but very subtle, indirect pressures reporters feel during times of fee increases and LDP complaints about NHK, he also was realistic about the need for a public broadcaster to be sensitive about the ruling party. He even felt that "one of NHK's merits as a news network in comparison to the commercial broadcasters is that it doesn't take an extremely negative position." Gōdō saw NHK's future as possibly either a completely state-run network, in which case their budgetary problems would be solved but their freedom lost, or a commercial broadcaster, in which case they would have more freedom but continued financial problems. Critical, but professional and pragmatic, would probably best describe my impression of his views about NHK during this interview.

Two years later, in May 1987, the title of a weekly magazine article concerning the death of a former city desk reporter caught my eye as I perused a bibliography of recent work on media in Japan. When I obtained the maga-

[33]*Shūkan Asahi,* May 17, 24, 31, June 7 and 14, 1985 issues.
[34]June 17, 1985.

zine and read the article, I was shocked to discover that it was about Gōdo. He had thrown himself off a cliff near his home in Kanagawa Prefecture. The letter he left behind to be published in a weekly magazine revealed he had committed suicide as a protest against the tendency of NHK to lose its independence to political authority.[35] He had sent a letter to President Kawahara about his feelings—he had never received a reply.

Questions of Omission

During 1988, Kawahara's last year in office, two events occurred that made Gōdo's suicide look less like the erratic behavior of an obsessed individual and more like the tragically extreme response of a man who genuinely loved NHK and could not stand to see its autonomy corrupted. In February, right before the end of the NHK live telecast of Budget Committee hearings from the Diet, Hamada Kōichi, veteran LDP politician and chair of the committee, suddenly shouted, "The Communist Party's (chairman) Miyamoto Kenji is a murderer!" Hamada was undoubtedly referring to longstanding charges that during the prewar years Miyamoto had tortured to death a suspected police spy discovered in the party, hardly a new accusation. What was news was the image of a Diet member and committee chair shouting such epithets about a fellow Diet member on live nationwide television in a totally inappropriate context. When the Diet erupted in chaos and confusion, NHK suddenly cut off the telecast, and it did not show the incident on its main 7 P.M. news that evening.[36]

In May of the same year, a more ominous type of omission occurred on the part of NHK and its respected professional polling unit, NHK Broadcast Survey Research Institute (NHK HYC), which periodically conducts surveys on "Life and Politics" (*kurashi to seiji*). One of the biggest and most controversial issues facing the LDP at this time was its nationwide sales tax proposal, but the December survey showed 46 percent approving the tax and a minority opposed. The results were broadcast repeatedly on NHK television and radio.

The March results, however, showed that opinion had swung drastically against the LDP plan: 46 percent *opposed* the tax, with only 19 percent in favor (the rest did not care or did not know about it). This time NHK never

[35] The weekly magazine article and Gōdo's final letter appeared in *Shūkan Asahi*, May 15, 1987, 33–34; see, Ninagawa Masao, "Aisuru NHK yo: Hōdō genron kikan toshite tuyoku nare" ("I Love NHK!: Make It Stronger as a News and Freedom of Expression Organ"), in the same issue, 28–33. On Gōdo's death and increasing frustration with NHK policy, see Ise, *NHK daikenkyū*, 41–51.

[36] On the "Hamakō" incident in retrospect, see the "medeia insido" column, "Terebi jishin ga sozai ni natta toshi" ("The Year Television Itself Became the Subject Matter"), *Asahi Shimbun* (evening edition), December 28, 1988, 7.

broadcast the results but only published them in its magazine on broadcasting and survey research, circulation 2,000.[37] The printed press was delighted to publicize NHK's contradictory treatment of the two polls. NHK defended itself merely by saying it had a right to edit its programs however it wished.[38] The most pernicious aspect of these omission incidents was that they appeared to be the result of NHK's own self-censorship, rather than of the LDP's direct pressure.

THE RISE AND FALL OF TWO PRESIDENTS

Kawahara's six years in office stirred unease among some within and outside of NHK concerning his administration's commitment to impartial news and to NHK as an independent institution responsible to the public. Yet neither the LDP nor the business community had much reason to be dissatisfied with Kawahara's tenure. To cope with budget deficits, he had begun the process of making NHK smaller and more efficient, and the influence of Ueda and the leftist union had been substantially curbed. The LDP's perception of NHK's "leftist bias" ceased to be an issue.

Ikeda, the "Zaikai" President

Yet new forms of dissatisfactions were stirring that would deprive Kawahara of the third term he wanted. The heavy costs of NHK's new media program were more than making up for any savings accomplished through personnel cuts and austerity, and technical problems with the program had begun to try the patience of viewers and their representatives. There was still no end to financial problems and the need to raise more revenue through fee increases and expected fees for the new media. Giant public corporations such as the Japan National Railways (JNR) had been privatized successfully as part of Prime Minister Nakasone Yasuhiro's (1982–87) "administrative reform" program. If these other enormous public bureaucracies could be made more efficient, why not also the public broadcasting corporation? Perhaps new leadership was needed to better respond to this age of new media and new thinking.

In this context, the Board of Governors began to consider its options after Kawahara's term expired in July 1988. Their "private" but nonetheless very well-covered decision-making process reveals much about the way the post of NHK president was viewed, treated, and influenced by the political

[37]*HKTC (Broadcasting Research and Surveys)* (May 1988).
[38]See, for example, *Asahi Shimbun*, May 8, 1988, 1; *Mainichi Shimbun*, May 9, 1988, 26; in English, *Japan Times*, May 11, 1988, 3; and the *Asahi Shimbun* editorial "Nattoku ikanai NHK no ronri" ("NHK's Theory Which Can't Be Assented To"), May 15, 1988, 5.

and business elites in Japan in the 1980s. With only a few variations, there seems to be a general consensus about what occurred.[39]

Sometime in late winter, Isoda Ichirō, chairman of the Board of Governors and president of Sumitomo Bank, began polling all the other Board members as to their ideas about the presidential selection. It was soon established that although most felt Kawahara had done a good enough job, few favored a third term because he was viewed as too weak managerially or politically to cope with NHK's pending problems. Isoda strongly felt that NHK needed a president from the business world (*zaikai*). He unsuccessfully approached several leading candidates, some of them uninterested because although the position of president was legally a full-time job and could not be combined with any other, the salary was low by business world standards (about ¥26 million per year or more than $100,000 at exchange rates then). Finally, Chairman Isoda settled on his fellow alumnus from Kobe schools, Ikeda Yoshizō.

This choice seemed exactly right for what the chairman believed NHK needed. A veteran leader of the business world, Ikeda had been president of Mitsui Bussan, one of Japan's great trading companies. In the course of his career there, he had acquired the nickname "the Lion"; whether because of his personality or physical resemblance to that regal animal is not clear. As president of Mitsui Bussan, he had been a major architect behind the company's involvement in the ambitious multi-billion dollar joint venture in the Middle East, the Iran-Japan Petrochemical Company (IJPC), one of the largest overseas Japanese investments ever made. Due to the Iran-Iraq war that project had to be cancelled, however, and Ikeda took responsibility by resigning his position. Although 77 years old, Ikeda remained active only by busying himself with ceremonial posts and committee work for Keidanren (Federation of Economic Organizations), the most elite and influential of large enterprise peak associations. From Chairman Isoda's perspec-

[39]The following description is based upon, "Zaikai shudō, irei no jinji—NHK kaichō ni Ikeda-shi naitei" ("Business World's Leadership, Exceptional Personnel: The Informal Decision to Make Mr. Ikeda NHK President"), *Asahi Shimbun*, June 1, 1988, 3; "'Minna-sama no NHK' jiki kaichō no jōken wa . . ." ("The Circumstances of the Next President of 'Everyone's NHK' . . ."), *Shūkan Asahi*, June 3, 1988, 20–23; Nishimae Teruo, "NHK ga abunai!" ("NHK in Danger!"), *Asahi Jānaru*, June 17, 1988, 14–18; "Iron mo atta NHK kaichō erabi no tenmatsu" ("The Particulars about the Choice of NHK's President about Which There Is Disagreement"), *Keizaikai*, June 28, 1988, 33–37; "Nanmon sanseki no NHK Ikeda taisei" ("The NHK Ikeda System for Which Tough Problems Pile Up"), *Asahi Shimbun*, June 16, 1988, 4; "NHK 'kaichō jinji' no uragawa" ("Behind the Scenes of NHK's 'Presidential Personnel'"), *Shūkan Shinchō*, June 2, 1988, 34–35; "Kenryoku no Teni: NHK 'posto-Kawahara' de kyū ukabiagari no 'rion Ikeda' to 'Shima Geji Tennō'" ("The Power Transition: 'The Lion Ikeda' and 'Emperor Don Shima' Who Quickly Surface in NHK's 'Post-Kawahara'"), *Sande-Mainichi*, June 12, 1988, 20–23; Koitahashi Jirō, "'Kōkyō hōsō' NHK no sōdai naru kyokō" ("The Fiction that 'Public Broadcasting' NHK Will Become Great"), *Tsukuru*, July 1988, 34–44.

tive, his old friend Ikeda was perfect: a leading business figure with great managerial experience but no full-time competing responsibilities.

Granted, there was room for doubt about Ikeda's appropriateness for the post. His advanced age was one concern. There was also the fact that he knew nothing either about NHK as an organization or about journalism, yet he would be heading the largest institution affecting public opinion and culture in Japan. Furthermore, he lacked direct experience with politics in the glare of public scrutiny, yet he would have to testify effectively before the Diet each year on behalf of NHK's budget.[40]

Isoda, nevertheless, believed he had found his man, and he proceeded to carry out the necessary consensus building to make the appointment possible. It is said to be customary for the chairman of the Board of Governors to touch base with the business elite on presidential selections by visiting the head of Keidanren and discussing the possible candidates in advance, but in this case, there was no problem lining up Keidanren's support, as Ikeda was one of the vice presidents of the organization. On May 21, 1988, just a few days before the Board was to meet officially to discuss the presidential selection for the first time, the newspapers leaked the information that Ikeda was the probable choice. This "appointment by the newspapers" (*shimbun jirei*) probably was a calculated leak to prepare the ground for him.

At the Board of Governors' meeting on May 24, the only two candidates who received multiple votes in a poll of members were Ikeda, with three, and Managing Director Shima, with four. It is unclear whether Shima's votes represented genuine support for him as president, strategic votes to position him for the vice presidency, or something of a protest vote among members who resented the pressure to appoint Ikeda.[41] Whatever the reason, following this meeting, Isoda's attempt to gain a consensus shifted into a higher gear.

Until this point, Prime Minister Takeshita Noboru had left the presidential search to Chairman Isoda. This was uncharacteristic restraint, given the precedents of previous premiers who actively designated the heads of NHK. It was unthinkable, however, that the appointment would not get at least the tacit approval of the prime minister, so Isoda visited Takeshita. The two knew each other well since Takashita's days as Finance Minister, and he quickly gave his approval. Takeshita then met with former Prime Minister Nakasone Yasuhiro, still leader of another important faction in the LDP, which also, not coincidentally, was the faction to which the MPT minister belonged. The minister also did his own consensus building with the higher bureau-

---

[40] See the articles in the previous footnote for background on Ikeda. Also, the "Hito" ("Person") column on Ikeda in *Asahi Shimbun*, June 16, 1988, 3. A prescient view of Ikeda at the time of his appointment is found in "Iron mo atta NHK . . . ," *Keizaikai*, June 28, 1988, 34.

[41] On this stage of the process, see "NHK 'kaichō jinji' no uragawa," *Asahi Shimbun*, June 16, 1988, 34; "Iron mo atta NHK . . . ," *Keizaikai*, June 28, 1988, 36; Nishimae, "NHK ga abunai!" 15.

crats in the Ministry. This was an important step because apparently some in the Ministry would have preferred one of their own as NHK president.[42] Finally, the prime minister consulted with Kanemaru Shin, Takeshita's faction lieutenant, but more importantly also the independently powerful "don" of the Postal policy tribe in the LDP.

By May 30–31, the Board's informal decision again began to appear in the press.[43] The remaining, more difficult, decision, however, was the vice presidential post. Shima, with his long experience as an NHK insider and his initial support for president from at least some of the Board, would seem to have been the logical choice to complement Ikeda. Apparently, however, the MPT was resistant. Further, since Shima's days of covering former Prime Minister Ikeda, he had remained especially close to that faction of the LDP, now led by Miyazawa Kiichi. Miyazawa's rival for the prime ministership, Abe Shintarō, was supposedly not happy with the choice of Shima as either president or vice president of NHK. Nevertheless, the Board decided to go along with the Ikeda-Shima combination, ratifying this publicly at its June meeting.[44]

On July 2, 1988, Ikeda Yoshizō became the tenth president of NHK, the ninth since the Occupation. Ikeda was the second businessman to head NHK but the first to have spent his entire previous career in the business world. He did not last long. Less than nine months later, in April 1989, Ikeda resigned.[45] During his tenure, he had been particularly ineffective politically. In public testimony to the Communications Committee of the Diet, he had been an embarrassment: several times he gave inappropriate responses to Diet Members' questions, and once he even started speaking in English.[46] At a party for the new chairman of the House Communications Committee, he publicly suggested that the "unbiased, non-partisan" (*fuhen futō*) principles

[42]See, for example, *Nihon Keizai Shimbun*, May 25, 1988, 5; note, however, that while this was occurring, at a House of Councilors meeting on May 26, the Minister of Posts publicly stated that everything concerning the selection was being left in the hands of the Board of Governors as "the Ministry of Posts has no right to meddle concerning personnel." See ibid., 35.

[43]See, for example, *Asahi Shimbun*, May 30, 1988, 1, and May 31, 1988, 1.

[44]On the Postal Ministry and the Abe faction's attitude, as well as the lack of clarity on where Nakasone stood, see Nishimae, "NHK ga abunai!" 15–16; *Asahi Shimbun*, "Zaikai shudō irei no jinji"; *Keizaikai*, "Iron mo atta NHK . . . ," 36, claims having Shima as vice president was a condition of Ikeda's appointment.

[45]Ikeda's intent to resign was reported in all the national dailies, usually as page 1 news, in their April 1, 1989, editions.

[46]For the specifics of these misstatements, see Ishii Kiyoshi, "Kairō Ikeda kaichō ga no-shiaruita NHK" ("NHK in Which the Bizarre Old Man Ikeda Swaggered"), *Bungei Shunjū* (June 1989): esp. 160–63; "Ikeda Yoshizō NHK kaichō ga kokkai de nokoshita chintōben no sūsū" ("The Number of Remarkable Replies NHK President Ikeda Yoshizō Left Behind in the Diet"), *Shūkan Yomiuri*, April 16, 1989, 32–33. On the background and general problems Ikeda had at NHK, see his successor's views in Shima, "*Shima Geji*," 195–200.

of NHK, as embodied in the Broadcast Law, should be rethought.[47] His un-persuasive negotiations with the MPT and also with the Diet led to the post-ponement of the receivers' fee increase NHK needed to raise revenue.[48]

Criticism of Ikeda mounted both within and outside NHK. After the Diet approved NHK's budget at the end of March, Chairman Isoda, due to step down from his post, took the opportunity to persuade his old friend Ikeda to resign, too, for "health" reasons.

A few days later, the Board of Governors informally decided to name Shima Keiji as Ikeda's successor. After appointing a successor to Isoda as chairman, the Board of Governors made the Shima appointment official on April 12, 1989.[49] They also named as vice president, a former MPT adminis-trative vice minister, appointed apparently to pacify the MPT's previous op-position to Shima.

The Fall of Shima the Powerful

Long the "kuromaku"—behind-the-scenes wire-puller—and the most influential individual within NHK management, Shima now finally combined power with authority at the relatively young age of 61. Tireless in his pursuit of his vision for NHK, he intensified his efforts to implement the new media; to reduce NHK's personnel and production costs; to reform its management and organization, in part by spinning off private subsidiary companies; and to make NHK a global media force. Internally, he consoli-dated his control by moving out those close to former President Kawahara and appointing his own former newsroom political reporters to key posts as directors and managing directors.[50]

The technology of satellite broadcasting, however, was not something Shima could control. Several technical failures on NHK communications sat-ellites had already slowed down progress. In mid-April 1991, Broadcast Satel-lite BS3H, built by General Electric (GE) and launched from Florida, failed while Shima was traveling in the United States. A few days later, while testi-fying about the failure in a House of Representatives Committee, Shima was asked whether he had been physically present to see the launch failure. His

[47]On Ikeda's public gaffe at the party, see Ishii, *NHK fukumaden no shinsō*, 163; "Kūkagetsu de orosareta NHK 'rōgai' kaichō Ikeda Yoshizō-shi" ("NHK Age-Suffering President Mr. Ikeda Yoshizō Who Was Brought Down in 9 Months"), *Shūkan Asahi*, April 14, 1989, 26–27; Shima, "*Shima Geji*," 200–201.

[48]See, for example, *Asahi Shimbun*, April 1, 1989, 1; *Aera*, April 11, 1989, 66. Also, Ishii, *NHK fukumaden no shinsō*, 164.

[49]On Shima and his appointment, see, for example, the "Hito" column on him in the *Asahi Shimbun*, April 13, 1989, 3.

[50]Nishimae Teruo, "Nagata-chō no gyakushū de kaitai shita dokusen ōkoku" ("The Ab-solute Monarchy That Was Dismantled by the Counterattack of Nagata-chō"), *Asahi Journal*, July 26, 1991, 22. Nagata-chō is the Japanese equivalent of Capitol Hill in Washington, D.C.

reply implied that he had watched it at GE headquarters. Almost immediately, however, and continuing for the next three months, doubts began surfacing about his answer. The LDP made an inquiry to the MPT for further information. At first, Shima stuck to his original story, but after a three-hour meeting with the chairman of the Board about the problem, he confessed that he had actually been in Los Angeles at the time of the launch.[51] Both the Diet and the LDP took this "misrepresentation" to the Diet very seriously and began pressuring the Board and Shima to resign.[52]

At a tearful news conference on July 16, 1991, Shima did resign, taking responsibility for having brought into question everyone's trust in public broadcasting. He further said, however, that the movements of the MPT and the House Communications Committee had forced NHK to try to protect itself from interference by those in power. He saw the new opportunity for interference that his error had invited as representing a "great danger to public broadcasting."[53] Many of his newsroom colleagues who had been elevated to director and managing director status subsequently had to resign their administrative positions.

The puzzle as to why the LDP pursued Shima relentlessly on his statements to the point that they drove him from office is probably answered by later media stories. These publications, by reputable journalists (one a close friend of Shima's) and in respectable journals, claim Shima was done in not by a misrepresentation to the Diet but by a vendetta by LDP factions he had alienated. Shima had differences with a director, Ebisawa Katsuji, a former political reporter, and he did not reappoint Ebisawa to a directorship, sending him out instead to be head of one of NHK's subsidiary companies. Ebisawa was a long-time intimate of the Takeshita faction, and this move, made without their consultation, severely angered them. Especially the chairman of the House Communications Committee, who was a Takeshita faction leader, and the "don" of the faction, Kanemaru Shin, was said not to have understood why Shima didn't check beforehand with them regarding this move. The committee, it was also said, was so angry that they then went after Shima's head.[54] This time, even Shima's ties to the weaker Miyazawa faction could not save him.

[51] It later came out that Shima was also in the company of a young lady in Los Angeles. He claimed she was the daughter of a former colleague and was like a niece to him. This was never the focus of the scandal—it always centered on problem of stating falsehoods to the Diet.

[52] See Nishimae, "Nagata-chō no gyakushū"; Okada Tokio, "Shima Keiji: Saigo no hinichi" ("Shima Keiji: The Final Days"), *Bungei Shunjū* (August 1991), 170–81; also the citations below on Shima's resignation. On the Board meeting with Shima and his statement that he was in Los Angeles, see *Asahi Shimbun*, July 10, 1991.

[53]*Asahi Shimbun*, July 16, 1991, 1; also the *Asahi Shimbun* editorial on July 17, 1991, 2.

[54]Nishimae, "Nagata-chō no gyakushū"; Okada, "Shima Keiji," 170–81. At the time, Okada and Shima had known each other for 40 years. On Communications Committee Chairman Nakano's role, see Okada, "Shima Keiji," 174–75.

Shima paints a more complicated picture of intrigue in his subsequently published book about his NHK journalistic and executive career.[55] In the background to any specific personnel decision that alienated the Takeshita faction was a general and increasing antipathy to Shima's strategies at NHK. His moves to spin off commercial companies had provoked fear and anger among commercial broadcasters, and his use of foreign satellites and launchings had alienated the communications tribe of the LDP and the MPT. Also, his reluctant acquiescence to Takeshita faction boss Ozawa Ichirō's plan to have Shima's former NHK colleague and once popular newscaster, Isomura Naoki, run against the incumbent governor of Tokyo in the April 1990 local elections resulted in Shima being blamed for Isomura's humiliating loss. Shima's career lived by his political connections and seems to have died by them as well.

The political machinations on this occasion did not end with Shima's resignation. The Board of Governors had seen two presidents resign under embarrassing circumstances within a two-year period. They did not want to appoint another businessman or anyone associated with the Shima administration, including his vice president, a former MPT bureaucrat who was known to want the position. So they immediately sought someone above both reproach and politics who could reestablish the credibility of the office and the Board of Governors' image of independence, as well as try to make a decision quickly so as not to give a margin for political interference. They offered it to a man who had served as former NHK auditor, Tokyo University emeritus professor, and High Court judge. He declined, however, and in their haste to reestablish NHK's credibility, they offended the LDP again, especially the Tanaka faction, who felt with such an external candidate, Shima's influence would remain from behind the scenes.

The Takeshita faction also was outraged that the Board had not consulted with them and followed the "proper procedures" when selecting a president. As one exasperated LDP executive said, apparently unaware of the spirit and letter of the Broadcast Law, "It's usual for the Prime Minister's Office and the Party to provide the candidates, and from among these the Board of Governors chooses. And there's also consultations in advance." Within a few days, however, Prime Minister Kaifu Toshiki, in response to criticism from within his own party that the difficulties resulted from insufficient *nemawashi,* or prior consultation, felt compelled at a press conference to reaffirm publicly that "because it (NHK) is a public service broadcaster and not government personnel, the government cannot interfere."[56]

[55]Shima, *"Shima Geji,"* 206–38.
[56]*Asahi Shimbun,* July 24, 1991, 3. On the successor to Shima process, also see *Asahi Shimbun,* July 22, 1991, 1; July 25, 1991, 2.

With parts of the LDP and the Postal Ministry wary of anyone that seemed close to Shima, the Board chose Kawaguchi Kaneo, former NHK managing director and, at the time, director of the NHK Symphony Orchestra. Kawaguchi's background was in entertainment and production, not news, and under his administration, NHK followed a most conservative course. He dismantled or trimmed back many of Shima's innovations and visions, especially in the area of new media and international broadcasting, as we will see in chapter 7.

Kawaguchi was reappointed in 1994 to a second term, the first second-term NHK president in almost a decade.[57] During both terms, his administration was seemingly content to play the role of noncontroversial, reliable public broadcaster, carefully avoiding offending either the commercial broadcasters, who had been threatened by Shima's aggressive repositioning of NHK through new media and other strategies, or the LDP.

How far NHK and its Board of Governors would now go to protect its flanks against the LDP was soon demonstrated in its appointment of Ebisawa Katsuji, first as vice president for Kawaguchi's second term in 1994 and then as his successor in 1997. Recall that Ebisawa was the very same NHK executive who may have played a major role in precipitating Shima's downfall.

Ironically, Ebisawa's career has many parallels to Shima's. He entered NHK in 1957 and, after the usual stint in a local bureau, he returned to Tokyo and his lifelong calling as a political reporter covering the LDP. He observed Prime Minister Satō Eisaku's long terms in office, and he was the reporter assigned to the faction of Tanaka Kakuei. Like Shima, he developed very close, career-long ties to an LDP faction, but unlike Shima, his ties were to the party's most powerful faction, especially in the area of media and telecommunications. In his case too, ties to the LDP and this faction even preceded his career as a journalist: his father had been an executive of the candidate support organization (*kōenkai*) of Hashimoto Tomisaburō, former LDP secretary-general under the Tanaka Cabinet and the political *eminence gris* of the NHK organization.

Ebisawa had risen from head of the News Bureau to managing director (*riji*) before his falling out with Shima sent him to become head of NHK Enterprises, an important NHK commercial spin-off company. In 1993, after Shima's downfall, Ebisawa was brought back into the executive ranks as a special managing director (*senmu riji*) with responsibility for all those spin-off companies before being elevated to the vice presidency. Observers at that time noted that Ebisawa's major qualification seemed to be, given Pres-

[57]On Kawaguchi's terms and reappointment, see *Asahi Shimbun* (evening edition), August 1, 1991, 1; "Shin kaichō de sofuto rosen ka minna sama no NHK" ("Everyone's NHK: Is It the Soft Alignment with the New President?"), *Aera*, August 13, 1991, 64. *Asahi Shimbun*, July 27, 1994, 29.

ident Kawaguchi's status as a political neophyte with a background in production, the need for someone with expertise and extensive contacts in politics to handle the Diet at the time of NHK's budget negotiations. In July 1997, the Board of Governors, without controversy, appointed Ebisawa as NHK's president.[58]

The turmoil of the late 1980s and early 1990s had come full circle. Following the disastrous attempt at appointing a businessman, the ambitious but politically destructive Shima years, and finally the retrenchment years under the noncontroversial Kawaguchi, the organization had at its helm another NHK former political news reporter who had risen through the ranks and who possessed extensive ties to the LDP. Like Kawahara, but unlike Shima, he was likely to use those contacts to protect NHK from political attack by not straying too far from the government's wishes, rather than using them to attempt to gain more political independence for the broadcaster.

PRESIDENTS AND POLITICS

Clearly, the Japanese political world maintains an intimate involvement with NHK presidents' appointments, tenures, and terminations. Of the ten successive presidents after NHK's postwar formation in 1950, four left office prematurely for reasons related to politics. Even the terms of presidents who remained in office and completed their terms, however, can hardly be characterized as politically neutral, recalling, for example, Maeda's appointment and later his land deal for the new Broadcasting Center, the Lockheed scandal reverberations for Sakamoto, or the controversies over news cuts during Kawahara's tenure. Interference from the LDP, the bureaucracy, and the business community came over many different types of issues: the selection or retention of the president, the purported leftist influence within NHK, the content of the news, among others.

Two structural dimensions of NHK as an organization stand out as sources of the politicization of the position of NHK president. The first is the appointment process. The Broadcast Law's provision that the Board of Governors appoint the president, thus making the chief executive officer of NHK only indirectly responsible to political authority, is not the way the selection process actually works. The provision fails to insulate the post from pressure from external actors. Occasionally, the Board has taken action independently or has attempted to assert its own prerogatives in presidential personnel decisions. Generally, however, it seems to have developed into little more than the intermediary or broker for arranging and ratifying the outcomes of power struggles among far more influential actors.

[58]Information about Ebisawa's background and career above from *Nihon Keizai Shimbun*, October 10, 1994, 36, and July 9, 1997, 15; *Asahi Shimbun*, July 9, 1997, 3.

The prime minister, the factions of the LDP, the business community, and the MPT wield the real influence over the selection process, and they determine who becomes president of NHK and how long each president stays in office. However, their influence is not equal. The prime minister is certainly the most important of the actors, and although different prime ministers have been more or less assertive in actually choosing the president, it is unthinkable that any prime minister would not have at least veto power over the decision. However, because the prime minister is only *prima inter paras* in the loose factional coalition that is the LDP, other factions have became involved, and sometimes the NHK president's post becomes a political football in the internecine warfare of factional politics. Most especially, the Tanaka and Takeshita factions within the LDP seem to have had more influence in these decisions than other factions because they have "colonized" the MPT and the policy area of telecommunications.

Compared to the LDP, both the business community and the Postal Ministry are distant second and third in influence. Apparently, no appointment would be make without at least consultations with Keidanren and MPT bureaucrats, but to actually determine outcomes, they must be allied with a powerful LDP faction and prime minister.

The consequence of this selection process is that the post of NHK president becomes part of the more general game of ruling party personnel decisions—almost as in the distribution of Cabinet positions. The selected incumbent requires, at most, a patron within the party, and, at the least, the effort to avoid alienating the prime minister or any major faction leader.

The second institutional mechanism that makes NHK management vulnerable to ruling party pressure, as was pointed out in chapter 4, is the need for the Diet to approve fee increases, with vulnerability increasing at times of budget deficits and fee increases. In particular, the LDP communications policy tribe can use their approval decision to put tremendous pressure on NHK's president. The forced resignation of Ueda and the dropping of yobisute may well have been especially overt cases of the LDP's ability to gain its wishes on internal organizational matters through this mechanism.

Whether the LDP uses crude pressure or not, the threat of retaliation and the fear of alienating the ruling party during a fee increase season can communicate itself down to the newsroom in subtle and not-so-subtle ways, as the cases of the Miki cut and the suppression of the consumer tax survey demonstrate. Self-censorship can accomplish the same results as overt interference.

These institutionalized vulnerabilities, through which especially the LDP threatens NHK and its leadership, were exacerbated during the last 20 years both because of the increasing importance of the news to NHK's programming and identity and because of the subsequent rise to positions of leadership within the organization of former newsroom personnel, notably former political reporters, such as Shima and Ebisawa. These intimate ties of former political reporters to the LDP intensified the latter's involvement in presidential selection and increased self-censorship.

NHK, however, is not only the passive recipient of pressure from the conservative establishment. These pressures have also led NHK to adopt countermeasures both to ensure that its agenda gets a hearing from the political elite and to try to insulate its core mission of news gathering and presentation from controversy. As discussed, at times either the Board or the president has tried to resist some of these pressures (as in Nomura's response to the LDP delegation, in Kawahara's appointment, or in the attempt to make a quick decision on Shima's successor), taken initiatives to persuade political and economic elites of the need for a particular kind of appointment (as in Isoda's successful push for Ikeda's appointment), or adopted internal controls and self-censorship to protect itself from attack by the LDP (as during the *Anpo* crisis, in cutting Hamada's outburst, and in the handling of the survey with negative implications for the LDP).

The other responses of NHK as an organization are taken up in subsequent chapters. On balance, however, the history of NHK's presidents through the postwar period makes it clear that the Occupation's attempt to provide NHK with a structure that would buffer its management from political interference has failed to do so completely.

CHAPTER 6

Occupational Roles and Politics

One reason NHK came to have an external "enemy" called the ruling party is that it held within it an absurd monster called *Nippōrō* (Japan Broadcasting Union).

—SHIMA KEIJI, FORMER NEWS EXECUTIVE, MANAGING DIRECTOR,

AND PRESIDENT OF NHK, *"Shima Geji" fūunroku*

Successive Prime Ministers have come to think of NHK as their own broadcasting agency.

—UEDA TETSU, FORMER CHAIRMAN OF JAPAN BROADCASTING

UNION AND DIET MEMBER FROM THE SOCIALIST PARTY,

CITED IN SHIGA NOBUO, *Buraun-kan no uragawa*

The relationship of presidents and Boards to the state is not the only factor affecting NHK's decisions and behavior. Indeed, management must also respond to, and mediate between, the state and their own organizational culture. The latter is crucially shaped by how management recruits, socializes, and structures the careers of its employees and by its labor-management relations.

NHK's personnel policies generally follow the standard model of postwar Japanese organizations. This pattern includes highly selective recruitment by merit through examination, resulting in the hiring of key, educated personnel from elite universities; pay and advancement based primarily on seniority; careful attention to matching personality and skill to position; frequent rotation to different units to build generalized skills and knowledge of the organization; lifetime employment; and a union based on the company.

The specific organizational task of a media organization, however, often requires additional modifications to this model. In this regard, NHK maintains personnel practices similar to Japanese newspapers, such as a clear, labor-intensive, news-gathering and editing hierarchy; systematic rotation between the central newsroom and local branches; and a high value placed on informal and difficult-to-measure journalistic skills learned from experience.

The consequences of these patterns, also typically, are employees whose primary identification is to their organization rather than to their profession or specialized skill; the infusion of personnel decisions with patron-client considerations and factional power struggles based on intraorganizational networks; and (because of the rather impermeable organizational boundaries of such a system) the need to use the available personal networks of employees to attempt to influence other organizations, including the state.

PERSONNEL AND PAYROLLS

The most striking characteristic of NHK's personnel is the sheer size. In 1955, NHK employed about 8,500 persons; by 1980, it had reached about 17,000 before financial pressures forced an austerity policy and cutbacks by attrition. During this period, and especially in the late 1950s and early 1960s, NHK had hired perhaps 10,000 new employees. By the early 1980s, these hires were reaching middle and upper management ranks with their consequently high pay based on seniority. The budget deficits that resulted, as well as the investments required for its new media strategy, discussed in previous and subsequent chapters, forced NHK to gain control of its personnel costs. Salaries, by the early 1980s, represented a full third of all ordinary revenues and of all ordinary operating expenditures.

Consequently, in 1980 President Kawahara Masato instituted an "administrative reform" policy to make NHK more efficient (*kōritsuka*). The subsequent programs that were implemented accomplished their goals to a large extent by reducing the number of employees through attrition. By 1984, the total number of employees had declined to about 16,500, and after a decade, the numbers had been successfully cut by another 14 percent to about 14,600 in 1991 and, as mentioned in the introduction, to about 13,000 by 1996. Personnel costs had been reduced to represent closer to one-quarter of ordinary revenues and of ordinary operating expenses.

News-gathering and editing employees by the 1980s occupied nearly 10 percent of the total personnel. More than 1,400 persons gathered, edited, and produced the news, excluding program technicians, about two-thirds of them in the Tokyo News Center.[1] This huge news staff was perhaps the

---

[1] Data on personnel, revenue, and changes from Tokunaga Masaki, *NHK fushoku kenkyū* (*Research on NHK's Rot*) (Tokyo: Seibunsha, 1981), 182; NHK HBCK, ed., *NHK nenkan '96*, 42; *NHK nenkan '91*, 3, 38, 43; and *NHK nenkan '84*, 61, 66 (*Radio and Television Yearbooks, 1996, 1991, and 1984*) (Tokyo: NHK, 1996, 1991, 1984, respectively); also "Suzuki Kenji-shi no arubaito to NHK ga mukaeru chūnen gyōkaku" ("Suzuki Kenji's Part-time Work and the Middle-aged Administrative Reform NHK Faces"), *Shūkan Bunshun*, March 3, 1983, 170–71.

largest in the democratic world, larger than the BBC and far larger than U.S. network television.[2] As we will see in chapter 8, its news-gathering resources also dwarf Japan's private broadcasters' flagship stations that are at the center of their news "networks."

Significantly, news-related employees have been reduced proportionately less than other types of employees in these attrition programs and therefore actually comprise a higher percentage of personnel than they did earlier. For example, in 1984, the 1,397 news-related personnel constituted 8.6 percent of all employees; but by 1990, the 1,429 news-related employees actually equaled about 9.75 percent of total personnel.[3]

BECOMING AN NHK REPORTER

All Japanese organizations, whether in large business, bureaucracy, or journalism, recruit through formal written examinations, designed to stringently select only the most intelligent employees for key posts. These written examinations are supplemented by formal and often informal interviews. The latter are designed to determine which of the select few who passed the written examination—and thus have the skill base necessary for their tasks—also will fit into the organization's culture.

Each year at the end of the summer, mass media organizations such as NHK administer and grade their written examinations and interview those who passed during an incredibly hectic period for Personnel Bureau staff.[4] Although its status as a place of employment has declined in the 1990s, NHK usually ranked among the top 20 corporations in popularity among college graduates seeking employment during the postwar period through the 1980s. Competition on the examinations therefore has been quite keen. In 1984, for example, of the 3,500 persons taking the exam, only 131 men and 9 women were hired, an acceptance rate of only about 4 percent.[5]

Those 3,500 applicants were effectively prescreened. NHK sends a limited number of application forms to universities, so the universities only give them to students considered to possess the qualifications for NHK. Further,

[2]Anthony Smith, *The Shadow in the Cave: The Broadcaster, His Audience, and the State* (Urbana: University of Illinois Press, 1973), 261.

[3]NHK Shichōsha Kōhōshitsu, *NHK Poketo Jiten, 1984* (*NHK Pocket Dictionary, 1984*) (Tokyo: NHK, 1984), 77; and *NHK Poketo Jiten, 1990* (Tokyo: NHK, 1990), 70. "News-related personnel" is defined as those engaged in news gathering (*shuzai*), whether reporters or visual (*eizō*) news gatherers; program technicians are categorized separately.

[4]Interview with T3, former NHK executive, in Tokyo, August 27, 1984. Before and during the early 1980s, the examinations were administered in November.

[5]Uchida Kōichi, "Saiyōshasū 'chōzō' no hōsōkai shoten wa NHK" ("Broadcast World's Hiree Numbers 'Superincrease,' NHK Focal Point"), *Hōsō Bunka* 39, no. 9 (September 1984): 7–71. Also interview with T3, August 27, 1984.

the number of forms each university receives is determined by both the size of the university and the level of development of their mass communication programs.[6] Although NHK publishes no statistics on the universities from which they draw their new applicants, my impression and those of others were that the elite national university, Tokyo University, and the two elite private universities known for their mass media academic programs and historically for providing news media personnel, Waseda and Keio Universities, predominated among reporters. This pool of bright students from elite universities is in fact the same as that of Japan's most prestigious newspaper, the *Asahi Shimbun,* and frequently the same students apply to both media organizations. By the mid-1980s, NHK was beginning an informal attempt to widen its recruitment base among regional universities, where few had been recruited in the past, by identifying and encouraging exceptional regional university students to apply.[7]

If a prospective recruit to NHK has attended one of these universities and performed well in a mass communications program, the next step is to apply to take the written examination. Even before taking the examination, however, a student can enhance his or her chances by visiting NHK. As is common with many Japanese companies, NHK has a "company visitation system" (*kaisha hōmon seido*) whereby prospective applicants can visit an organization and have informal talks and interviews with personnel department employees. If a student, even before passing the written exam, can make an impression on the personnel employee, he or she may have a better chance of being hired.[8]

The next step then is to pass the written examinations, no mean feat. The NHK examination is one of the most difficult of all employment exams in Japan, supposedly ranking with the higher civil service examinations that recruit Japan's elite bureaucrats. There are two parts to the written examination process: a general examination and a specialized one for reporters or technicians, and so forth.

The first, general, part of the examination for college graduates usually consists of about 40–60 multiple choice questions drawn from all fields of knowledge, including politics, economics, current events, history, statistics, geography, science, meteorology, literature, and English language. Following this part, there is a section on the Japanese language, emphasizing the identification of the correct Japanese character (*kanji*) for a word. The exam then moves to an English language section that always includes at least two or three reading comprehension questions. The applicant is given about

[6]Interview with T3, August 27, 1984.
[7]Ibid.; also Aoki Sadanobu, *NHK: Sekai saidai no masukomi shūdan* (*NHK: The World's Largest Mass Media Company*) (Tokyo: Asahi Sonorama, 1980), 148.
[8]Interview with T3, August 27, 1984.

70 minutes for these three parts. There is also a 1,000 character essay that must be completed in 60 minutes. To illustrate the nature and difficulty of the exam, I've selected a few questions as illustrations from the multiple choice and English reading comprehension sections of the test. These appear in tables 5 and 6. One can understand why one high-level news executive has said, "If the present executives (of NHK) took the exam, they'd probably all fail."[9]

Should he manage to pass this stringent general exam, the prospective reporter would then have to pass the more specific examination for reporters and the formal interview process. Through these methods, a highly select and elite group of very bright graduates from the nation's top universities, all of whom also seem to fit the personality type of an NHK reporter, are selected.

The system ensures top quality personnel and individuals prescreened for their ability to fit into the corporate organization. One of its other consequences, however, is to also guarantee that its key news personnel have very similar educational backgrounds to Japan's political and economic elites, and, most probably, friends who are joining ministries and business corporations at the same time.

REPORTERS' CAREERS

The new recruit immediately enters a two-month training program according to the specialization—news, production, announcer, or clerical—that will define his career. Then the unseasoned NHK reporters, similar to all the other new recruits, will be sent to local bureaus for their first jobs. There is a fairly fixed rotational pattern of center-local experience at NHK. After about four or five years, the new employee probably will be rotated back to the NHK headquarters in Tokyo for an assignment—although there is no guarantee of this.[10] After another five years or so, he may be sent back to a local bureau, often as head of that bureau. Then, in the next rotation five years later, he may return to Tokyo to a more important position, such as head of a desk or of the NHK team at a reporters' club beat. Such center-local rotation ensures that every reporter gains broad experience both in the field and in the Tokyo News Center.

Every summer, as such *tenkin* (job transferring) decisions approach, an extra bit of tension pervades the newsroom. The decision making starts as early as April when News Center executives enter into informal discussions both with the reporters, whose preferences are noted, and with each other

[9]Quoted in Aoki, *NHK*, 148.
[10]Description of process in ibid., 149.

Table 5.   Sample Questions from the 1985 NHK Entrance Examination

12. Which of the following statements are correct:

   (1) A and C   (2) A and D
   (3) B and C   (4) B and D

   A. To change the names of the House of Representatives and the House of Councilors to the Lower House and the Upper House, constitutional reform is necessary.
   B. Because membership in the House of Representatives is restricted to people over age 30, constitutional reform is necessary.
   C. To transform elections with the proportional representation system for members of the House of Councilors (nationwide districts) and elections with local districts, constitutional reform is necessary.
   D. To create four-year terms of office for members of the House of Councilors, constitutional reform is necessary.

15. In the following text, when the words A to D are used to fill in the blanks, which combination is correct?

   From the standpoint of the school of economic thought termed mercantilism, in a nation's foreign trade, exports should exceed imports. However, this attitude is a convenient argument for the protection of domestic A. Underlying this philosophy is the view that a nation must both economize resources and focus on the interests of B. However, C does not fund investment, and this results in a recession. It is impossible for every nation to follow a mercantilist policy successfully, as all countries cannot export more than they import. When countries practice this philosophy, generally this causes D to decrease.

   (1) A=producers, B=companies, C=consumption, D=imports
   (2) A=producers, B=households, C=savings, D=exports
   (3) A=consumers, B=households, C=consumption, D=imports
   (4) A=consumers, B=companies, C=savings, D=exports

28. Arrange the descriptions A–D in the correct chronological order.

   A. In order to restrain the spread of India's independence movement, England enacted the Rowlatt Acts, strongly suppressing the movement.
   B. Called Europe's powder keg, Serbia, located in the Balkan peninsula, was the site of the murder of Austria's crown prince.
   C. The Africa policy of England, which owned shares in the Suez Canal, was opposed by an anti-colonial campaign in Egypt led by Arabi Pasha.
   D. Constitutional provisions for universal suffrage were enacted, fulfilling a major aim of the Chartist movement. The six provisions included the abolition of property requirements for elected representatives.

   (1) DCBA   (2) CDAB
   (3) CBAD   (4) DACB

37. The descriptions A, B, and C refer to painters who were famous representatives of the Renaissance. Which of the following artists match these descriptions?

   A. Person who was influenced by the Jesuit movement, which spread around Spain, and who adopted a dark style that made his works famous. One of his representative works is called the "Burial of the Count de Orgaz."

(continued)

Table 5. (*cont'd.*)

B. "St. Francis Preaches to the Birds," which is exhibited in the Assisi temple, is said to be his work. He liberated interpretations of paintings from the influence of Christianity and exalted art for art's sake. He is said to be a pioneer of the Italian Renaissance.

C. He painted many works of the Madonna and Child. His lines of painting harmonized rhythmically. Because the subjects of his paintings have a quiet, innocent look, his work creates the image of a original, attractive world. One of his representative works depicting the Madonna and Child is called "La Belle Jardinere" ("The Beautiful Gardener").

(1) A=Rubens B=Giotto C=Botticelli
(2) A=El Greco B=Friar Angelico C=Botticelli
(3) A=El Greco B=Giotto C=Raphael
(4) A=Rubens B=Friar Angelico C=Raphael

38. Which of the following descriptions are correct:

(1) only A   (2) A and C
(3) only B   (4) only C

A. In the international tennis federation, a professional player's performance was recognized more in the Davis Cup competition's cherished international tournament than in the British Open, even with the latter's long history.

B. According to the federation for international sporting events on land, while fees given to players for displaying advertisements in public forums were approved, such things as cash prizes and rewards for a player's participation in an athletic event are all prohibited.

C. In the international soccer federation, beginning in the preliminary selection trials for next year's Olympic games in Los Angeles, professional players will actually be allowed to participate.

41. Of the following descriptions related to a metal's propensity to rust, which are accurate?

(1) A   (2) A and C
(3) B   (4) B and C

A. An alloy of iron and other metals is more resistant to rust than iron alone. That explains why alloys tend to ionize more than iron.

B. A sheet of galvanized iron resists rusting because of a surface plating made from zinc. Zinc reacts with water more easily than iron does, and the zinc coating gives iron a negative attraction.

C. The reason stainless steel is resistant to rusting is the fusion of a component molecule of the metal, which changes the metal's physical properties.

48. If in the set (a, b), b is larger than a and in the set (a, b) b is smaller than a, what is the value of x in the following equality: $(x - 2, x - 1) - (2x + 1, 2x - 12) = (4x - 1)$

(1) 4   (2) 5
(3) 6   (4) 7

Source: "NHK nyūsha shiken mondai, 58-nen jūichigatsu futsuka jisshi" ("NHK Hiree Examination Problems, Administered November 2, 1984"), *Hōsō Bunka* 39, no. 9 (September 1984): 86–95.

Table 6. Part of an English Language Comprehension Question (from the August 1991 examination)

The cultured man is a man of integrity, of sound moral principle. (A) *To himself being true* he cannot be false to any man. (B) *The principle of expediency is repugnant to him,* and never on any account will he trade with his conscience. He is a just man, but not so just that he is unaware of human frailty. He knows that in order to be kind it is necessary to be just, but he knows also that in order to be just it is necessary to be kind, for the essence of the law is love, (C) *justice being love expressed through rational calculation.*

(1) Which of the following is *most appropriate* as the content of the underlined part (A):

    a. True as he was to himself
    b. Were he true to himself
    c. As he is true to himself
    d. Whereas he is true to himself

(2) Which of the following is *not appropriate* as the content of the underlined part (B):

    a. The principle of expediency is practical to him.
    b. The principle of expediency causes repugnance to him.
    c. To him the principle of expediency is very unpleasant and offensive.
    d. He strongly disagrees with the principle of expediency.

(3) Which of the following is *most appropriate* as the content of underlined part (C):

    a. While fairness and love should be given based on reasonable calculation.
    b. As the quality of being just is love expressed though reasoning.
    c. Because a judge considers a case through a logical process with love of humanity.
    d. Since the action of the law intrinsically represents love taken through sensible reasoning.

Source: "Masukomi nyūsha shiken mondai: NHK" (Nippon Hōsō Kyōkai), 91-8-6 ("Mass Media Hiree Examination Problems: NHK" [Japan Broadcasting Corporation], August 6, 1991), *(Gekkan) Shimbun Daijyesto,* no. 298 (January 1992): 198–207.

to try to match individual talents and preferences to various jobs. This mixture of reporter preference and executive control over personnel decisions is reflected in the News Bureau high executive's response to my question as to whether a reporter who does a good job covering a major story in a local area may make it back to Tokyo a bit earlier:

> Well, for example, if there is an election campaign in Fukuoka and we know of a very promising reporter in Fukuoka who aspires to a position in the political desk (*seijibu*) we'll send him to do the story. If he does a good job, we keep an eye on him. If the political desk in Tokyo likes him they may suggest to us to move him up. But unless that reporter makes it clear that he wants to be a political desk reporter and works hard, nothing will come of it. It's very competitive.[11]

The News Bureau executives submit their suggestions to the personnel staff (*jinjibu*), who are also collecting the proposals for job transfer from

[11]Interview with O, high-level news executive, September 1, 1983.

broadcasting stations throughout NHK, and they make the final decisions. The Personnel Bureau's decisions are no rubber stamp. A news executive estimated that only about one-third of the personnel suggestions made by the News Bureau are eventually implemented.[12] Yet obviously news executives can sometimes influence the Personnel Bureau's decisions. I observed a few news personnel bowing low and sincerely thanking an assistant director of the News Bureau for their latest postings.

Let us say a reporter has done a stint at a local bureau, where he carried out fairly unspecialized tasks, covering stories about any important event that occurred in that region, from natural disasters to murders to local elections. Transferred to Tokyo subsequently, he would be assigned to one of the specialized "desks" (*bu*), whose role in the process of news editing is discussed in chapter 3. If he had an interest in and talent for political reporting, he would be assigned to the political desk (*seijibu*).

Most desk reporters will be given an assignment in one of the specialized beats based in a reporters' club at one of the major government agencies or important societal organizations. These assignments typically last only a year, or two at most, before the reporter is reassigned to another club or to the desk in the News Center. NHK customarily transfers its employees to new positions fairly frequently, even if within the same desk. A former head of the city desk reports in his autobiography that he was moved an average of once every three years during his 33-year career.[13]

In a few cases, an assignment has been prolonged to allow a reporter to gain additional experience covering a particularly difficult beat. An experienced political reporter, then serving as the kapu (captain, or "cap") of NHK reporters at an important reporters' club, told me that although they had lengthened the assignments for certain difficult postings from the usual one to two years, young reporters in complex ministries often would like more time. Nevertheless, a great deal of emphasis is put on training reporters for a beat, even though the frequent rotations are acknowledged to make it difficult for reporters to be adequately prepared in some cases for their assignments. In the opinion of the same veteran political reporter, "the three big networks in America are soft" because they don't pay enough attention to training.[14]

Veteran reporters often train and act as mentors for young reporters. This necessitates passing on sources to the cub reporter, leading to some sensitive questions in their relationship. This was frankly described also by the same "cap":

[12]Interview with News Bureau executive, June 4, 1985.
[13]Gōdo Shirō, *NHK shakaibu kisha* (*NHK Society Desk Reporter*) (Tokyo: Asahi Shimbunsha, 1986), 245–46.
[14]Interview with H, veteran political reporter, May 28, 1985.

Every reporter places great importance on his own information sources, but the way he passes this knowledge on to the next reporter varies. In my case, I take the new reporter to my source (*shuzaigen*) and say "please rely on him" (*yoroshiku tanomu*). I also take him on my night rounds. I would be in trouble, though, if my sources gave the new reporter all of his information, so I must convince him to continue to confide in me; but it would also be a problem if I got all the information and discouraged the new reporter. You've got to get the new reporter into a competitive spirit with his senior (*sempai*).

In discussing what advice he passes on to novice political reporters, the cap said he emphasizes the importance of aggressively concentrating on sources, citing the adage "write a story with your feet." Most importantly, he urged new reporters to see their sources and talk to them face-to-face, as that is the only way to get a feeling for the credibility of the source. He derided the American reporters' habit of using the telephone to get information from sources.[15]

Thus, after several years, an NHK reporter has accumulated local experience of a general nature, knowledge of the methods and practices of veterans through a personal mentoring system, and experience with several specialized beats in Tokyo. At some point, he may be selected to work at one of the desks coordinating the reporters in the field, to produce segments for the evening news, or to be posted to one of the special assignment teams producing programs other than the evening news. Toward the middle of his career, he will probably take another turn at a local bureau, but this time as bureau chief. Later still, he will become eligible for the higher reportorial positions at the Tokyo News Center, such as cap of a reporters' club team, head or assistant head of a desk, or chief producer of a program. Those interested in international affairs may be sent to an overseas bureau. Some veteran reporters land at one of the six positions on the "main desk," where the major decisions are made for the evening news program.

A few will advance to become, for example, an assistant director (*jichō*) or even the director of the News Bureau (*hōdōkyokuchō*) or to take a position in the office attached to the president's office that reviews programs, including news programs, for conformity to NHK standards. The even more select will cap their careers in positions as director (*riji*), or managing director (*senmu riji*), with responsibilities for news or personnel.

By the end of his career, an NHK reporter will typically have had extensive experience in all aspects of broadcast reporting: from news gathering to production, from source relationships to managerial and coordinating responsibilities, from general local reporting to beat reporting. This expe-

[15]Ibid.

rience, however, would have been gained in one specialized organizational niche at a time, in a clearly defined hierarchy, within the boundaries of one organization, and in a system in which he was initiated, trained, promoted, and rotated to assignments based almost completely on the judgments of veteran reporters who had very similar experiences. He will be expected to do the same for those younger than he.

Spending his entire career within this hierarchical and paternalistic bureaucratic system, the Japanese reporter will become, to a greater extent than many of his Western counterparts, an "organization man." Many Western reporters can and do move from one media organization to another relatively freely, both laterally in terms of region or size of media organization or up to better positions at larger companies. These reporters also develop early and lasting identifications with the profession of journalism as much or more than with the particular organization that happens to employ them. They have frequent contact with a wide range of reporters from other media organizations. This is less true of Japanese reporters, including those at NHK. One NHK reporter who had spent time in Washington, D.C., as an overseas correspondent told me he thought the chief difference between journalists in the United States and those in Japan was that American reporters develop an individual style in reporting because they changed companies; Japanese reporters, on the other hand, tended to write relatively homogeneously because they were basically company men who interacted primarily with others of the same organization.[16]

PERSONNEL AS CONDUIT AND RESOURCE

If NHK's personnel practices and organization mitigate the development of horizontal professional ties, and encourage vertical organizational identifications, they develop human resources through which the organization may exert influence externally into the political world to achieve its goals. At the same time, however, these practices and this structure make NHK vulnerable to penetration by politicians and cooptation by the state.

NHK and Constituent Services

NHK political reporters make sure politicians' pedestrian demands for favors for themselves and for their constituents are satisfied. The political reporters covering the LDP factions bring to the public relations executives and producers requests for everything from tickets to Ōsumo (traditional Japanese wrestling) and other NHK broadcast events to requests to

---

[16]Interview with NHK foreign desk correspondent, Tokyo, December 18, 1991.

stage and film popular programs in their constituencies, especially near election time. How and whether requests are responded to depends on the "rank"—in other words, influence—of the politician making the request.[17]

A few powerful politicians have done much more than ask for trivial favors—they have used NHK to supply them with patronage jobs. Although most NHK personnel, and certainly all reporters, are hired through the difficult entrance examination process, some politicians have been able to provide employment to friends and constituents through alternate means. By using the authority of NHK's division directors, who can hire temporary employees, powerful politicians have procured jobs for the families of voters and for their own circles of acquaintances. These patronage employees take a special examination, offered every couple of years to provide the opportunity for temporary employees to gain permanent status. This examination is much easier than the regular entrance exam.

All major faction leaders have taken advantage of this backdoor to NHK employment, but one powerful member of the *yūseizoku* (posts and telecommunications policy tribe), Hashimoto Tomisaburō, was notorious for it. Hashimoto's wife was a former NHK announcer and he was a former newspaper reporter. In his political career, he both climbed to the heights as a secretary-general of the LDP, the most powerful leadership position in the party after the prime minister and president, and fell to the depths as one of those arrested in the Lockheed scandal investigations. Hashimoto may have placed more than 300 persons into NHK through this and other methods, and former NHK executive and President Shima Keiji describes this group as performing the function of a "branch" (*shibu*) of Hashimoto's personal candidate support organization (*kōenkai*) in Ibaraki Prefecture.[18]

A former NHK reporter I interviewed did not think these employees within the organization had a direct "pipe" into the News Center, but rather were loyal conduits to Hashimoto, providing him with information about the organization that he could then use to threaten NHK management.[19]

Political Reporters as Channel

NHK, on the other hand, also uses its employees, especially political desk reporters, to advance its own agendas with politicians. We have seen

[17]Shima Keiji, *"Shima Geji" fūunroku—Hōsō to kenryoku, 40-nen* (*The Troubled Record of "Shima Geji": Broadcasting and Politics, 40 years*) (Tokyo: Bungei Shunjū, 1995), 93–94.

[18]Ibid., 90–93; Shiga Nobuo, *Anata no Shiranai NHK* (*The NHK You Don't Know*) (Tokyo: Denpa Shinbunsha, 1975), 115–20; Shiga Nobuo, *Buraun-kan no uragawa* (*The Hidden Side of the Television Tube*) (Tokyo: Nihon Kogyo Shinbunsha, 1977), 46–47. Tokunaga Masaki, *NHK fushoku kenkyu* (*Research on NHK's Rot*) (Tokyo: Seibunsha, 1981), 183.

[19]Interview with K2, former NHK city desk reporter and newscaster, March 27, 1995.

how reporters' clubs serve several functions in news gathering and news predicting for mass media organizations in Japan and how they have the potential to induce conformity and source dependence. Little recognized, however, is the fact that these reporters' clubs also serve as a crucial mechanism by which NHK develops internal specialists to achieve its goals and protect its interests externally in the state, even while politicians also use them to accomplish their aims and interests involving NHK.

NHK maximizes their political reporters' access to those who may make the policies and decide on the budgets that affect their organization. As former NHK reporter, executive, and president Shima Keiji describes it, the political reporters are given a special mission every budget season to act as the "hands and feet" of NHK executives, lobbying the policy tribe politicians responsible for NHK's budget.[20] A former NHK city desk reporter put it even more forcefully and directly, noting that the Politics Desk at NHK really had not one but two "missions": the first was gathering news about politics; the second, getting information on how NHK's budget will fare. In his judgment, political desk reporters were actually evaluated more on the budget process information they delivered than on any journalistic scoop. He went on to say that this use of political reporters for budget lobbying purposes began early in NHK's history. These reporters assumed it was their job to get information on the NHK budget process and to influence politicians. Further, he thought that the political desk was proud to be "keeping the organization alive."[21]

This use of political reporters is only one part of the connection between these reporters and those in power. Through the reporters' clubs, the journalists may develop personal relationships with their sources that include long-lasting friendships that then affect how NHK will use them in their future careers. Discussing NHK's activities in lobbying the MPT and the Diet about its plans and goals, an NHK executive described a separate group of personnel within NHK who specialize in listening and talking to either the LDP or to opposition politicians. When asked the background of these government and opposition relations specialists, he acknowledged that they were political reporters who had known the Diet members from previous assignments.[22]

The ubiquitous Shima Keiji's career represents an extreme case of an otherwise typical career-long linkage between political reporters and their former sources. A former political reporter who had covered former Prime Minister Ikeda Hayato and his faction in the early 1960s, Shima maintained

[20]Shima, *"Shima Geji,"* 85.

[21]Interview with K2, March 27, 1995.

[22]Interview with K4, NHK executive with experience in the president's office, May 28, 1991.

close ties to this group for the rest of his career at NHK. His career biography is replete with examples of his attempting to persuade key LDP politicians of NHK's views and serving as a source of information for the organization about the political world. For example, when leaders of this faction, Ohira Masayoshi and Suzuki Zenkō, respectively, each became prime minister in the late 1970s and early 1980s, it is said that Shima proved very useful to them by providing political information gathered by NHK reporters in the course of their jobs.[23] If Shima used his power in the NHK newsroom to increase his influence among political friends, conversely his intimate hobnobbing with the political elite impressed and added to his power among his NHK colleagues as well.[24]

The inevitable other side of the coin, however, is that his career is also filled with anecdotes about how politicians and prime ministers attempted to use him to influence or obtain information about NHK. For example, when Nakasone Yasuhiro was in office from 1982 to 1987, Shima would be called to the prime minister's residence about once every two months to be told Nakasone's complaints about news broadcasts, often with the prime minister holding a transcript of the program that had been prepared by his staff.[25]

It is difficult to avoid the impression that Shima's relationship with political leaders was more like that of a close consultant on media issues than that of an independent journalist.[26] The reputed intimate connections of a later president of NHK, Ebisawa Katsuji, with the Tanaka/Takeshita faction, based on his prior news career as a political journalist covering that faction, provides another example of the two-way, mutual dependence of NHK and influential politicians.

Advisory Councils and Amakudari

Personnel connections between NHK and the state extend to the more formal ties established by NHK personnel serving on government public advisory bodies, including the *shingikai* (advisory councils) attached to administrative agencies.[27] Such advisory councils, common in most in-

---

[23]Nishimae Teruo, "NHK ga abunai!" ("NHK in danger!"), *Asahi Jānaru*, June 17, 1988, 15.

[24]Interview with K2, March 27, 1995.

[25]Shima, "*Shima Geji,*" 168–70; see also Nishimae, "NHK ga abunai!" 17.

[26]Shima, "*Shima Geji,*" 22, 26–27, 45, 48–52, 73, 153–54, 156–58, 168–69; also on another former political desk reporter with close connections to LDP leaders, see 227–28.

[27]On these bodies in Japan, see for example, Ehud Harari, "The Institutionalization of Policy Consultation in Japan: Public Advisory Bodies," in Gail Lee Bernstein and Haruhiro Fukui, eds., *Japan and the World* (London: Macmillan Press, 1988), 144–57; Frank Schwartz, "Of Fairy Cloaks and Familiar Talks: The Politics of Consultation," in Gary D. Allinson and Yasunori Sone, eds., *Political Dynamics in Contemporary Japan* (Ithaca: Cornell University Press, 1993), 217–41; also see Frank Schwartz, *Advice and Consent: The Politics of Consultation in Japan* (New York: Cambridge University Press, 1998).

dustrialized democracies, are composed of "experts," most from outside government, whose purpose is to advise the bureaucracy on policy.

What seems unusual in Japan, however, is the presence, and not in insignificant numbers or proportion, of personnel from the mass media on these bodies. Frank Schwartz found, for example, that about half of all active *shingikai* in 1973 (49 percent) and 1983 (55 percent) contained personnel from the mass media, including NHK.[28] In 1992, Ehud Harari similarly found that a bit more than half (110 out of 205) of those *shingikai* listed in the official advisory council directory had a member from a mass media organization.[29] This is a lower proportion than members from business and agriculture, university scholars, and government bureaucrats, but nonetheless, still a not insubstantial percentage. Also, considering that in few other countries do media personnel regularly serve in these official capacities on such state organs without resigning from their media positions,[30] it indicates the uniquely close relationship between journalism and the state in Japan.

NHK is particularly active. Harari found in 1992 that it sent more individuals (30, or 19 percent of the sample) to such bodies than any other media organization, and when multiple memberships of these individuals was taken into account, its proportion was accentuated further (47 persons in total membership, or 21 percent of the sample).[31] Similarly, a 1993 study found that 25 NHK personnel were members of *shingikai*, occupying 45 positions. This did not include the five positions occupied by five former NHK employees. Almost half (26) of NHK's positions were filled by present or former members of its Commentary Committee (*kaisetsu iinkai*), veteran and senior personnel who are responsible for the occasional commentary programs, the mild equivalent of editorials on NHK, and who come from backgrounds in many fields at NHK, including former news reporters and executives. Among those filling the other half of the positions were the vice president, the director and vice director of the Broadcast Division, and some of the most important executives at NHK, as well as producers, directors, and announcers. In one case, the vice president of NHK served on an advisory panel on electrical communication technology (*denki tsūshin gijutsu shingikai*) attached to the Ministry of Posts and Telecommunications, the nominal regulatory agency of NHK in the Japanese government.[32]

[28]Schwartz, "Of Fairy Cloaks," table 9.1, p. 221, and also *Advice and Consent*, table 2-2.
[29]Ehud Harari, "The Government-Media Connection in Japan: The Case of Public Advisory Bodies," unpublished paper, 1997, 4. I am grateful to Professor Harari for both sending this paper and giving me permission to cite it.
[30]Ibid., 2, 4, 14.
[31]Ibid., table 3, p. 44.
[32]Data from Maruyama Masaru, "Kenryoku to no yūchaku!! Masu komi no shingikai sanka" ("The Integration with Power: The Advisory Council Participation of Mass Media"), *Tsukuru* (February 1994): 76, and the list of media positions in these bodies, 82–89.

Harari notes the ambivalent consequences of media personnel serving on these official government advisory bodies. On one hand, as media representatives come neither from government nor from industrial interest groups, their participation in the policy-making process could make these bodies' private deliberations somewhat more transparent and also could bring into the process criticism and alternative perspectives including those in the public interest. On the other hand, their involvement in the formal policy-making process of government could alter the perspectives of the participants, who might also share the information and viewpoints to which they are exposed with their reporter colleagues, and thus may indirectly and more subtly affect the coverage of the news.[33]

Other conduits, these from the state into NHK, are the retired higher government bureaucrats "descending from heaven" (*amakudari*) into the policy and regulatory areas of public corporations and private firms that their former administrative agencies oversee. In the case of NHK, it is the MPT that serves as a post-retirement source of personnel for NHK's executive ranks. We've already noted the most famous of the bureaucrats who "parachuted" into NHK: Ono Yoshirō, former MPT vice minister who eventually became president of NHK and then was forced to resign. Both his ascension and his resignation were connected to his relationship with Tanaka Kakuei.

This is but one example. During the 10 years from 1988 until 1997, one former administrative vice minister and one bureau chief of MPT became NHK executives and eventually managing directors. The commercial broadcasters also are staffed with such former officials. From 1985 to 1993, four former MPT bureau chiefs became executives at the private networks.[34] Indeed, "of the six terrestrial (non-cable, non-satellite) channels available in the Tokyo area, Nihon Television Broadcasting Network seems to be the only one that has not yet taken an MPT *amakudari*."[35]

The function of *amakudari* remains a source of debate in the field. Does it afford bureaucrats influence over recipient organizations? Or is it merely the "spoils" of that control? Or is it a two-edged sword, also providing recipient companies with the potential for influence on the bureaucracy that regulates them?[36] Ulrike Schaede's argument that *amakudari* officials also serve the function of helping the state monitor compliance with discre-

[33]Harari, "The Government-Media Connection," 18, 20, 22–23.

[34]"Yakunin Tenkoku: Yūseisho-hen" ("Officials' Paradise: Ministry of Posts Edition"), *Shūkan Gendai*, May 9, 1997, 5.

[35]Koichi Nakano, "Becoming a Policy Ministry: The Organization and *Amakudari* of the Ministry of Posts and Telecommunications," *Journal of Japanese Studies* 24, no. 1 (winter 1998): 110. Italics in original.

[36]Ibid., 113–16; Ulrike Schaede, "The 'Old Boy' Network and Government-Business Relationships in Japan," *Journal of Japanese Studies* 21, no. 2 (1995).

tionary regulation—especially where regulation is "extralegal" because this is where compliance is most difficult to ascertain—is worth noting in the case of NHK.[37] Given the Broadcast Law's prohibition on interference in programming, much of government's "regulation" of NHK is necessarily extralegal. Having former bureaucrats from MPT in higher executive ranks—and, as we have seen, at least one also on the Board of Governors—provides the regulatory agency for broadcasting with at least a channel of information about NHK's activities, and perhaps more.

The very fact that media personnel are incorporated into the state's official organs and processes and engaged in activities that help to legitimize particular national policies, as well as the fact that high-ranking bureaucratic officials join NHK's executive ranks after retirement, severely blurs the boundaries between the state and the media and between the official and the journalist. These exchanges also provide the media organizations, including NHK, with channels into the state. These channels allow NHK both to communicate with and exert some influence on government, and they facilitate government efforts to communicate with and exercise some influence on NHK.

LABOR UNION: NIPPŌRŌ

The Company Union

NHK has one major labor union, Nippon Hōsō Rōdō Kumiai (Japan Broadcasting Union), or Nippōrō for short. As with many Japanese unions, Nippōrō is neither a craft nor an industrial union. Rather, it is an enterprise union: the membership confined to NHK employees without regard to occupation. In 1988, it listed almost 12,000 members, or 80 percent of the NHK total staff of 15,000 employees.[38] All those in supervisory positions in management, as well as those in staff positions who attain a certain managerial level (*fukubuchō* or Assistant Bureau Chief), are automatically excluded from union membership, and these numbers account for part of the remaining non-union members.

The organizational structure of the union is three-tiered: a central office, regional branches, and local chapters. The central office and regional

[37]Schaede, "The 'Old Boy' Network," 300–302. Note that Nakano, "Becoming a Policy Ministry," 115, rejects this relationship because, he asserts, MPT doesn't need "spies" to inform it of compliance. The evidence of MPT's use of its former officials on NHK's Board of Governors, and the LDP's use of former reporters' club reporters, however, supports Schaede's interpretation.

[38]Interview with Nippōrō Central Executive Committee member, Tokyo, June 15, 1988. This is down from the 13,500 in the union five years earlier. See Ishii Kiyoshi, "Gekiretsu na jinji kōsō de NHK wa hōkai sunzen da" ("NHK Is on the Verge of Collapse by Its Violent Personnel Struggles"), *Sekai Ōrai* (May 1983).

branches each have a central executive committee including a chair, vice chair, and secretary-general. Ten union leaders in the central office and two each (the chair and secretary-general) at the 10 regional branches are full-time union leaders who do not work at any other task. With the approximately 15 clerical staff and receptionists included, the number of full-time union staff comes to about 45 nationwide. The central executive committee prepares an annual policy program and presents it to the annual general meeting of the union each October, which approves it and elects the central office chair, vice chair, and secretary-general. Since the early 1990s, the number of candidates have often not exceeded the number of positions and the elections, while free, have been less competitive.[39]

The Union as "Watchdog."   As a union leader concisely described the twin goals of the organization: "The union deals not only with improvement of payroll but with freedom of speech, the protection of media's freedom, or ways to protect NHK as a public broadcasting service . . . ." He went on to say that, whereas efforts to improve pay and benefits for employees tend to be concentrated around the "spring offensive" (shuntō), protecting the freedom of broadcasting is a year-round daily activity. The union considers this role crucial due to NHK's vulnerability to political pressure at budget time:

> What we worry about are the cases in which some requests were made regarding NHK's programs, news, and reports in exchange for the budget. We consider that one of our important roles is to check this matter. In other words, we continue to ask NHK's top managers to be dauntless and to remind the LDP not to intervene in the freedom of expression guaranteed in the Constitution.[40]

Note the assumption that NHK and its managers need someone to prod them to stand up to the LDP and that only the union can perform that function.

Concern for politics and freedom of broadcasting has been intimately involved in the union's birth and development. After the Occupation began, NHK employees constituted themselves as a chapter of the Japan Newspaper and Broadcast Labor Union (*Nippon shimbun tsūshin rōdō kumiai*), or Newspaper Union, a labor federation that represented workers at 33 media organizations at its formation in February 1946.[41] The union was part of the Sanbetsu (Congress of Industrial Unions) Federation led by the Japan Communist Party.

A few months later in October 1946, workers at the newspaper, *Yomiuri Shimbun,* went on strike and at first most of the other chapters supported

[39]Above information from interview with Central Executive Committee member, June 15, 1988.
[40]Ibid.
[41]*Nippōrōshi henshū iinkai (History of Japan Broadcasting Union)* (Tokyo: Nihon Hōsō Rōdō Kumiai, 1981), 4.

them, preparing to walk out. Before the targeted strike day, however, all but a few of the chapters, including NHK's, called off the action. When three days of the shutdown of broadcasting at NHK produced no solution, the government took over NHK facilities and the Communications Ministry itself broadcast basic information services in the Tokyo area.[42]

Within a few weeks, the strike petered out, the government relinquished control, and normal broadcasting resumed. The strike, however, increased many chapters' dissatisfaction with the revolutionary policies of the Newspaper Union leadership and Sanbetsu that had led to the failed strike that had, in turn, isolated the broadcast workers; with the lack of internal union democracy; and with policies that neglected more conventional trade union economic issues. By the end of 1947, a new union of broadcasting employees, independent of the Newspaper Union, Sanbetsu, and the Communist Party, was formed. By March of 1948 when it held its founding convention, the new union, Nippōrō, had the loyalty of about 83 percent of NHK's approximately 7,000 employees, with the original Newspaper Union and a third small union dividing the rest.[43]

The Japan Socialist Party (JSP) emerged as the chief opposition party after the April 1947 elections. Around this time, the Occupation went into "reverse course," de-emphasizing democratization and demilitarization and focusing more on stability and anti-Communism as a result of the initiation of the Cold War and the new fear of Communist subversion in Japan. Following the Socialists' emergence and the Occupation's change of focus came a renewed interest in a non-Communist but leftist labor federation alternative. Sōhyō (the General Council on Trade Unions) was formed in March 1950, and composed to a large extent of Socialist-leaning public employees unions, such as the Teacher's Union and National Railway's Union. Nippōrō joined in 1953 and has maintained its affiliation with Sōhyō and the Japan Socialist Party.[44]

Nippōrō's subsequent history shows its efforts to maximize the two major goals that led to its founding: improving the working and economic conditions of its members and advancing political issues, including broadcasting freedom. Soon after joining Sōhyō, the union for several years focused pri-

---

[42]This was the only time in Japan's history, even during the military period, when the state took total control over broadcasting. In English, see NHK Radio and TV Culture Research Center (NHK RTVCRI), ed., *50 Years of Japanese Broadcasting* (Tokyo: NHK, 1977), 159–60; NHK RTVCRI, ed., *The History of Broadcasting in Japan* (Tokyo: NHK, 1967), 156; in Japanese, *Nippōrōshi henshū iinkai*, 5–6.

[43]*Nippōrōshi henshū iinkai*, 7–12.

[44]Ibid., 14–15. On Sanbetsu's rise and fall with Communist fortunes in the immediate postwar period, see Robert A. Scalapino, *The Japan Communist Movement, 1920–1966* (Berkeley: University of California Press, 1967), 68–70. On Nippōrō joining Sōhyō, see Shiga, *Anata no Shiranai NHK*, 256. The Japan Socialist Party changed its name a few years ago to the Social Democratic Party (SDP) of Japan (Nihon Shakai Minshu-tō).

marily on internal matters, particularly "wage struggles" and establishing the right to strike during such wage conflicts. Then, in response to the computer and television age, union and NHK management entered into an arrangement called the "EDPS Basic Agreement." Both sides committed to prior consultation in organizational planning, no reduction of personnel, agreement on distribution of posts, and an upgrading of working conditions.

So with the 1960s, Nippōrō began to turn also to external political issues, many of which involved the attempt to mobilize public opinion. In 1967, it opposed a Broadcasting Law revision and started the Mass Media Citizens' Movement (*masu komi shimin undō*), including the magazine *masu komi shimin* (*Mass Media Citizen*) with 40,000 readers. In 1969 the union began a movement on behalf of a "Defending Broadcasting Freedom Month," and in 1971, it combined an internal and an external theme in what was called the "General Struggle" for both Okinawa reversion (without nuclear weapons) and higher wages. One of Nippōrō's histories classified such struggles into three categories: (1) the struggle with power—pursuit of the responsibility of political power, management; (2) the struggle to build public opinion—pursuit of rights for the people; and (3) the struggle toward self-regulation—responsibility for cultural creativity.[45]

One reason for the union's external orientation in the 1960s and 1970s was Ueda Tetsu, the frequent chair of Nippōrō after 1962. In 1968, the union helped elect him to the National Diet.

The Rise and Fall of Ueda Tetsu

In the fairly voluminous postwar literature about NHK up until the 1980s, probably a higher proportion of pages are devoted to this man than any other subject. His rise to power within NHK, his perceived power over NHK personnel policy and practice, his rivalry with Shima Keiji, his political career and the reaction it provoked from the ruling LDP, and his and Nippōrō's consequent decline in influence within the broadcasting organization have all been well documented.[46] Certainly, Ueda's rise and fall had

[45]The post-Occupation development of the union is found in Shiga, *Anata no Shiranai NHK*, 255–59.

[46]A small sample: Ishii Kiyoshi, *NHK fukumaden no shinsō* (*The Truth about NHK Pandemonium*) (Tokyo: Jiyū Kokuminsha, 1983) and his "Gekiretsu na jinji," 96–113; Shiga, *Anata no Shiranai NHK; NHK ōkoku no uchimaku* (*Behind the Scenes of the NHK Kingdom*) (Tokyo: Nisshin Hōdō, 1972), 52–76, 223–47; *Buraun-kan no uragawa*, 21–23; 44–49; *Terebi eitei* (*Television '80*) (Tokyo: Kioi Shobō, 1980, 189–92, 200–206; Gōdō Shirō, *NHK shakaibu kisha* (*NHK Society Desk Reporter*) (Tokyo: Asahi Shimbunsha, 1986), 208, 214; Ise Akifumi, *NHK daikenkyū* (*Large Research on NHK*) (Tokyo: Poru Shuppan, 1988), 167–72, 175–93; Sase Monoru, "Ueda Tetsu: NHK no 'Yami Shōgun'" ("Ueda Tetsu, NHK's 'Shadow Shogun'"), *Bungei Shunjū* (April 1981): 94–123.

important consequences internally for personnel relations at NHK, externally for the broadcaster's relationship with the state, and overall for the connection between the two.

Ueda Tetsu, born in Tokyo in 1928, went to the same high school in Niigata Prefecture as his contemporary and future nemesis, Shima Keiji. After a checkered occupational history, including teaching in high school, he completed his education at the prestigious Faculty of Law of Kyoto University, graduating in 1954, and entered NHK as a reporter.

His spectacular rise to influence within NHK followed a career route more common in the earlier postwar period—the union. In those days, the breadth of experience and vision of union leaders was viewed by NHK management as indications of the qualifications for advancement to organizational leadership, not to mention as a good way to co-opt and manage relations with the potentially troublesome union. One of Ueda's closest colleagues and a mentor for a while, for example, was Nakazuka Masatane, his predecessor as Nippōrō chairman, who went on to become an NHK special director and then vice president to President Sakamoto Tomokazu.[47]

Thus, Ueda's power came not from his professional positions in NHK but from his union leadership. His career as a reporter was only typical: after serving for several years in local areas, he was brought to Tokyo and the News Division's city desk (*shakaibu*) in 1959 and assigned to cover the National Policy Agency. Ueda joined the News Division in Tokyo just as it was expanding in size and status under the direction of President Maeda Yoshinori.

The pivotal event of Ueda's career, however, was not related to his reporting; rather, it was a campaign against polio launched by NHK's city desk and in which Ueda played a leading role as union branch chief of both the politics-economics (these were later separated) and city desks. This led to his appointment in July 1962 to Nippōrō's Central Committee as a representative of the News Division, as well as his selection to be its organization bureau chief (*soshiki buchō*). From these positions, he consolidated his power within the union and expanded his and the union's influence within mass media's labor unions in general and in Sōhyō.

Just 10 years after graduating from college and entering NHK, he became chairman of Nippōrō. In 1964 there was even a movement in the Socialist Party to nominate him as a party candidate in the House of Councilors election, but his enemies influenced Nippōrō's Central Committee to reject him. Returning to the News Division briefly, he was back as chairman of Nippōrō in 1966.

When the special managing director for labor relations was found to have attempted to promote an anti-Ueda movement in local branches of the

[47]On Ueda's early life and career, see Ishii, *NHK fukumaden*, 26–28.

union, he was forced to resign and a colleague of Ueda's, Nagazawa Taiji, took his place. Ueda now had a close ally in management, especially concerning labor relations, and successors in that position also were allies of Ueda. He also forged a strategic modus vivendi with President Maeda, who had a vested interest in stabilizing that area of management. Ueda and Nagazawa could now influence personnel policy and purge the enemies of the union within NHK, as well as extend Ueda's influence into other areas of the organization.[48]

In July 1968 Ueda had his previously aborted political ambitions fulfilled when he was elected to the House of Councilors in the national constituency as a Socialist, with some sources suggesting that he used his Nippōrō position to succeed in the national arena. As union chairman, he had pushed for collapsing the classifications of high school and college graduates in the pay scales and thus won the loyalty of the less educated but numerous collectors of receivers' fee, who then helped him mobilize the vote in the election.[49] Undoubtedly, the ability of Nippōrō to deliver and mobilize votes from their branches all over the country, the votes of Socialist Party supporters attracted to this dynamic new candidate, and memories of Ueda's role in the anti-polio campaign also played a major role in his winning the third most votes of all the candidates in the nationwide races. The two placing ahead of him were well-known "talent" names, including the famous novelist and archconservative Ishihara Shintarō, who was to become a major critic of Ueda in the future.

Ueda continued to serve as chairman of the union even after his election to the House of Councilors, a fact that raised the hackles of the LDP, as well as some concern even within the union. But despite some pressure put on President Maeda to do something about this, nothing was done. Maeda's successor, Ono Yoshirō, who owed much of his career to Tanaka Kakuei, also continued the alliance of convenience with Ueda and Nippōrō, even elevating a close ally of Ueda's, to become Ono's vice president in 1973–74.

The Lockheed scandal and the campaign of Ueda and Nippōrō to name a "homegrown" NHK executive to succeed Ono, who was forced to resign after his visit to the indicted Tanaka, led to the appointment of Sakamoto Tomokazu as president. Meanwhile, in February 1977, Ueda finally stepped down as the chairman of the union, but took on the honorary title of "emeritus chair" (*meiyo iinchō*).[50]

---

[48]For an account of the anti-polio campaign and Ueda's role in it by a fellow reporter and participant, see Gōdo Shirō, *NHK shakaibu kisha*, 76–92; for the union's personnel power and Shima's as well, see 226–28. On Ueda's career rise in NHK, see ibid., 26–36.

[49]Interview with K2, March 27, 1995; Sase, "Ueda Tetsu," 103–4.

[50]On Ueda's political career and consolidation of power within NHK, see Ishii, *NHK fukumaden*, 36–47. On his "resignation" as chair, see 156; also Ishii, "Gekiretsu na jinji," 103.

This nominal concession to the independence of broadcasting from politics nonetheless could not conceal the fact that Ueda's power had become even stronger. Under Sakamoto, the so-called "UNN Line" (i.e., the "Ueda-Nakazuka-Nagazawa Line") was firmly established at NHK. With Ueda as the "shadow shogun" (*yami shōgun*) of the union; Nakazuka, Ueda's long-time ally, in an important management post; and Nagazawa, mentor to both Ueda and Nakazuka, on the management board with responsibility for labor relations,[51] the UNN Line soon flexed its muscles, first in a clash with Kawahara Masato, the personnel division chief who was known as a antiunion hardliner, over the choice of a new director for the News Division. Ueda won.

Then, after President Sakamoto was appointed to a second term, union power was confirmed when Nakazuka was appointed Sakamoto's vice president in 1979 and his likely successor. Ueda and his allies now purged antiunion executives such as Kawahara, banishing them to some minor executive posts, and installed more pro-union executives into management.[52] The attitude at NHK was, it was said, "If you're not Nippōrō, you are not a person" (Nippōrō de nakeraba hito de nai). When Ueda was elected to a seat in the more important House of Representatives, both the union's power within NHK and Ueda's political career, even as a major Socialist Party figure at the national level, seemed unstoppable.

That very year, it all fell apart. The LDP, especially the Tanaka faction, resenting what they saw as bias in treatment of the Lockheed scandal and their still powerful, if indicted, former leader and warily watching the growing power of Ueda and the union within NHK, now launched a major counterattack. Angered at the role that Nippōrō had played in Ono's resignation, the LDP intensified its denunciation of Ueda, accurately claiming he had an undue influence on personnel and more tenuously charging that he influenced other decisions affecting coverage at NHK. In April 1979, as was discussed in chapter 4, the LDP turned up the pressure further by very briefly establishing a subcommittee of the Communications Committee of the Diet to investigate NHK. That NHK was requesting a receivers' fee increase from the Diet at the time was not lost on NHK management. Ueda announced his resignation as leader of Nippōrō in December 1979.

Ueda never disclosed the exact reasons for his resignation, but there have been intimations of various possible scandals involving, among other things, his personal finances that might have been used by NHK to pressure him out. Ueda's resignation speech, however, implied he was sacrificing himself

[51] See the diagram of Ueda's personnel connections in Sase, "Ueda Tetsu," 99, and the chart on p. 114 of Nippōrō's Central Committee Members advancement in NHK.
[52] On these developments see Ishii, *NHK fukumaden*, 156–70; "Gekiretsu na jinji," 97–102.

to gain the fee increase for NHK. Rumors within NHK even have it that Ueda's resignation was a condition imposed on Sakamoto by the LDP when he became president for a second term.[53]

His resignation did not, however, stem the LDP attack. In March 1981, the House of Representatives' Communications Committee discussed Ueda's influence and use of NHK for his own political purposes in two days of meetings during which LDP Diet members vociferously criticized the practices. Both President Sakamoto and his formerly pro-union vice president Nakazuka, who had ambitions to succeed Sakamoto, began to backpedal and distance themselves from the union, but it was too late. The presidency was lost to both of them. As we have seen, Nippōrō's enemy and victim, Kawahara, was appointed by the Board of Governors to succeed Sakamoto, and the anti-Ueda and anti-union Shima Keiji, with close connections to the ruling party, became a managing director. After taking office in July 1982, Kawahara conducted a thorough purge of Ueda supporters, driving 40 employees from their executive and special posts.[54]

By all written accounts and of those I interviewed, the influence of Nippōrō within NHK declined precipitously after Ueda's fall, even as Shima Keiji's power increased. The 1980s NHK would be dominated internally by Ueda's political and professional archrival, Shima.

The 1980s: Internal Editing

As early as the late 1960s, Nippōrō had become concerned with institutionalizing the autonomy of the editing process within NHK. To this end, it proposed the establishment of an "Editing Council" (*henshū kyōgikai*), composed of NHK employees, to make the final decisions on editing. With Shima's growing internal power, his close relationship to LDP leaders, and the "Miki cut" incident described in the previous chapter, the union became even more concerned about this issue during the 1980s.

NHK's management, on the other hand, fiercely opposes giving over ultimate editing responsibility to a council in which the union participates.[55] It argues that such a council of employees determining editing decisions with labor union representation would violate the Broadcasting Law's proscription against any group's interference in programming.

---

[53]On the resignation, see Shiga, *Terebi eitei*, 198–206; see also Ise, *NHK daikenkyū*, 170–71, on the pressure on Ueda and NHK.

[54]On the LDP attack and its consequences, see Ishii, "Gekiretsu na jinji," 104–12; Ise, *NHK daikenkyū*, 168–71.

[55]Noguchi Satori, "Naibuteki hōsō no jiyū ron" ("The Theory of Internal Broadcasting Freedom"), *Masukomi Shimin*, no. 234 (March 1, 1988): 58–59. Noguchi was head of the Planning and Research Bureau of the Central Executive Committee of Nippōrō at the time the article was published.

Noguchi Satori, a Nippōrō executive, argues in an article[56] that management's contention is based on the assumption that broadcasting freedom only protects the broadcaster's right to operate freely and treats the broadcaster almost as an individual whose right of expression must be protected from the state and external social groups by control over editorial decisions.

Noguchi supports instead an approach particularly espoused by Germany's Social Democratic Party and certain regions in that country, in which broadcasting is seen as performing an important social function in the formation of democratic public opinion and the audience's right to receive diverse information must be guaranteed. Therefore, broadcasting autonomy is not an "individual right" but a "societal right." The state is not just a potential threat to the media organization's autonomy, it also has a positive role to play as one guarantor of society's right to receive various information and opinions.

Broadcasting employees also have a responsibility to protect broadcasting freedom, and the union should be thought of not only as a workers' union under labor law but also as an occupational group that organizes journalists and therefore has rights of participation in editing. Because of the special role of public broadcasting to provide a forum for diverse opinion in a democratic society and the increasing threat from manipulation by authority, it is especially important to protect and widen freedom within NHK by giving such rights to its employees and the union.

At first it may seem strange that a leftist labor union—the history of which includes a struggle against the postwar conservative government's interference with NHK's operations—would see a positive role for state regulation and emphasize internal participation in editing decisions over defending broadcasting freedom from external threat. Nippōrō's view of the threat to media freedom, however, inextricably links internal participation in editing decisions and defense of NHK against the state. In a democratic society with formal press freedom rights guaranteed, a crude repression by the state as in prewar Japan is not an imminent danger.[57] It is the indirect manipulation by authority to which management voluntarily submits that represents the real danger to NHK's autonomy.

In the aftermath of the "Miki cut" and the Ueda resignation incidents, the union developed a more sophisticated conception than the simple, earlier postwar left's view that the chief danger to freedom came from direct state repression as in prewar times. "Self-censorship" by management under covert pressure from those in power realistically poses a greater threat to broadcasting freedom than overt governmental regulation. If so, then only

[56]The following discussion comes from ibid., 60–73.
[57]Noguchi, "Naibuteki hōsō," 62.

the union's enhanced power within NHK through formal rights of participation in editing decisions—in other words, checking management internally—can provide the necessary antidote.

There are four ways in which NHK's personnel policies and practices have had consequences for its relationship to the state. First, personnel practices have had major implications for NHK's fiscal situation, particularly in helping to create or manage the budget deficits that affect its vulnerability to political interference. Second, personnel policies and practices provide the background for reporters learning the news values and priorities that determine their norms, behavior, and modus operandi in covering the news, including political news.

The third important influence of personnel practices is that recruitment and socialization practices for reporters mitigate cross-organizational, professional contacts and identifications, but stimulate organizational and professional identifications and relationships that create strong linkages to governmental personnel, especially politicians and bureaucrats. These relationships involve NHK personnel heavily with the state and its policy-making processes. Both NHK and the state use these relationships to communicate with and persuade the other, and thus they become two-way conduits and channels of influence.

Finally, labor-management relations have played a major role in some of the conflicts involving NHK and the state in the postwar period. In these conflicts, an employees' union affiliated with the leftist opposition has attempted to defend NHK's autonomy from state influence, within and without, putting pressure on management and the LDP to resist intervention in broadcasting autonomy. It has also, however, through its own activities and the power of its former chairman, Ueda Tetsu, provided the rationale and motivation for the LDP's attempted interference in NHK as a way of preventing leftist influence on personnel and broadcast decisions. The ruling party without, and the leftist union within, have both justified their attempts to extend their power over NHK using the perceived threat of the other to NHK's autonomy and neutrality.

CHAPTER 7

New Media Strategies
and Organizational Change

Technology does not drive choice, choice drives technology.
—MICHAEL BORRUS AND JOHN ZYSMAN, *The New Media,*
Telecommunications, and Development

Certainly, there is much useful discussion of the economic, social
and political determinants of the *choice* between different technological options . . . but much less on *why those options have developed*
as they have.
—DONALD MacKENZIE AND JUDY WAJCMAN,
The Social Shaping of Technology

The primary thing I grappled with as an executive and in my time
as President was to reform this predisposition (of NHK's need to
please politicians). To do this we had to break the vicious circle of
embellished budgets, perennial red ink, and fee increases. How to
do that? It was simple. We should earn money independently.
—SHIMA KEIJI, FORMER NHK PRESIDENT, *"Shima Geji" fūunroku*

If NHK's personnel policies and labor-management relations were
studies in continuities and the reflections of previous eras, its corporate
strategy and approach to technology in the 1980s looked to the future and to
change. Strategy and technology were linked, as the organization's strategies
for survival, financial reconstruction, and continued broadcasting dominance involved innovative "new media" technologies, such as satellite broadcasting and high-definition television. These technologies in turn necessitated changes in organizational structure and strategy to escape from NHK's
bureaucratic hierarchy and in-house production through the spinning off
of subsidiary companies that could link up with the private sector and engage
in commercial activities. Inextricably intertwined with these changes was
NHK's attempt to respond to, or gain more autonomy from, state influence.

SATELLITE BROADCASTING

The Development of NHK's Broadcasting Satellite Program

NHK's interest in satellite broadcasting began early as the mid-1960s. The first successful live satellite transmission between the United States and Japan took place during the Tokyo Olympic games in 1964. The following year NHK established the Broadcast Satellite Research Committee and produced a broadcast satellite plan.[1]

This rapid response to the new technology derived in part from NHK's obligations under its charter, the Broadcast Law. Article 7's statement of the "purpose" of the corporation obligates NHK's signals to be received all over Japan, and Article 9 empowers NHK to "conduct research and investigations necessary for the improvement and development of broadcasting and the reception thereof."[2] Satellite broadcasting was seen both as a potential solution to the major problem inherent in efforts to broadcast all over Japan and as a means to fulfill the mandate of Article 9. Estimates were that one to two million households had great technical difficulties receiving NHK broadcasts because of their isolated locations amidst Japan's mountainous and island topography. Satellite broadcasting could redress the problem by bypassing the natural and human-created land-based obstacles to reception. If NHK was to remain current with global technological evolution, satellite research and development was imperative.

NHK President Maeda Yoshinori acknowledged these two motivations in testimony before the House of Representatives Communications Committee's deliberations on NHK's 1966 budget, citing as concerns the lack of full nationwide television coverage and the international isolation of Japan as satellites for television broadcasting were developed. In 1972, Maeda proposed the development of an experimental satellite.[3]

Soon, however, NHK's interest in satellite broadcasting became intertwined with the government's desire to develop Japan's fledgling aerospace

[1] Matsuda Hiyoshi, "NHK wa doko e iku—Nyū medeiya jidai o mukaete" ("Where NHK Is Going: Confronting the New Media Age"), *Sekai* (November 1986): 79; Ōtsuki Hiroyoshi, "NHK ga nomerikomu eisei hōsō no aya: Kyodai soshiki no kike na sentaku" ("Suspicions about Satellite Broadcasting that NHK's Throwing Itself Into: The Dangerous Choice of a Giant Organization"), *Bungei Shunjū* 68, no. 1 (January 1990): 188.

[2] JBC, *The Broadcast Law* (Tokyo: NHK, n.d.), Article 7, p. 7 and Article 9(2), p. 11; see also Nozaki Shigeru, Higashiyama Yoshiyuki, and Shinohara Toshiyuki, *Hōsō gyōkai* (*The Broadcasting Industry*) (Tokyo: Kyōikusha, 1983), 56.

[3] On NHK's concerns and response, see Ōtsuki, "NHK ga nomerikomu eisei hōsō," 188–89; Ogino Yoshikazu, "Nyūsu, kyō, asu: NHK eisei hōsō" ("News, Today/Tomorrow: NHK's Satellite Broadcasting"), *Mainichi Shimbun*, July 8, 1987, 4; Richard A. Gershon and Tsutomu Kanayama, "Direct Broadcast Satellites in Japan: A Case Study in Government-Business Partnerships," *Telecommunications Policy* 19, no. 3 (April 1995): 220.

industry. The Science and Technology Agency, the Ministry of Posts and Telecommunications, and the Liberal Democratic Party's telecommunications policy tribe all wanted NHK's plans integrated with the government's policy to cultivate Japan's satellite launching and communications technology. As a result, NHK's push for satellite broadcasting came to be guided by the national industrial policy goal of achieving technological autonomy through the "indigenization" (*kokusanka*) of technology, absorbing, diffusing, and nurturing it to build a competitive domestic industry.[4]

If NHK used domestic technology, domestic manufacturers would benefit from higher demand and thus greater economies of scale, cutting costs through efficiencies and gaining profits to offset the high costs of development, all of which would nurture the competitiveness of a domestic industry vying against more advanced foreign rivals. NHK's first satellite in 1978 used a U.S. "Delta 2914" rocket; but for its BS-2 and BS-3 satellites, it used Japanese-developed "N-II" and "H-I" rockets. President Maeda admitted that much of the impetus behind satellite broadcasting was fueled by state interests: "The broadcast satellite concept is not at all being driven by the interests of NHK. I am acting on behalf of government policy."[5]

In January 1977, Japan received eight bands from the World Administrative Radio Conference—Broadcast Satellite (WARC-BS) division and in April 1978, launched its first experimental broadcasting satellite, "Yuri." By June 1980, however, all its transmission functions stopped. In January 1984, Japan launched the BS-2a (named "Yuri 2a" after launch), its first communications satellite intended to eliminate the problems of reception for many households and for actual broadcast use. Yuri 2a was also the world's first high-powered Direct Broadcasting Satellite (DBS). Two months after launch, however, it developed major technical problems that left it with only one of its three channels (two regular and one reserve) operational. Forced to alter its plans to begin regular satellite broadcasting, NHK instead carried out further experiments on the one remaining, not always properly functioning, channel and postponed the launch of the next satellite in the series.

When "Yuri 2b," with another three channels, was finally launched successfully in winter 1986, the program seemed back on track. After it was in orbit, however, power circuit and telemetry problems forced broadcasting to be

[4]Ogino, "Nyūsu, kyō, asu," 4; Tahara Sōichirō, *Medeia ōkoku no yabō* (*The Ambitions of a Media Kingdom*) (Tokyo: Bungeishunjū, 1992), 170; Shima Keiji, '*Shima Geji" fūunroku—hōsō to kenryoku, 40-nen* (*The Troubled Record of "Shima Geji": Broadcasting and Politics, 40 years*) (Tokyo: Bungei Shunjū, 1995), 232–33. See Richard J. Samuel's definitive work, "*Rich Nation, Strong Army": National Security and the Technological Transformation of Japan* (Ithaca, N.Y.: Cornell University Press, 1994), 42–56 on "kokusanka."

[5]Matsuda, "NHK wa doko e iku," 78. On the use of domestic rockets, see Nozaki Shigeru, Higashiyama Yoshiyuki, and Shinohara Toshiyuki, *Hōsō gyōkai* (*The Broadcasting Industry*), rev. ed. (Tokyo: Kyōikusha, 1986).

switched to reserve equipment. Critics also charged that NHK had been rushed into a premature effort to implement an unstable technology because it was pressured by its commitment to the government's space development agenda.[6]

Insurance costs for such launchings, in part because of these failures, were increasing more consistently than the costs of the satellites themselves, adding to the expense of the program. As the programming on the two Yuri-2b channels was the same as on its land-based channels, sales of the receiver dishes attained only about 140,000 receivers. With such low "economies of scale," manufacturers of the receivers could not lower unit prices rapidly and the cost of the parabola antenna and tuner together was still almost $1,700 by mid-1987.[7]

Not to be deterred, in 1987 NHK applied to the MPT for a revision of its satellite broadcasting license to combine Yuri 2b's previously separate two channels into one, thus creating a separate channel for special satellite programming. On the morning of July 3, 1987, the MPT granted NHK a new license changing the previous designations of the channels. On the following day, NHK began broadcasting experimentally on the world's first 24-hour broadcasting channel. These broadcasts included, for example, world news, containing live feeds from its New York and London studios; the United States's ABC and Britain's BBC news with simultaneous translation in captions; live sports events; and music programs in digital sound.[8]

NHK's heavy advance publicity created a sudden, heavy demand for receiver sets that, in turn, created a shortage by the time the channel was actually initiated. Within two months, the number of sets installed jumped to 170,000, and the average rate of installation (4,000 per month) had tripled. Within less than a year, the price was down to about $1,000 for a conve-

[6]See the following on these satellite technology failures and criticisms of NHK: Nozaki et al., *Hōsō gyōkai*, 43; Ōkura Yūnosuke, "NHK no Zasetsu," *Nyū Medeia* (November 1986): 16. Gershon and Kanayama, "Direct Broadcast Satellites," 221; Shirakawa Michinobu, *Eisei hōsō to haibijyon (Satellite Broadcasting and Hivision)* (Tokyo: Kyōikusha, 1990), 63–64, 67–71; Matsuda, "NHK wa doko e iku," 76, 77; Umehara Kiyoshi, "NHK: Kaji o ushinatta kyosen" ("NHK: The Rudderless Ocean Liner"), *Sekai*, no. 515 (June 1988): 279–80, 284–85; Ōtsuki, "NHK ga nomerikomu eisei hōsō," 186.

[7]Shirakawa, *Eisei hōsō to haibijyon*, 71, says that by 1990 insurance fees came to comprise 35 percent of the launching costs; also "Hōsō eisei—Atama itai hōkenryō kōtō" ("Broadcast Satellite Headache: Insurance Fees Dramatic Jump"), *Asahi Shimbun* (evening edition), March 2, 1990, 17; on sales, see Ogino, "Nyūsu, kyō, asu," 4.

[8]On the license revision and satellite programming, see "NHK no shineisei hōsō: Kōhyō no sutāto" ("NHK's New Satellite Broadcasting: A Well-Received Start"), *Denpa Taimuzu*, July 10, 1987, 1; Ogino, "Nyūsu, kyō, asu," 4; "NHK 24-jikan eisei hōsō hajimaru" ("NHK's 24-hour Satellite Broadcasting Begins"), *Nyū Medeia* (September 1987): 6–14; see also NHK, *Supēsu chyanneru: Uchū kara no "new" messēji (Space Channel: The New Message from Space)*, inaugural edition, 1987 (a brochure); *NHK Newsletter*, no. 7 (August 1987).

niently sized dish, and the programming was receiving favorable reaction from Japanese and foreign residents alike. In June 1989, full-scale DBS service began on two channels, and two months later, NHK requested and received from the Diet a new category of receivers' fee for satellite service, despite critics who then and later questioned the fee for a service that had no back-up satellite in place.[9]

The critics had a point. In February 1990, NHK planned to send a new BS-2x satellite into space to back up and supplement Yuri 2b's two channels. Because domestic satellites had proven so expensive, NHK decided to try less expensive foreign-built technology, a General Electric (GE) satellite, launched on a French Ariane rocket from French Guiana. The rocket exploded shortly after take-off. The next satellite, BS-3H, also a GE satellite, was launched by an American Atlas-Centaur rocket in Florida, but it also had an abortive launch. It was questions about NHK President Shima's whereabouts at the time of this launching that precipitated his resignation.[10]

In August 1991, a Japanese H-1 rocket finally succeeded in putting BS-3b into orbit. It provided two channels for NHK, one for the private stations' Japan Satellite Broadcasting (JSB) company, and one a combined NHK-commercial station channel transmitting high-definition television broadcasts. Future satellites were planned to supply more channels. As of the mid-1990s, about seven million households received NHK's satellite services (about 15 percent of the 40 million households with television in Japan). Another one and a half million received the commercial broadcasters' service.[11]

The Shifting Goals: Political Background and Strategy

This direct satellite broadcasting experience raises some obvious questions. What happened to NHK's initial motivation of eliminating reception problems for rural households? How and why did it wind up with a separate 24-hour satellite channel with its own programming? Given the

[9]"NHK no shineisei hōsō," 1; "The Big Hit Nobody Expected," *Nikkei*, no. 2 (December 1987): 8. This article is an abridged version of an article in the *Nikkei High Tech Report*, October 12, 1987. For criticism of the fee, see Van Buren, "NHK's satellite broadcasts commendable," *Japan Times*, May 27, 1988, 16; "NHK ni shinkoku na kōishō: Eisei shippai—Towareru 'yūryōka'" ("Serious Aftereffects for NHK: 'Satellite Failure—Charging a Questionable Fee'"), *Mainichi Shimbun* (evening edition), February 24, 1990, 7.

[10]*Asahi Shimbun* (evening edition), February 23, 1990, 1; in English, "Panel of Experts to Examine Explosion of Ariane Rocket," *New York Times*, February 24, 1990, 7. On the background and politics surrounding BS-3H, see Tahara, *Medeia ōkoku no yabō*, 172–73.

[11]Junji Matsuzaki, "The Scenario for Hi-Vision Broadcasting in Japan" (paper presented at the Conference on High Technology Policy-Making in Japan and the United States, Washington, D.C., June 8, 1993); Gershon and Kanayama, "Direct Broadcast Satellites," 226; "Japanese Television: The Slow March of Progress," *Economist* (July 15, 1995): 49.

enormous costs and failures along the way, why did NHK persist in its expensive commitment to this "new media"?

The answer to these questions lies in a major shift in NHK strategy that occurred in the mid-1980s in response to its political and economic environment. If NHK's satellite program had as its original purpose the elimination of reception problems for a half million households in the 1960s, 20 years later this justification had become moot. By 1984 improvements in the technical development of land-based broadcasting had reduced the number of such households to 400,000; just two years later, the number was down to 100,000. Meanwhile, the money that NHK had invested in satellite broadcasting development, ostensibly for accomplishing what had already been accomplished by other means, had increased. The development and launching of Yuri 2a and Yuri 2b had cost more than a quarter of a billion dollars,[12] of which NHK had borne about 60 percent of the costs. This represented almost a full 10 percent of NHK's yearly budget, and had this expenditure not been made, the receivers' fee increase of 1984 might not have been necessary. It became increasingly difficult for either NHK or the government to justify such expenditures to improve reception for such a small part of the population. "In desperation" (*kurushimagire ni*), as NHK former President Shima puts it, the MPT proposed new purposes for satellites, especially the broadening of programming options by creating additional broadcasting bands beyond land-based broadcasting and the providing of new services.

After the costly series of "Yuri" satellite failures, NHK reevaluated how much it could support "national policy." Putting the payload into orbit using domestic rockets cost more than twice as much as using U.S. or European rockets and five to seven times as much as launching with either Russian or Chinese rockets.[13] NHK was spending an enormous sum of money, exacerbating its financial problems, and forcing it to raise receivers' fees in order to subsidize national space development—facts that did not go unnoticed in the media or by the public. The Americans also were putting increasing pressure on the Japanese government because the cheaper foreign satellites were not being used. Using indigenous satellites was becoming less politically viable, both domestically and internationally.[14] Thus NHK's use of foreign satellites and rockets in 1990 and 1991, a change that sparked angry

[12]600 "oku" yen; depending on the exchange rate, these have been between a quarter (at ¥160) to one-half a billion dollars (at ¥120 to $1).

[13]Shima, *"Shima Geji,"* 233. He also subsequently implies that the number of households not receiving service had actually been reduced to only 20,000–30,000; see also Umehara, "NHK: Kaju o ushinatta kyosen," 279; Ogino, "Nyūsu, kyō, asu," 4; on satellite costs, see ibid., 4; Nozaki et al., *Hōsō gyōkai,* rev. ed., 188. Matsuda, "NHK wa doko e iku," 76–77.

[14]Ōkura, "NHK no Zasetsu," 16.

reaction from the MPT and especially the LDP's communications policy tribe. These groups accused NHK of conspiring with foreign manufacturers and violating "national policy." Indeed, Shima claims that this alienation of NHK's political patrons was one of the significant factors precipitating his downfall.[15]

Why then did NHK persist in pursuing its investments in broadcasting satellites if it cost so much money and the broadcaster's technology choices created hostility from the bureaucracy and key politicians? The answer is that "new media" had become NHK executives' long-range strategy for securing greater financial, and thus political, independence. Recall that fee increases, each necessitating approval by the Diet and LDP, left NHK vulnerable to political pressure. Such increases, which became necessary in the early 1980s due to NHK's worsening financial situation, rankled viewers and their representatives, and the latter began pressuring NHK to deal with the structural causes of the problem. Austerity and personnel reduction programs were not going to work sufficiently or rapidly enough.

NHK executives needed to find new revenue sources in order both to respond to the political pressure and to gain some freedom from it. As early as 1982, NHK's "Long-term Vision Advisory Council" (*chōki bijyon shingikai*), an advisory board to the president of NHK, urged the broadcasting organization to "play a leading role in the development and operationalization" of new media, to consider multiple applications for satellite broadcasting in addition to eliminating reception difficulties, and to establish new fees for its new media services.[16] If NHK could no longer easily justify raising land-based receivers' fees, it could justify a new, separate fee for initiating a different service, direct satellite broadcasting.

The political environment also added some motivation. Prime Minister Nakasone Yasuhiro (1982–87), like his conservative counterparts Ronald Reagan and Margaret Thatcher and with the strong backing of the business community in Japan, had committed the government to "administrative reform." This included the privatization of two of Japan's huge public corporations, NTT (Nippon Telephone and Telegraph) and JNR (Japan National Railways). Not a great fan of NHK, Nakasone believed it to be biased against conservatives, and at least some other conservative elites wanted NHK included in the list of organizations to be "reformed."[17] This motive provided one impetus to big business and the LDP politicians to push for a business leader like Ikeda Yoshizō to be named NHK president in 1988. NHK was not

[15]Shima, *"Shima Geji,"* 232–35; Tahara, *Medeia ōkoku no yabō,* 170.
[16]Nozaki et al., *Hōsō gyōkai,* 239–40.
[17]On some LDP politicians' antipathy to NHK, see Shima, *"Shima Geji,"* 168–71, 176; also, a personal conversation in August 1983 with Nakasone in which he indicated he thought NHK was biased.

about to be privatized or commercialized, and the business community still supported NHK's broadcasting dominance to maintain a "cultural standard." Nevertheless, the organization had an incentive to find a new raison d'être and a means to retain its dominance in Japan's "duopoly" broadcasting system.

"New media," such as satellite broadcasting and high-definition television, seemed to offer means to that end. Ogino Yoshikazu, in answering the question of why NHK chose in the mid-1980s to push satellite broadcasting despite its costs, calls it NHK's "wishing star" (*kibō no hoshi*) to carry out the reconstruction of its deficit finances, while Isomura Hisanori, then NHK's News Division director, in 1984 called it NHK's "trump card" (*kiri fuda*) to establish NHK's overwhelming presence in the "new media" age.[18]

This strategy was unintentionally abetted by the late and difficult entrance of the commercial broadcasters into satellite use. Initially, the commercial broadcasters were very slow, indeed antagonistic, in their response to direct satellite broadcasting. In 1973, an executive of the Commercial Broadcasters Association (*Mimpōren*) expressed the fear that direct satellite broadcasting would be implemented under government supervision and would therefore threaten freedom of expression. The real fear, however, was that direct satellite broadcasting would destroy the local affiliates system of the commercial broadcasters. Despite this initial reluctance, established commercial broadcasters after 1973 gradually came to accept the idea of direct satellite broadcasting because they saw that the MPT was committed to it, it was becoming important internationally, and they realized that if they did not participate, new entrants would undermine the position of existing commercial broadcasters.

MPT and its advisory groups pushed for an organization that would be able to bring together and coordinate all the private sector groups interested in the Direct Broadcasting Satellites. In December 1984, Japan's first commercial broadcasting satellite company, Japan Satellite Broadcasting (*Nihon eisei hōsō*) was established with authorized capital of ¥28 billion from 190 companies. MPT awarded the management contract for the first DBS channel for private firms on its planned BS-3 satellite to Keidanren (Federation of Economic Organizations) and then asked the powerful business peak association to advise it on allocating participation in the company. Keidanren promised to form one company with representation from all the interested parties.[19]

---

[18]Ogino, "Nyūsu, kyō, asu," 4; Isomura quoted in Matsuda, "NHK wa doko e iku," 79.

[19]On commercial broadcasters and satellite broadcasting, government policy, and JSB, see Nozaki et al., *Hōsō gyōkai*, 45–47; Gershon and Kanayama, "Direct Broadcast Satellites," 221–25; interview with D, a director (*riji*) of JSB, Tokyo, June 10, 1988, conducted jointly with Prof. Eleanor Westney (my thanks to Prof. Westney upon whose interview notes I am relying);

The process was marked by conflict over proportion of shares to be allocated, first over non-media companies' holdings, especially the division between new entrants diversifying into the communications industry and "neutral" passive investors. Ultimately, existing media firms would hold about 40 percent of the capital, the rest split up among electronics manufacturers, banks, utilities, and various commercial and industrial groups.

The second issue was the desire of the commercial networks—which were, as might be expected, central to this private broadcasting enterprise—for a majority (51 percent) of the shares; ultimately, however, they obtained slightly less than 20 percent of the investment capital. Neither MPT nor business leaders, concerned about "cultural standards," the low quality of commercial programs on TV (for example, nudity on late night shows), and a lack of educational programming for children, wanted the commercial networks to have that much influence on satellite broadcasting.[20] In April 1991, JSB began the commercial broadcasters' first satellite television channel, "WOWOW," primarily a non-advertising, subscriber movie channel broadcast.

By then, however, NHK's early entrance in the field, its mid-1980s enthusiastic conversion to support for new media, and the commercial broadcasters' late and difficult entrance into the field, gave the public broadcaster a commanding lead in both technology and market position over its commercial rivals.

Finally, NHK executives hitched their institution's wagon to the DBS star because it was a stepping-stone and the preferred means to implement an even more significant new medium to bring financial relief and maintain NHK's dominance: high-definition television.

HIVISION (HDTV)[21]

In the aftermath of the 1964 Tokyo Olympics broadcast, engineers in the NHK Technical Laboratories set as their goal the development of "television having ample future performance viewed both socially and technically, along with being the most appropriate for human beings."[22] Con-

---

and Japan Satellite Broadcasting, "Introductory Notes of Japan Satellite Broadcasting, Inc." (Tokyo: Japan Satellite Broadcasting, Inc., 1986) provided during that interview.

[20] Nozaki et al., *Hōsō gyōkai*, rev. ed., 193–96; and interview with D, June 10, 1988; Gershon and Kanayama, "Direct Broadcast Satellites," 225–26, discuss the reduced private broadcasters' role, but not the "cultural standard" issue.

[21] Parts of this section on HDTV appeared previously in my "Competition among Japan, the U.S., and Europe over High-Definition Television," *Pew Case Studies in International Affairs*, case no. 151, The Pew Charitable Trusts, 1992, 1–22.

[22] Quoted in Sugimoto Masao, *Kankaku kakumei haibijyon* (*Sensory Revolution Hi-Vision*) (Tokyo: Yomiuri Shimbunsha, 1991), 30.

sidering the existing U.S. National Television Standards Committee (NTSC) standard, also used in Japan, Korea, and Canada, among others, incapable of great improvement, they assumed that they would have to invent a whole new system that would be incompatible with any of the existing television formats.[23]

At first HDTV was but a small experiment within NHK Labs, engaging only a few people and using trial-and-error methods to set technical parameters. By 1972, however, enough progress had been made for NHK to notify both manufacturers and the government that they had a system they believed would be the future of television. In 1978, with the successful launching of its first experimental broadcast satellite, NHK decided that technically and financially HDTV was best transmitted via DBS, especially as cable television was relatively undeveloped in Japan compared to the United States.[24] The technical problem was the need to compress the very wide spectrum band needed for HDTV broadcasting to fit on the narrower satellite channels.

The Political Economy of HDTV in Japan

Despite the government's and business's interest in aiding the development of DBS and the satellite industry, both the MPT and electronic firms until the mid-1980s were actually more interested in Enhanced-Definition Television, an improvement over current television systems, than in a whole new technology. Meanwhile, the Ministry of International Trade and Industry (MITI), presiding over Japan's industrial policy, was keeping tabs on developments through its private sector sources, but it had yet to realize the full commercial implications of HDTV.[25] Constantly educating government and the electrical manufacturers about HDTV's progress and future implications, NHK, until the mid-1980s, was the only driving force behind HDTV's development.

Best estimates are that over the course of nearly 25 years, NHK probably spent about $100–150 million dollars developing HDTV.[26] Part of its motivation was the same as it had been for satellite broadcasting: new sources of

[23]Interview with S, NHK managing director and former head of NHK Technical Laboratories, May 27, 1991. NTSC is named for the National Television Standards Committee, which originally approved the standard. The other existing TV standards were the PAL (Phase Alternate Line) or SCAM (Sequential Couleur Avec Memoire) formats that originated in Europe.

[24]Interview with S, May 27, 1991; on cable penetration, see "Industrial Survey, Media: On the March," *Journal of Japanese Trade and Industry,* no. 1 (1989): 37.

[25]Interview with MITI official with knowledge of HDTV development, Tokyo, May 1988.

[26]Interview with Kumabe Norio, NHK and NHK Enterprises executive, on NBC program, *20/20,* February 17, 1989; for a similar estimate, see Japan Economic Institute (Jon Choy), "Developing Advanced Television: Industrial Policy Revisited," *JEI Report,* no. 2A (January 13, 1989): 1–9.

revenue from yet another category of fee for the new service. NHK wanted to ensure its future dominance in Japan's mixed public-commercial media system with more resources and an initial development advantage. Other incentives included receiving licensing fees from the manufacture of HDTV equipment and enhancing sales of its programming to other nations, especially if the rest of the world also adopted NHK's technical standards.

With the increasing technical feasibility of HDTV, especially NHK's development in 1984 of its MUSE (Multiple Subnyquist Sampling Encoding) system that compressed the HDTV frequency band and thus enabled satellite transmission, both government and industry finally began to take an active interest in HDTV's commercialization.[27] As one part of this new thrust, NHK and the MPT decided to push for NHK's technical format—referred to as "Hivision" in Japan after February 1985[28]—to be adopted as the global production standard.

The history of video technology offered ample evidence of the need to do this. Because of national or commercial competition, there were no global standards for either television or videocassette recorders, resulting in a need for different equipment, manufacturing facilities, translation of videos and programs to other formats, with consequent added business costs, obstacles to global communication, and (in the case of VCRs) consumer confusion.[29] Having the NHK standard adopted globally made sense for the world's businesses, broadcasters, and consumers. It also ensured that NHK's programming would find a larger international market and that Japanese manufacturers would have an almost insurmountable lead in the production of the equipment needed to produce, transmit, and receive HDTV around the world.

NHK's and Japan's International "Strategy"

NHK and the Japanese government had not made any secret of the broadcaster's progress in developing HDTV. As early as 1972, Japan's representatives proposed an HDTV research plan for discussion and resolution of regulatory and other problems to a conference of the Consultative Committee on International Radio (CCIR), a part of the International Telecommunications Union (ITU) under United Nations auspices. Two years later, CCIR formally adopted HDTV as a research theme. In the United States, the Society of Motion Picture and Television Engineers (SMTE) formed an

[27]Interview with S, May 27, 1991.

[28]Wakui Kōtarō, "Kōhini terebi no shōrai" ("The Future of High-Definition Television"), in Bunka toshite no sentan gijutsu o kangaerukai, eds., *Bunka toshite no sentan gijutsu* (*Leading Edge Technology as Culture*), vol. 1 (Tokyo: Nippon Hōsō Kyōkai, 1985), 131.

[29]See Heather Hazard, "Zenith and High-Definition Television, 1990," *Harvard Business School Case No. 9-391-084* (Boston: Harvard College, 1991), 4–5.

HDTV study group in 1977, and manufacturers and broadcasters set up an Advanced Televisions Systems Committee.

By the early 1980s, HDTV had moved up on the agenda of the CCIR, and NHK and manufacturers had stepped up their efforts to settle on final standards with preliminary international support. The technical issues are complex, but basically three standards are involved: studio or production standards, transmission standards, and receiver standards. Ideally, all should be the same to attain the best picture without loss of information, but they can differ as long as it is technically possible to translate the key initial studio standard, in which the original "software" is created, to the others.

The studio standards are the number of lines in the picture (the more lines, the more information conveyed and the clearer the picture); the aspect ratio (horizontal to vertical length of picture frame); and the number of fields per second that are scanned to display the picture. NHK had originally proposed 1,125 lines (more than double the National Television Standards Committee's 525 lines); an aspect ratio of 5:3 (a 25 percent increase over the standard TV picture); and 59.94 fields per second (the NTSC standard). Around 1982, NHK turned to American CCIR representatives and engineering groups for their reaction to the proposal. The Americans suggested changes such as a 16:9 aspect ratio, the same used in modern movie screens, to satisfy Hollywood. They also suggested a 60 frames-per-second standard—different from both the European and American standards—so that the Europeans would not object to the change because the Americans would have to revise their system, too. NHK accepted these suggestions and completed their development of Hivision, using these standards that ironically would later become known as "the Japanese standards" (also as the "1125/60" system).[30]

Comparison of Hivision and U.S. and European Conventional TV and Movies[31]

	Japan (HIVISION)	U.S. (NTSC)	Europe (PAL & SECAM)	MOVIES
No. of lines	1,125	525	625	
Aspect ratio	16:9	4:3	4:3	16:9
Fields/sec	60	59.94	50	

[30] 1,125 seems to have been picked because it is more than the 1,000 lines minimum NHK thought necessary for picture quality and halfway between double the U.S. NTSC standard of 525 (1,050) and the European PAL and SECAM standard of 625 (1,150). The 5:3 aspect ratio was determined by scientific visual and psychological testing. Interview with C, a former American representative to CCIR, Washington, D.C., March 8, 1989, and interview with S, May 27, 1991. S also was a representative to CCIR until 1986.

[31] For a similar but more detailed chart, see Seiji Ohara, "Progress of HDTV Technology and Its Applications," *Optoelectronics* 5, no. 1 (1990): 33.

NHK then set out to build support for Hivision especially among U.S. movie producers and broadcasters because of Hollywood's importance as a supplier of video "software" (i.e., movies and programs). If U.S. filmmakers and broadcasters adopted a different type of system, it would undermine both Japanese manufacturers' worldwide markets for their equipment and NHK's desire to easily exchange programming. Japan's "hardware" and America's "software" expertise in audio and video, on the other hand, would be a potent alliance indeed.[32] In Europe, NHK sold or loaned Hivision equipment to broadcasters and filmmakers, especially in Italy and the United Kingdom.[33] Japan intended to propose Hivision as the universal standard for HDTV at the 16th Plenary Assembly of CCIR, meeting in Dubrovnik, Yugoslavia, in May 1986.

Initially, the major European electronics manufacturers had been generally supportive of a single standard. Giant European consumer electronics firms, such as Phillips (the Netherlands) and Thomson (France), however, began to realize that a worldwide standard based on Japan's Hivision represented a threat because, unlike U.S. firms, these companies continued to dominate their consumer electronics markets as well as parts of the third world on Europe's PAL (Phase Alternate Line) and SECAM (Sequential Couleur Avec Memoire, or sequential color with memory) systems. Japanese firms had captured less than one-sixth of the color television market in Europe, for example, although they were stronger in the VCR field. Should NHK's Hivision system become the global standard, with such a head start in technology and backed by the production prowess of Japanese electronics firms, the European firms could foresee losing their markets. Consequently, Phillips and Thomson lobbied their own governments and European Community (EC) bureaucrats for action.[34]

EC nations often had trouble agreeing on telecommunications policy, for example on a unified DBS system called MAC (multiplex analog component) because of the diverse interests of companies, broadcasters, bureaucrats, and countries on issues regarding standards and technologies.[35] In the case of a single standard, however, some national as well as EC bureaucrats saw a combined cultural and manufacturing threat, a twenty-first century

[32]Adam Watson Brown, "The Campaign for High Definition Television: A Case Study in Triad Power," *Euro-Asia Business Review* (April 1987): 7.

[33]Ibid., 7–8.

[34]On European and other markets, see Jeffrey A. Hart, "Consumer Electronics," in Bjorn Wellenius, et al., *Electronics Industry Development* (Washington, D.C.: World Bank, 1993). In interviews in Washington, D.C., March 8, 1989, U.S. government officials and M attributed the initiative to electronics manufacturers, but EEC (European Economic Community, now known as European Union [EU]) consultant Brown, "The Campaign for High Definition Television," 8, implies it came from EEC officials.

[35]Ibid.

in which Europeans would watch American programs on Japanese-built televisions.

The United States supported the "Japanese" standard of 1125/60 and tried to broker a compromise between Japan and Europe. At the 1986 CCIR meeting in Dubrovnik, the governments of the United States, Japan, and Canada, as well as CBS and the North American National Broadcasters Association, attempted to get Hivision standards officially adopted as the worldwide production standard, but the Europeans blocked the measure and successfully insisted on further study of the matter until the next Plenary Assembly in 1990.[36] This opened the door to intense national economic competition.

Hivision as "Industrial Policy"

Despite the setback at Dubrovnik, Hivision's domestic promotion was advancing. In 1987, the Japanese broadcasters and manufacturers in the Broadcasting Technology Association (BTA) agreed on the 1125/60 standards as the common one for all HDTV equipment such as cameras and VCRs. Hivision had quickly been established as the only standard in Japan.

Meanwhile, the Japanese government became more active in creating a potential market for HDTV in Japan. Considered in the postwar era to be a second-rank, politicized agency, the MPT tried to raise its status in the 1980s by assuming industrial policy strategies toward telecommunications. This course put the MPT in competition with the Ministry of International Trade and Industry, which considered industrial policy toward any industry to be under its jurisdiction, and led in the early 1980s to the so-called Telecom Wars over several telecommunications-related issues. In these skirmishes, the MPT won more than it lost to the vaunted, powerful MITI.[37]

The MPT seized upon HDTV as its next area of telecommunications policy strategy and announced several programs to stimulate future consumer demand for Hivision. For example, in July 1987, the MPT announced plans to launch, in cooperation with NHK, a Hivision broadcast demonstration project for the 1988 Seoul Olympics to stimulate consumer interest in the technology. Two hundred Hivision receivers were set up throughout Japan

[36]See Subcommittee on Telecommunications and Finance, Committee on Energy and Commerce, House of Representatives, "High Definition Television," 101st Cong., 1st Sess., March 8 and 9, 1989, serial 101-34 (Washington, D.C.: U.S. Government Printing Office, 1989), 139–45; interview with M, March 8, 1989.

[37]See Chalmers Johnson, "MITI, MOPT, and the Telecom Wars: How Japan Makes Policy for High Technology," in Chalmers Johnson, Laura D'Andrea Tyson, and John Zysman, eds., *Politics and Productivity: How Japan's Development Strategy Works* (New York: HarperBusiness, 1989), 177–240.

at 81 public locations, such as train stations and department stores, and the games in Hivision were seen by an audience estimated at 3.7 million.[38]

Also that year the MPT began a savings program through which consumers could earmark monthly deposits at the Postal Savings Banks for purchase of HDTV receiver sets when they became available in the early 1990s. Efforts to create a market for a particular new technology, even in advance of its maturity, is a common technique of Japanese industrial policy.[39]

Again interministerial competition appeared. In 1989, MITI initiated a project called Hivision Communities to stimulate local industries and local governments to develop HDTV services. By 1990, 19 "model regions" had been designated by MITI. The same year, MPT began a "Hivision City" project with similar aims, and by the end of 1990, the ministry had designated 23–24 local cities and regions as "model cities."[40]

In late 1990, the first HDTV sets went on sale to the public in Japan. As NHK was only broadcasting in Hivision one hour per day at this time and each set initially cost about $34,000, HDTV was hardly a mass market item initially. Almost exactly a year later, in November 1991, NHK began eight hours of experimental broadcasting daily in Hivision, via the BS-3b satellite, as part of a consortium with commercial broadcasters. In November 1994, NHK started regular broadcasting 10 hours per day, despite the $5,000 cost per receiver and the fact that only 30,000 receiver sets had been sold to homes. By mid-1995, about 55,000 households received it. Forecasts predicted that there would be four million Hivision receiver sets in operation by the year 2000.[41]

The American Battleground

NHK and Japanese electronics manufacturers redoubled their efforts to secure U.S. support for the 1125/60 standard, hoping to establish Hivision as the de facto American standard. Demonstrations were set up on

[38]See *Nikkan Dempa Times* (*Daily Radio Times*), July 8, 1987, 2; *NHK Newsletter,* no. 14 (October 1988): 1.

[39]Fred Hiatt, "Defining a Market for High-Definition TV," *Washington Post National Weekly Edition,* September 21–25, 1988, 21; Daniel I. Okimoto refers to this important and often neglected industrial policy dimension as "demand pull" in his *Between MITI and the Market: Japanese Industrial Policy for High Technology* (Stanford: Stanford University Press, 1989), 97–98ff.

[40]See Haibijyon Fukyu Shien Senta (Hi-Vision Distribution Support Center), eds., *Haibijyon nenkan, 1991-nenpan* (*Hi-Vision Almanac, 1991*) (Tokyo: Tsusan Sangyo-sho [MITI], Shin-Eizo Sangyoshitsu [New Visual Industry Office], 1991), 114–23.

[41]On the development of Hivision programming, set sales, and costs, see David E. Sanger, "The New TV Makes Debut in Japan," *New York Times,* December 6, 1990, C1 and "Few See Japan Make TV History," *New York Times,* November 26, 1991, C1, C5. Also Hōsō Bunka Foundation, "NHK cites ISDB as its Future Multi-Media Broadcast System," *HBF Report,* no. 6 (April 1995): 9; "Japanese Television: The Slow March of Progress."

Capitol Hill, sponsored by the Public Broadcasting Service (PBS) and the Canadian Broadcasting Corporation, which were cooperating with NHK. In 1989, the Sony Corporation bought Columbia Pictures and a year later Matsushita Electric Company purchased MCA, the parent company of Universal Studios. Both acquisitions were directly related to these companies' HDTV strategies: purchase of an American studio and its film library ensured control over a major source of "software" for broadcast and distribution in HDTV. Japanese electronics manufacturers knew that consumer acceptance of the new technology would depend as much on the availability of "software" for their sets and VCRs as it would on technical quality, a lesson learned when the VHS standard beat out the technically superior Beta by capturing more of the video rental market. They also knew that owning Hollywood studios that would adopt the Hivision standard would contribute to making it the de facto standard in the United States.[42]

In the meantime, European producers and governments, under the EC's "Eureka" high-technology R&D program, began to develop in October 1986 an HDTV system incompatible with Hivision but compatible with their own 50 frame per second MAC satellite system. Their motivation was primarily "to ensure it does not lose out to a standard that would give the advantage to the Japanese." In September 1987, French, Dutch, and British telecommunications companies, including Thomson and Phillips, and broadcasters set up a consortium to produce an HDTV system of 1,250 lines (125 more lines than Hivision) that later became known as the HD-MAC system.

In 1989, Thomson acquired a foothold in U.S. television by acquiring General Electric's RCA television and audio business. (Phillips already owned Magnavox and GTE's television business through earlier acquisitions.) In 1990, Phillips and Thomson combined in a five-year plan to invest $3.6 billion to develop HD-MAC in time for the 1992 Winter Olympics in France. The French government gave Thomson more than half a billion dollars to help the company pay its share of the costs.[43]

[42]John Burgess, "Attention, Couch Potatoes—HDTV Is Coming, Eventually," *Washington Post National Weekly Edition*, October 25, 1987, 19; see also Richard W. Stevenson, "Pushing Video in the Film Capital," *New York Times*, November 6, 1991, C1 and C3; Eamonn Fingleton, "Japan's Yen for Movie Studios: ¥MCA," *The New Republic* (December 31, 1990): 14; also Japan Economic Institute (Jon Choy), "U.S. HDTV Picture Still Fuzzy," *JEI Report*, no. 44B (November 17, 1989): 9. On the VHS-Beta case, see Gregory W. Noble, "The Industrial Policy Debate," in Stephan Haggard and Chung-in Moon, eds., *Pacific Dynamics: The International Politics of Industrial Change* (Seoul and Boulder: CIS-Inha University and Westview Press, 1989), 72–77.

[43]On European HDTV development, see David Allen, "Shoot-Out at the HDTV Corral," *Videography* (January 1987): 47–49. The quote is by George Waters, head of the European Broadcaster's Union technical center, in "European HDTV to Challenge Japanese," *Japan Times Weekly*, March 12, 1988, 2. Brown, "The Campaign for High Definition Television," 9. See also the references in Ellis S. Krauss, "Competition Among Japan, the U.S., and Europe Over High-Definition Television," *Pew Case Studies in International Affairs*, Case No. 151, The

The Europeans also set about thwarting, through political means in Washington, what NHK and Japanese producers were attempting to impose through the market. They engaged in an active campaign in 1987–88 to stir up American politicians' and the U.S. computer and electronic industry's fears about Japanese competition and future domination of the technology.[44] Among their allies were the many local broadcasters who were unenthusiastic about quick adoption of Hivision because of the large expense involved in having to replace much of their present equipment. The European campaign coincided with the U.S. trade deficit with Japan. The resulting trade friction and the concern of many American policymakers and businessmen about the American industry's competitiveness with Japan were reaching very high levels. It was perfect timing for a European-American alliance to develop.[45]

Indeed, influential American representatives in telecommunications policy had become very interested in HDTV and the U.S. government's seeming lack of concern for ensuring American competitiveness in this new industry. From late 1987 through mid-1989, Congressman Edward Markey's (D-Mass.) House subcommittee with jurisdiction over telecommunications would hold four hearings on the HDTV issue. Other House committees also held hearings during the same period, and Congressional researchers began to write policy options reports. By the end of 1989, 11 separate bills relating to government support for U.S. HDTV development had been introduced into Congress.[46]

Many American businesses also became interested in HDTV and its potential. In November 1988, the American Electronics Association's (AEA) Advanced Television Task Force released a report that argued that, because it used so many computer chips and its screens would eventually become

---

Pew Charitable Trusts, 1992, 9, notes 25–28, and "French Government Gives Thomson $545-mil for HDTV Research," *Variety*, July 25, 1990, 2. There was both broadcaster and consumer resistance, however, to the changeover to MAC systems.

[44] In an interview with F, a former FCC source knowledgeable about HDTV, September 21, 1990, he said, "I've been to a lot of events, public and private, where the Europeans have done a lot of bashing of the Japanese"; an interview with M, a former CCIR representative, March 8, 1989, and R, a U.S. government expert on HDTV standards, September 21, 1990, Washington, D.C., confirmed the lobbying.

[45] Interview with R, September 21, 1990.

[46] STF/CEC, "High Definition Television," 100th Cong., October 8, 1987, June 23, and September 7, 1988; and 101st Cong., 1st Sess., March 8 and 9, 1989; and Science, Space, and Technology Committee, "High Definition Television," 101st Cong, 1st Sess., March 22, 1989 (Washington, D.C.: U.S. Government Printing Office, 1988 and 1989). Also David B. Hack, "High-Definition Television (HDTV) in the United States—What Does An 'Even Playing-Field' Look Like (With Policy Options)," *CRS Report for Congress* (Washington, D.C.: Congressional Research Service, Library of Congress, May 6, 1988, revised May 31, 1988); data from an annotated list of legislation, no title, dated "1-05-90," provided me during interview with congressional staffer familiar with the HDTV issue, Washington, D.C., March 9, 1989.

computer video terminals, "HDTV will provide the very lifeblood for existing and future technologies," and that the United States must therefore become competitive in this area. Although often with large misconceptions about NHK's or the Japanese government's development role and funding, both the mass media and academia soon were focusing attention on HDTV and its potential spin-off effects on national competitiveness. Not all agreed about HDTV's impact, however, or that government should be involved in promoting or funding it.[47] Early interest in executive branch efforts in this field among parts of the Bush administration were ultimately quashed in the name of the American economic ideology of laissez-faire.[48] The previous inclination to accept Japan's Hivision standard quietly as the de facto American standard, however, had been halted.

Hivision Made Obsolete

This delay proved crucial. First, the Federal Communications Commission (FCC) in November 1990 announced plans to test competing HDTV systems and to choose one as the U.S. standard in 1993. In this competition, an American firm, General Instrument Corporation, succeeded in developing a digital HDTV system, a major improvement over the Japanese MUSE analog system. This success stimulated the other competitors to move to a digital system, leaving NHK's MUSE as the only analog system still competing.

In February 1993, the FCC concluded that all five tested systems were flawed and recommended that four of them be retested after improvements were made—NHK's Hivision was the fifth. It had dropped out of contention. The others began discussions on various forms of cooperation. In May of that year, a "grand alliance" was formed by the remaining participants to design an HDTV (increasingly called ATV for "Advanced Television System" in the United States) with the best characteristics of the previous proposals.

[47]The American Electronics Association report is "High Definition Television (HDTV): Economic Analysis of Impact; A Working Document Prepared by American Electronics Association ATV Task Force Economic Impact Team" (Santa Clara, Calif.: American Electronics Association, 1988); see also Japan Economic Institute, "Developing Advanced Television," 7; neutral and skeptical media articles during this period would include Harry F. Waters, "The Future of Television," *Newsweek*, October 17, 1988, 84ff.; "Super Television: High Stakes in High-Definition TV," *Business Week*, January 30, 1989, 56ff.; Peter Passell, "The Uneasy Case for Subsidy Of High Technology Efforts," *New York Times*, August 11, 1989, C1 and C4; "Plug into Tomorrow's Telly: Technical Standards Are No Place for Politicians to Meddle," *Economist* (November 4, 1989): 16. For a fuller list of media articles, see Krauss, "Competition Among Japan, the U.S., and Europe," 15, footnotes 59 and 60. For a deeper academic perspective, see Jeffrey A. Hart and Laura D'Andrea Tyson, "Responding to the Challenge of HDTV," *California Management Review* (summer 1989): 132–45.

[48]For details on how free market proponents triumphed, see Krauss, "Competition Among Japan, the U.S., and Europe," 16–17.

Within the next two years, the FCC made its decisions, choosing a better method than NHK's MUSE to compress signals before transmission and a system originally designed by Zenith for sending digital signals over the air.[49]

Although the future of HDTV in the United States remained both ambiguous and highly contested, it was widely acknowledged that the American HDTV digital technology had now leapfrogged over all analog systems, making them obsolete. In 1993, the EC virtually abandoned plans to impose its own analog HDTV television system on broadcasters and acknowledged that a form of the American technology would likely become the global norm.[50]

Their "sunk costs" and the advanced stage of implementation kept NHK and manufacturers committed to the analog MUSE system in the short term. When in February 1994, Egawa Akiasa, director-general of the Broadcasting Administration Bureau of MPT, dared to suggest that the government was considering abandoning Hivision for the more advanced digital variety, the political reaction from the electronics firms and NHK was swift, furious, and extensive. Forced to backtrack from his statements the following day, Egawa said that MPT would continue to support the analog Hivision system after all, at least until after the turn of the century.[51]

Whichever system emerges in the two countries, which region's firms will do the bulk of manufacturing? Will the merging of computer, Internet, and visual media into a true multimedia technology present very different future technological and marketing choices? The stakes are enormous globally, as well as in Japan. A survey by NHK and the Nomura Research Institute predicted that the audience for HDTV would reach 5 million by the turn of the century, although sales by early 1998 indicated that this figure may be

[49]See Andrew Pollack, "Format Emerging for Advanced TV," *New York Times*, March 23, 1990, C1 and C12. On Zenith's enthusiasm for HDTV, see Krauss, "Competition Among Japan, the U.S., and Europe," 16. Zenith eventually was sold to a Korean firm. Joel Brinkley, "Advanced-TV Systems Are Called Flawed," *New York Times*, February 12, 1993, C2. Lori Valigra, "Do Not Adjust Your Set: Manufacturers Await a Decision on Advanced TV," *Japan Scope* (summer 1994): 29–30; Kathryn Jones, "Zenith Wins Competition for HDTV," *New York Times*, February 17, 1994, C1.

[50]See, for example, Jube Shiver, Jr., "FCC to Seek Closer Look at Regulations for HDTV," *Los Angeles Times*, July 27, 1995, D1; William J. Broad, "U.S. Counts on Computer Edge in the Race for Advanced TV," *New York Times*, November 28, 1989, 19; Andrew Pollack, "A Milestone in High-Definition TV," *New York Times*, December 3, 1991, C1. For further references, see Krauss, "Competition Among Japan, the U.S., and Europe," 19, footnote 73. See also Richard W. Stevenson, "Europe Gives Up Its Advanced-TV Project," *New York Times*, February 20, 1993, 26, and Simon Mansfield, "Whatever Happens, the Japanese Makers Are Ready," *Japan Times Weekly International Edition*, February 3–9, 1992, 17.

[51]On sales see Japan Economic Institute, "Future of Japan's Advanced Television System Debated," *JEI Report*, no. 9B, (March 24, 1994): 6–7. On Egawa's statement, see Andrew Pollack, "Japan May Abandon Its System for HDTV," *New York Times*, February 23, 1994, C1, and "Under Pressure by Industry, Japanese Retreat on HDTV," *New York Times*, February 24, 1994, C1; Japan Economic Institute, "Future," 5–6; Valigra, "Do Not Adjust Your Set," 29.

difficult to achieve, and another study estimated that the Japanese market was potentially worth about $17 billion per year for broadcasting applications alone.[52]

The Move to Digital and a New Regulatory Environment

Just a few years later it was clear that analog Hivision was on its way out. In February 1997, an HDTV advisory group to MPT recommended a digital format for the BS-4 broadcasting satellite that was to be put into orbit in 2000. In their rejection of NHK's analog system, the group specifically cited digital's technological superiority and international acceptance. No doubt remained about Japan's transition to digital format when the interim report of the Advisory Committee on Digital Terrestrial Broadcasting to the MPT in June 1998 specified that current land-based television broadcasting should be replaced by digital broadcasting beginning in 2000 in the Kantō (Tokyo-Yokohama) region and that all analog broadcasting should end after 2006. Also, digital satellite broadcasting (DBS) was to start in 2000, primarily to provide HDTV broadcasting.[53]

Meanwhile, the MPT's previous telecommunications policies had changed, and new commercial competition emerged in, for example, the areas of communications satellites and cable. Neither had been promoted strongly by the MPT, but as these technologies have blossomed in other countries, domestic criticism for deregulation mounted. Recognizing the potential for providing many more channels to the viewer and enhancing the linkages between the broadcasting and telecommunications industries, the MPT reversed course. Beginning in April 1992, several new broadcasters began operations using communications, instead of broadcasting, satellites, and in 1996, they began digital broadcasting as well. The MPT also allowed for multiple cable companies in an area and foreign capital participation.

As a result, new Japanese-foreign ventures in cable formed and between 1993 and 1998 the percentage of households subscribing to cable nearly tripled. By spring 1998, 102 television channels were operated on communications satellites by 64 broadcasters, and the cable television industry, after years of relative stagnation, improved its market share from 1.4 percent of the broadcasting media in 1991 to 3.7 percent in fiscal year 1995. Many

---

[52]Matsuzaki, "The Scenario for Hi-Vision," 1–2, 9. Although the Hivision receiver distribution had increased 1.6 times over the previous year, by March 1998 it amounted to only 586,000 sets. See NHK HBCK, *NHK nenkan, '98* (*NHK Radio and Television Yearbook, 1998*) (Tokyo: NHK, 1998), 88.

[53]Ebitsubo Isamu and Nakamura Tokuji, "Chronology, December 1996 through February 1997," *Japan Quarterly* 44, no. 2 (April–June 1997): 117; NHK, *Broadcasting Culture and Research*, no. 5 (summer 1998): 3, 5–7.

non-broadcasters and foreign firms, including Rupert Murdoch's News Corporation, rapidly entered the satellite and cable programming business. As the distinction between communications and broadcasting satellites disappeared, and the possibility of a single set receiving both became likely, questions were raised about how much and how the drastically changed field of "broadcasting" would be regulated.[54]

In part to respond to these changes, the MPT proposed revisions to the Broadcast Law to accommodate digital broadcasting's ability to transmit data. These revisions include changing the definition of "television broadcasting" to include non-moving information. An *Asahi Shimbun* editorial pointed out the potential dangers to freedom of expression in putting printed information under the Broadcast Law's injunction of "political fairness" and MPT's power of enforcement. In the new age of multiple channels and crossover of information technologies, the editorial also called for rethinking the need for the Law's "fairness principle," as occurred in the United States when the Federal Communications Commission dropped this requirement.[55]

These dramatic changes complicated relationships among NHK, commercial firms, and the government. Although initially resenting NHK's bold entrance into satellite broadcasting, commercial stations, worrying about declining or stagnant advertising revenues, the profitability of digital satellite broadcasting, and their shortage of "software" for the multiplicity of new channels, seemed content to let NHK, with its huge resources and inventory of programming from a decade in the field, take the lead in this area. Meanwhile, NHK proposed joint digital satellite broadcasts with commercial stations for the 2000 Olympics in Sydney, Australia. NHK had entered into innovative commercial new tie-ups with business, but nonetheless, it resisted new business entrants and competition in digital satellite broadcasting. The MPT, after allying with NHK's new media strategy in the 1980s, pushed ahead with regulatory changes that cut into NHK's broadcasting dominance, even while future reliance on NHK's leadership for digital broadcasting seemed likely. NHK, after hoping to achieve more autonomy from the LDP

[54]On communications satellites, see NHK, *Broadcasting Culture and Research*, no.3 (spring 1998): 8–9; on the vanishing satellite distinctions, see "Eisei hōsō no kakine hiku" ("The Fence of Satellite Broadcasting Lowers"), *Nihon Keizai Shimbun*, May 10, 1999, 17; on relative market shares by various technologies, including cable, and on recent changes in the broadcast industry, see Greg Noble, "Let a Hundred Channels Contend: Technological Change, Political Opening and Bureaucratic Priorities in Japanese Television Broadcasting," *Journal of Japanese Studies* 26, no. 1 (winter 2000); Ministry of Posts and Telecommunications, *White Paper 1997: Communications in Japan* (Tokyo: General Planning and Policy Division, Minister's Secretariat, Ministry of Posts and Telecommunications, 1997), 32–37.

[55]"'Genron no jiyū' ga shimpai da" ("'Freedom of Expression' Is a Worry"), *Asahi Shimbun*, April 22, 1999, 5.

through its new media strategy of alliance with the MPT in the 1980s and resisting digitalization, began cooperating with the MPT's testing of digital terrestrial broadcasting formats, suggesting the possibility of using public funds "under government guidance" to achieve early diffusion of digital broadcasts, and planning to initiate digital satellite broadcasting and 7-channel digital Hivision by the end of 2000.[56]

After 30 relatively stable years of color television characterized by a highly regulated environment and NHK's technological leadership, NHK and the broadcasting world as a whole is trying to cope with new and much more varied technical, financial, and policy choices. Through it all, NHK continues to attempt to maintain technological leadership, provide new sources of revenue, and push toward integrated, multimedia, and interactive broadcasting. In the long-range, the broadcaster hopes to develop true three-dimensional TV in the twenty-first century.[57]

COMMERCIALIZATION AND DECENTRALIZATION

While NHK was embarking on its new media strategy with such ambiguous consequences, it simultaneously initiated a related course of organizational innovations that included building a conglomerate of related companies to engage in commercial activities and strengthen its international linkages.

Creating the "NHK Conglomerate"

In the early 1980s, NHK executives realized that the new media technology alone would not solve NHK's basic financial problems. These executives began going to the Diet—often in concert with the MPT—and asking for revisions of the Broadcast Law that had previously prevented NHK from investing in commercial activities. For example, Article 9, Section 4 of the Broadcast Law prohibited the public broadcaster from conducting business with an aim toward profits. The 1982 revision, and later revisions in 1988, widened NHK's allowable investments and activities with related companies and also established guidelines to regulate them. Article 9, Sec-

---

[56]On the commercial stations and digital broadcasting, see "'Kōseisai' ippon ni" ("To One Channel HDTV"), *Asahi Shimbun*, June 1, 1999, 30; on NHK's Olympic, digital broadcasting, and funding ideas, see "Public Broadcasting's Role in the Digital Age" (an address by NHK President Ebisawa Katsuji), and "Pioneer of the Digital HDTV Broadcast Era," *Broadcasting Culture and Research*, no. 8 (spring 1999): 2, 1, respectively.

[57]See the discussion in "Fukyōge no meisō—terebikai yo, doko e iku" ("Running Confused under the Recession: Where the TV World Is Going"), *Tsukuru* (April 1994): 16–31; Matsuzaki, "The Scenario for Hi-Vision," 10–12; the 3-D TV plans were mentioned in interview with S, May 27, 1991.

tion 3 allowed NHK for the first time to "entrust" part of its authorized activities to others outside the organization as long as the business was conducted in accordance with the standards NHK stipulated and would not interfere with its mandated activities. Article 26, Sections 5–9 strengthened NHK's reporting and accounting control over such companies.[58]

Related organizations were nothing new to NHK. Its world-renowned NHK Symphony Orchestra was one of Japan's many forms of "public corporations." In addition, NHK had long sunk capital into NHK Publishers, an actual stock company (*kabu kaisha*), that was established in 1931 to publish books, magazines, and journals with a connection to NHK broadcast programs.

In the 1980s, however, both the numbers of these companies and their breadth of activities expanded enormously. NHK's 1984 yearbook lists only the orchestra and one other organization; by January 1986, the number had increased to 20 related organizations and by 1989, 23. Two years later the number was up to 28, of which almost half (13) were "private" (i.e., shareholding, for profit) companies related to the production and sales of media, with the remainder primarily support services, foundations, health and welfare, and educational and cultural organizations. Generally, the financial principle was that the more directly related the organization was to broadcasting, the greater NHK's investment in it.[59]

The most important of these companies was NHK Enterprises, the "cornerstone of NHK's management strategy aiming to emerge as a general information industry confronting the new media age," as one commentator labeled it. Established in January 1985, NHK Enterprises was designed as an outsourcing production company to produce many of NHK's programs. Until the mid-1980s, about 97 percent of NHK programs were produced in-house. Prior to embarking on this strategy, NHK managers studied foreign public broadcasters for models of possible strategies to reduce costs by outsourcing, and the British Broadcasting Corporation and its BBC Enterprises was selected for emulation. This represented a major policy change for NHK and, along with the commitment to personnel reduction, was one of

[58]NHK HBCK, ed., *NHK nenkan, '91* (*NHK Radio and Television Yearbook, 1991*) (Tokyo: NHK, 1991), 231, 332; Tsuji Hideo, "Sabaibaru o kaketa kigyōshūdanka e o yabō" ("The Ambition to Make an Enterprise Group on Which It Gambled Its Survival"), *Tsukuru* (June 1986): 48; "38-nen buri no hōsōhō kaisei" ("Reform of the Broadcast Law After 38 Years"), *(Shin) Hōsō Bunka*, no. 10 (summer 1988): 88–92; JBC, *The Broadcast Law*, 10, 13–14, 20–21; NHK, ed., *NHK nenkan, '91*, 332.

[59]NHK, ed., *NHK nenkan, '84* (*NHK Radio and Television Yearbook, 1984*), *NHK nenkan '89, NHK nenkan '91* (Tokyo: NHK, 1984, 1989, and 1991), 305–60, 537, 568–70, respectively; also, interview with A2, a former NHK top executive in charge of planning for subsidiaries and also of NHK Enterprises, May 23, 1991.

the major pillars of its rationalization program in administration to reduce costs.[60]

Initially capitalized at only about three-quarters of a million dollars with NHK providing 55 percent of the capital and the rest from private investors, NHK Enterprises began small, doing about $10 million worth of business and at first primarily producing programs for NHK's *Broadcast University*, a media educational extension program. Soon, however, the company began to produce more, more important, and larger programs for NHK, including some of its "signboard" (*kanban*) or signature programs, such as *NHK tokushū*, its famous documentary series. By 1991, it was doing 20 times the business of its first year, or around $200 million.

NHK Enterprises became an investor in other commercial companies, too. In 1986, it joined with Dentsū, the world's largest advertising agency, to become the two major shareholders (25 percent each) to form Sōgō Vision with more than 60 other companies, including major banks, movie companies, and advertising agencies. Initially capitalized at about $1.75 million, Sōgō Vision's major functions were to sell NHK programs and materials abroad for a profit, to coproduce or codistribute programs with U.S. and European broadcast companies, to market the reuse and rebroadcast of NHK programs for a profit, and to obtain broadcast rights to major sporting events. Many of these activities particularly revolved around Hivision programs.[61]

Simultaneously, NHK more actively cultivated profitable relations with many local regions and governments. Eager for the tremendous publicity and possible tourist revenue, many cities, towns, and villages began to compete for the chance to become the site of one of NHK's high-profile and very popular dramas, such as its historical drama programs. In return for choosing a particular site, NHK entered into a contract with the local government to build a very expensive set and then pay only to lease it for filming. Such an arrangement saved NHK enormous production costs. One of NHK's related companies also increased its participation in the sponsorship of local special and sporting events.[62]

---

[60]On NHK Enterprises, see, "NHK Enterprises Dives Into Commerce," *Variety*, October 15, 1986, 129; "Mimpō shinsutsu wa NHK shidai" ("Commercial Broadcaster's Progress Depends on NHK"), *Hōsō Hihyō* (January 1987): 15–27. *NHK Newsletter*, no. 14 (October 1988): 2; interview with A2, May 23, 1991; Shima, *"Shima Geji,"* 194; Matsuda, "NHK wa doko e iku," 71.

[61]Matsuda, "NHK wa doko e iku," 71–72; Ishii Kiyoshi, "Dentsū to tekei shita 'Sōgō Bijyon' seiretsu no nerai" ("The Aim of Establishing "Sōgō Vision" that Linked Up with Dentsū"), *Tsukuru* (June 1986): 58–61; interview with A2, May 23, 1991; all dollar values calculated at ¥125/$1.

[62]On NHK's local tie-ups, see Editorial Board, "NHK ga nerau furusato senden shikin" ("The Home Town Public Relations Capital that NHK Aims for"), *Hōsō Hihyō* (January–February 1992): 2–7.

Commercial broadcasters understandably saw in this NHK "conglomerate" an invasion of the private sector's territory and the creation of a powerful, publicly funded and government-backed rival for commercial profits. They considered NHK's new activities to be an undermining of the postwar division of labor between the public service and commercial broadcasters of Japan's "duopoly" broadcasting system. Media commentators worried that NHK had "crossed the Rubicon" and was well on its way to losing its identity and future as a true public broadcaster.[63]

Despite the criticisms, NHK's management—especially the ubiquitous Shima Keiji, first as a managing director and later as president, and his group within NHK—saw the spinning off of commercialized companies as performing many necessary functions. First, it bypassed NHK's huge and rigid bureaucracy and created small firms that could flexibly respond to the needs of the competitive new media age. Experience in the domestic and international private sector would create a new type of manager at NHK, one who could operate more efficiently and effectively and could resuscitate NHK's stifling hierarchical organization. Another important purpose was, as we have seen, to cut costs of production by producing outside the over-staffed NHK organization. On average, an organization like NHK Enterprises could generate a production for 20 percent less than NHK's costs.

The companies helped trim costs in other ways, primarily by enabling NHK to reduce the number of personnel on the payroll, something it had promised to do when it obtained a receivers' fee increase in 1984. Accomplishing this reduction essentially through attrition, these new organizations helped the broadcaster get employees "off the books," much as smaller subcontractors (*shitauke*) do for larger firms in Japanese business. These vertical subcontracting systems are known as *keiretsu*. Of the 700 persons cut from the payroll in 1991, for example, perhaps half were sent to related firms. That these transfers also represented a real commitment to the purposes for which these firms were established, however, is shown by the fact that among such employees were some of NHK's rising stars, such as Aoki Kenji, a former vice director of the News Division, and top producers.

These related firms also provided an additional income to the now-stagnant receivers' fee receipts. The Subcommittee on Special Legal Corpora-

[63]Ishii Kiyoshi, *NHK uchimaku* (*Behind the Scenes at NHK*) (Tokyo: Sanichi Shinsho, 1993), 110–18. On the commercial broadcasters' responses, see, e.g., Noma Eiji, "NHK ga shitauke shōbai ni hongoshi" ("NHK's Strenuous Efforts in Subcontractor Business"), *Tsukuru* (April 1985): 164–67; "Jōhō no shoten: hōsōhō kaisei no ugoki de fujyō shita 'NHK mineika' ron" ("The Focus of Information: the 'NHK Privatization' Theory That Surfaces in the Movement of the Broadcast Law Revision"), *Tsukuru* (December 1986): 28–29; Tsuji, "Sabaibaru o kaketa kigyōshūdanka," 51–52; Shima, *"Shima Geji,"* 208. For a summary of the Commercial Broadcasters Association's report "NHK no arikata" ("The Way NHK Should Be"), January 1987, see *NHK Hōsō Kenkyū to Chōsa* (March 1987): 72.

tions (*tokushu hōjin mondaira shōiinkai*) of the Provisional Administrative Reform Promotion Council put out a report in May 1986 urging NHK to broaden its activities and increase its secondary income. By the early 1990s, the investment in all these spin-off companies was beginning to pay off. In 1991, such companies' profits represented less than 2 percent of NHK's total budget, about $65 million, and were never expected to provide more than 10 percent.[64] Nevertheless in an era when NHK's receivers' fee income was lagging behind is needs, every bit helped.

Behind, and intertwined with, these firms' financial and organizational strategic purposes was an important political aim, as attested to by the quote of the strategy's architect, Shima Keiji, that opens this chapter. NHK needed to earn independent money to become more autonomous from the politicians. Shima goes on to explain how the programs NHK produced had unrecognized value:

> We could use the programs we made once in various ways, for example, reusing programs and selling them to other broadcasters. At least we could lengthen the time we had to raise (fees) from three years to five, six years. We had to make the effort. . . . Decentralizing and creating various related companies and organizations began with this conception.[65]

An integral part of this strategy was to make NHK more international. In July 1990, MICO (Media International Corporation, *kokusai medeia coporēshyon*) was formed to engage in large-scale joint production with international companies; buy and sell visual "software"; invest in, and engage in, visual and high-definition activities; and be a base for transmitting news and information about Japan overseas. With the investment of more than 45 companies, including some very large firms and banks, MICO's capitalization soon increased to about $50 million. The firm's capital was not at the level of NHK Enterprises, but its president was a former NHK Enterprises vice president, one of its managing directors had come directly from being head of an NHK Satellite Broadcasting unit, and 14 of its 30 employees had formerly worked at NHK. The fact that Sumitomo Bank, the company of former NHK Board of Governors chairman Isoda Ichirō, was one of the major financial backers of MICO added to the widespread belief that the corporation had been planned by Shima and Isoda to make NHK dominant in the media production and distribution market, domestically and internation-

---

[64] On the spin-off companies' functions, see Shima, *"Shima Geji,"* 194, 206; interview with A2, May 23, 1991; Matsuda, "NHK wa doko e iku," 71–72. NHK entered into specific contracts with each company for a specified portion of the firm's profits.
[65] Shima, *"Shima Geji,"* 81.

ally.[66] Shima also had other grandiose international plans. He began efforts to form a rival international network, Global News Network (GNN), to compete with CNN and the BBC, but, with his downfall, subsequent NHK administrations retreated from Shima's plans to placate critics: GNN was completely scrapped and MICO was scaled back both in personnel and in function to become just another program supplier.[67]

THE RISE AND FALL OF NHK'S NEW MEDIA STRATEGIES

Confronting a major fiscal problem in the early 1980s, NHK executives adopted various strategies to provide new sources of revenue, reduce personnel and costs, gain more organizational flexibility to meet the demands of new technology and international markets, maintain NHK's dominance in the broadcasting system, and achieve more autonomy from political interference. They had, at least initially, the support of important state and private sector actors, each for their own interests and reasons.

These strategies can be deemed only partially successful, but they had major consequences for NHK and broadcasting in general. The commercial networks eventually entered the satellite broadcasting field. NHK's analog HDTV technology was leapfrogged by the Americans and was slow to catch on in terms of sales in Japan. Partially because of these domestic and international "failures," the MPT pushed for NHK's analog system finally to be replaced by digital systems and other new communications technologies.

The future of the new and dramatic technological and policy developments is murky, but it is clear that in the late 1990s more changes were underway in Japan's broadcasting industry than in any other time since the beginning of television broadcasting in the 1950s. For the first time in the postwar period, NHK, while still central to the system's future, faced much more commercial competition in a complicated variety of broadcasting technology service options, with a policy environment more tolerant of pluralism in the broadcasting marketplace than previously. Furthermore, with Shima's fall, NHK's plans to become more international and create an NHK *keiretsu* were scaled back.

Nonetheless, NHK retains an advantage over the commercial networks in satellite broadcasting. It has 9.4 million subscribers to its satellite color television service a decade after its June 1989 full-service launch, while the commercial stations' WOWOW channel claims about 2.5 million subscribers;

---

[66]Tahara, *Medeia ōkoku no yabō*, 17, 20–22. Iwasaki Yasuhiro and Onoue Yukio, *Masukomi gyōkai (The Mass Communications Industry)* (Tokyo: Kyōikusha, 1993), 62, including the chart of MICO's organization.

[67]Kyoko Sato, "Far-Flung Expansion Plans Scaled Back," *Nikkei Weekly*, August 1, 1992, 10; Gregory W. Noble, personal communication, June 29, 1999.

communications satellite providers, about 1.4 million.[68] Many of NHK's spin-off companies continue to exist, generating revenue and providing alternative positions for personnel.

The continued dominance and autonomy NHK had hoped to achieve with these alliances in the 1980s had mostly disintegrated by the 1990s as at least some of the other players pursued their own interests in ways that either did not involve or might actually actively compete with NHK. Although NHK's new media strategies in part were designed to give LDP politicians less opportunity to hold NHK's budget and receivers' fees "hostage" to good behavior, paradoxically, the strategies had the effect of making NHK more dependent on the MPT and big business in other ways. In the post-Shima age, NHK's autonomy in new media fields is probably less than ever before. In digital broadcasting, it hopes for and needs cooperation with and support from politicians, the MPT, business, and commercial broadcasters.

As NHK was forging these new, more complicated alliances with state and private actors, but failing to achieve many of its ambitious aims, its core competence in the news was being challenged for the first time in a quarter century from an unexpected source.

[68]NHK, *Broadcasting Culture and Research*, 22.

CHAPTER 8

"Casters," Commercial Competition, and Change

And somebody introduced smallpox, bubonic plague and the Black Death. And somebody is minded now to introduce sponsored broadcasting.

—LORD REITH, FORMER DIRECTOR OF THE BBC, QTD.

IN BARRIE MACDONALD, *Broadcasting in the United Kingdom*

Much of what passes for quality on British television is no more than a reflection of the narrow elite which controls it and has always thought that its tastes were synonymous with quality.

—RUPERT MURDOCH, ADDRESS TO THE

EDINBURGH TELEVISION FESTIVAL

In public service broadcasting you get money to make programmes and in commercial broadcasting you make programmes to get money.

—BILL COTTON, FORMER MANAGING DIRECTOR FOR

BBC TELEVISION, QTD. IN STUART HOOD AND

GARRET O'LEARY, *Questions of Broadcasting*

By the early 1990s, NHK faced a challenge perhaps more serious than the failure of its "new media" strategy to ensure its technological and broadcast leadership at home and abroad: for the first time in 30 years, commercial competition struck at the heart of its long-term dominance of the news. Unlike some other public broadcasters in Europe that had once enjoyed a monopoly over broadcasting, NHK has always had commercial competition in the "marketplace" in the postwar period. Ever since the early 1960s when President Maeda Yoshinori had developed NHK's News Division into the premier broadcasting information service in Japan, the 7 P.M. news had been the flagship news program for all of Japanese broadcasting. In the late 1980s, TV Asahi, a commercial competitor, adopted an innovative news format for its new program, *News Station,* that NHK could neither emulate nor overcome. This new program has had a major impact on both television news and politics in Japan. Ironically, its format was in part pioneered by another of NHK's news programs, *News Center 9 P.M.* (*NC9*), the first Japanese news program more in tune with the technology and methodology of television than the 7 P.M. news.

NHK VERSUS COMMERCIAL TELEVISION NEWS: THE REALITY OF NHK DOMINANCE [1]

After the buildup of NHK's News Division in the late 1950s through the late 1960s, its dominance in this field became a fact of life for the commercial broadcasters. As early as 1962, even before this build-up was completed, NHK's news programs constituted 25 percent of its total broadcast time, with the commercial networks ranging from about 7.5 percent to 16.7 percent.[2] Indeed, NHK's share of the 2,000 minutes per week of news on the air in Japan has always exceeded 30 percent.[3]

After the 1960s, there were many reasons for private broadcasters' reluctance to devote more time and attention to the news. News was considered quite expensive to produce, especially for a broadcaster competing with NHK's huge personnel advantage in its national and international news gathering apparatus. NHK's News Division employed more than 1,000 reporters nationwide[4] and about 800 people total in the News Center in Tokyo.[5] By comparison, in 1985, TV Asahi, the Asahi News Network's (ANN) "key" station in Tokyo that was responsible for much of the national news for the network, had a total of 190 permanent employees and about 36 additional people who were contracted for services, with about 80 reporters covering the capital region.[6] Given NHK's status in the media world, it also attracted some of the best graduates from the elite private and public universities.

Confronted with NHK's advantage in human resources, commercial broadcasters did not believe news could be very profitable before the late 1980s. An NHK top news executive confirmed that, because the costs of a news organization can be "bottomless," most broadcasters "didn't put a lot of effort into such programs."[7]

---

[1] Parts of the following sections were published in Ellis S. Krauss, "Changing Television News in Japan," *Journal of Asian Studies* 57, no. 3 (August 1998): 663–92.

[2] Shima Nobuhiko, *Media no kage no kenryokusha-tachi* (*The Powerful People of Media's Shadow*) (Tokyo: Kōdansha, 1995), 176–77.

[3] Tahara Shigeyuki, *Terebi no uchigawa de* (*Inside Television*) (Tokyo: Sōshisha, 1995), 72.

[4] Interview with T, NHK News Division executive, December 18, 1991.

[5] Interview with Y, NHK News Center producer, June 24, 1985.

[6] Kyōikusha, ed., *Terebi Asahi* (*Asahi Television Station*) (Tokyo: Kyōikusha, 1983), 29, and interview with TV Asahi News Division executives, Tokyo, June 25, 1985.

[7] Interview with T, December 18, 1991.

Financially, NHK had other major competitive advantages that constituted obstacles to commercial stations. NHK, for example, had more than three times the revenue of the average individual key commercial broadcasting station in Tokyo.[8] Less obvious was the fact that NHK's salaries were lower, and the public broadcaster did not have to pay for its own capital construction costs.[9] Further, unlike NHK, the commercial stations had to show a profit and thus were much warier about sinking their resources into what might prove to be a risky venture given NHK's dominance in the field.

Individual private broadcasters came to believe they could not compete with NHK's personnel, financial, organizational, and technical resources and advantages. A vicious cycle was created: as long as NHK was dominant in news and commercial stations thought this field was unprofitable, they were unlikely to devote much effort or resources to trying to compete with NHK's advantages; as long as they did not even attempt to compete seriously, the commercial stations would continue to believe NHK's dominance in news to be impregnable and the field unprofitable.

The commercial broadcasters also faced diminished incentives to becoming truly nationwide news-gathering broadcasters like NHK. For various historical and legal reasons, Japanese commercial broadcasters never developed the full, exclusive "affiliates" system found in the U.S. networks.[10] They instead established news "networks," using their "key stations" in Tokyo to provide national news.

Each of the major television news networks is partially owned by one of the large national newspapers. For example, the second largest newspaper, the *Asahi Shimbun*, which some consider the "paper of record" in Japan and the most liberal of the national papers, is partial owner of TV Asahi. With this connection to the national press, "the television companies themselves put relatively few resources into building an organization to gather and present the news."[11] When I interviewed TV Asahi executives in 1985, they quite adamantly insisted on their separate identity from the newspaper, asserting that "there are rarely any cases where a story covered by someone from *Asahi*

---

[8]Kōmoto Hisahiro, *Ichinichi de wakaru tsūshin, hōsō gyōkai* (*Understanding the Telecommunications/Broadcasting Industries in a Day*) (Tokyo: Nippon Jitsugyō Shuppansha, 1999), 163.

[9]Shima Keiji, *"Shima Geji" fūunroku—Hōsō to kenryoku, 40-nen* (*The Troubled Record of "Shima Geji": Broadcasting and Politics, 40 years*) (Tokyo: Bungei Shunjū, 1995), 86–87.

[10]D. Eleanor Westney, "Mass Media as Business Organizations," in Susan J. Pharr and Ellis S. Krauss, eds., *Media and Politics in Japan* (Honolulu: University of Hawaii Press, 1996), 60–61. For example, in 1985, TV Asahi in Tokyo was the "key" station for the Asahi News Network (ANN) and provided national news to a total of 20 stations. Including the Tokyo station, 12 were full network stations and the rest were "crossnet" stations that combined ANN as a programming source with Fuji Television, while others combined Nippon TV and Fuji. Interview with TV Asahi News Division executives, June 25, 1985.

[11]Westney, "Mass Media," 61.

(Shimbun) becomes news" and that the newspaper's information is used only as a basis for a story that then must be covered by the broadcaster's own reporters in order to get on the air. Nonetheless, they also said:

> We have a hot line connecting the editorial department (*henshū-kyoku*) of *Asahi Shimbun* and our news desk. We also work closely with people at the local bureaus of the *Asahi Shimbun* across the country . . . . We get information and Tokyo or a local bureau will cover a story based on this information. . . .[12]

The TV Asahi executives felt that it was a mutual relationship of "sharing information."

In other words, commercial stations, to at least some extent, rely on external sources, such as the national newspaper that partially owns it, to alert it to the potential "pool" of news stories that day. This enables the commercial broadcaster to select among these stories to assign its cameras and reporters. Japan's commercial stations are not vertically integrated like NHK. More a news production than a news gathering service, they have little motivation to build up a more complete news organization.

In the mid-1980s, the future looked worse than the past for Japanese commercial broadcasters. The "new media" revolution had begun and satellite broadcasting and later high-definition television were due to be introduced. The commercial broadcasters initially resisted satellite broadcasting, but NHK pushed for it with the support of the MPT and would have an initial monopoly of direct satellite broadcasting before the commercial stations even had a single shared channel.

NHK's present and future dominance in the news looked fairly invulnerable in 1985. Thus, when I visited TV Asahi news executives in the summer of that year and they told me of their plans to begin a new type of news program that autumn, none of us would have imagined that it would change Japanese television news styles and potentially alter its politics.

The Commercial Stations' Hidden Advantages   As it turned out, the reasons underlying NHK's dominance turned out to be either ephemeral or easily challenged. If NHK's personnel resources were impressive, in quantity and quality, the commercial broadcasters could call upon their own strengths. First, the operating revenues of the commercial broadcasters had increased exponentially, especially in the period 1967–85. In 1966, the total of all commercial stations' operating income (eigyō shūnyū) was about double that of NHK's; by 1984, its income advantage had increased to about four times NHK's, or about ¥1.3 trillion ($10.4 billion at ¥125/$1), with income

---

[12]Interview with TV Asahi News Division executives, June 25, 1985.

per employee more than double that of the public broadcaster.[13] These private sector broadcasting employees generally were also younger, more entrepreneurial personnel who worked in a more flexible, profit-driven, less bureaucratic and hierarchical system, making them much more efficient. Consequently, production costs were much lower at the commercial stations than at NHK.[14]

Thus, years before NHK even began to integrate journalists' and visual editors' roles for its 7 P.M. News production, TV Asahi's news personnel exhibited a mixture of expertise and backgrounds as part of its more flexible production process. A News Division editor was expected to serve in all three of the major news-gathering operations (political-economic, societal, and foreign) before becoming an editor, announcers could gather news, and some personnel had backgrounds in entertainment. In contrast to NHK's emphasis on specialization, TV Asahi executives espoused a very different organizational philosophy: "You can't be a good television reporter unless you're an all-round player," and "You can't say that you're a full-fledged television journalist unless you've learned how to produce images on the screen."[15]

The introduction of new technology such as ENG (electronic news gathering, such as video camcorders) and satellites made news gathering a more mobile and quicker process, which served to further reduce NHK's huge advantage in personnel. This technology allowed commercial stations to respond quickly and flexibly to breaking news events and to provide pictures with visual impact faster and more easily.[16]

Besides, NHK held a numerical advantage in personnel only in Tokyo. Commercial stations are more decentralized and have affiliates that are full-fledged stations. Comparing NHK with his and other commercial news operations, a TV Asahi executive admitted that NHK's resources and coverage were unmatched in Tokyo, but, he confidently argued, if the reporters in the private broadcasters' local affiliates were included, these broadcasters' human resources and initial news from outside Tokyo were better than those of NHK. Furthermore, between their local bureaus and affiliates, commercial broadcasters often have a personnel and equipment advantage in a particular region. "So, in the case of NHK, if something happens locally, their

[13]Nozaki Shigeru, Higashiyama Yoshiyuki, and Shinohara Toshiyuki, *Hōsō gyōkai* (*The Broadcasting Industry*) (Tokyo: Kyōikusha Shinsho, 1986), fig. 1.3, pp. 33, 34; also, Ishizaka Etsuo, *Masu media sangyō no tenkan* (*Changes in Mass Media Industry*) (Tokyo: Yūikaku Sensho, 1987), table 2, p. 148, chart 3, p. 72.

[14]Shima Keiji, former NHK news executive and president, estimated that it takes at least twice as much to produce a program at NHK than it does an equivalent program at the commercial stations; see Shima, *"Shima Geji,"* 87–88, 189–90.

[15]Interview with TV Asahi News Division executives, June 25, 1985.

[16]Tahara, *Terebi no uchigawa de,* 76.

initial report is weak. In the initial report . . . commercial networks are strong locally."[17] Even if after the initial report, NHK's superior resources from the capital are brought to bear, the TV Asahi executives claimed that commercial networks were superior when nationwide coverage is viewed in total.

Commercial networks also had increasing resources to devote to the news. Television advertising expenditures increased more than 100 percent per year over the previous year from 1970 to 1986, and television's share of advertising (35.2 percent in 1985) permanently surpassed that of newspapers (28.7 percent in 1985) as early as 1975.[18]

By the 1980s the market opportunities in news—especially in certain niches—were becoming more and more tempting. The early to mid-1980s represented the height of a trend among the Japanese public toward greater interest in news and information programs. In 1984, more people—about 70 percent of viewers over 15 years of age—paid attention to news and news shows than any other type of program.[19]

Additionally, audience factors had been undermining some of NHK's apparent dominance. Many rural areas had no local commercial stations, or only one, and thus NHK had an artificial monopoly in these areas that increased its ratings in the news. Even in the early 1980s in large metropolitan regions where there was more competition, NHK news was not as dominant. Thus, the 7 P.M. news had about half the ratings in Tokyo, Osaka, and cities of 500,000 or more, and among business, technical, and service people than it did in towns, villages, farm households, and cities of fewer than 100,000.[20]

This artificial ratings advantage in rural areas hid a glaring weakness for NHK news: urban white-collar workers in Japan generally did not return home until much later than 7 P.M., so there was an unfulfilled audience potential in this socioeconomic strata. In addition, while NHK was particularly strong in its news ratings among the older generations, it was weaker among those in their 20s and 30s and among those more interested in sports, performing arts, and softer news subjects.[21] By the 1980s, this was exactly the type

---

[17]Interview with TV Asahi News Division executives, June 25, 1985.

[18]Ishizaka, *Masu media sangyō no tenkan*, table 2, p. 148, chart 3, p. 72, respectively.

[19]Fujiwara Norimachi, "Terebi sodachi no otona-tachi wa terebi ni nani o mitomete iru ka" ("What Are Adults Raised on Television Approving on Television?"), *Hōsō Kenkyū to Chōsa* (August 1984): 8.

[20]NHK HYC, *Terebi-rajio bangumi shichōritsu chōsa: Zenkoku-sōbetsu kekka hyō* (*Television, Radio Programs Audience Rate Survey: Charts of Findings Nationwide and By Strata*), November 1982, 32.

[21]Yoron Chōsabu Shichōritsu Gurūpu, "Terebi-rajio shichō no genkyō" ("The Current Circumstances of the Television-Radio Audience"), *Hōsō Kenkyū to Chōsa* (September 1984): 23, 25, respectively; Fujiwara Norimichi and Miya Eiko, "Terebi hōdō wa dō uketomerarete iru ka" ("What Are You Accepting on Television?"), *Hōsō Kenkyū to Chōsa* (July 1987): 3; NHK HYC, *Terebi-rajio bangumi shichōritsu chōsa*, 32.

of viewer who was ready for something different in the way of news. Lacking a commitment to any political or economic cause and enjoying an unprecedented array of material possessions and possibilities, this generation felt alienated from society and cynical toward politics and leaders.[22] To these viewers, NHK offered only predictable, old-fashioned, and stuffy news about bureaucrats, government ceremonies, and policy changes, told in a bland, neutral, but somehow didactic manner. Its content and style lacked appeal for this younger generation.

The "new media" technological innovations developed under NHK's leadership also proved increasingly less daunting, as we saw in the previous chapter. By concentrating on a structural technological approach of new media to retain its dominance, NHK may have neglected the more important factor in audience marketing—programming.

In retrospect, it is clear that there was a potential audience of urban, younger viewers for a commercial network's later evening news program, especially if that program presented a new and more interesting form of news. Ironically, NHK first perceived this need as early as the 1970s. Its introduction of a new kind of news would lay the basis for its commercial competitor, TV Asahi, later to carry the concept beyond anything that NHK could accomplish.

NC9: "CASTER NEWS"

As early as the 1960s, some NHK executives had been dissatisfied with NHK's slavish emulation of newspaper news and had unsuccessfully pushed for a new kind of news program that would take advantage of the special characteristics of the broadcasting medium.[23] The idea was revived in 1973 by some of the same executives and none other than the future managing director and president, Shima Keiji, who was converted to the idea in part because of his experience as a foreign correspondent in Washington, D.C.[24]

News Center 9 P.M., first broadcast in April 1974, was designed to provide a later-evening alternative for the younger, urban and suburban, commuting white-collar worker, who was rarely home for the main evening news, rather than for the older, less urban audience who liked NHK's 7 P.M. program.[25] As a News Division executive in 1983 explained it:

[22]Susan J. Pharr, *Losing Face: Status Politics in Japan* (Berkeley: University of California Press, 1990), 3–4; Joseph A. Massey, *Youth and Politics in Japan* (Lexington: Lexington Books, 1976), 21–44.

[23]Shima, *Media no kage no kenryokusha-tachi,* 105–9.

[24]Ibid., 110–14.

[25]The description of *NC9* is based primarily on my observation of the production of the program and my interviews with News Division executives, producer-directors, casters, and journalists on both news programs in 1983 and 1985.

NC9, in comparison, has the set as the center of attention, with young anchors and foreign news. It's done very colorfully as a contrast to the traditional presentation of the 7 P.M. news. If we had programs like *NC9* going from morning to night though, we'd fail to please the older audiences, executives, and NHK fans, and so forth. The 7 P.M. news is something that they can feel comfortable with. *NC9* tries to escape traditional boundaries. We take the good things we see in Western news programs and copy them for *NC9* . . . and the younger audience in Japan likes "caster news."[26]

If the 7 P.M. news announcer was merely a news "reader" in the BBC tradition, *NC9* was to have instead a "caster" (the shortening of the English word for "broadcaster" is used in Japanese), who was much more like the American "anchor." The caster had reporting experience and was supposed to inject his or her personality into the program, occasionally offering commentary—although not "opinions"—about the news to elucidate background or meanings. The program set was a studio *and* a newsroom, giving the impression, as on American network news, that the viewer was in the work environment with the news crew and observing journalists in action.

Because the target audience was the better educated, more cosmopolitan urban "salary man," *NC9* would give more weight to international news and provide more depth and different angles on the news, explaining background and eliciting more viewer interest, than the 7 P.M. program. Instead of announcer narration from the studio, reporters would appear from remote locations more often. According to plan, *NC9* would be a longer (40-minute) "news show," not just a news program.[27]

The first person chosen for this new role of "caster" was Isomura Hisanori, a man with wide international experience, both in the United States and Europe, and an appealing personality. Isomura admired Edward R. Murrow and had no intention of becoming a "talking machine" like the 7 P.M., nonjournalist news announcers. He requested and got final editorial responsibility.[28] Isomura's more conversational, relaxed style contrasted with the formal presentation of the 7 P.M. news announcers, and his charm and personality were intentionally integrated into the program. He could deviate from the reporters' drafts of straight factual reporting to insert a brief comment. The "caster" in many ways plays the role of intermediary between the audience and the event, and consideration was given to what might be of interest to the viewer, rather than only to what the journalist considered im-

[26]Interview with O, NHK News Division executive, August 25, 1983.

[27]NHK reporters compared *NC9* to ABC's *Nightline* program or PBS's *McNeill-Lehrer Report.* But unlike these U.S. programs, NHK presented the full range of news, instead of focusing on a few items with guest interviews. *NC9* might better be described as a rather unique format, falling almost exactly between the 7 P.M. news and the above mentioned U.S. news shows.

[28]Shima, *Media no kage no kenryokusha-tachi,* 117–18.

portant. These innovations set a precedent for a new type of "caster news" in Japan.[29]

In one major respect, however, Isomura could not deviate from NHK's traditional news. Any commentary he gave could not truly be his own opinion or criticism. News Division executives set the ground rules for what Isomura could add and how: he had to use NHK-gathered news as the basis for the news item and, because it was felt that using the public airwaves for a personal opinion might violate NHK's charter under the Broadcast Law, any commentary had to be done citing the foreign press. For example, he would say after presenting a factual news, "To this the French newspaper *Le Monde* responded today with. . . ." Isomura could exercise editorial choice in his selection of the foreign press commentary, but he could never say "I think. . . ." Indeed, his catchphrase, "Chotto kiza desu ga . . . ," ("It's a bit rude/presumptuous of me, but . . .")—as famous in Japan as Walter Cronkite's "And that's the way it is" in the United States—served a functional purpose on the program to clearly mark what followed from the purely factual news that had preceded it.[30]

Within a few short years, Isomura was to become one of the most popular TV personalities in Japan, so popular that he has been called "Mr. NHK," ensuring the show's slow climb in the ratings.[31] Retiring as "caster" in 1977, Isomura had risen to higher executive positions within NHK by the mid-1980s, and he eventually resigned to run in an abortive bid to become governor of Tokyo.[32]

Several successors to Isomura had come and gone by the time I visited the *NC9* studios in the mid-1980s. By then the male-female team of "casters" were Kimura Tarō and Miyazaki Midori, both intelligent, charming, cosmopolitan persons. A veteran reporter of the city desk as well as overseas assignments, Kimura anchored the program with solid journalistic skills, a desire to transcend the limitations of the 7 P.M. news, and a pleasant demeanor and smile. Although not a journalist, Miyazaki was young, attractive, and she possessed both a master's degree in international relations and good English interviewing skills.[33]

[29]As Kazutami Yamazaki, in "Broadcast Views: TV Newscasters and Their Role in Shaping Public Opinion," *Japan Scope* (summer 1994): 59, has said, NHK's *NC9* "both pioneered the role of the newscaster and entirely changed the way news was presented on Japanese television."

[30]Shima, *Media no kage no kenryokusha-tachi*, 123–24. See also Isomura's autobiography: Isomura Hisanori, *Chotto kiza desu ga* (*It's a Bit Rude of Me, But . . .*) (Tokyo: Kōdansha, 1982), 223–58.

[31]Shima, *Media no kage no kenryokusha-tachi*, 124–27.

[32]While Isomura was backed by the national LDP organization, the Tokyo branch backed the aging but still lively incumbent.

[33]On Kimura and Miyazaki's background and how the latter was chosen for her position, see Shima, *Media no kage no kenryokusha-tachi*, 128–29.

NC9 was produced by a separate unit of the News Bureau, a small team of two executive producers who rotated weekly, the casters, and several reporters, producers, and editors, who produced the particular segments, supported by a technical staff. Although most of the segments on *NC9* were gathered by the same reporters and camera crews that supplied items for the 7 P.M. news (its longer length often allowed *NC9* to air footage and reports that the 7 P.M. program could not use), the newer program also had a few of its own reporters and cameramen to produce some reports independently.

Visuals were given at least equal weight to the scripts on *NC9*. The visuals were edited to an already written script for the 7 P.M. news, but the two were edited simultaneously for *NC9*. Furthermore, visuals played an important role in determining the news value of an item. The visuals' inherent interest could determine both what was shown in the item and the order in which items would appear.

The decisions as to what items would appear and in what order were made in a relatively collective and consensual process at two informal afternoon meetings attended by the entire team. There were few fixed norms regarding the ordering of items except for the determination—ultimately made by the executive producer and Kimura but informed by the collective discussions—of what item was most "interesting" in terms of drama, impact, or visuals. One implicit norm, though, was that the *NC9* program should try to differentiate itself from the 7 P.M. broadcast. As one of the casters told me in 1985, "We purposely change our news order watching the 7 P.M. show, and we hate to put on a story which the 7 P.M. news put on top on the top of our show."[34]

Like the anchors on U.S. network news, the *NC9* casters read from a teleprompter, appeared in a working news studio, and used the same "remote" journalists on the program night after night. This arrangement was designed intentionally to build up audience identification with the reporters.[35]

NC9's innovations in Japanese news were considerable. In contrast to the specialized, bureaucratized process for the 7 P.M. news, *NC9* was assembled by a team in which specific roles were not as clearly defined. Reporters worked with producers and editors to put together an item, moving away from the tradition of news that is clearly controlled and defined by reporters. News from the reporters' clubs was supplemented with special footage gathered by *NC9*'s teams, and casters played a major role in decisions, along with the executive producer. Instead of relying solely on "hard news" based on a journalist's script, the *NC9* team considered the inherent interest of the

---

[34] Interview with K2, May 30, 1985.

[35] In the case of the political reporter, they also hoped that politicians would be more likely to give an NHK reporter information if they knew he would definitely get on the air each night.

Fig. 16. Kimura Tarō, *NC9* newscaster, rehearses in the *NC9* studio set, 1985. The *NC9* program led to changes in the 7 P.M. news and was a precursor for TV Asahi's *News Station.*

story and visuals when determining segment inclusion, length, and priority. In short, if the 7 P.M. news was much like a Japanese newspaper, *NC9* was more like American network news.

In the 1980s, *NC9* enjoyed solid, but not spectacular ratings in the low teens. Although consistently more popular among older males, college graduates, and the managerial strata, it was not necessarily more popular in urban than in rural areas.[36] Nevertheless, *NC9* had two major consequences for television news in Japan: it influenced the style of the 7 P.M. news, which adopted some of its visual-centered approach, and it served as a forerunner for *News Station,* which would take its caster- and audience-centered approach in a new direction.

CHANGES IN THE 7 P.M. NEWS

Because of its somewhat revolutionary differences with the long-established and core 7 P.M. news, *NC9* was not introduced without major tension and conflict within the News Division. Especially in the beginning, the older reporters, originally trained as newpapermen, and the younger ones trained by these veterans resisted the new style of news. In turn, casters, producers, and some reporters on *NC9* often felt a keen sense of competition with the 7 P.M. program. At an editorial meeting I attended in May 1985, I

---

[36] See for example, NHK HYC, *Terebi-rajio bangumi shichōritsu chōsa* 8, 32ff.

sensed that a ratings report generated excitement not so much because it suggested they were doing well compared to a commercial network competitor but because it indicated *NC9* was catching up to the 7 P.M. news. When I checked this out with the caster afterward, he said, "Oh yes. We feel the 7 P.M. news is, how do you say, our biggest competition."

By the early 1980s, the 7 P.M. news had changed: more frequent use of reporters reading their own stories, rather than announcers; somewhat more attention to visuals; and a bit less rigid emphasis on politics and economics.[37] Yet, these were minor changes: the basic newspaper structure and process deriving from the early 1960s remained virtually untouched. NHK's fiscal difficulties, however, fueled the concern of some executives, who saw the highly expensive, personnel-intensive, specialized, and bureaucratic 7 P.M. news process as being a luxury that NHK could not continue to afford.

Gradually, and only over the objections of the large, entrenched reporters' faction who believed in the traditional newspaper news norms, these news executives introduced changes in the 7 P.M. news organization and process. With no intent to change the primarily domestic and purely factual nature of that news, they nevertheless hoped to meld the reporters' and editors' functions in the editing process so that producers and visual editors without journalist backgrounds would have more equal status with reporters and to make visuals as important as the written drafts of reporters. When I first begin this research in 1983–85, the tension over this transition was palpable, with reporters and executives talking openly of the problems, contrasts, and trade-offs between the two news styles.

As part of this transition, the News Center was reorganized. The coordination desk was folded into a new general, larger organizational unit called the "Editing Center" (*henshū sentā*). The collection of videos from all the different programs was centralized in this center. Previously, the videos collected by specific programs, like *NC9*, were not always shared with the other programs. The head of the Editing Center and one of the five department heads below him came from a directing, not a reporting, background. The reorganization also included putting all the desks to which field journalists reported and all that collected information into a new "News Gathering Center."

Some of the barriers between the specialized reporter and producer roles, and among reporters, producers, and visual editors, were being broken down in order to merge these work activities. Segments came to be edited and produced by reporters simultaneously working with the visual editors, who once merely illustrated with video scripts written by desk reporters.

Not all the problems of changing the 7 P.M. news had to do with different ideas about the style of the news. The union, Nippōrō, was very concerned

[37]Interview with O, News Division executive and a long-time NHK reporter, May 28, 1985.

with concrete questions of status and pay involved in the transition in professional roles. The fixed career advancement line of reporters, editors, and other employees blurred as the newsroom structure changed. Nippōrō went along with the transition, however, partially because it provided individuals the challenge and skills afforded by new tasks.[38] Finally, news judgments were altered to give visuals more emphasis when deciding on the "news value" of an item and in producing the segments. In 1985, when I asked a producer whether the editing process was still the same as it had been two years earlier, he replied, "Basically yes," but then added:

> The story written by the reporters doesn't mean everything anymore. . . . The producer, the director, and others who only made programs, are now working together with the reporters, . . . the story is no longer given priority, but now there are many cases where video is given priority. . . . It wasn't like that before. Images were always an add-on.[39]

The function of the desks, however, seems to have been virtually unaltered by this change. When I asked a key political desk executive in 1985 how his desk had changed in the reorganization of the newsroom, he responded, "Basically it didn't change a bit. But you can say we moved places a little," referring to the physical reorganization that accompanied the organizational one.[40]

In April 1988, the News Center moved to new quarters in a partially underground, specially-designed modern facility next to the main NHK building, another innovative concept that Shima Keiji helped push to fruition. When Shima became vice president under Ikeda Yoshizō in 1988, he also lobbied for a further reorganization of the News Center, merging the News Gathering Center and the Editing Center into one unit, advancing the breakdown of traditional roles and moving editing and production more into the video age with a less specialized, less bureaucratic, more integrated organization.[41] Personal computers became common in the new News Center, and this electronic network became the means for communicating and editing stories.

Nonetheless, the reporters' club system of news gathering, with its advanced warning functions and its specialized desks[42] linking the field reporters with the final editing process; the personnel-intensive, separate

---

[38]Interview with K, News Center producer, August 13, 1985. All NHK personnel begin with equal base pay that advances with seniority, but there is also a small component of salary that is merit-based.

[39]Ibid., June 13, 1985.

[40]Interview with O2, political desk leader with extensive experience in reporters' clubs, August 4, 1985.

[41]Shima, "*Shima Geji*," 188–90.

[42]Now they constitute separate "groups," rather than "desks," within the more general News Center, but a differentiation still exists.

Fig. 17. NHK News Center studio, 1998.

segment production; and the news order priority decision process did not change substantially. In 1991 I asked a top executive in the News Division, whether the fact that some stories with more entertainment value, human interest, and visual appeal were more likely to be covered on the 7 P.M. news meant that the priority once given to political and economic stories had been fundamentally altered. He replied:

> I don't think we'll go that far. . . . Our coverage started with political news, then economic, then incidents including accidents and crimes; such items were our mainstay. But now, in addition to what I just mentioned, we may take up social phenomenon; for example, the world is shocked because a girl posed in the nude. Or now that we are in the computer age, when we want to know what our children are thinking about . . . maybe children today are different from children yesterday. So you can see that our news coverage is becoming wider, but the focus of our news is still political and economic news, and news about incidents and accidents.[43]

That these developments in organization, process, and news value did not substantially change what the viewer saw and heard about politics and government is indicated by the results of our content analysis in 1996/97, presented in chapter 2. The fundamental orientation of NHK toward ob-

[43]Interview with T, December 18, 1991.

Fig. 18. NHK News control center in the 1990s. The facilities are modern, but the process has changed relatively little.

jective, "factual" news remained—commentary and analysis was confined primarily and carefully to what was known and confirmed by sources. TV Asahi's *News Station,* however, would take *NC9*'s innovations and carry them much further than NHK's limited altering of the 7 P.M. news and turn the public broadcaster's strict neutrality into a competitive advantage for itself.

News Station: THE PROGRAM

Of all the commercial stations, TV Asahi had less to lose than others by challenging NHK's news dominance. Of the five major commercial "networks" in Japan, it was fourth in operating revenue in 1985, with about a 9 percent share of the total commercial television income.[44] Its executives were quite attuned to television audiences' almost insatiable desire for information, and these executives were aware that sponsors were beginning to make more offers to news programs than previously and that "people associate news programs with the station's image."[45]

[44]Ishizaka, *Masu media sangyō no tenkan,* table 1, p. 145. Kase Kazuaki analyzes TV Asahi's continuing financial and program weaknesses in "'Nyūsu sutēshon' tayori terebi asahi no 'meisō'" ("TV Asahi's 'Troubled Run' Relying on 'News Station'"), *Tsukuru* (July 1988): 72–74.

[45]Interview with TV Asahi News Division executives, June 25, 1985.

Meanwhile, a few executives at Dentsū, Japan's mammoth commercial advertising agency, believed that commercial stations could not only put together a news show like *NC9*, but even better, produce one that broadcast the news the audience wanted to have rather than what journalists thought they should have. These ideas coincided with the views of a young and successful radio and television personality who was looking for new professional challenges, Kume Hiroshi. Kume, a wildly successful radio and television host, harbored an ambition to host a serious television news program that would make better use of the medium, appeal even to viewers who did not read the newspapers, and be presented in an accessible manner. At 34, he resigned from his station affiliation to work freelance, then he hooked up with Dentsū executives, who considered him the perfect host for their innovative, developing news show, *News Station*.[46]

Airing a news show in prime time (7–11 P.M., the 7–10 P.M. portion of which is specifically referred to as "Golden Hours") posed a huge risk and would be a hard sell to sponsors and to the networks both because of NHK's dominance in the field and because traditionally commercial networks showed only entertainment in prime time. Dentsū shouldered most of the huge financial risk of the program, and after several of the other networks turned it down, TV Asahi's president, over the resistance of his own News Division, approved the program in spring 1985. The industry widely viewed the project as TV Asahi betting the company and indulging in "suicidal behavior."[47]

Dentsū, TV Asahi News, and the production company, Ofuisu Tou Wan, (Office 21) that developed *News Station* were in agreement about the kind of new program they wanted, a conception that accorded well with Kume's own view of what television news could be: news from the perspective of audience tastes, not journalists' traditional norms; an interesting and stimulating program that could compete with NHK; content that was understandable even to a middle school student; a focus on people; and full use of the sound, visual, and other capabilities of live television.[48] Thorough research was carried out to implement and develop these concepts, including critically dissecting and questioning every aspect of *NC9*'s format, style, impact, effectiveness, and comprehensibility. Pre-launch marketing of the program included some unprecedented techniques, including publicly recruiting some of its on-air personnel from among average citizens. Thirteen were recruited from the 5,762 applications and appeared on the first program.

Finally, in the fall of 1985, Kume Hiroshi looked into the camera and said "It's come round to October 7th, Monday, 10 P.M. I'm Kume Hiroshi. Good

[46]Shima, *Media no kage no kenryokusha-tachi*, 69–77. For a fuller discussion of the development of *News Station*, see my "Changing Television News in Japan," 667–69.

[47]Shima, *Media no kage no kenryokusha-tachi*, 55, 79–88.

[48]Ibid., 58–59, 86, 90.

evening everyone. Today is finally *News Station*'s first day. I'm also nervous about doing a news program for the first time."[49] Thus began the first Japanese commercial news program in prime time.

TV Asahi's News Division, as mentioned above, consists of about 200 persons, of whom approximately half are reporters. The News Division puts together the morning, noon, and evening news programs on TV Asahi, but not *News Station*, which is produced by a separate team of 40 persons, including *News Station*'s own journalists. One of the programs producers interviewed in 1995[50] explained the system to me. The program will often use the raw news data that TV Asahi's regular news staff gathers, including that gathered at reporters' clubs, but also often adds its own angle and sends out its own reporters on special assignments and for supplementary material. No *News Station* reporter belongs to a reporters' club. Subjects for special teams to cover are decided at a joint meeting of the News Desk and producers. Producers of the program consider *News Station* a joint venture with TV Asahi's News Division, but one in which they independently add their own perspective on the news.

Since its conception, *News Station*'s purposes have remained the same—to give background understanding to the news to people who might otherwise not be interested in it and to communicate that understanding in interesting ways. The producer further explained that *News Station* was a bit like the afternoon edition of a newspaper in that the audience already knows the basic outlines of that day's news and is ready to ask "so what?" *News Station* was conceived to provide the "because . . ." part and to go "inside the news." In words almost identical to those used by the founders of the program a decade before to describe the fundamental distinction between traditional, journalist-centered news and the perspective *News Station* brings, the producer said "there's news we want to broadcast to everyone and that which the audience would like to know." Even when covering items that interest few in the audience—for example, national budget matters—*News Station* strives for originality in its presentation. Flip charts and other creative visual devices that "remain in the eyes" (*me ni nokeru*) are often used in an attempt to overcome one of the problems of television—namely the brief appearance, then quick disappearance, of visual images.

The process of decision making for the program stands in marked contrast to the highly specialized and bureaucratic system that produces the 7 P.M. NHK news and is even more informal in some ways than *NC9*'s process. Most of the decisions are made by the producer on duty (they operate in shifts), the head of the news desk, and three of those who appear on the

[49] Ibid., 52. My translation.

[50] Interview with W, *News Station* producer and veteran TV Asahi journalist, February 14, 1995. The description of the program's aims and decision-making processes that follows is from this interview.

Fig. 19. TV Asahi's *News Station* team, 1998. Kume Hiroshi is second from right.

show, Kume, his female co-anchor—for a long time Komiya Etsuko—and a veteran journalist colleague, usually a former *Asahi Shimbun* commentator or editor who acts as both a foil and a counterpoint to Kume.

The decision-making process takes place in very informal meetings that begin in the late afternoon with a rough plan for what will be included in the program that night. These meetings often extend almost up to show time. Kume does not always participate in all these discussions. In the general mode of operation on the air, Kume reads exactly the news scripts prepared for him by the journalists; then he reacts to the news, even expressing his own opinions, which are a subtle combination of planning and spontaneity. In discussing the news at one of the editing meetings prior to the show, the producers and other decision makers come up with a general theme in reaction to the important items that they've agreed need to come out and that they should "beat" (*tatakō suru*). They also decide on the visual aids, such as charts or dolls, for example, that should be used. Exactly what phrase or particular words or intonation will be used on the air to express that theme concretely is left up to Kume.

Kume has always said, often in the face of criticism that he is violating journalistic norms of objectivity, that "I am not a newscaster; I'm a representative of the viewer." He frequently compares himself to a "master of ceremonies (*shikaisha*) who worries about advancing the program."[51]

[51] Tahara, *Terebi no uchigawa de*, 82.

News Station: COVERAGE

Quantitative Analysis

To understand the concrete differences between *News Station* and NHK's main news at 7 P.M., I conducted a content analysis of the same four weeks of weekday news of both programs, two weeks in 1996 and two weeks in 1997. Although the results of this quantitative analysis cover a short period and may be influenced by the particular news events that occurred during analysis, the fact that both programs covered the same news period allows us to compare the general tendencies of each station's coverage relative to the other.[52] The following indicates the relative percentages of each program in terms of the general categories of subject:

	News Station	NHK (7 P.M.)
Government	47%	52%
Society	64%	55%
Economy	10%	17%
Foreign/defense	40%	30%

As can be seen in the table, both programs pay most attention to societal subjects, stories about disaster, crime, environment, health, education, transportation, media, culture, religion, and news items about sports. Around half the items on both stations cover government and politics. NHK's 7 P.M. news has somewhat more coverage of economics; *News Station* has more coverage of foreign news items.[53]

More importantly, I analyzed differences in coverage of specific actors in government and politics, as shown in figure 20. These data represent only items related to domestic government and politics stories and excludes for-

[52]John Nylin, a former graduate student at my school, conducted under my supervision the initial content analysis of the data for both programs. The same person conducting both analyses means that any errors or bias should be consistent across programs. I spot-checked his work to ensure that the procedures and definitions followed were consistent with the intent of the analysis. The dates of the analysis were the 10 weekday programs of each station between August 19 and August 23, and August 26 and August 30, 1996, and the nine programs between April 7 and April 11 and April 14 to 16 and April 18, 1997. Technical difficulties prevented us from receiving the April 17 program. Each item was coded in up to two general categories, and thus the percentages do not compute to 100 percent. Readers who compare the results of only the 1996 two-week period in Krauss, "Changing Television News in Japan," will find very little difference with the four-week period presented here, indicating little variation between the samples eight months apart, and that these are consistent differences with NHK.

[53]When the analysis is done according to the amount of time, the results are similar, with only a few exceptions. Looking only at domestic news, the relative proportions and rankings of each kind of news were not very different from the overall results described above.

cign coverage.[54] Here, an item could be categorized into up to three sub-categories. Both programs give the most coverage to the bureaucracy: adding in the percentage of coverage given to the advisory councils (*shingikai*) attached to the bureaucracy, then 43 percent of NHK's and 38 percent of *News Station*'s coverage related to the administrative arm of the state. NHK's coverage of new policy, however, exceeds that of *News Station* by a considerable margin (28 percent to 4 percent). Although both give a fair amount of attention to administration and policy, NHK's focus on these subjects is greater.

News Station gives more attention and time to local government (24 percent to 15 percent), to the Cabinet (19 percent to 10 percent), and to the police (8 percent to 3 percent). Both pay a fair amount of attention to political parties, but NHK emphasizes this topic more, with two or three of every ten items in domestic politics having some content related to them. Neither allot substantial coverage to the Diet. Although both stations cover the prime minister more in foreign stories, he does not play a significant role in news broadcasts about domestic politics.

Thus, the main news programs in Japan, whether public or commercial, pay most attention to the bureaucracy, even though much academic research and many journalists acknowledge the importance of politicians in policy making and even when Japanese electoral and party politics is in a major transition period. NHK, however, focuses on policy much more than *News Station,* and political parties rank as the second most covered subject by the public broadcaster. Where the two broadcasts differ is in the coverage of subjects, such as crime and the affairs of the local governments, that are closer to the average citizen. *News Station* emphasizes these topics more and that may be more in tune with their philosophy of providing news from the perspective of the viewer.

The chief difference between NHK and *News Station,* however, is not so much in how much they cover government or particular political actors, but in *how* these topics are covered. Reporters or anchors give a commentary or analysis far more often on *News Station* than on NHK, as is shown in figure 21, where the interjection of commentary and analysis is broken down by type of segment. NHK's commentary is roughly equally distributed across categories—8 percent overall and in each category except the economy, which shows 5 percent. *News Station*'s commentary also is relatively equal across categories but with a much wider variance (between 31 percent and 42 percent): there is at least four times as much commentary in a news segment on

[54]Domestic news was news that was primarily about the actions or activities of Japanese persons or institutions that took place within Japan's national borders. Thus, a story about the prime minister's foreign visit was considered a "foreign" story, but one about his meeting his Cabinet to discuss foreign policy was considered a "domestic" story.

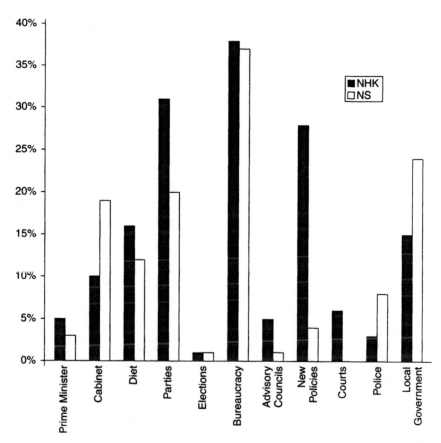

Fig. 20. Political subjects in NHK 7 P.M. and *News Station* news: NHK, 1996–97; *News Station,* 1996–97.

Kume's program as on the public broadcaster's main news, and sometimes even greater multiples. Almost two-thirds (63 percent) of *News Station*'s overall time is composed of items that have some commentary, whereas on NHK, this portion is only about one-third (32 percent). These findings conform to data found in a study of American and Japanese media coverage of the other country: two commercial broadcasters, TV Asahi and TBS, were more than twice as likely as NHK to have a reporter or anchor insert an overt personal opinion or commentary into the items concerning the United States.[55]

[55]Whereas only one-fifth of the items on NHK news contained such personal opinion or commentary, the results were twice that for TBS and attained nearly half of all items on TV Asahi. Data are from "Portraying the Other Nation: Images of the United States and Japan on American and Japanese Television News," a project conducted on all major TV news programs in both countries for seven months in 1992, sponsored by the Mansfield Center for Pacific Affairs, the NHK BCRI, the Research Institute of Japanese Commercial Broadcasting, and the NHK Joho Network.

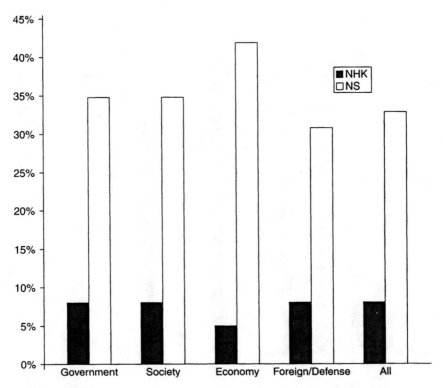

Fig. 21. Items with analysis or commentary by type of news: NHK, 1996–97; *News Station,* 1996–97.

Significantly too, there is more commentary and opinion presented with regard to the bureaucracy (more than half of the items) than in segments about any other political actors. *News Station* may cover the bureaucracy about as much as NHK, but it is approached much more interpretively than NHK's straightforward factual news about administration.

Qualitative Analysis

When we look concretely at how these subjects are handled and the kind of commentaries that are made, we find the two programs are very different. On NHK, the commentary is rather descriptive and usually apparent, providing additional objective information. Usually, it is either a recapitulation of the story in different words or a rather obvious statement about future implications or development. *News Station*'s commentary, in contrast, is more pointed and critical. Take, for example, a story on a raid by Osaka prosecutors on the offices of a pharmaceutical firm, Green Cross. The firm was being investigated in the death of a man who had contracted the HIV virus from unheated blood products after the company allegedly knew that heated blood was safer. The NHK reporter merely offered a description of how the case against the company was likely to proceed. By contrast, in the *News Station* segment on the same story, Kume interviewed the mother of the victim, during which he agreed with her that the company may be no different than a murderer for allowing this to happen.

In another case, the Supreme Court ordered the governor of Okinawa to force residents to lease their land again to the American military, turning down his appeal that they be allowed to abrogate their leases. The NHK journalist remarked only that the government had to give careful attention to a referendum, scheduled for the following month, in which Okinawans would vote on related issues. Kume, however, said in his report that the Court was not thinking of the Okinawan people.

On some issues NHK gives no commentary at all in their coverage, while Kume provides direct commentary. After a couple of segments concerning doubts about the Ministry of Health's initial report that the source of a serious E. coli (O-157) epidemic in Japan was radish sprouts, Kume commented that blame for the cause of the outbreak may have been placed too quickly and that radish farmers should probably receive compensation.

A brief comparison of the first and main news portion of a typical *News Station* program suggests the differences in the style of coverage in general, and political coverage in particular, of both programs. The broadcast is on the night of August 22, 1996, the same date as the program I described for NHK's 7 P.M. news in chapter 2.

The first half of the program has fewer segments than NHK because *News Station*'s segments are usually longer on average, including a long sports report as the fifth item that, with its commercials, encompasses a full 19 minutes, and there are six commercial breaks. The contrast with NHK is striking.

The first story, about the kidnapped Sanyo executive's return to Japan, is introduced in a straightforward fashion by Kume and his female co-anchor. The story includes longer excerpts from the executive's press conference, including a portion showing him near tears and a more extensive remote report on the Tijuana police investigation. At the end of the NHK story, the announcer merely notes the police leads concerning the suspects. *News Station*'s Kume, in contrast, laughs cynically and remarks to the Asahi editor to his right that despite reports that they are about to catch the suspects, it never seems to happen. He then contrasts this to what would happen in Japan. After the Asahi editor briefly commiserates with the difficult situation of the Mexican government, which is currently hosting the Japanese prime minister and receiving Japanese foreign aid, Kume reiterates his doubts as to whether the Mexican police will really ever catch the kidnappers.

The second *News Station* story of the evening, lasting about seven minutes, reports on the possibility of Hatoyama Yukio breaking from the Sakigake party to form a new party. The report begins with Kume cutely playing tag with the camera while sitting in front of a stand with a sign that says "Hatoyama New Party" and a display of dolls whose faces bear the likenesses of key current Sakigake and Social Democratic political party leaders, among others. Kume giggles as he introduces a "ghost story" (*bake banishi*), a video montage of Hatoyama's threat to bolt Sakigake and form a new party, in part because of dissatisfaction with his party leaders' consideration of merging with the Social Democrats. Playing on the theme of the ghost haunting the parties, the montage is replete with a musical score and subtitles sarcastically providing an implicit commentary and subtext to the interviews with politicians on the screen.

Kume comes back on air and, in an exchange with a reporter stationed at the Diet Press Building, remarks on the complexity and difficulty of the situation. The Diet reporter then proceeds to elaborate on what is going on, with the camera occasionally cutting back to the faces of the dolls of the politicians he is discussing. His report is supplemented by a filmed interview with a New Frontier Party politician. Next, Kume has a conversation with the Asahi editor about the difficult position of Mr. Kan Naoto—a Sakigake leader and Health Minister in the coalition cabinet with the Social Democrats and Liberal Democrats—who is thinking of joining Mr. Hatoyama's new party. Kume wonders whether it can really be called a "new party" if the individuals involved are all familiar faces and whether politicians would want a merger so soon before an election. Reaching in front of the doll stand, Kume pulls out the figure of Kan and, as the camera focuses on it, he says that this one is the "key man" and that he was in Osaka today—a segue into the next item.

This is the cue for his female co-anchor to introduce a filmed story about Kan's visit to Osaka to discuss the outbreak of food poisonings with the prefectural governor and local officials. This story, and the following one on the prosecutors raiding the offices of Green Cross, are very similar to their counterpart items on NHK. Even the *News Station* video footage is similar, with no humorous remarks or commentary, but the segments on these stories are about half the length of NHK's coverage, even though, on average, NHK's stories are shorter.

These stories are followed by the long sports report, and then Kume is back with a young, vivacious female reporter who begins a conversation with him by referring to the story about political "apparitions," the theme used in the story about Hatoyama and the possibility of new parties. She then makes a deft transition with this theme to the next segment, which lasts almost eight minutes, about another kind of apparition, a bizarre phenomenon (called *kamaitachi* or "weasel's slash") in which people, in one specific location in Niigata Prefecture, bleed from inexplicable cuts. Again, a skillful video montage is mixed with the reporter's script, using a scale model of the topography of the area and graphics to explain to Kume why the phenomenon probably occurs.

Continuities and Contrasts

As we have seen in previous chapters, NHK has portrayed the Japanese state in a factual manner as salient, as a bureaucratic state impersonally engaged primarily in ritualized rule making, and as a paternal active guardian engaged in managing conflict or counteracting infringements of the moral order or the safety and well-being of citizens. Even in the 1990s, despite more appealing sets, a longer format with a more rapid pace, and a bit more attention to parties, much of this content and presentation remains the same.

For *News Station,* the state is important and the bureaucracy and political parties also receive significant attention. New policies are much less salient on Kume's program, however, and segments about police investigations, local governments, and individual politicians appear more frequently than they do on NHK. Further, stories that are interesting and unconnected to the state, whether about unusual phenomena or of human interest, are pushed more toward *News Station*'s center stage.

More importantly, each broadcaster's approach to subjects involving political authority is different. The bureaucracy is viewed interpretively on *News Station,* with commentary and opinion, and the state becomes personalized. Political figures and officials are treated as individuals and the consequences of their decisions for the average citizen are emphasized. This personalized state may try to portray itself as the paternal guardian of the people's interests, but this claim is treated warily and sometimes with skepticism. Scandals and mistakes often form the focus of stories on the bureaucracy, and this institution's activities are not merely reported, they are interpreted, often cynically. As often as not, the state—not only in Japan but also in foreign countries—is portrayed as creating conflict and problems through its actions or inactions. The subtext is that Kume, as the people's representative, is there to watch out for their interests. The behaviors of elected and appointed officials need explanation to be understood, but also are the objects of pessimism, drama, incredulity, or sarcastic entertainment. Kume's skillful, selective, and interesting insertion of comments signal to the viewer when the state's claims and behavior should be treated with suspicion, cynicism, or humorous disdain.

Although Kume's intervention in the program is often characterized as "opinion" and can be so labeled in a general way if the contrast is primarily to NHK's factual and neutral style, it really comes closer to subverting commentary, critique, and skepticism. The state is not clearly opposed with alternative policies offered; the state and its policies are deconstructed in an entertaining and interesting way.

News Station's *Appeal and Impact*

News Station was not an immediate hit. Ratings did not rise much from the initial 9 percent, and they were even lower weekdays in the Tokyo region.[56] Coverage of the space shuttle *Challenger* disaster of January 1986, in which *News Station* used visuals from CNN to put together an effective program and achieved a 14.6 percent audience rating, and its interesting and dramatic coverage of the Philippine citizens' revolution against the Marcos regime in February 1986, boosted the program's ratings to nearly 20 percent.[57]

By late 1987 its average ratings in the Kantō and Kinki areas around Tokyo and Osaka had surpassed that of *NC9*, and in the latter region, it had become one of the top 20 most watched programs.[58] By 1989 it had reached a nationwide peak of about 18 percent before sliding back a little in the early 1990s, settling into a range slightly above the mid-teens, representing similar ratings for NHK's 7 P.M. news, but even higher than the NHK program in the urban Kantō and Kinki areas.[59] The two programs were equally the most popular sources of television news for Japanese citizens. This trend continued into the 1990s. Although NHK outdistanced *News Station* in ratings in their coverage of the horrendous Kobe earthquake in January 1995, the latter was still the second most turned-to station, and *News Station* surpassed NHK's 7 P.M. news in ratings on the first night of coverage of the Aum Shinrikyo cult's Sarin gas attacks on Tokyo subways in March, achieving ratings of more than 20 percent.[60] These are unprecedented ratings for a commercial station's coverage of important news events, especially when,

---

[56]Yoron chōsabu—Kantō Shichōritsu Chōsa Gurūpu, "Aki no bangumi kaitei to shichō jōkyō" ("Fall Program Revisions and Audience Conditions"), *Hōsō Kenkyū to Chōsa* (December 1987): table 5, p. 23; Shima, *Media no kage no kenryokusha-tachi*, 94, 142.

[57]Ibid., 150–53.

[58]Yoron Chōsabu, "Aki no bangumi kaitei," table 5, p. 23; Yoron Chōsabu, "Terebi/rajio shichō no genkyō" ("Current Conditions of Television and Radio Audiences"), *Hōsō Kenkyū to Chōsa* (March 1988): table 10, p. 8.

[59]Oshima Hiroshi et al., "Terebi/rajio shichō no genkyō" ("Current Conditions of Television and Radio Audiences"), *Hōsō Kenkyū to Chōsa* (March 1994): tables 15, 16, 32; Tahara, *Terebi no uchigawa de*, 80; Iwai Tomonobu, "Gojyūgo-nen taisei no to masu medeia" ("Mass Media and the Destruction of the 1955 System"); Nihon seiji gakkai, *Nenpō Seijigaku: 1996 (Political Science Annual, 1996)* (Tokyo: Iwanami Shoten, 1996), fig. 1, p. 78; Yamazaki, "Broadcast Views," 60, gives both the 7 P.M. NHK news' and *News Station*'s ratings as tied at 15.6 percent in April 1994.

[60]Fujihira Hōki, *Shichōritsu '96 (Audience Ratings, 1996)* (Tokyo: Ōzorasha, 1996), 11, 20–21.

in times of disaster, Japanese viewers had previously turned to NHK's trusted reports from its extensive network of correspondents.

What Japanese viewers in the late 1980s especially liked about *News Station* is shown in the responses to one question on an interview survey conducted by NHK's reputable Survey Research Division.[61] The survey, a random sample of more than 2,300 viewers over the age of 16, asked the viewers to compare *News Station* to NHK's then later evening news program, *News Center 9 P.M.*, considering production values, substance, timing, presentation, and style of the news programs. Had the comparison been to the more domestic, fact-based, and conservative news style of presentation of the 7 P.M. news, the results might have been somewhat different.

NC9 topped *News Station* in such areas as the timing and length of the broadcast, the integration of the days' events, the comprehensibility of the background of the news, and the presentation of foreign news. Even in a major area of *News Station*'s avowed strengths and purposes—presenting easily understood news—*NC9* and *News Station* both rated well among viewers and to an equal degree. *News Station* seemed to achieve its greatest advantage in its impact on viewers via its style of presentation: its variety, vividness, freshness, and relaxed atmosphere. In short, although *News Station* used Kume to achieve its purpose of making the news comprehensible to the average viewer, it is the production values that are associated more with entertainment that clearly differentiated the program from *NC9,* its rival on NHK.

News Station had a profound impact on NHK and the entire television news industry. Commercial sponsors began lining up and competing for a spot on Kume's show, and for the first time on the private networks, news came to be seen as a profitable venture.[62] As an NHK news executive put it, "Because of *News Station*'s success, commercial broadcasters have invested more and more money in the news, and I think that now this investment is beginning to bear fruit."[63] As other commercial broadcasters upgraded their television news, they also improved the quality of their coverage, including that of foreign news, an area where NHK once reigned supreme because of its superior human resources. By the early 1990s, the commercial stations were covering major foreign events with a concern and a verve that captured the attention both of viewers and of NHK. An NHK executive explained that while, at the time of the Gulf War in 1991, NHK was confident that it still was ahead of its commercial rivals, after the 1992 attempted coup in the Soviet Union, they saw the competition rapidly catching up, becoming more capable, and attracting the talent needed for good news programs. He went on

/

[61] Fujiwara and Miya, "Terebi hōdō wa dō uketomerarete iru ka," table 8, p. 6.
[62] Yamazaki, "Broadcast Views," 59.
[63] Interview with T, December 18, 1991.

to say, "It's often said that NHK's audience rating is going down, but it's rather that the commercial stations' ratings are improving and they are eating away at our ratings. So I believe that we've really entered the era of competition."[64]

Indeed, the commercial competition greatly undermined NHK's later evening news "show." *NC9*'s casters, Kimura Tarō and Miyazaki Midori, left NHK to work for commercial stations. Kimura went to a late-night news program on Fuji Television. Believing that "there is no journalism without editorial expression" and that "In the name of neutrality NHK is killing the expression of opinion," Kimura includes opinion and interpretation on the show. Yet unlike Kume, he thinks that, as a professional journalist, he must keep the news and commentary separate.[65]

With both these anchors gone, and late evening news audiences in urban areas deserting to the commercial stations, ratings for *NC9* and two successors, *News Today* and *News 21*, dropped and each was scrapped by NHK. By 1997, NHK's later night news programming consisted of a short news roundup at 9 P.M. and an 11 P.M. news show featuring the nephew of Isomura Hisanori, the first *NC9* caster.

The success of *News Station* prompted the other commercial stations to change their style of news to more interesting formats containing commentary. Most notably, TBS (Tokyo Broadcasting System) introduced its own news show at 11 P.M. *News 23* was anchored by veteran journalist Chikushi Tetsuya, who, if anything, is often clearer and more definite than Kume in his on-the-air opinions.[66] *News 23* and other *News Station* emulators, however, have not succeeded in capturing more than a fraction of the audience that regularly watches *News Station*.

News Station's success has created a diverse set of options for the Japanese viewer. A 1992 content analysis of all news items related to the United States that appeared on the major Japanese television news programs of the five networks over a seven-month period yielded results illustrative of these options. Its findings are shown in table 7.[67] NHK and TV Asahi resembled each other in that they emphasized political, international, and business news, that is, "hard news" coverage as opposed to the "soft news" of the other networks. These findings are consistent with the NHK and *News Station* comparison presented above. As we have seen, however, there is another dimension of "news style" in addition to news content. *News Station*, TBS's *News 23*, and NTV's news have an opinionated and critical news style, compared to the factual news emphasis of NHK and Fuji. The two-by-two relationships

---

[64]Ibid.

[65]Interview with Kimura, March 27, 1995.

[66]This seems to be the consensus in Japan among Japanese journalists to whom I have talked; on this comparison, see also Tahara, *Terebi no uchigawa de*, 81.

[67]See note 55.

Table 7. News Item Content by Network (percentage of all items related to U.S. on that network)

Content	NHK	Asahi	NTV	TBS	Fuji
Politics (n=328)	41	42	30	37	19
International (n=351)	58	47	31	46	14
Business (n=225)	39	32	19	23	10
Culture (n=385)	33	28	32	38	37
Society (n=509)	37	46	49	37	48
Social issues (n=309)	11	21	31	13	37
People's lives (n=338)	6	6	23	19	51

Note: Items could be categorized into as many categories as applied, thus totals equal more than 100 percent. As for types of subjects in each category:
Political includes government, administration, policy, elections, protests. International includes the U.S.-Japan relationship, military and national security, foreign policy, international organizations. Business includes economic policy, trade, specific industries, financial markets. Culture includes education, science and technology, art, popular entertainment, mass media, etc. Society includes natural disasters, accidents, violence and crime, labor, race, human rights, justice system, environment, social conflicts, civic movements, scandals and corruption. Social issues includes morality, religion, emperor's or president's family, general gossip, local activities, medicine, public welfare issues. People's lives includes ordinary life and human interest stories.

shown in figure 22 illustrate the pluralistic news market in Japan today. This market is more diverse certainly than the U.S. market where the networks, PBS, and CNN all share a similar news style and content.

SUBVERTING NHK VIA THE MARKET

News Station's successful challenge to NHK's quarter-century dominance of news in Japan arguably represents the most drastic and dramatic change in the source of Japanese citizens' information about politics and government in the postwar era and certainly since NHK established its dominance in the 1960s. This change was brought about in the face of NHK's consistent support by the political and bureaucratic elite of the Japanese state.

Three general reasons may explain why the change occurred. First, as we have seen, there was a *shift in the relative material and human resources* between NHK and commercial networks, a gradual change occurring under the surface of NHK dominance for 20 years.

Accompanying this change in resources was a *shift in market opportunities.* Affluence had brought with it a generation of urban men and women whose appetites for information, both from within Japan and from around the world, seemed insatiable. This new generation, with lifestyles and tastes unlike those of their elders, found NHK's 7 P.M. news program unappealing. *NC9* had served that niche market for a while, but, by the late 1980s, the urban younger generations below the age of 40 decreasingly watched either of these NHK programs with their fairly traditional styles of "objective" and

CONTENT TENDENCY OF NEWS

	"Hard News"	*"Soft News"*
"Factual"	NHK	Fuji
STYLE OF NEWS		
"Opinionated"	Asahi	TBS, NTV

Fig. 22. Japanese TV networks: content and style of news.

fact-oriented news. This generation was a neglected segment of the news market.

These factors, however, provided the potential and the opportunities for change. They resulted in change because TV Asahi's *strategies were synergistic with the market structure* in the news field in Japan. NHK's very dominance and support from, and for, the state created the opportunity for commercial broadcasting to appeal to a new audience in a different way.

In Western Europe and Britain, public broadcasters' monopoly or oligopoly of broadcasting had been broken by state policy decisions to create competing public broadcasters or to allow commercial competition. In the United States, the oligopolistic dominance of the three major commercial networks in the news field was broken by a new technological medium, cable television, introducing CNN's all-day, all-news format, and the establishment of a public broadcasting network. Japan lists among the very few democratic nations with a mixed public-private broadcasting system since the early 1950s—the norm to which most the rest of the industrialized world has now moved. In the news field, however, Japan's public broadcaster had dominated the field, leaving the five other commercial "networks" to divide and segment the remainder.

As a public broadcaster with a large, cross-sectional audience, with budgets requiring approval of the people's representatives in the Diet, and with conservative politicians always waiting to pressure its executives, NHK had to present traditional, "safe" news without controversy or even the inkling of bias. TV Asahi was the first commercial broadcaster to realize that this was NHK's great vulnerability. In a market where the dominant news broadcaster had to serve the broader cross-section of the audience, TV Asahi could target just a segment of that audience—youth—who did not find NHK's news appealing and provide that audience with a type of news with which NHK could not possibly compete—that is, news intermixed with opinion and entertainment. Public broadcasters in a monopolistic system (as formerly in Western Europe) could not adopt this style of news because they are public with a monopoly or oligopoly granted by the state. Neither could commercial networks in a dominant oligopoly (as formerly in the

United States) adopt such a style because, each network's cross-sectional audience makes it commercially inexpedient to alienate any portion of the viewership by appearing biased or injecting controversy into the news. Thus, it was left to TV Asahi in the particular hybrid Japanese broadcasting system to "invent" a new news form to use the market, rather than a state decision or a new technological medium, as a means to challenge the dominant public broadcaster.

POLITICAL CONSEQUENCES

One of the most important of *News Station*'s political consequences is that it has stimulated a belief among a segment of the public, but most especially a fear among the conservative political elites, that it is molding public opinion. In 1996 surveys of the public and politicians about the mass media, the *Yomiuri* newspaper asked respondents about their perceptions both of the impact of newspapers versus television and of the truthfulness and accuracy of each medium.[68] While virtually all politicians and almost three quarters of the public thought that television news programs and the opinions of television newscasters have some influence on voting behavior, fully two-thirds of the politicians, compared with less than a quarter of the general public, thought news programs and newscasters had a "great deal" of influence.

Given a list of the major newscasters on television and asked which ones had societal influence, 85 percent of politicians and 54 percent of the public chose Kume Hiroshi. Chikushi Tetsuya ranked second, with 74 percent of the politicians and 46 percent of the public considering him influential.

Television reporting, on the other hand, was not necessarily deemed accurate or truthful. When asked about the accuracy of newspapers and television, only about 46 percent of the politicians and a nearly equal proportion of the public believed that television was accurately or even fairly accurately reporting the events of the world. The figures for newspapers were in the 60 percentile range by comparison. Only a quarter of politicians and about 42 percent of the public thought television could be trusted; the response for newspapers, on the other hand, was about double that for each sample. In an earlier survey in 1987, two years after *News Station* began, three-fifths of the respondents acknowledged that NHK news was transmitting the truth and reporting on important issues accurately. One-fifth to one quarter of those surveyed said the same about newspapers, but almost none of the respondents believed the commercial television stations reported truth-

[68] *Yomiuri Shimbun,* June 12, 1996, 14; see also p. 1 article; results for politicians were also published separately in an earlier edition, April 10, 1996, 1, 2–3.

fully or accurately.[69] This combination of more biased but influential news was especially noted by the political elite.

As early as 1989, when the LDP lost its majority in the upper (House of Councilors) election, many of its leaders blamed *News Station* for the defeat, citing its insistent criticism of the consumer tax introduced by the government. Reports appeared of LDP politicians communicating their dissatisfaction to TV Asahi executives, implying threats to the broadcasters' licenses, and pressuring the sponsors to drop the show.[70]

LDP dissatisfaction increased after the 1993 general election in which the party lost power for the first time in 38 years and an unusual coalition of former LDP conservative splinter groups and former opposition parties took power under the leadership of Prime Minister Hosokawa Motohiro. This election has been called Japan's first "television election" because of the important role television played, from creating the conditions and themes under which the election was held to bringing about the new ruling coalition. Kume and *News Station* fomented public anger against Kanemaru Shin, the powerful second-in-command of the Takeshita faction, the largest in the LDP, and "don" of some of its policy tribes, while he was under investigation in a 1992 corruption scandal. The public campaign resulted in Kanemaru's indictment and resignation.

His downfall contributed to the split in the LDP. Another factor contributing to the rift was Prime Minister Miyazawa's promise of reform, delivered during an interview with Tahara Sōichirō, the moderator of TV Asahi's *Sunday Project*. His inability to keep his promise ultimately forced his resignation and the calling of the election.[71] So great was television's influence on the election's origins, themes, and atmosphere that the ensuing Hosokawa-led coalition was dubbed by pundits the "Kume-Tahara administration" (*Kume-Tahara seiken*).[72]

Many LDP politicians attributed their loss of power to TV Asahi and its new style of critical public affairs broadcasting. The opportunity for coun-

[69]*Hōsō Kenkyū to Chōsa* (May 1987): 5. In contrast to the recent surveys, however, NHK was seen as having the power to influence national politics by about a quarter of the respondents, compared to almost none who viewed commercial TV as influential.

[70]Shima, *Media no kage no kenryokusha-tachi*, 228–29.

[71]See, for example, Kristin Kyoko Altman, "Television and Political Turmoil: Japan's Summer of 1993," in Susan J. Pharr and Ellis S. Krauss, eds., *Media and Politics in Japan* (Honolulu: University of Hawaii Press, 1996), 171–74; Jacob M. Schlesinger and Masayoshi Kanabayashi, "Japanese TV News Anchor's Antics Stirred Sentiment against Kanemaru," *Wall Street Journal*, October 16, 1992, A11; Duncan McCargo, "The Political Role of the Japanese Media," *Pacific Review* 9, no. 2 (1996): 255; Paul M. Berger, "Exploring the Intersection of Government, Politics and the News Media in Japan: The Tsubaki *Hatsugen* Incident" (working paper, MIT Japan Program, Center for International Studies, Massachusetts Institute of Technology, 1995), 2–5.

[72]See Iwai, "Gojyūgo-nen taisei no to masu medeia," 67.

terattack came when conservative newspapers leaked the transcript of a private talk in late September 1993 by the head of TV Asahi's News Division, Tsubaki Sadayoshi, in which he candidly revealed he had encouraged (but not directed) the news staff to "conduct our news reporting with a view to assisting the non-LDP forces in establishing a coalition government."[73]

The resulting controversy, some of it spearheaded by conservative newspapers, led to Tsubaki and the president of TV Asahi being summoned to appear before a Diet committee for testimony. Major broadcast anchors joined together publicly to protest the violation of freedom of the press by this summons, but ultimately Tsubaki resigned. By coincidence, TV Asahi's broadcasting license was up for renewal during this period, and many felt this incident gave the LDP even greater leverage to attack the station. The license was renewed, but with the condition attached that the station conduct a thorough internal investigation into the allegations of biased coverage during the elections. Almost exactly a year after Tsubaki's controversial presentation, that internal investigation concluded that there had been no bias. The Newspaper Publishers Association, on the other hand, gave an award to the newspaper that had leaked the Tsubaki story, a most controversial decision among the press.

The Tsubaki case illustrates the great perceived impact that this innovative news show has had in politics, the reaction it has generated among Japan's conservative political elite, and the continuing means still used by the latter to punish what they perceive as biased and irresponsible reporting that sways voters.

The conservatives' fear of Kume both under- and overestimates *News Station*'s impact on politics in Japan. On the one hand, *News Station*'s impact on citizens and politics may be more profound than a perception of Kume's direct influence on voters. For the first time since the polarized politics of the late 1940s and early 1950s, a major source of information offers a critique of those in power to a significant segment of the Japanese public. This negative, cynical information is not primarily the province of intellectuals, not a systematic and systemic critique, and not conveyed in the weighty tones of establishment journalism. Rather, the news source assumes the legitimacy of the democratic state, criticizes its incumbents in an ad hoc manner for not living up to its principles, and is delivered by a skillful entertainer and aimed at a younger audience. Unlike the alleged role of the press in the earlier postwar period, the long-term consequences of this form of journalism may not be polarization as much as fragmentation and anti-governmental

[73]The following discussion of the Tsubaki Incident is based on McCargo, "The Political Role of the Japanese Media," 257–58; Berger, "Exploring the Intersection," 5–6, 14–27; Shima, *Media no kage no kenryokusha-tachi,* 232–38; Altman, "Television and Political Turmoil," 180–82.

distrust in the polity and not so much alienated opposition as armchair alienation.

In a democratic political system where reporters' clubs function as "information cartels"[74] and where establishment press reporters often act as an integral part, rather than independent critics, of the political process,[75] the information pluralism provided now by these more free-wheeling news programs may be functional for Japanese democracy. If a democratic political system requires both allegiance and criticism to function appropriately and cannot operate smoothly with too much of one and too little of the other, Japanese citizens now have access to news styles that provide political images of both. Thanks to this new form of television news, it is unlikely that the LDP, should it reestablish its electoral and parliamentary dominance, will also easily reestablish complete symbolic hegemony.

On the other hand, Kume's conservative critics exaggerate both his influence on voters and the extent to which he represents an opposition to conservative values and policies. Lost in the rush to attribute such pernicious electoral power to television was the fact that, even if TV Asahi's shows did influence the key events leading up to the election, there is little evidence that they influenced the actual outcome, inasmuch as the LDP hardly lost any votes or seats from its pre-election strength.[76]

Nor does *News Station* provide either a marked alternative viewpoint or true investigative journalism. Rather, this newfound diversity in television news may merely be contributing to the trend toward a new form of conservative polity rather than to true oppositional politics. *News Station* is sponsored by large business corporations and owes its existence to the largest advertising agency in the world, Dentsū. Kume is as much a reflection of the growing power of business in society as NHK is of the relatively diminishing power of the state compared to the earlier postwar period. Less a vanguard of a new form of principled political opposition in Japan than a "trickster," he plays a dual role as existing apart from and against the powerful and wealthy but also as an integral and supportive part of the same establishment.[77]

The content of Kume's program in terms of subjects covered is not dramatically different from NHK's content. Both focus on the bureaucracy and

[74] Laurie Anne Freeman, "Ties That Bind: Press, State, and Society in Contemporary Japan" (Ph.D. diss., University of California, Berkeley, 1995), a revised version published as *Closing the Shop: Information Cartels and Japan's Mass Media* (Princeton: Princeton University Press).

[75] Ofer Feldman, *Politics and the News Media in Japan* (Ann Arbor: University of Michigan Press, 1993), esp. 201–5.

[76] McCargo, "The Political Role of the Japanese Media," 256–57.

[77] Susan Pharr, "Media as Trickster in Japan: A Comparative Perspective," in Pharr and Krauss, eds., *Media and Politics*.

political parties. Kume's news style is to deconstruct political reality, not to oppose it or provide real oppositional alternatives to the conservative political elites and their cultural hegemony that have dominated Japan for most of the postwar period. In this sense, he represents the changed landscape of party politics in Japan. The Japanese voter today is faced with a choice between the LDP and an array of smaller parties, beginning with the largest "opposition" parties (that seem to splinter and recombine in bewildering ways), such as the now-defunct New Frontier Party or the Democratic Party, composed in part of former LDP politicians. These parties' principles and behavior are usually more populist than the LDP, but only marginally different—or they are different in ways that seem to be opportunistically adopted for political gains alone. Political opposition is a form of cynical alienation combined with vague conservative populism, rather than real opposition of principle. Disagreements are over means rather than ends.

The new electoral system adopted in 1994 and first used in the October 1996 elections was supposed to usher in a new politics of parties competing on issue differences. Instead, it seems likely that this system will lead to slightly different varieties of conservatives competing for the same median voter. In 1990, 56 percent of the members of the House of Representatives were Liberal Democrats; after the 1996 election, 66 percent were LDP or former LDP politicians. There were more incumbents, fewer new faces, and an average older age of elected official after the 1996 election than under the prior system.[78] The earlier postwar Japan's deep and abiding political divide between a conservative party, supported by big business, and a socialist party, supported by leftist labor unions, that clashed over fundamental value issues of security and peace, foreign policy, and democracy[79] no longer exists. *News Station* has brought more political diversity to broadcast journalism than when NHK dominated the news, but it is still more a contributor to and reflection of the much diminished former political cleavages in Japan than any true opposition to conservative rule.

POSTSCRIPT

At the end of September 1999, TV Asahi's president announced at a press conference that Kume was taking a three-month furlough from the program because of "fatigue of mind and body." On the evening of October 6,

[78]Albert L Seligman, "Japan's New Electoral System: Has Anything Changed?" *Asian Survey* 38, no. 5 (May 1997): 422–24.

[79]Joji Watanuki, "Patterns of Politics in Present-Day Japan," in S. M. Lipset and S. Rokkan, eds., *Party Systems and Voter Alignments* (New York: Free Press, 1967), 447–66.

Kume signed off his program, saying that the evening's performance was his last and thanking everyone for their longtime support. TV Asahi insisted that this was merely his furlough farewell and that he would return. This incident and Kume's temporary absence raised serious questions about the program's long-range future, even though a seemingly more relaxed and informal Kume returned as promised early in 2000.

CHAPTER 9

The Politics of Broadcasting
and the Broadcasting of Politics

The key to the relationship between a state and its society is the source of the legitimacy that exists between them.

— CHALMERS JOHNSON, *Japan: Who Governs?*

Broadcasting is too important to be left to the broadcasters.

— TONY BENN, BRITISH PARTY LEADER, QTD. IN ASA BRIGG,
The History of Broadcasting in the United States, vol. 1

We are permeated with the spirit of public broadcasting and are going to carry out fair, impartial program editing. Our supplying the seven o'clock news and then *NewsCenter 9 P.M.* is an expression of those efforts. We aim for broadcasting in a form which doesn't become a problem.

—NHK PRESIDENT SAKAMOTO, FEBRUARY 8, 1981, RESPONDING
TO CRITICISM OF NHK BEFORE THE LDP's EXECUTIVE COUNCIL

N HK's political coverage is unique among the major industrialized democracies' public and commercial broadcasters in that it provides disproportional attention to the national bureaucracy, portraying it as the prime actor engaged in governing, managing conflict, and making societal rules and as an impersonal and active guardian of the interests of the average citizen. It is also idiosyncratic in the extreme to which it carries its factual, opinionless, and dramatically anemic style. This type of very traditional coverage of public affairs has been remarkably consistent through time, representing a news organization, process, and product that has not changed except in minor ways (for example, devoting more attention to visual elements) from the 1960s through 1990s.

What explains the unique coverage of politics produced by NHK? What has formed the media organization and processes that create it? What has the role of the state been in influencing NHK's structure and practices?

In one sense, the explanation for NHK's political news product is simple: the organization and processes that gather, edit, and transmit the news are designed to produce exactly that type of product, as we saw in chapter 3. The news-gathering process revolves around the reporters' clubs, which disproportionately focus on the bureaucracy and ensure that field reporters remain dependent on official sources. The news editing process is highly bureaucratized, and though it insulates the journalists from direct political pressure, it also guarantees little leeway for controversy or interpretation. Journalists' norms gave political news priority over other news fields, emphasized the text over the visuals and content over audience and dramatic elements, and adhered consistently to factual presentations.

From the perspective of organizational sociology of the media, these structural and process characteristics make apparent why this type of news results from this type of organization. But such a narrow approach to explanation fails to account for the broader and deeper questions concerned with *how and why* this particular combination of organizational characteristics were adopted and maintained by NHK but not by public broadcasters elsewhere or by private broadcasters in Japan.

Similarly, approaches that focus only on the political structure[1] would not provide a full explanation because such approaches demonstrate only that political institutions provide incentives for politicians to manage the media upon which their reelection chances and power depends.[2] Japanese politicians did try to influence NHK and had political incentives to do so, but these facts do not necessarily tell us *why they chose to influence it the way they did*. Why didn't LDP politicians, who consistently had the votes in the Diet to change the Broadcast Law to bring NHK more firmly under their legal control, do so if it was important to the fortunes of their party, their factions, and their policy tribe? Why did they choose instead to leave the legal safeguards in place but to attempt to subvert them and influence the public broadcaster behind-the-scenes? Such a purely structural approach also would not include an analysis of NHK's means and motivations to preserve

[1] On how political structures change incentives see, for example, Matthew Soberg Shugart and John M. Carey, *Presidents and Assemblies: Constitutional Design and Electoral Dynamics* (Cambridge: Cambridge University Press, 1995).

[2] They also tend to focus on individual journalists' relationships with their sources. See, for example, John Zaller, "A Theory of Media Politics: Politicians, Reporters, and the Struggle Over News" (paper prepared for delivery at the Conference on the Future of Fact, Annenberg School For Communication, University of Pennsylvania, 1997).

some autonomy from the state.[3] If the LDP's incentives were to subvert NHK's autonomy, to what extent were NHK and its journalists able to prevent or counter this? To what extent were they not, and if not, why not? What were the incentives for the media, as well as for politicians, and what were their options?

To answer these questions we must look at the *interaction* of *both* the political pressures and the media organization, and we must add a *historical dimension* to the analysis. NHK's organization is the product of history and of the formal and informal "rules of the game" and relationships that developed over time with other organizations in its environment, including the state and other mass media.

ORGANIZATION, ORIGINS, AND TIMING

Leadership, timing, and choice all play crucial roles in the establishment of institutions and the consequent patterns of behavior shaped by institutions. Most especially, times of "institutional choice and change" may reveal the role of choice and intentionality, as well as the importance of the "unintended consequence of political battles fought over other issues."[4] In the field of broadcasting and politics, Raymond Kuhn, for example, argues convincingly that the French state's control over, and the partisan politicization of, the medium in that country owed much to television's period of diffusion coinciding with de Gaulle's attempt to legitimize the Fifth Republic and the institution of the presidency.[5] Japan's more complicated mixture of control and autonomy also owes much to the timing of the origins and development of NHK's news organization and processes.

The crucial, formative period in the timing of the building of NHK's News Division was the late 1950s to the late 1960s under President Maeda Yoshinori. It is during this period that the dissemination of television occurred, but these years also represented the height of the polarized conflict between left and right in postwar Japan that reached its apex with the 1960

[3]Terry M. Moe, "An Assessment of the Positive Theory of 'Congressional Dominance,'" *Legislative Studies Quarterly* 12, no. 4 (November 1987): 480–82, argues that rational choice approaches neglect the "agent," concentrating on the incentives of the "principal." Its outcomes are also "indeterminate" because more than one could logically follow from the same incentive structure. See, for example, Sun-Ki Chai, "Entrenching the Yoshida Defense Doctrine: Three Techniques for Institutionalization," *International Organization* 51, no. 3 (summer 1997): 400.

[4]Kathleen Thelen and Sven Steinmo, "Historical Institutionalism in Comparative Politics," in Sven Steinmo, Kathleen Thelen, and Frank Longstreth, eds., *Structuring Politics: Historical Institutionalism in Comparative Analysis* (Cambridge: Cambridge University Press, 1992), 21, 27.

[5]Raymond Kuhn, *The Media in France* (London: Routledge, 1995), 113–23.

U.S.-Japan Security Treaty crisis. The coincidence of these events had a profound impact on the nature of NHK's news organization.

The expansion of the News Division required, as it does in all organizations growing in size and complexity, greater structural and functional differentiation to process the news. In building the News Division, Maeda and other NHK executives, as has already been discussed in previous chapters, looked to the organizational structure of the giant Japanese newspapers. Indeed, Maeda came from a newspaper background, as did many other News Division executives or their original postwar mentors. The organizational structure of the News Division, closely modeled on the Japanese newspaper, became firmly established.

This structure was partially motivated by, and served, important political functions. In the polarized political situation of this era, in which the LDP was just establishing itself as the ruling party, the fledgling television news organization and NHK as a whole were extremely vulnerable. It was becoming clear that at least some LDP leaders understood the potential of the new medium and were determined to try to prevent it from serving its ideological enemies' purposes. As most individual journalists from elite universities were perceived as sympathetic to the left, conservative politicians were especially concerned that this powerful new technology with mass appeal not be put in the service of the opposition. As we saw in chapter 4 on the history of NHK management, Tanaka Kakuei's tenure as Minister of Posts in the late 1950s manifested the LDP's initial intent to try to control broadcasting. Not only did he use the licensing power as a lever in this age of the rapid expansion of television stations—NHK had to apply for a license for every new local station it opened—but he also threatened to change the Broadcasting Law to have the president of NHK directly appointed by the prime minister

The newly formed LDP attempted to consolidate its rule in the late 1950s, survived the 1960 treaty crisis, and thereafter avoided polarizing controversial issues to concentrate instead on non-factious policies, such as rapid economic growth.[6] Conservative politicians also became more interested in reaching the public in order to govern: note that the Public Relations Office of the prime minister's office (*Sōrifu Kōhōshitsu*) was established on July 1, 1960, just a few weeks after the culmination of the 1960 Treaty Crisis shook the government.[7]

---

[6]See Michio Muramatsu and Ellis S. Krauss, "The Conservative Policy Line and the Development of Patterned Pluralism," in Kozo Yamamura and Yasukichi Yasuba, eds., *The Political Economy of Japan*, vol. 1, *The Domestic Transformation* (Stanford: Stanford University Press, 1987), 522–26.

[7]Ide Yoshinori, *Gyōsei kōhōron* (Tokyo: Keisō Shobo, 1967), 97. My thanks to Michio Muramatsu for pointing out this fact.

All public broadcasters in all democracies have to satisfy a wide cross section of the public and thus must be perceived as "neutral." In Japan, the Broadcasting Law specifically mandates such neutrality, but in the polarized political situation of the late 1950s–60s when NHK built its news organization, it was especially important to the public broadcaster that it not be perceived to be part of either political camp. The newspaper model's very functionally differentiated and hierarchical editorial management mechanisms simultaneously performed crucial internal and external functions: carry out the mission of NHK for impartial news; protect the news organization from direct interference by insulating it organizationally within NHK; and, at the same time, ensure that the news was factual, uncontroversial, authoritative, and politically safe so that it would not offend the ruling party or the left in this era of political confrontation.

These three functions, although ostensibly separate if concurrent, are, in fact, directly intertwined in complex ways: the turbulent political environment and growth of NHK's television news staff and programs induced many to buy television sets to follow the unfolding events;[8] accessibility to television news by large numbers of citizens and the intense political polarization made the content of NHK evening news important to the LDP government and motivated them to try to influence such an important broadcasting organization; the mass audience for television news, the political polarization, and the potential for intervention made the construction of a news organization bureaucracy in NHK imperative, both to provide access to these events of interest to the public and to manage NHK's vulnerability to political pressure.

During this formative first decade of LDP rule, the relationship of journalism and NHK to power was shaped and institutionalized. As Iwai Tomonobu has argued, the "1955 system" of a dominant but fractionalized LDP confronted by a leftist Socialist party was also "internalized" into the newspapers' approach to the state.[9] So too at NHK.

Reporters in reporters' clubs also became the basis for NHK television news. As we have seen, because of the sheer number of journalists in reporters' clubs in administrative agencies and because of the particular nature of television's need for an advanced warning system, news from the national bureaucracy became the particular kind of factual, noncontroversial news emphasized at NHK. Reporters' clubs also suited the functional political needs of NHK as an organization as it built its news structure: the clubs provided "news you could trust" from authoritative sources that would neither

---

[8]NHK, ed., *Nippon Hōsōshi*, vol. 2 (Tokyo: Nippon Hōsō Shuppan Kyōkai, 1965), 570–71.
[9]Iwai Tomonobu, "Gojyūgo-nen taisei no hōkai to masu medeia" ("Mass Media and the Destruction of the 1955 System"), in Nihon Seiji Gakkai, *Nenpō Seijigaku: 1996 (Political Science Annual, 1996)* (Tokyo: Iwanami Shoten, 1996), 69ff.

offend the ruling party who presided over these agencies nor the leftist opposition party who challenged the ruling party.

NHK's managers may have preferred autonomy, as many organizations' managers do,[10] but they had to accommodate the ruling party. They needed to do so, however, by appearing neutral. Because of the opposition parties in the Diet and the leftist union within their organization, NHK could not appear to be submitting to LDP pressure. This was accomplished by careful organizational controls on "bias" through internal bureaucratic methods. With reporters' club organization for news gathering and the norms of journalism inherited from the newspapers, NHK's coverage was inclined toward the bureaucracy in any case, but this inclination proved functional in the political conditions of the late 1950s and early 1960s. Thus, the focus on bureaucracy was partially "path dependent" because of Japan's journalistic institutions, but the focus was also the product of contemporary organizational needs in a time of conservative dominance but polarized ideological conflict.

Another feature of this 1955 system of media-state relations was the importance of the *ban kisha,* the duty reporter assigned by the newspapers exclusively to the major LDP party leaders and factions. These reporters developed close relations with their sources and became closely involved in the internal politics of the LDP. Their political connections also affected their career paths and advancement within their companies. As a result of these close relationships with conservative leaders, reporters did not reveal much of the behind-the-scenes information in the press, and much reporting about the ruling party became *tatamae,* that is, only the public face the sources wanted presented.

In these regards, NHK was similar to the major newspapers. In contrast, the commercial networks, emphasizing news much less during this period, were less dependent on the 1955 system and thus freer from its internalization into journalism. Although commercial broadcasters also sent their reporters to the clubs, they were less involved with news at the time of the historical development of the 1955 system and less dependent on the state than NHK. Thus, later in their careers, these former political reporters did not play as great a role as a means for the ruling party to penetrate and influence the private broadcaster. It was the commercial networks, such as TV Asahi, therefore, that in the 1990s could challenge and undermine the 1955 system politically and journalistically with a different approach to politics and government.[11]

[10]R. Kent Weaver posits three major "strategic options" or goals that managers of public enterprises may seek to maximize, "security, autonomy, and public service," but that they prefer security and autonomy. See his *The Politics of Industrial Change* (Washington, D.C.: Brookings Institution, 1985), esp. 149–60.

[11]Iwai, "Gojyūgo-nen taisei," 73–76.

THE STATE AND NHK: COVERT INFLUENCE

As shown in the empirical chapters, other institutional arrangements added to and reinforced the basic patterns established in NHK's formative period. What is striking is the extent to which NHK has been embedded in a web of diverse relationships with the Japanese state. In the area of management, we have seen how NHK's president, ostensibly chosen by a Board of Governors intended by the Occupation to be a buffer between the state and the broadcaster, instead has been approved at least by the prime minister and been as much a pawn of factional LDP politics as a Cabinet post. The Board of Governors has been appointed by the prime minister to ensure that a majority of members and its chair would be responsive to the LDP's vision of NHK's role and manner of broadcasting as a neutral conveyor of political news. Even the Ministry of Posts and Telecommunications, a minor player compared to politicians in this policy field and one that is to a large degree politicized by the postal tribe of the LDP, usually has an appointee on the Board of Governors and also often "parachutes" its former high officials into NHK's management after their retirement from government.

In regard to financing, I have shown how the LDP has the potential to punish or threaten NHK for past or potential perceived behavior against the interests of the party by the threat of delaying approval of its budget or rejecting requested increases in the receivers' fee.

In personnel, we have seen how, through source-journalist relationships in reporters' clubs, politicians have affected what is broadcast, and, through former political reporters to whom they remain close, politicians have also influenced to some extent the selection of the News Division executives who decide what is broadcast. These former reporters also continue to keep LDP leaders informed about NHK's plans and operations. Even in pursuing its technological goals in new media, NHK had to give in to politicians' pressure to use indigenous satellites rather than cheaper foreign ones.

Given NHK's large degree of formal-legal autonomy under the Broadcast Law, how is the state able to be so heavily and deeply involved in the public broadcaster's affairs? To what extent is this involvement of a different nature than that experienced by public broadcasters elsewhere in the democratic world?

The State and NHK: Covert Governmental Influence

Through the formal authority, granted to them as representatives of the public, to hold public broadcasters responsible and accountable to public authority, politicians and governments in all the industrialized democracies use (and sometimes abuse) these institutional powers for their own partisan and personal political benefit. The BBC's travails in the 1970s and 1980s under Margaret Thatcher are well documented,[12] and certainly offer a corrective to any idea that NHK is somehow peculiarly subject to political pressure, manipulation, or management in these respects.

Japan seems unusual, however, in the extent to which politicians have been able to exert nonlegal, informal, and less overt influence over NHK. After the abolition of the Radio Regulatory Commission (*dempa kanri iinkai*) at the end of the Occupation, the conservatives never fundamentally altered the liberal provisions of the Broadcast Law, which protects the autonomy of broadcasting. Japan's uniqueness lies in the contradiction between the formal and legal structures providing ideal protection from political interference and in the depth of political penetration through personal, informal, indirect, and covert relationships.

"Privatization of conflict" from public arenas to institutional and organizational channels and the disparity between formal authority and de facto power are common themes in the literature on the Japanese state, as I noted in chapter 1. This study indicates that broadcasting, though, is an area of state "power without authority" more than "authority without power." Nonetheless, there is a fundamental commonality between this study and these others in that conservative political elites in Japan, rather than trying to change the laws to attain and exercise specific legal authority, have consistently used indirect, "private," and informal means of influence to attain their political ends. Law and formal authority are not necessarily used as a means of power, and the exercise of power is not necessarily synonymous with law and authority in postwar Japan.

It is tempting to see this contradiction as just another example of the *tatamae* (formal) and *honne* (actuality) duality of traditional Japanese culture.[13] The real explanation of this disparity, however, at least in the case of broadcasting and probably in other areas of well, is both more profound and less exotic—it was the inevitable result of the postwar political conditions in which the major actors found themselves.

On the one hand, Japanese political leaders have been denied, by the very stringency of Occupation-created broadcasting autonomy and the existence of an opposition ready to confront any perceived deviation from that autonomy, the use of more formal and overt methods of influence, such as those possessed by British political leaders (for example, charter renewal and the legitimacy of making a formal request to cancel an offending program). The lack of acceptance of the norm of "majority rule" in parliamentary pol-

---

[12]For example, see Steven Barnett and Andrew Curry, *The Battle for the BBC* (London: Aurum Press, 1994); Tom O'Malley, *Closedown? The BBC and Government Broadcasting Policy, 1979–1992* (London: Pluto Press, 1994).

[13]This disparity with a cultural explanation is one of the major themes of Karel van Wolferen, *The Enigma of Japanese Power* (New York: Alfred A. Knopf, 1989).

itics also provided a major disincentive for LDP leaders to opt for changing laws and policies formally, as the political "cost" of doing so through the Diet process was very high.[14] By the mid-1960s and afterward, the conservatives were intent on avoiding the controversial ideological issues surrounding democracy and foreign affairs that had polarized the nation between 1955 and 1965. With the liberal safeguards of the Occupation established in law and with the cost of openly challenging them too high, as the previous period had clearly proven, the conservatives overtly accepted the formal "rules of the game." Without changing the law, they had only informal, indirect, and covert methods at their disposal.

The multi-member, single nontransferrable vote system also encouraged vote mobilization based on candidates' personal organization and connections, rather than on inter-party competition and emphasis on issues. This system led members to concentrate on constituency benefits, rather than on public goods legislation.[15] It also made even more ambiguous the winning party's claim to a policy "mandate" that could be used formally to change laws in a controversial area like "freedom of the press." Thus, although it was important to manage this new, influential medium, both political and institutional arrangements raised the political costs of relying primarily on formal authority, law, and institutional change, but limited the resources that could be used to do so.

On the other hand, as it became apparent in the late 1960s that the opposition was not going to take power anytime soon, there were also fewer restraints on LDP's attempts to influence NHK and more motivation for NHK not to resist these too strenuously, as I argued in chapter 4 about the differences between alternating and one-party dominant regimes.

The 1957 compromise of Minister of Posts Tanaka Kakuei, in which he dropped the proposal to formally change the Broadcast Law in exchange for the informal agreement on his candidate for president of NHK, in effect proved to be the forerunner of the de facto strategy the conservatives followed after the mid-1960s: accept the formalities of the institutional separation between the state and the public broadcaster but establish and use informal processes to ensure that it does not become useful to the opposition. This strategy gave politicians a partial detour around the legal autonomy of NHK.

The LDP was not alone in its reliance on covert and informal means of influence. In the late 1960s and early 1970s, Ueda Tetsu and the left were

[14]See my "Conflict in the Diet: Toward Conflict Management in Parliamentary Politics," in Ellis S. Krauss, Thomas P. Rohlen, and Patricia G. Steinhoff, eds., *Conflict in Japan* (Honolulu: University of Hawaii Press, 1984), 243–93; see also T. J. Pempel, "The Dilemma of Parliamentary Opposition in Japan," *Polity* 8, no. 1 (fall 1975).

[15]J. Mark Ramseyer and Frances McCall Rosenbluth, *Japan's Political Marketplace* (Cambridge: Harvard University Press, 1993), 20–31.

attempting clandestinely to influence NHK too, only from within the organization instead of from without. Indeed, the fear of this influence only heightened the motivation of LDP leaders to ensure NHK's neutrality. NHK became a partially penetrated and permeable organization in which the previous period's overt clashes between left and right were transferred from the streets and halls of the Diet to covert ones within other key institutions.

Does this disparity between legal principles and informal reality make NHK's formal autonomy and its legal protections a sham? Not necessarily. To assume so may be to ignore that this pattern of disparity between formal and informal power results from the fact that the principles are maintained because there is so much support for them. This fact forces the conservative political elite's self-interested aims to be partially achieved in a covert manner. The Occupation's liberal framework was not a failed but rather an incomplete adaptation.

Professionalism and State Control

Why did these indirect methods of control succeed to the extent they did? Why was there not more resistance by management or journalists to political leaders' informal penetration of NHK? The answer to these questions may lie in the nature of large media organizations in Japan.

Very much in line with organizational resource dependency theory, those who can manage or influence "the flow of critical resources from external sources" can become powerful within the organization.[16] Shima Keiji's and Ebisawa Katsuji's careers illustrate this principle and the fact that there is little incentive for managers to keep an arms-length relationship with the political world when both the organization and their own careers depend on their developing close ties with politicians.

As for reporters, chapter 6 on NHK personnel indicated that horizontal professional identifications and relationships are weaker than those in American media organizations, and vertical and hierarchical administrative identifications and relationships are stronger. This pattern undercuts one of the major norms girding journalistic independence from government—identification with like professionals in a separate community of interest, independent of a particular organization or the state. This has been seen as a cultural characteristic of Japanese society,[17] but again, there are fewer cultural explanations. It may simply be the natural organizational consequence of the barriers to workers exiting the firm because of the "lifetime" employ-

---

[16]Richard P. Rumelt, Dan E. Schendel, and David J. Teece, "Fundamental Issues in Strategy," in their *Fundamental Issues in Strategy: A Research Agenda* (Boston: Harvard Business School Press, 1994), 33.

[17]Chie Nakane, *Japanese Society* (Berkeley: University of California Press, 1970).

ment system, with restricted labor mobility inducing stronger identifications with the organization and less inclination to protest within it.[18]

All media organizations everywhere contain pressures on journalists to identify with, and conform to, company policies. In Western media organizations, however, vertical organizational identifications and pressures tend to be balanced with horizontal professional identifications, whereas in Japanese media organizations, the vertical organizational norms have only weak competition.

In the Japanese mass media, there are only two areas where horizontal professional norms can be developed and exercised: the reporters' clubs and the labor union. The reporters' club represents one of the few opportunities for Japanese print or broadcasting journalists to interact on a daily basis and to develop a sense of common professionalism that transcends individual organizations. Ironically, this is also the context most under the influence of, and subject to, the control of governmental sources, a fact that mitigates its ability to serve as a source of professional autonomy from government.

Reporters' clubs also generate close ties between journalists and public officials. These links and external conduits to power through personal relationships may last through the entire career of the (former) reporter, as we have seen in the case of Shima. NHK has sought to lobby politicians and bureaucrats on behalf of its plans and goals and, at the same time, to insulate NHK from their interference, all through the informal personal connections with powerful leaders that develop out of the reporter-official relationship.

It would be a mistake to see the American lobbyist and the Japanese present and former political reporter as equivalents, however. The lobbyist attempts to persuade the official, but the official has no direct equivalent means of influence over the lobbyist. This (former) reporter-politician relationship may give the media organization access to power, but it also gives those in power access to the media organization. It is a two-way channel of influence that can also be used to advance the political world's interests in NHK.

The second area where professional norms of autonomy from government can be expressed is in and through Nippōrō, the labor union. Nippōrō indeed serves in a sense as the "conscience" of NHK, constantly thrusting the issue of the broadcaster's independence from government to the forefront of its public positions. The problem, however, is that this issue, instead of being an integral dimension of the average political reporters' daily professional life, becomes externalized as a political issue that lies outside normal organizational processes and affects labor-management relations. Furthermore, a politicized labor union, as was seen in the case of Ueda, can be isolated and controlled by the LDP through pressure on NHK management.

---

[18]Albert O. Hirschman, *Exit, Voice, and Loyalty: Responses to Decline in Firms, Organizations, and States* (Cambridge: Harvard University Press, 1970), esp. 92–98.

The result of the "organizational domestication" of professional norms of autonomy in the reporters' club and the "externalization" of them into politicized labor union issues is that the counterbalance to organizational norms and hierarchy of command is weak. If government can manipulate and control the management of the organization, it has little to worry about from individual reporters. If questions involving freedom of the press are sublimated into the politicized arena of labor-management confrontation, the ruling party can use its leverage and advantage in this arena, where it is not the journalist as representative of the public confronting the government but opposition labor union as biased political group versus the government. The latter is a confrontation the government is more likely to win.

Bernard Silberman's comparative analysis of the development of the administrative state in Japan and Western countries in the nineteenth century is relevant here. He argues that the ideal typical Weberian model developed in the United States and Britain and was characterized by: a "professional orientation"; pre-professional training in educational institutions; internalization of a body of knowledge and techniques in individuals; less emphasis on hierarchical control and status; more self-regulation; and vertical and horizontal mobility between organizations. In contrast, Japan is the archetypical case of "organizational orientation": specified and early career paths into administration; highly predictable patterns of promotion based on seniority; great specialization in roles; an emphasis on organizational status and hierarchy; and little mobility between organizations. In the latter, the state can dominate through the "organizational control of knowledge."[19]

The Japanese newspaper model of organization, also adopted by NHK, resembles this "organizational mode" of administration, and their similarities may be the natural result of the dependence of media organizations for their crucial resource of information on government.[20] As we have seen, such organizations inhibit the formation of strong self-regulating and autonomous professional orientations and behavior.

In media organizations based on the "professional model," as in the United States and Britain, government's influence, even if it could manipulate management, would not be able to control the working journalists completely. This may be why, as in Britain under Thatcher, politicians intent on

[19]Bernard S. Silberman, *Cages of Reason: The Rise of the Rational State in France, Japan, the United States, and Great Britain* (Chicago: University of Chicago Press, 1993), 10–15, 416, 424.
[20]See Walter W. Powell and Paul J. Dimaggio, eds., *The New Institutionalism in Organizational Analysis* (Chicago: University of Chicago Press, 1991), esp. chaps. 3, 15, pp. 63–82, 361–89; on pp. 74–75, their hypotheses include: "The greater the dependence of an organization on another organization, the more similar it will become to that organization in structure, climate, and behavioral focus," and posit a similar relationship with centralization of resource supply, both of which would fit media organizations' dependence for information on government, especially bureaucracy.

influencing the public broadcaster either had to use their formal powers to gain conformity or try to change the structure and function of the organization and market itself, for example, by commercializing it. With little interchange of personnel across organizations, NHK, by contrast, is vulnerable to outside influence from political leaders who, through informal and covert methods, use personal relations with managers and current and former political reporters. Lacking the U.S. and British reporters' strong sense of professional, self-regulating norms of journalistic autonomy and enclosed in such a hierarchical organization, Japanese reporters are less likely to be successful in resisting such indirect interference and manipulation or they must channel such resistance through the labor union where it is less likely to be successful.

NHK AND THE STATE: "BOUNDED" RATIONALITY AND AUTONOMY

Despite the efforts—and partial success—of politicians to ensure that the news is not biased against them by influencing the news organization, NHK has been able, to some extent, to limit, counter, and manage that influence and thus to maintain some degree of autonomy. There are several reasons for this. One is, as we have seen, the legal prohibitions against interference in broadcasting content have provided at least a partially protecting wall for the news, even if it is one that has been breached on occasion—the LDP cannot overtly challenge its autonomy but must do so covertly.

Second, as noted earlier, the News Center editing process seems fairly well insulated. The paradox is that the very hierarchical bureaucratic procedures and processes that help keep NHK news within its relatively narrow and strict definitions of neutral and objective—factual news from authoritative sources, especially the bureaucracy—also generally protect it from direct partisan pressures for blatantly favorable treatment of the LDP.

The third reason is that there have also been counterpressures within the organization not to bias the news too much toward the LDP. Nippōrō, despite its decline in influence since the 1960s and 1970s, serves some function as an internal watchdog, ready to warn and possibly resist any clear signs of overt control by the state.

Fourth, we have also seen that the channels to the state that give politicians an informal means of gathering information about NHK and exerting some influence on it simultaneously give the public broadcaster a way of defending itself or persuading the powers-that-be on behalf of its own interests. Former political reporters like Shima and current ones in the reporters' clubs can also act to try to ward off LDP politicians' interference in the organization and to persuade politicians to help pass NHK's budgets or to revise the Broadcasting Law in ways that fit NHK's long-term strategy (for example, regarding subsidiary companies or new media).

Finally, NHK is not without some margin to employ strategies in an attempt to affect its own fate. For example, although the Ministry of Posts has not played as great a role as LDP politicians in broadcasting politics, the MPT having some supervisory role and its own self-interests means that NHK can exploit it as an ally when the MPT's interests converge with those of NHK. The development of new media is an excellent example. Taking advantage of the MPT's ambitions to become an industrial policymaker, NHK temporarily was able to gain MPT's support first, in quietly converting satellite broadcasting from a minimal plan to overcome transmission difficulties to a strategy for maintaining dominance in the broadcast system and then, in establishing HDTV as a major technology. NHK's spin-off and commercialization strategy, discussed in chapter 7, also represented a potentially fruitful, if ambiguous and abortive, strategy to avoid past financial and thus political vulnerability.

Such strategies, however, had uncertain consequences for autonomy. In effect, Shima was counting on a complicated multiple dependence on several sources (for example, private capital through commercialized related firms, MPT for new media development support, NHK's political masters in the LDP for budget approval) for revenue to give NHK some degree of autonomy from singular financial and political dependence on politicians for fee increases. Multiple dependence has been recognized by organizational theorists as a viable way to increase autonomy from a single supplier.[21] To the extent NHK can keep from running a deficit by such means, it deprives the LDP of one of its major weapons for ensuring NHK's compliance: the threat to not raise the receivers' fees when NHK is in financial difficulty.

NHK management, caught between external preferences and pressure from the LDP and the internal preferences of reporters and its union, has attempted to maintain some autonomy in order to fulfill its mission of serving the entire range of Japanese citizens, including supporters of the opposition parties.

These findings suggest that there may be institutional conditions that can provide a measure of autonomy to a media organization like NHK even when politicians seek to control or manage its behavior. For example, politicians may have to choose among competing preferences and thus give up the maximization of one preference in favor of attaining another. In the case of the LDP and broadcasting, the party chose not to maximize its pref-

[21] See, for example, the work of Jeffrey Pfeffer, "Bringing the Environment Back In: The Social Context of Business Strategy," in David J. Teece, ed., *The Competitive Challenge* (New York: Harper & Row, 1987), 127; Jeffrey Pfeffer and Gerald R. Salancik, *The External Control of Organizations: A Resource Dependence Perspective* (New York: Harper & Row, 1978).

erence for control over NHK by changing the Broadcast Law because it understood that it would face a long and expensive public battle with "audience costs" that might cost it other aspects of its legislative agenda.[22]

Thus, politicians' rationality is "bounded," and they spend a great deal of time "satisficing":[23] they accept second-best alternatives or less than their preferences in order to save resources of time, credibility, information, or energy to gain other preferences. In our study, LDP leaders accepted the neutrality of broadcasting rather than attempting to maximize the preference of totally favorable coverage. Even a conservative ideological leader like Margaret Thatcher, when faced with recalcitrance from other leaders in her party, the Home Office, and the Peacock Commission, on which she pinned her hopes for commercializing the BBC, had to accept less than she had desired.[24]

Media organizations too must often accept less than their ideal preferences. As R. Kent Weaver has argued, in the case of public enterprises, managers may have to seek compromises among the goals of security, autonomy, and public service.[25] In responding to LDP preferences, NHK usually preferred organizational strategies that gave priority to security and public service at the sacrifice of some autonomy. Nonetheless, it never surrendered completely to the LDP's desires to be portrayed positively, but chose instead the safe and partially autonomous route of strict neutrality and coverage of the bureaucracy. Under Shima, the strategies of spinning off commercial subsidiaries and seeking new media options that would help NHK attain more financial stability and organizational autonomy from government were temporarily but unsuccessfully pursued.

These compromises with preference maximization, and choices among plural preferences, represent the heart of the political process in all countries. The outcome was one that suited both the LDP's minimum preference of neutral broadcasting content and NHK's minimum desire to retain at least a degree of independence in its journalistic processes and product. In NHK-state relations, both the LDP and NHK "satisficed" and eventually established an equilibrium, although one occasionally punctuated by attempts to widen the scope of control or autonomy. Once the LDP accepted that the political costs of revising the Broadcast Law or of overt control were too high,

[22]As Moe, 'An Assessment," 481, has put it, indicating the limitations of some principal-agent theory: "The rational principal will voluntarily make trade-offs. While he may ideally want total control, in fact he will choose that level of control—however low it might be—at which the costs of additional expenditures begin to outweigh the benefits."

[23]What Herbert A. Simon postulated about administrators more than fifty years ago is probably even truer of politicians. See his *Administrative Behavior*, 4th ed. (New York: Free Press, 1997), 118–20.

[24]Barnett and Curry, *The Battle for the BBC*, 22–25, 35, 45–55.

[25]Weaver, *The Politics of Industrial Change*, 157–64. See also footnote 10.

it monitored NHK through various informal methods. It intervened primarily when it had a strategic opportunity (for example, a request to increase receivers' fees) to tighten or reinforce its perception of the acceptable boundaries of NHK's behavior or when NHK seemed to exceed those boundaries (for example, in its view of Nippōrō's increasing influence within the corporation).

NHK usually accepted the government-defined boundaries, except when a strategic opportunity (such as new media) or a shift in the internal or external political situation (such as Nippōrō's influence within NHK or Tanaka's downfall through the Lockheed scandal) induced the broadcasting organization to attempt to attain more autonomy.

In the normal equilibrium that developed, NHK executives were the "middle persons" who had to balance and handle political power, ideological rivalry, and conflict externally (among factions and other groups within the LDP and between it and the opposition parties) and its reproduction internally through former political reporters close to the LDP or Nippōrō. NHK's organization, process, and product are the compromise equilibrium between the ideal preferences of the politicians and the ideal preferences of the journalists and media organization: the organization is neither a total puppet of the LDP nor really fully autonomous.

The media-state relationship in Japan, as a result, is an intimate and complicated pas de deux of two partners with mutual interests, rather than the more arms-length dance of two wary and ultimately incompatible partners, circling each other, that is found in some Western countries and in ideal democratic theory. Does the extent and nature of NHK's involvement with the state undermine its autonomy to the point that it cannot perform its journalistic functions toward government in a democratic polity?

We should be careful not to hold NHK to an unrealistic standard. Very few broadcasters in the democratic world are adept at or equipped to produce a great deal of investigative journalism, and all public broadcasting agencies must be careful not to offend particular political forces. The way in which, and the extent to which, public broadcasting agencies do not offend, however, varies by the institutional relationships developed within and between the media organization and the state over time, as we have seen. These in turn affect the images of the state that citizens see and ultimately how they perceive their state. The most important consequence of the combination of formal and informal means of influence by the LDP on NHK has been a particularly effective self-censorship. Of course, the British government's use of formal political power against the BBC may lead to greater timidity on the part of the broadcaster to avoid punishment or conflict with political authority, but because such means of pressure are overt and transparent, public opinion, the legal norms of press freedom, and the professional norms and identifications of journalists can be mobilized against such actions to limit their effectiveness or raise the political costs of attaining their objectives.[26]

Informal influences are more insidious and difficult to combat as they are, by definition, nontransparent and thus more difficult to challenge with public or professional opposition. Weaker professional norms and identifications in Japan make a less effective counter against attempts by government to influence NHK. Therefore, the union must become the institutional watchdog to resist attempts at LDP pressure. Nippōrō's decline in influence and its ultimate loss of power following Ueda's downfall, however, rendered it a weak reed against a stronger wind. Whatever their ideological motivations, the union's fears in the 1980s about self-censorship have quite a rational basis.

NHK and the BBC are both "free" and "unfree," but in different ways. On the one hand, NHK's formal institutional and legal arrangements and the LDP's political environment make it difficult to overtly change the state's formal relationship to broadcasting, and the LDP prefers a public broadcaster it can control to a commercial one it may not be able to control. This provides NHK some protection against the kind of attempt at commercialization and change of legal structure that Thatcher could attempt with the BBC.

On the other hand, NHK is less free because, through informal and covert means, the LDP can gain what it wants—noncritical broadcasting—without resorting to formal and legal attempts to change the structure. The BBC has more leeway in its selection and presentation of the news, but its leadership knows that if the ruling party is sufficiently alienated and can gain a consensus, the stakes of punishment—structural change—are somewhat higher. At the same time, fundamental reforms may be less likely to be enacted in Britain because of the good possibility that the opposition party can take power and undo them.

In Japan, on the other hand, there has been no need for the LDP to try to change the structure because it was likely to retain power for some time, and it had other means to influence the public broadcaster. NHK has less leeway, but the stakes of punishment for alienating government leaders are lower, if surer, than those for the BBC. Control in Japan is not exercised through the threat of potentially large but less certain *ex post* sanctions, as in Britain, as much as through likely *ex ante* controls with smaller stakes. The latter seems to work more effectively and consistently at inducing self-control in the broadcaster, much as a degree of internalized controls often prevents

[26]Shima Keiji, *"Shima Geji" fūunroku—Hōsō to kenryoku, 40-nen* (*The Troubled Record of "Shima Geji": Broadcasting and Politics, 40 years*) (Tokyo: Bungei Shunjū, 1995), 69, sees the difference between NHK and the BBC in terms of the political pressure of the prime minister becoming a public issue in the latter case but not in the former.

deviant behavior more effectively than promised large punishment after deviation.

Tom Burns refers to the BBC's relationship to the state as "liberty on parole," that is, although the BBC believes it has the autonomy it needs, the terms of that autonomy "can be altered, without notice, by the Government."[27] The truth of Burns's observation was demonstrated distinctly by the actions of Margaret Thatcher. NHK's autonomy and lack thereof are of a different nature. Despite the legal barriers to interference, the state possesses consistent informal means to keep NHK from straying too far from its role as provider but not interpreter of government information. "Liberty on an invisible leash" might be a better metaphor for NHK.

What specific roles does such a public broadcaster play in Japanese democracy? Perhaps the function most commonly attributed to a democratic press is that of the *watchdog:* it exposes government's wrongdoing, corruption, and blunders. This, however, is only one of the important functions that the media can perform in modern democracies. It can also be a *guard dog,* pursuing stories of wrongdoing and being influential in the punishment of the wrongdoers after they've been exposed elsewhere. More fundamentally, the press can perform the role of *guide dog,* providing citizens with the information and counsel necessary to make political judgments and decisions and to become participants in political life. Finally, often neglected is the media's role in facilitating government's communication with the public to mobilize its support for political authority, institutions, and policies. Call this the media as *lapdog.*[28] This analysis leaves no question that NHK has been a far better guide dog and lapdog than watchdog or guard dog.

IMPACT: NHK AND THE DEVELOPMENT OF JAPANESE DEMOCRACY

Does all this matter? After all, NHK has not been the only source of news about public affairs. The giant newspapers with their mass circulations and extensive coverage of the political realm provided an alternative source of information about the state. Even if the print coverage of the bureaucracy and policy making resembled NHK's, the newspapers did sometimes manage to fit in critical and oppositional perspectives and, through their emphases on stories and their series of feature articles, such as those detailing the pol-

    [27]Tom Burns, *The BBC: Public Institution and Private World* (London: Macmillan Press Ltd., 1977), 20.

    [28]I discuss these roles in "Japan: News and Politics in a Media-Saturated Society," in Richard Gunther and Anthony Mughan, eds., *Democracy and the Media: A Comparative Perspective* (Cambridge: Cambridge University Press, 2000); see also Maggie Farley, "Japan's Press and the Politics of Scandal," in Susan J. Pharr and Ellis S. Krauss, eds., *Media and Politics in Japan* (Honolulu: University of Hawaii Press, 1996), 133–63, esp. 159–60.

lution problem in the early 1970s, to convey, at least occasionally, a different agenda and different priorities to that of the conservative-dominated elite. Weekly magazines and intellectual journals also provided dissimilar information and views about government and politics to their audiences. Below I argue that, nevertheless, NHK has mattered and continues to matter quite a bit.

In the introduction I pointed out that the question of *how* the Japanese state was legitimated is the most neglected fundamental one in the literature on postwar politics in Japan. Below I construct a case to argue that NHK television news provided at least part of that legitimacy, and the way it accomplished this has important ramifications to the present day.

Let us consider some of the possible alternative explanations for how the postwar state was legitimated. Is it not possible that the conservatives' moderation of their ideological stance after 1960 and the avoidance of polarizing issues contributed to diminishing political conflict and the ability of the LDP to stay in power? Most assuredly, as I have argued previously.[29] Legitimation requires more than just the diminishing or relative absence of intense conflict, however. It requires the development of a positive orientation to the state rather than just the lack of a negative one.

This positive orientation might have been created by the strategy of concentrating on rapid economic growth and the distribution of disaggregable goods through the political process. Increasing affluence and the state's distribution of economic "payoffs" to favored client groups is thus a second alternative hypothesis for the creation of legitimacy.

This undoubtedly is part of the answer to the puzzle of postwar legitimacy. As Kent Calder has shown, the LDP used the expanding economic "pie" after the 1960s to shore up its political base especially with agriculture and small business, large proportions of the electorate.[30] Yet, as Calder also emphasizes, economic growth was often episodic, based on a large amount of corporate debt, and generated social dislocation and demands for change. This, in turn, created a sense of vulnerability for the business and political elites[31] that may well have also been felt by the public as well.

Although rising affluence levels in the general population and specific distribution of "private goods" to particular client groups certainly must have created some loyalty to the regime and to the LDP over time, an orientation only to the material performance of the political system is a fragile form of stability. All theorists of political authority, from Gramsci and other Marxists to Weber and pluralists, have emphasized the normative, affective,

[29]Muramatsu and Krauss, "The Conservative Policy Line," 526–28.
[30]Kent Calder, *Crisis and Compensation: Public Policy and Political Stability in Japan, 1949–1986* (Princeton: Princeton University Press, 1988).
[31]Ibid., 42–54.

symbolic nature of authority: legitimation and long-term stability cannot be based solely on materially-based loyalties.[32] When there are no underlying symbolic underpinnings to the legitimacy of a regime, the regime may become vulnerable if economic growth and affluence declines or stagnates. Japan underwent recessions in the 1970s after the "oil shocks" and has experienced a 10-year structural recession after the economic "bubble" of the 1980s burst. Yet during these periods no one questioned the fundamental stability of the democratic polity in Japan. How did that underlying symbolic attachment to the regime develop?

Political socialization in the schools also may provide part of the answer. Younger generations educated to be loyal to the democratic regime may have produced cohorts of citizens who accepted the authority of the postwar democratic state. Indeed, studies show that by the 1970s the schools did succeed increasingly in forming a positive attachment to the concept of "democracy" as the postwar period progressed, even if was not quite as important a symbol as it is in the United States. These same studies, however, also found that school children had little affective attachment to the prime minister and that a conception of the Japanese executive's competence and honesty fell precipitously in higher public school grades, decreasing to an extent not found in any other industrialized democracy. This and other studies also have shown that Japanese of all ages often have both a cynical view of elected politicians and their responsiveness to the average citizen and a weak identification with political parties.[33] Other than a vague attachment to the concept of "democracy" then, with what specific referent of the state might the Japanese public identify?

This brings us to our final possibility, represented by the "developmental state" model of Japan and its argument that the bureaucracy inherited the mantle of prewar power under the Occupation when all other prewar institutions had been discredited and democratically elected politicians had not mobilized citizens' attachments. Thus, Chalmers Johnson's seminal work on

[32]Gabriel Almond and Sidney Verba, *The Civic Culture* (Princeton: Princeton University Press, 1963), 251, 429, 489–97, argue that systems based heavily on output orientations and performance are less stable in the long run, as do almost all theorists of authority. See Gramsci's cultural "hegemony," analyzed in Joseph V. Femia, *Gramsci's Political Thought* (Oxford: Clarendon Press, 1981), esp. chap. 2, pp. 23–60; Robert A. Dahl, *Modern Political Analysis,* 2d ed. (Englewood Cliffs: Prentice-Hall, 1970), 33–34; Amitai Etzioni, *A Comparative Analysis of Complex Organizations* (New York: Free Press, 1961), esp. chaps. 1, 3.

[33]"Peace" actually seemed to be the symbol that played the emotive symbolic role that "democracy" did for Americans. See Joseph Massey, *Youth and Politics in Japan* (Lexington: Lexington Books, Inc., 1976), 64, 104–5; on the prime minister, see 27–31; on cynicism and parties, see 39; Bradley Richardson, *The Political Culture of Japan* (Berkeley: University of California Press, 1974), 69–78; Scott C. Flanagan et al., *The Japanese Voter* (New Haven: Yale University Press, 1991), 19–27, summarizes the Japanese findings on party identification and attitudes toward politics in cross-national perspective.

MITI and the "developmental state" posited a Japanese state that had as its key purpose and its legitimizing function the achievement of economic growth and where politicians reigned, but bureaucrats ruled.[34] Although politicians held nominal power in postwar democratic institutions, national bureaucrats, as heirs to a prewar tradition of bureaucratic authoritarianism, were master strategists, using their derived expertise, autonomy, legal powers, informal influence, and institutionalized connections to the private sector to retain predominant policy influence even within postwar democratic institutions.[35]

In this conception, internal power and external legitimacy of the state are connected in complicated ways. The authority and prestige of the prewar imperial bureaucratic legacy was seen as continuing into the postwar period in the form of de facto power, whereas explicit authority was now ostensibly held by elected representatives, setting up another variation of the traditional Japanese separation of power from authority, the "ruling" versus "reigning" dichotomy. The fact that the national bureaucracy was the least purged or changed of prewar institutions and that in order to maintain order, feed a starving and largely homeless population, and impose its reforms on Japan, the Occupation actually preserved, reinforced, and expanded the bureaucracy's powers under U.S. rule only exacerbated this dichotomy between power and authority.[36]

Johnson's singular attempt to confront the legitimacy question directly is noteworthy. There also is more than a little validity to this attribution of divergence between formal authority and informal influence within the state, as we have seen; but from the perspective of how that authority became established and Japanese politics stabilized after 1960, however, this formulation contains some logical problems and contradictions.

First, even if it was the least changed of all prewar institutions and even if it had more influence on policy during this period than the politicians, why should the bureaucracy have retained any great legitimacy among the public in the postwar period? If all other institutions associated with the prewar emperor system were mostly or partly delegitimized by the defeat in war and the new democratic ideology brought by the Occupation, so too surely was

[34]Chalmers Johnson, *MITI and the Japanese Miracle* (Stanford: Stanford University Press, 1982), esp. chap. 9, pp. 305–24, and *Japan: Who Governs? The Rise of the Developmental State* (New York: Norton, 1995), 67–68.

[35]See also Bernard Silberman, "The Bureaucratic State in Japan: The Problem of Authority and Legitimacy," in Tetsuo Najita and J. Victor Koschman, eds., *Conflict in Modern Japanese History: The Neglected Tradition* (Princeton: Princeton University Press, 1982), 226–57. Ramseyer and Rosenbluth, *Japan's Political Marketplace,* 100, criticize Silberman's dictum that the bureaucrats continue to enjoy high status and prestige even under a different institutional structure in the postwar period as indicating unrealistic continuity.

[36]Johnson, *MITI,* esp. 34–45.

the bureaucracy, which had, after all, exercised the leadership under the prewar system. Why should the bureaucracy have been spared such "guilt by association?" Even if the Occupation largely perpetuated or even expanded the bureaucracy's personnel and formal powers, this still does not explain how or why the symbolic power of the bureaucracy continued into the postwar period.

If we assume for some reason that it did, we are still left with several fundamental contradictions: one can have authoritative bureaucratic rule without stability, or stability without authoritative bureaucratic rule, but logically not both. If the bureaucrats inherited respect, status, and prestige and were the focus of legitimacy even in the postwar authority vacuum—thus reigning with symbolic power and ruling with effective power—why then was the polity so unstable? If the bureaucrats retained their symbolic appeal even after the war, then why didn't this transfer to the regime and prevent the political chaos of the immediate postwar era?

If, on the other hand, the bureaucracy ruled but did not reign and political authority was not yet established in the earlier postwar period, then that rule was not legitimized at the time and we are thrown back to the question of how the establishment of a stable postwar regime was accomplished. How did a bureaucracy with de facto but not de jure authority bring stability and legitimacy to the postwar democratic state after 1960? And, if these were established because of rapid economic growth, then how did those bureaucrats gain credit for that achievement in a political system where authority was nominally vested in political, not administrative, leaders—especially when it was politicians like Prime Ministers Ikeda Hayato and Kishi Nobusuke who articulated the famous "Income-doubling Plan" of 1960 that led to that growth?

Any complete explanation of the state's increasing legitimation also would have to take into account symbolic power, that is, the legitimacy of the state in society, not just the actual exercise of influence within the state; how this developed *after* the 1960 period; and how it was transferred to the entire democratic political regime. I agree that indeed the symbolism of the national bureaucracy was crucial for legitimizing and stabilizing the Japanese state after the instability of the late 1940s and 1950s. Neither the automatic transfer of the bureaucracy's prestige and power nor its role in creating Japan's postwar economic growth alone provided that crucial transition; it was instead NHK television news' new image of the bureaucracy as a paternalistic, competent actor looking after the interests of the ordinary citizen in the new democratic framework. Although other ideological factors, such as the influence of the Cold War, and other media too may have played an important role in this transition, television news was at least one crucial missing link in understanding the puzzle of the transition from bureaucratic power without full regime legitimacy in the earlier postwar period to a legitimized regime in which both politicians and bureaucrats have policy-making influence.

Prior to the 1960s, with the prewar institutions discredited, a legitimacy vacuum existed. Through Occupation propaganda and with new generations of school children socialized by a new democratic curriculum, the concept and general symbol of democracy gradually became accepted. For those who grew up under the prewar emperor system or under the Occupation and immediately after, however, developing specific attachments to the new institutions must have been complicated.

For those on the left who rejected the prewar symbols and everything associated with them and who embraced the Occupation's promotion of democracy and the new Constitution, the attachment to the new framework was more immediate. Nevertheless, they still distrusted the rightist politicians who led the conservatives and suspected that these politicians wanted to turn the clock back to the prewar era. Beginning in the 1960s, the image of a "neutral" state bureaucracy, looking after the public interest and the average citizen rather than pursuing ideological goals associated with a totally discredited past, surely allowed for identification with not only the principles underlying the postwar state but with some of its nonelected government officials as well.

What of those on the right and in the center who found the foreign-imposed democratic institutions too foreign and liberal for Japan's traditions and for their own inclinations? Here especially, the positive images of the national bureaucracy created by NHK television news would have provided a source of reassurance and an attachment to the new regime. It was not just the continuity represented by this bureaucracy's activities; it was that the bureaucracy, however little it had been changed in personnel or procedures, was now portrayed as acting on behalf of the average citizen's interests in this new democratic order. Television news provided a crucial bridge between stability and the new democracy for these citizens.

Thus, for the left, NHK's images of the omnipresent bureaucratic state provided reassurance that the state was not all neo-fascist LDP politicians and prime ministers trying to undermine the new Constitution and their rights, but neutral officials who cared about the public. These same images also assured the center and right that the same foreign-imposed Constitution could nonetheless provide stability and taught them that the state could be both democratic and secure. For all sides, administration as symbol was infused with the image of competence, expertise, and protection of the interests of all. As Murray Edelman has argued, the symbolism of "reassurance" may be at the heart of citizens' relationships to their state. And from the late 1950s through the 1980s, NHK provided those symbols focusing on the national bureaucracy.[37]

Much as the symbol of the emperor in Meiji Japan was not the unchanged cultural tradition of Japan's past history, but the creation of the young oligarchs after the Restoration,[38] the status and authority of the bureaucracy from the early 1960s through the 1980s was not an unmitigated continuity from prewar Japan, but it was somewhat artificially manufactured. This time the creator was not a political elite intentionally using the resources and tools of the state, but rather journalists, who were using the new medium of television to create this product inadvertently.

I cannot "prove" these assertions in a narrow social scientific sense. The kind of longitudinal data of both viewing habits and political attitudes that might confirm it do not exist. The circumstantial case for television's role, however, is fairly compelling. First, public opinion surveys do support the likely great impact NHK had on postwar generations from the late 1950s to the late 1980s. As I mentioned in the introduction, television news has been the prime source of information for the average Japanese citizen since the 1960s, and surveys also confirm that, since the 1960s at least, Japanese have been as attached to their video tubes as Americans and as dependent on television news as on newspapers, relying on television in many ways more. As we also have seen, NHK was the dominant form of television news for most of the postwar period.

NHK was the preferred source of political information for more Japanese, with newspapers a distant second, and commercial television far behind. A survey in the late 1980s asked respondents which media they most frequently used to get information on different types of news. NHK dominated with both sexes and in all age groups, although NHK TV news was somewhat more important with those over 30 years of age.[39] We have also seen that on the subject of trust, a major intervening variable between media message and media impact, surveys beginning in the 1970s showed that NHK was the most trusted institution in Japanese society during that period and that those who believe NHK "is transmitting the truth" far outnumber those who believe in any other medium. The far greater trust in NHK's news

---

[37]Murray Edelman, *The Symbolic Uses of Politics* (Urbana: University of Illinois Press, 1980), esp. chaps. 1, 2, 3, pp. 1–72.

[38]Carol Gluck, *Japan's Modern Myths* (Princeton: Princeton University Press, 1985).

[39]The results for politics and economics news were: NHK, 54 percent; commercial television, 12 percent; newspapers, 23 percent; other, 3 percent; no interest, 6 percent. Fujiwara Norimichi and Mitsuya Keiko, "Terebi hōdō wa dō uketomerarete iru ka: 'Terebi to hōdō' chōsa kara" ("How Are You Accepting Television Information? From a 'TV and Information' Survey"), *NHK hōdō kenkyū to chōsa* (July 1987): table 1, p. 3; chart 2, p. 4. The survey was conducted by NHK HYC.

than in that of the commercial networks has been consistent at least since the mid-1970s.[40]

Finally, although NHK's 7 P.M. audience tends to be older and more rural than the national average, there is evidence that its viewers are only slightly more likely to be interested in national politics and that its impact did not vary by socioeconomic level or political orientation.[41] NHK viewers were not "self-selected."

The argument for NHK's impact on the "videolegitimation" of the postwar Japanese state thus goes like this: NHK television news has been, for most of the postwar period, the primary source of television information, particularly political information, for a staggeringly large percentage of the Japanese public, who consider it an eminently trustworthy source, enhancing the possibility that its message—a positive image of the bureaucratic state—may have an impact. When we consider that there exists some indirect evidence in Japan indicating that there may be a link between the amount of coverage given to particular political actors and viewer's positive attitudes toward those actors,[42] we begin to see the potential for state legitimation in NHK's extensive coverage of news about the bureaucratic state.

Given NHK's diverse audience structure, there is no evidence that it had a predominant influence on one particular socioeconomic class more than others or that it converted supporters of a partisan political orientation to another. Indeed, as we have seen, the "message" in NHK's news is not a partisan bias toward a particular party or ideology per se; NHK actually gives more even-handed coverage to the opposition parties than do the commercial networks.[43] Rather, from the late 1950s to the mid-1980s, NHK's news helped to legitimate the role, efficacy, and capacity of the national bu-

[40]NHK HYC, "Nihonjin no terebikan chōsa" (Tokyo: NHK Broadcast Research Institute, 1978). For "transmitting the truth": NHK, 61 percent; commercial television, 3 percent; newspapers, 19 percent; other, 1 percent; no interest, 9 percent. Similar results were found for which medium covers the news thoroughly and with proper priorities. Fujiwara and Mitsuya, "Terebi hōdō wa dō uketomerarete iru ka," chart 1, p. 3. When respondents are asked to compare "TV" (NHK and commercial stations combined) to newspapers, however, newspapers usually do better on "accuracy" and "trustworthiness." See Nihon Shinbun Kyokai, "Newspapers in Japan & Trust in Them," *Japan Times*, October 19, 1997, 19.

[41]NHK political news viewers are a bit *less* likely to identify themselves as "conservative" (59 percent) than commercial network watchers (64 percent) based on my recalculations of data from a 1986 survey in the Tokyo suburb city of Machida, conducted by Prof. Akuto Hiroshi and his associates. See Toshio Takeshita and Ikuo Takeuchi, "Media Agenda Setting in a Local Election: The Japanese Case," in Pharr and Krauss, *Media and Politics in Japan*, 339–50.

[42]Kobayashi Yoshiaki, "Terebi no nyūsu no hōdō ni kansuru naiyō bunseki," *Keiō Daigaku Hōgaku Kenkyū* 55, no. 9 (September 1982): 35–36, found that there were more LDP supporters among viewers of the stations that covered the LDP more. As he points out, it is impossible to know whether this was the result of the coverage or due to the selection of the channel by particular party supporters.

[43]Ibid.

reaucracy as a central positive symbol to Japanese citizens and through that attachment integrate these citizens into the postwar democratic state.

No claim is made here for NHK's sole impact in this regard. Newspapers and other media may have played a role as well. Nor am I arguing that NHK's messages were the only source of legitimacy: the symbolic messages of a paternalistic administrative "guardian" state actively protecting the people's interests reinforced the other material and normative bases for legitimacy that existed. The nature of the party system, and the LDP's ability to more skillfully mobilize large segments of society, compared to the opposition parties,[44] may have contributed to stability in postwar Japan. Economic growth and the LDP's distributive benefits undoubtedly provided the material basis for increasing stability and legitimation. The general concept of "democracy" as taught in the schools provided the overarching, vague symbol of positive attachment to the regime. Its concrete symbolic referent, however, was an effective public bureaucracy making policy on behalf of the average citizen in a democratic state.

This image also contributed to the ability of the LDP to establish its symbolic hegemony as a dominant party after the mid-1950s. In addition to other forms of symbolic mobilization that helped create the conservatives' long-running dominance,[45] the LDP's ability to create an identity as the party that could work well and effectively with the state bureaucracy to govern must rank as one of the most important elements in developing its 38-year continuous reign. NHK television news, in turn, helped the LDP-bureaucratic state create this "official version of the social world"[46] and maintain its symbolic dominance.

NHK television news alone was not a sufficient condition for the legitimation of the democratic state in postwar Japan. Indeed, it was the simultaneous occurrence of the LDP's minimizing ideological issues and maximizing economic affluence and distributive benefits, combined with the symbolic reassurance of NHK's portrayal of the effective bureaucracy behind that regime, that probably enabled such a stabilization. But the argument and evidence presented indicate that it was a necessary condition, one hitherto not given the attention it deserves. Without the images of a paternalistic, public-interested bureaucracy that NHK conveyed to so many citizens so often, the legitimation of the democratic state probably would have occurred less quickly, less solidly, and in a different manner than it did.

[44]T. J. Pempel, "Conclusion: One-Party Dominance and the Creation of Regimes," in T. J. Pempel, ed., *Uncommon Democracies: The One-Party Dominant Regimes* (Ithaca: Cornell University Press, 1990), for example, 346–48.

[45]Ibid.

[46]These phrases are from Pierre Bourdieu. See Richard Harker, Cheleen Mahar, and Chris Wilkes, eds., *An Introduction to the Work of Pierre Bourdieu: The Practice of Theory* (New York: St. Martin's Press, 1990), for example, 13.

This latter point—the manner in which legitimation occurred—is important. The consequences of legitimation through *this* particular image of the state, probably remain with us to this day. I would argue that the influence of television news on Japanese politics continues and that NHK's and its challengers' brands of television news also help us to understand the issues and styles of Japanese politics in the 1990s. In this political system, the fundamental issues are no longer legitimacy and stability, but alienation, cynicism, and the demand for reform within a legitimate, stable, and increasingly pluralist democracy.

After the early 1960s, education inculcated the intrinsic value of democracy; older generations became aware of the importance and value of voting for politicians who brought concrete benefits to their locales and to their interest groups; affluence justified faith in the state that helped create it; the right traded holding power for changing the Constitution and the left exchanged protection of the Constitution for radical programs; and new issues, like economic growth, pollution, and welfare supplanted the old issues that had so divided the immediate postwar generation. Through all this, NHK continued to transmit the symbols of that state, including its apparently effective and caring bureaucracy, to its middle-aged and older citizens especially. And so, the new democratic state became widely accepted, stabilized, and fully legitimized.

Japanese politics also became more pluralistic as interest groups grew in wealth and power, as new middle-of-the-road opposition parties emerged and focused on new issues, and as LDP politicians were reelected again and again, learning the substance of policy and how to acquire and use influence within the policy-making process. As that process became more diverse and influenced by politicians within the state, the private sector became relatively more powerful vis-à-vis the state as "the balance of skills, talents, and therefore, influence shifted between the public and private sector at the beginning of the third postwar decade."[47] As this trend continued, the shift in resources by the mid-1980s abetted the shift to pluralism and more influential players within the political process, as negotiations among more multiple actors became necessary.

NHK executives were not totally insensitive to these changes: the creation of *News Center 9 P.M.* in the early 1970s was an attempt to appeal to the growing ranks of urban, affluent salaried men who worked for large corporations with overseas subsidiaries and connections and who would respond to more international news presented in a more interesting manner. More visuals, "casters" with personality and journalistic skills, and more news from over-

<hr>

[47]Gary D. Allinson, "Analyzing Political Change: Topics, Findings, and Implications," in Gary Allinson and Yasunori Sone, *Political Dynamics in Contemporary Japan* (Ithaca: Cornell University Press, 1993), 3.

seas could be incorporated into this new form. Alliances with business could be developed to pursue new media aims. NHK, however, could not change in the more fundamental sense of incorporating more interpretation, including less news about the bureaucracy, and paying much more attention to society. The institutional networks with the state were far too embedded by then to risk such change.

The political rise and demise of Shima Keiji in this context is the tale of a man with vision who sensed that the balance between state and society had been shifting and knew that NHK had to respond, but who ultimately was too much the product of the very institutional networks that needed changing. His downfall illustrates how deep and embedded those media-political networks were, and how little NHK could do about them. Finally, in the late 1980s, others responded more directly and successfully to the shifts in state-society relations. While NHK continued to present bureaucratic officialdom as the center of the news, TV Asahi debuted Kume Hiroshi's *News Station*. Kume's target audience, viewers between 20 and 30 years of age, had been socialized in schools to positive values of democracy, but they also had cynical attitudes toward political leaders. And, for the most part, they did not tune into NHK for news.

NHK dominated the news until the late 1980s, but its inability to respond to these trends, combined with *News Station*'s appearance, may have had important, continuing political consequences. Had NHK news reflected the changing political and social balances and forces more realistically and as they were occurring, there might have been a gradual transition in the public's perception of government and society. Instead, NHK's offerings of bureaucrat-centered, factual news of the paternalistic state gave the (increasingly distorted) impression to Japan's mature citizens that little had changed: the state was still relatively as powerful as it had been in the earlier postwar period, the bureaucrats were at least as or more influential than the politicians, and these incorruptible career officials were looking after the interests of the public, even if the venal politicians were not. Surveys indicate that Japanese citizens have always manifested high levels of cynicism and distrust toward politicians, but bureaucrats have been viewed more positively. Until the 1990s, that is, when revelations of bureaucratic misconduct created within the public a level of distrust that rivaled what they had long felt for politicians.[48] Here *News Station* helped.

The LDP's conviction that Kume swayed elections is an extreme, exaggerated, and unsupported allegation that one television news personality

[48] Susan J. Pharr, "Officials' Misconduct and Public Distrust: Japan and the Trilateral Democracies" (paper presented at the Conference on "Public Trust and Governance in the Trilateral Industrial Democracies," Bellagio, Italy, June 29–July 3, 1998), 26–27.

had the power to influence voters and elections. Kume's real influence may be at once more limited but also more profound: the unprecedented easy availability to a portion of the Japanese public, especially young adults, of negative images of the state and of its incumbents, including bureaucrats, wrapped in an appealing and entertaining package that stood in stark contrast to NHK's earlier coverage of officials. Kume's "deconstruction" of the state, and his merciless and entertaining follow-up to the 1990s scandals of both politicians and bureaucrats probably further exacerbated the bureaucrats' fall from the grace that NHK news had bestowed upon them through earlier decades.

For many middle-aged and older citizens, the long period of NHK's portrayal of the bureaucratic state as omnipresent, positive, active, and beneficent, quickly followed by revelations of official misconduct in the 1990s, may well have had a greater impact because of the sudden differences conveyed. The introduction of *News Station*'s skepticism, scandal, and images of the less omnipresent and corruptible bureaucratic state reinforced and expanded the alienated cynicism of younger Japanese adults. NHK's extensive coverage of the bureaucracy is now transformed to a negative, rather than a positive, state image, and when combined with Kume's relentless commentary on the subject, may well be undermining NHK's "videolegitimation" and introducing a form of unprecedented "video malaise"[49] to Japanese politics. A study by Susan Pharr indicates that the factors most associated with public distrust of government in Japan are media reports of officials' misconduct.[50]

Television news did not create the scandals in the 1990s. Neither did it create the desire for less administrative interference in society, upon which the rising cynicism and increasing anti-bureaucratic feelings in contemporary Japan are based. Television, however, may well have exacerbated the cynicism and the negative attitudes.

In the 1990s, television news also may have been one factor leading to the LDP facing a more cynical, critical, and alienated public that was less willing to tolerate its perennial corruption scandals and grasping at the hope of political "reform" brought by new politicians and parties not associated with the past. If Kume's *News Station* responded more perceptively to the new, more pluralist Japanese society, its broadcasts have also contributed to making the polity more pluralistic as well.

In recent political trends in Japan, parties present a more cynical and populist alternative to the old bureaucratic-centered conservatism, but they of-

---

[49] Michael J. Robinson, "Public Affairs Television and the Growth of Political Malaise: The Case of the 'Selling of the Pentagon,'" *American Political Science Review* 70 (June 1976): 428.

[50] Pharr, "Officials' Misconduct," 24–42.

fer little in the way of the framing of real political alternatives. The establishment, bureaucratized conservatism of the LDP and the skeptical, populist,
but ultimately nondissenting "opposition" parties find their journalistic
equivalents in NHK and *News Station,* respectively. I've argued that they have
done more than reflect this new political situation: they also may have been
partly responsible for creating it.

NHK's future is unclear, but one thing is certain: it will never again be as
dominant in television news as it was from the 1960s through the 1980s. The
competition from *News Station* and its emulators, as well as the new technological alternatives, discussed in chapter 7, that the MPT has finally allowed
and even encouraged, now offer the viewer too many choices for NHK to
maintain its pre-1960 domination. Whatever the ultimate fate of *News Station,* as new technical and viewing options come on line and as information
sources become more varied and available, NHK news' niche in the market
is likely to become smaller. As regulators and audiences begin to question
having a general receivers' fee in this environment, the public broadcaster,
in the not too distant future, may face partial "commercialization" as a "pay
per service" or "pay per view" provider or even a status resembling fuller
privatization.

For now, however, it remains a public broadcaster, and a major player in
broadcasting and in the news market. There are two important reasons why
it also has a chance of remaining so, if Kume and *News Station* continue and
maintain their current levels of popularity. The first is its huge control over
human, financial, and technical resources. No single existing commercial
broadcaster, and certainly not any new entrants into the field, can match
these. That this can give NHK an advantage is shown by the private broadcasters deferring to NHK's lead in developing and instituting digital broadcasting in the early twenty-first century.

The second reason is political. Japan is something of an anomaly in media politics among the industrialized democracies. Elsewhere, conservative
political elites usually perceive the public broadcaster to be too leftist or oppositional, perpetrating subversive values, and they target these broadcasters for criticism, even while the broadcaster attempts to continue a tradition
of journalism that is independent of the state. Margaret Thatcher's attacks
on the BBC and the attempt to renegotiate the whole traditional concept of
public broadcasting, even while the BBC continued to produce independent and investigative reports that provoked the government, is a clear
example.[51]

[51]Barnett and Curry, *The Battle for the BBC,* 29–34; O'Malley, *Closedown?* 53–64, 173–80.

Japan is almost unique in that its conservative political elites are not attacking the public broadcaster or trying to commercialize it, and business elites are entering into joint ventures with and supporting it for maintaining cultural standards.[52] Japan may be the only industrialized democracy where *commercial* networks are seen as antagonistic to a conservative party that is supported by large business and where that ruling party endows the commercial *News Station* with exaggerated powers and attacks its motivations. Thus, public broadcasting and commercial broadcasting, and the state and the market, are now in an implicit codependent relationship: commercial broadcasters require NHK's factual but turgid news of the state to create market appeal for their critical and opinionated style; NHK requires the commercial broadcasters' critical, opinionated, and controversial style to provide it with continued political support for public broadcasting's factual news of the state.

Whatever occasional criticism they may have of NHK because of a perception that it is not presenting their views accurately or sufficiently, the ruling party knows that NHK ultimately serves the LDP-dominated state far better than Kume's deconstruction of it or than a more plural, independent market. NHK is more vulnerable to their influence, provides a centralized source of neutral and factual news about bureaucracy, and represents no threat to its rule. Despite a significantly diminished role in the broadcast system since earlier in the postwar period, NHK stands a chance of not being fully dismantled, commercialized, or privatized as long as the LDP remains in power.

Public broadcasting in democracies represents an inevitable trade-off between two democratic norms and public goods: responsiveness and accountability. Public broadcasters must attempt to respond to and avoid alienation of all segments of the public (or their representatives) who are their ultimate masters. As an influential component of the "fourth estate" of journalism, however, they also are supposed to reveal embarrassing and critical information about the government in order to keep it accountable to the citizens. The task of balancing these often competing democratic values is mediated by the specific institutional arrangements in which governments representing the public keep public broadcasters responsive, even while the latter are expected to keep those governments accountable.

Ideally, the mutual "checks" of government and broadcaster should result in the public gaining at least a moderate amount of both responsiveness and accountability. When NHK is weighed in the balance, it has usually tipped

[52]Not all parts of the conservative elite find NHK congenial to their taste; however, unlike the BBC or other European public broadcasters, NHK has never invited widespread dissatisfaction from the ruling party or been made a target for potential privatization or weakening of influence.

the scales too far to the side of responsiveness and not far enough on keeping government accountable. The reasons for this tendency lie not in some inherent cultural inability of Japanese citizens to understand or appreciate the Western notion of "freedom of the press," not in the peculiar malevolence of Japan's political leaders, and not in a unique lack of will of Japanese journalists to stand up to authority. It lies in the way state and media institutions have developed and become linked to each other in postwar Japan.

Index

ABC news, 30–31, 70, 74
Abe Shinnosuke, 125, 127
Abe Shintarō, 143
Administrative reform policies, 152, 183
Advanced Television System (ATV). *See* High-definition television
Advertising, 90n, 210
Advisory Committee on Digital Terrestrial Broadcasting, 196
Advisory councils (*shingikai*), 164–66
Amakudari, 166–67
American Electronics Association (AEA), 193–94
Announcers, 70–71, 73, 90–91. *See also* Casters
Anpo crisis of 1960, 7, 124, 126–27, 243–44
Aoki Kenji, 201
Aoki Sadanobu, 116
Asahi News Network (ANN), 206, 207n
Asahi Shimbun, 54, 114, 115–16, 154, 197, 207–8
Audience: of *News Station*, 220, 221, 230–31, 233–35, 268; of 7 P.M. news, 4, 24, 84, 210–11, 230, 265; of U.S. network news, 74–75. *See also* Public opinion

Board of Governors (NHK). *See* Governing Board
British Broadcasting Corporation (BBC), 3, 47–50, 51, 54, 84, 199; governing board of, 102–3; political pressures on, 247–48, 252–53, 255, 256–58, 270; regulation of, 104–6
Broadcasting Center, 129–30, 131

Broadcasting Technology Association (BTA), 190
Broadcast Law, 94, 174, 178, 197, 198–99; neutrality requirement of, 83, 245; NHK autonomy under, 92–93, 96–97, 167, 248, 249, 254–55; NHK financing under, 98–100; and NHK leadership, 102–3, 148, 244; and NHK mission, 97–98; proposed fee revision of, 111, 114, 116–18, 119, 125–26
Broadcast Satellite Research Committee, 178
Budget (NHK), 101–2, 105–6, 109–13, 119–21, 163; covert negotiations regarding, 108–9, 113–14; and program content, 115–19, 121–22; and unions, 117–18, 168. *See also* Financing; Receivers' fees
Bureaucracy, 80–81, 120, 166–67; in developmental state model, 260–63; distrust of, 268–69; European coverage of, 44, 45, 47, 48, 51; on *News Station* and 7 P.M. news compared, 224, 226, 229; NHK emphasis on, 5, 10–11, 29–32, 33, 77–79; NHK portrayal of, 34–35, 38–40; during Occupation, 260–63; and reporters' clubs, 60, 77–79, 245–46; symbolic power of, 262–67. *See also* Ministry of Posts and Telecommunications
Burns, Tom, 3, 258

Cable television, 196–97
Calder, Kent, 259
Canada, 104, 105
Casters, 70–71, 212–13, 214. *See also* Announcers

273

ist, 33, 117, 169, 171, 172. *See also* Liberal
Democratic Party
Presidents (NHK), 103; selection of, 123–24,
125–26, 140–41, 148–50, 244, 247. *See also*
specific presidents
Press freedom. *See* Expression, freedom of
Prime ministers: coverage of, 58; and NHK
leadership selection, 123–24, 149, 247.
See also Diet
Privatization, 140, 183–84; of conflict, 248
Professionalism, 250–53
Provisional Administrative Reform Promotion Council, 201–2
Public broadcasters, 40–44; conflicting values of, 17, 271–72; French, 10, 44–47, 51,
104, 105; government attacks on, 270;
pressures on, 83–84; regulation of, 16–17,
102–6. *See also* British Broadcasting Corporation; NHK
Public monopolies, 93–94, 106
Public opinion: and *News Station*, 231, 235–
39; on news trustworthiness, 4, 83, 264–65;
on NHK's legal and financial status, 90–
100, 101; and Nippōrō, 170; on sales tax,
139–40. *See also* Audience; Ratings

Radio, 93, 96; prewar, 89–91; during Occupation, 88–89, 91–94
Radio Regulatory Commission, 93, 96n, 100,
248
Radiotelevisione Italiana (RAI), 41–42
Ranney, Austin, 12
Ratings, 210–11, 230–32
Receivers' fees, 3, 98–100, 104, 110, 112–14,
129, 173–74; Diet approval of, 84, 101, 108,
137, 149; legal nature of, 98–99, 110–111,
114, 116, 117–18; and NHK commercialization, 201–2, 270; for satellite broadcasting, 180, 183. *See also* Budget
Regulation, 16–17, 100–102, 167, 175–76,
197–98; international comparison of,
103–6
Reich, Michael, 12, 81n
Reporters, 63–64, 70, 73, 74, 214, 221; careers of, 155, 158–61, 217; freelance, 60;
images of, 34–35, 39, 42; as political channels, 161–64, 253–54; professional autonomy of, 250–53; recruitment of, 153–55,
156–58
Reporters' clubs (*kisha kurabu*), 54–55, 57–
62, 73, 159, 217, 251; advantages and disadvantages of, 75–77; and bureaucratic
emphasis, 77–79; and news values, 79–80;
political functions of, 76–77, 163, 245–46;

and predictability, 62–63, 77, 79. *See also*
Source-reporter relationship

Sakamoto Tomokazu, 112, 116, 133–35, 171,
172, 173, 174
Samuels, Richard J., 18
Satellite broadcasting, 178–81, 203–4, 208;
goals for, 181–85
Satellites, communications, 144–45, 196–97
Satō Eisaku, 128, 130, 147
Scalapino, Robert A., 7, 8
Scandals, 25, 111, 131, 268–69. *See also* Lock-
heed scandal
SCAP. *See* Supreme Commander of the Allied
Powers
Schaede, Ulrike, 166–67
Schwartz, Frank, 165
Science and Technology Agency, 179
Second NHK Basic Problems Investigation
Council, 112
Security Treaty crisis. *See* Anpo crisis of
1960
Seoul Olympics (1988), 190
7 P.M. news, 53–57, 63–64, 79–84, 205; audience of, 4, 24, 84, 210–11, 230, 265;
changes in, 215–19; characteristics of,
72–74; editing of, 55, 64–69, 70, 216; and
European public broadcast news compared, 40–44, 50–51; and BBC, 47–50;
and France 2, 44–47; feedback after, 71–
72; and *NC9* compared, 211–12, 214–15;
news order on, 32–33, 67, 69, 79–80, 214,
218; and *News Station* compared, 223–27,
228, 229, 230; production of, 69–71, 73;
typical program, 24–26; and U.S. network
news compared, 28, 29–31, 37, 74–75.
See also Political news; Reporters' clubs;
Source-reporter relationship
Shiga Nobuo, 113, 132
Shima Keiji, 108, 121, 138, 162, 217, 254,
255, 268; and broadcast satellites, 181,
182; fall of, 144–47; and Miki cut, 135;
and *NC9*, 211; and NHK commercialization, 177, 201, 202–3; political ties of, 137,
163–64, 250; rise of, 137, 142, 143; and
Ueda Tetsu, 170, 171, 174
Silberman, Bernard, 252
Social Democratic Party of Japan, 33, 117.
See also Japan Socialist Party
Society news, 28, 47, 223
Society of Motion Picture and Television En-
gineers, U.S. (SMTE), 187–88
Sōgō Vision, 200
Source-reporter relationship, 56–57, 74, 81,
115, 116, 159–60, 251; interdependence in,

CPSIA information can be obtained at www.ICGtesting.com
Printed in the USA
238144LV00002B/3/P